BORDERS, FENCES AND WALLS

Contrary to what we have been told by the globalization theorists that the world has become deterritorialized and borderless, the past decade has seen an upsurge in the construction of new fences and walls as part of the inter-state borders within the international system. This is largely due to the sense of fear of the 'outsider' in a post 9/11 world. Part of this is real, much of it is a social construction which enables governments to justify the establishment of new border fences as a means of keeping out the 'alien' and controlling their own territory. The collection of chapters in this book highlights diverse aspects of the ways in which walls and fences function in a globalized world, covering regions as far apart as America and Spain, and from the West Bank to Africa. The book is to be recommended for all students of the renaissant discipline of border studies.

David Newman, Ben Gurion University, Israel and Editor, *Geopolitics*

Notwithstanding all the post-Cold War 'endist' illusions, the contemporary world political map is marked by a growing number of boundaries and walls. This book presents an important aid in the understanding of this far from painless process. This set of contributions edited by Elisabeth Vallet moves a step towards a theory of walled borders, introducing at the same time a wide array of different case studies.

Elena dell'Agnese, Università di Milano-Bicocca, Italy

With its rich collection of contributions, this volume illustrates the diversity amongst physical borders in different parts of the world. It is an important and very welcome addition to the border studies literature.

Emmanuel Brunet Jailly, University of Victoria, Canada

Border Regions Series
Series Editor: Doris Wastl-Walter, University of Bern, Switzerland

In recent years, borders have taken on an immense significance. Throughout the world they have shifted, been constructed and dismantled, and become physical barriers between socio-political ideologies. They may separate societies with very different cultures, histories, national identities or economic power, or divide people of the same ethnic or cultural identity.

As manifestations of some of the world's key political, economic, societal and cultural issues, borders and border regions have received much academic attention over the past decade. This valuable series publishes high quality research monographs and edited comparative volumes that deal with all aspects of border regions, both empirically and theoretically. It will appeal to scholars interested in border regions and geopolitical issues across the whole range of social sciences.

Borders, Fences and Walls
State of Insecurity?

Edited by

ELISABETH VALLET
University of Quebec at Montreal, Canada

LONDON AND NEW YORK

First published 2014 by Ashgate Publishing

Published 2016 by Routledge
2 Park Square, Milton Park, Abingdon, Oxon OX14 4RN
711 Third Avenue, New York, NY 10017, USA

Routledge is an imprint of the Taylor & Francis Group, an informa business

Copyright © Elisabeth Vallet 2014

Elisabeth Vallet has asserted her right under the Copyright, Designs and Patents Act, 1988, to be identified as the editor of this work.

All rights reserved. No part of this book may be reprinted or reproduced or utilised in any form or by any electronic, mechanical, or other means, now known or hereafter invented, including photocopying and recording, or in any information storage or retrieval system, without permission in writing from the publishers.

Notice:
Product or corporate names may be trademarks or registered trademarks, and are used only for identification and explanation without intent to infringe.

British Library Cataloguing in Publication Data
A catalogue record for this book is available from the British Library

The Library of Congress has cataloged the printed edition as follows:
Borders, fences and walls : state of insecurity? / edited by Elisabeth Vallet.
    pages cm. -- (Border regions series)
  Includes bibliographical references and index.
  ISBN 978-1-4724-2966-7 (hardback) -- ISBN 978-1-4724-2967-4 (ebook) -- ISBN 978-1-4724-2968-1 (epub) 1. Border security--Case studies. 2. National security--Case studies. 3. Emigration and immigration--Government policy--Case studies. I. Vallet, Elisabeth, author, editor of compilation.
  JV6225.B674 2014
  355'.033--dc23

2014015347

ISBN 13: 978-1-4724-2966-7 (hbk)

Contents

List of Figures		vii
List of Tables		ix
Notes on Contributors		xi

	Introduction *Elisabeth Vallet*	1
PART I	**INSECURITY AND BORDERS IN EUROPE AND NORTH AMERICA**	
1	The Mediterranean Sea as a European Border: Trans-Mediterranean Migration, Forced Return and Violation of Fundamental Rights *Maria Chiara Locchi*	11
2	The Canary Islands' "Maritime Wall": Migration Pressure, Security Measures and Economic Crisis in the Mid-Atlantic *Josefina Domínguez-Mujica, Ramón Díaz-Hernández and Juan Parreno-Castellano*	27
3	A Community of Borders, Borders of the Community: The EU's Integrated Border Management Strategy *Denis Duez*	51
4	Border Games: From Duel to Russian Roulette at the Border *Markus Heiskanen*	67
5	Borders, Bordered Lands and Borderlands: Geographical States of Insecurity between Canada and the United States and the Impacts of Security Primacy *Victor Konrad*	85
PART II	**TOWARDS A THEORY OF BORDER WALLS?**	
6	Walls and Borders in a Globalized World: The Paradoxical Revenge of Territorialization *Jean-Jacques Roche*	105
7	Border Fences in the Globalizing World: Beyond Traditional Geopolitics and Post-Positivist Approaches *Serghei Golunov*	117

8	Is the Wall Soluble into International Law? *Jean-Marc Sorel*	131
9	Walls of Money: Securitization of Border Discourse and Militarization of Markets *Elisabeth Vallet and Charles-Philippe David*	143

PART III   FENCED BORDERS IN THE TWENTIETH AND TWENTY-FIRST CENTURIES

10	Walls and Access to Natural Resources *Sabine Lavorel*	159
11	Border Fences as an Anti-Immigration Device: A Comparative View of American and Spanish Policies *Said Saddiki*	175
12	Walls, Sensors and Drones: Technology and Surveillance on the US–Mexico Border *Rodrigo Nieto-Gomez*	191
13	Technologies, Practices and the Reproduction of Conflict: The Impact of the West Bank Barrier on Peace Building *Christine Leuenberger*	211
14	Towards a High-Tech "Limes" on the Edges of Europe? Managing the External Borders of the European Union *Vincent Boulanin and Renaud Bellais*	231
15	Towards the Wall between Nogales, Arizona and Nogales, Sonora *Irasema Coronado*	247
16	Border Wall as Architecture *Ronald Rael*	267

Index   *279*

List of Figures

2.1	Map of irregular migration routes from Africa to the Canary Islands (2006)	32
2.2	Links between migration stages and policing measures	40
2.3	Links between migration stages and the labour market regulation	44
5.1	Map of the Cascade Gateway	90
16.1	Different forms of barrier used along the US–Mexican border	268
16.2	Flooding in Nogales, Arizona caused by the border wall	270
16.3	Water catchment wall, El Paso, TX	271
16.4	Water treatment wall, Calexico, CA	272
16.5a	Solar wall	273
16.5b	Solar wall	273
16.6	Solar hot water wall	274
16.7	Water and life safety wall	275
16.8	Family visits across the wall	276
16.9	Yoga across the wall	277
16.10	Bike path and pedestrian wall	277

List of Tables

2.1	Landmarks in the management of unauthorized migration flows in the EU and in Spain (1985–2010)	33
2.2	Spain's economic indicators and immigration	45
4.1	Transformation of borders	70
14.1	Illegal immigration in Europe (detections or cases as reported by Member States)	233
14.2	Alternative aggregation technologies of public supply	234

Notes on Contributors

Renaud Bellais, ENSTA Bretagne, France.

Vincent Boulanin, École des Hautes Études en Sciences Sociales, Paris, France and Stockholm International Peace Research Institute, Sweden.

Irasema Coronado, Professor at the University of Texas at El Paso, USA and Executive Director of the Commission for Environmental Cooperation Montreal, Quebec, Canada.

Charles-Philippe David, Raoul-Dandurand Professor of Strategic and Diplomatic Studies, UQAM, University of Quebec at Montreal, Canada

Ramón Díaz-Hernández, Permanent Professor in the Department of Human Geography at the University of Las Palmas de Gran Canaria, Spain.

Josefina Domínguez-Mujica, Permanent Professor in the Department of Human Geography at the University of Las Palmas de Gran Canaria, Spain.

Denis Duez, Professor in Political Science and Director of the Institute for European Studies at the University of Saint-Louis, Brussels, Belgium.

Serghei Golunov, Research Fellow at the Centre for EU-Russian Studies, University of Tartu, Estonia.

Markus Heiskanen works in the research unit of the Finnish Border and Coast Guard Academy, Finland.

Victor Konrad, Adjunct Research Professor in the Department of Geography and Environmental Studies at Carleton University, Ottawa, Canada.

Sabine Lavorel, Lecturer in Public Law at the University of Grenoble II/CESICE, France.

Christine Leuenberger, Senior Lecturer in the Department of Science and Technology Studies at Cornell University, USA.

Maria Chiara Locchi, Member of the Department of Public Law at the University of Perugia, Italy.

Rodrigo Nieto-Gomez works at the Center for Homeland Defense and Security at the Naval Postgraduate School in Monterey, USA.

Juan Parreno-Castellano, Permanent Professor in the Department of Human Geography at the University of Las Palmas de Gran Canaria, Spain.

Ronald Rael, Associate Professor at the University of California, Berkeley, USA with a joint appointment in the departments of Architecture and Art Practice.

Jean-Jacques Roche, Professor at the University Paris II, Pantheon Assas, France.

Said Saddiki, Associate Professor of International Relations and International Law at Al-Ain University of Science and Technology, Abu Dhabi, UAE and Sidi Mohamed Ben Abdellah University, Fez, Morocco.

Jean-Marc Sorel, Professor at the Sorbonne School of Law (University of Paris 1) and Director of the IREDIES, France.

Elisabeth Vallet, Adjunct Professor of Geography and Scientific Director, Raoul-Dandurand Chair at UQAM, University of Montreal, Canada.

ID# Introduction[1]

Elisabeth Vallet

In 2013, Turkey became the fourth country in less than two years to announce plans for a new border wall. After Bulgaria, Greece (which completed a barrier along its border with Turkey in December 2012) and Israel (which completed the bulk of its barrier with Egypt in January 2013, began reinforcing the 56 kilometres of fortifications on its border with Syria,[2] and planned an upgrade and extension of its barrier with Jordan[3]), Turkey announced the construction of a border wall to solve its security problems on the Syrian border.[4] To be sure, the idea of fortifying a border is not new. From the building of the Roman Limes in the second century CE (which included Hadrian's Wall and the Antonine Wall in Scotland), the construction of the Great Wall of China begun in the third century BCE, King Gudfred of Denmark's Danevirke built in the seventh century, the Silesian Walls and the Japanese *genko borui* built to guard northern Kyushu Island against Mongol invasions, up to more modern structures such as the iconic Berlin Wall, the "wall" has been a constant in international relations.

However, the fall of the Berlin Wall (and the new international order that emerged at that time) opened an era of globalization that seemed to irrevocably doom the State to obsolescence (Balibar and Badie, 2006). With the apparent movement towards a world without borders (Ohmae, 1990; Badie, 1999, 2000; Galli, 2001; Zolo, 2004; Schroer, 2006) – or at least a world where borders are less and less important (Lévy, 2005: 40; Brunet-Jailly, 2005, 2010; Andreas, 2003a: 82) – academics began shifting away from State-centric interpretations of international relations (Paasi, 1998: 70–71). But while observers assumed that, following the fall of the Berlin Wall, the world would never be the same, the borders, walls and barriers that were symbolic of the bipolar world and were expected to perish with it returned with a vengeance in the aftermath of 9/11 (Jones, 2012; Brown, 2009; Vallet and David, 2009; Vallet, 2012; Paasi, 2009: 216), accompanied by a new border discourse (Newman, 2006).

Walls had not actually disappeared after the Cold War (12 remained standing, half of which served very conventional purposes[5]). But what leads us to speak of the "return"

---

1   This study was made possible by a research grant from the Social Sciences and Humanities Research Council of Canada.
2   "More than 90 per cent of the fence, which is about 130 kilometers long in total, was built shortly after the 1973 Yom Kippur War". It no longer meets current security needs, partly because "severe weather in the Golan Heights has battered the fence over the years to the point where in certain places, it barely exists" and also because of the situation in Syria. Gili, Cohen, 2012. "IDF reinforces security along border fence with Syria", *Haaretz*, September 14, 2012; "Israel to fortify Syrian border fence", *AFP*, January 6, 2013.
3   Largely because migrants from the Sinai have been forging new migration routes passing through Jordan.
4   "Turkey to build 2.5-kilometer-long wall on Syria border", *Hurriyet Daily News*, May 23, 2013.
5   The walls between South Africa, Mozambique and Zimbabwe, between Israel and Syria, Israel and Lebanon, China and Hong Kong, China and Macao, Rhodesia, Mozambique and Zambia, Cuba and the Guantánamo zone, the first phase of the wall between India and Pakistan, the wall in the

of border walls is the contrast between the "world without borders" discourse and the resurgence of wall-building, particularly after 2001. After peaking at 19 between 1945 and 1991 and declining to 12 by the end of the Cold War, the trend was reversed with the addition of 14 new walls during the decade following the Cold War. In the 20 years after the end of the Cold War, the total number of walls more than tripled.[6]

But despite the appearance of new walls in the post-Cold-War period, studies continued viewing walls through a stubbornly local lens, a consequence of the persistent "territorial trap" (Agnew, 1994). So the scholarly literature on walls essentially consisted of case studies – i.e. analysis of "a" wall from various point of views: anthropological (Latte Abadallah and Parizot, 2011), legal (Kahan, 2004; Araujo, 2004), biological (Su et al., 2003), historical (Martinez, 2009; Sterling, 2009) and sociological (Medina, 2007). With a few exceptions – such as the studies by the geographers Newman and Paasi (1998), Jones (2009) and Foucher (2007); the philosopher Brown (2009); the legal scholar Sorel (2010); and the political scientists Vallet and David (2012a, 2012b, 2013) – the wall was not regarded as a global phenomenon. And even in the latter cases, it was approached more often than not from within the confines of a single discipline. Exceptions include special issues of the magazines *Hermès* and *Diplomatie*, and of scholarly journals such as the issues of the *Journal of Borderland Studies* and *Études internationales* edited by Vallet and David (2012a and 2012b).[7]

However, the scope of the trend, combined with the changing nature and function of "the" wall, did prompt some researchers to draw distinctions between contemporary border walls and the border fortifications of the past. It has been suggested that the modern wall, as a "post-Westphalian" phenomenon (Brown, 2008: 54), extends beyond the limits of the military structures, such as the Maginot Line or the Siegfried Line, that typified the 1945–1991 period, being distinguished from classical border barriers by three features: control of the border, physical demarcation of the border and asymmetry (Hassner and Wittenberg, 2009). These walls are artefacts of a new era in international relations and of a new understanding of the very idea of the border. Border walls have become the "fault lines of globalization" (Ritaine, 2009a: 160) as well as markers of identity, instruments of differentiation (Foucher, 2008), tools at the service of State sovereignty (Brown, 2009; Parizot, 2009: 53; Latte Abdallah and Parizot, 2011).

What initially could be interpreted as a tightening of security spurred by 9/11 proved to be a ratchet effect produced by the reaction against fast-paced globalization, which had not been wholeheartedly embraced by many members of the international community. While 9/11 may appear to have ratified the return of the wall as a physical object and political instrument (Jones, 2010), the speed with which walls sprang up suggests the existence of a latent tendency that predated 9/11, at least at the ideational level. The apparent security-seeking reflex actually sprang from the pull of identity, which explains

---

demilitarized zone between the two Koreas, the separation line in Cyprus, and Morocco's wall in Western Sahara all survived the end of the Cold War (see Vallet and David, 2012a and 2012b).

6 Estimates of the length of the extant walls vary: 18,000 kilometres according to Foucher (2007), more than 41,000 kilometres according to Rosière (2009) (trimmed to 39,000 in 2010), a little more than 29,000 kilometres according to Vallet and David (2012). The differences are due to the fact that some counts may include not only completed walls but also those in the advanced planning stage, and that the numbers are generally based on government figures.

7 Every two years, an international conference on that issue takes place in Montreal. Most authors of this edited volume have participated in at least one of the four international conferences on the subject organized by the Raoul Dandurand Chair in 2009, 2011 and 2013.

why democracies also set about fortifying their boundaries (Jones, 2012; Foucher, 2007) in order to demonstrate their ability to regain control of their borders (Foucher, 2009: 6): as of 2013, the US, Israel, Greece, Spain and India had a total of 6,000 kilometres of walls.

Since 2001 (Jones, 2009; 2012), the purpose of new walls has been not so much to convert a front line into a *de facto* border as to address two threats: migrants and terrorists (the two sometimes overlap or blend together in the pro-wall discourse). The upshot has been the creation of a worldwide great wall of globalization (Davis, 2007: 172) that has become virtually impossible for migrants from the South to scale. The quest for absolute impenetrability (Bennafla and Peraldi, 2008; DeBardeleben and Neuwahl, 2005: 11, 23; Zielonka, 2002: 11–12) leads to the establishment of systems of norms, visas, exclusions and deportation processes which, by fragmenting the territory, ultimately create protected sanctuaries (Rekacewicz, 2009).

Still, walls are not truly impregnable (Lecumberri, 2006, although her argument is disputed: Staniland, 2005–2006: 31–34; Weizman, 2008: 90). In some respects, walls may even be said to be illusory, for they give rise to bypass strategies and alternative routes (Pallister-Wilkins, 2012; Wittenberg, 2009). It has been suggested that their true purpose is to maintain a sense of security and identity (Ritaine, 2009: 161). Walls provide tangible evidence that governments are doing something (Hassner and Wittenberg, 2009). To be sure, this has always been the case (Duffin, 2009), but in the wake of 9/11, optics seem to take precedence over reality and domestic politics over foreign policy and diplomacy: the image of a fortified border becomes more important than its actual effectiveness. In this age of risk management, the wall, its various functions (protection, pacification, separation and even segregation – see Karlin, 2012) and accompanying security mechanisms (El Maslouhi, 2009: 6; Beck, 1999) are all conscripted to serve the logic of perception: they are not only the most important functional elements but also the most visible components of interconnected surveillance processes (Ritaine, 2009; Gonzalez, 2012).

* * *

The wall, in the proportions it has now assumed, is a unique, almost unprecedented, object in international relations. But it is also an artefact that stretches back in time to antiquity. Over its history, the wall has embraced a heterogeneous range of structures built with diverse motivations on a variety of borders. This book considers walls as a global phenomenon, one that is expanding primarily because of States' perceived insecurity in a globalized world. Part I deals with Europe and North America, the two large free-trade blocs produced by the 1990s and the end of the Cold War, where this tendency is particularly evident. Maria Chiara Locchi, Josefina Domínguez-Mujica, Ramón Díaz-Hernández, Juan Parreno-Castellano, Denis Duez, Markus Heiskanen and Victor Konrad investigate the current state of affairs in European and North American States, which stands in contrast to the prevailing view at the end of the Cold War, and discuss how legal and political instruments are being mustered to support ever-stricter control over borders, up to and including the erection of walls, real and virtual.

In view of this closing of borders, we need to rethink the wall in view of its new meaning and the reconfiguration that has occurred since the end of the 1990s, and to analyse, at a theoretical level, the reterritorialization effected by border walls. In Part II, Jean-Jacques Roche, Serghei Golunov, Elisabeth Vallet and Charles-Philippe David and Jean-Marc Sorel bring theoretical perspectives to bear on the resurgence of border walls in an increasingly globalized world.

Finally, Part III consists of a series of case studies of the most important border barriers of the twentieth and twenty-first centuries and their impacts. Sabine Lavorel, Said Saddiki, Rodrigo Nieto-Gomez, Christine Leuenberger, Vincent Boulanin and Renaud Bellais, Irasema Coronado and Ronald Rael look at how the growth of border walls has ushered in new ways of thinking about border areas from every point of view: law, sociology, technology, the environment, art.

It is our hope that this multidisciplinary approach will serve to shed new light on the wall phenomenon as a whole, in all its aspects.

References

Agnew, J. 1994. The Territorial Trap: The Geographical Assumptions of International Relations Theory. *Review of International Political Economy*, 1: 53–80.

Andreas, P. 2000. The Wall after the Wall, in Andreas, P. and Snyder, T. (eds), *The Wall around the West. State Borders and Immigrations Controls in North America and Europe*. Oxford: Rowman & Littlefield Publishers.

Araujo, Fr. R.J. 2004. Implementation of the ICJ Advisory Opinion – Legal Consequences of the Construction of a Wall in the Occupied Palestinian Territory: Fences [Do Not] Make Good Neighbors? *Boston University International Law Journal*, 22: 349–385.

Badie, B. 1999. *Un monde sans souveraineté*. Paris: Fayard.

Badie, B. 2000. *La Fin des territoires. Essai sur le désordre international et sur l'utilité sociale du respect*. Paris: Fayard.

Balibar, E. and Badie, B. 2006. L'étranger comme ennemi. Sur la citoyenneté transnationale. CERI, Projets transversaux: http://www.ceri-sciencespo.com/cerifr/transversaux.php.

Ballif, F. and Rosière, S. 2009. Le défi des *teichopolitiques*. Analyser la fermeture contemporaine des territoires. *L'Espace Géographique*, 38(3): 193–206.

Beck, U. 1999. *World Risk Society*. Cambridge: Polity Press.

Bennafla, K. and Peraldi, M. 2008. Introduction. Frontières et logiques de passage: l'ordinaire des transgressions. *Cultures & Conflits*, 72, winter [En ligne], mis en ligne May 19, 2009: http://www.conflits.org/index17383.html [July 27, 2011].

Bocco, R. 2011. Pratiques de lieux, logiques des pouvoirs: une lecture foucaldiennes espaces israélo-palestiniens, in Latte Abdallah, S. and Parizot, C. (eds), *À l'ombre du mur – Israéliens et Palestiniens entre separation et occupation*. Arles: Actes Sud/MMSH.

Brown, W. 2009. *Murs – Les murs de séparation et le déclin de la souveraineté étatique*. Paris: Les prairies ordinaires.

Brunet-Jailly, E. 2005. Theorizing Borders: An Interdisciplinary Perspective. *Geopolitics*, 10(4): 633–649.

Brunet-Jailly, E. 2010. Introduction – Borders, Flows and Territories, in *Theorizing Borders and Borderlands*. Special Issue of *Geopolitics*, Guest Editor, 15(4).

Caldeira, T. Pires do Rio. 2001. Urban Segregation, Fortified Enclaves, and Public Space. *City of Walls. Crime, Segregation, and Citizenship in São Paulo*. Berkeley: University of California Press, 256–296.

Chamoiseau, P. and Glissant, É. 2007. *Quand les murs tombent – L'identité nationale hors la loi?* Paris: Galaade.

Clochard, O. 2003. La Méditerranée: dernière frontière avant l'Europe. *Les Cahiers d'Outre-Mer*, 222, April–June: http://com.revues.org/index862.html [July 30, 2011].

Crépeau, F., Nakache, D. and Atak, D. 2007. International Migration: Security Concerns and Human Rights Standards. *Transcultural Psychiatry*, 44(3): 311–337.

Cuttitta, P. 2007. Le monde-frontière. Le contrôle de l'immigration dans l'espace globalise. *Cultures & Conflits*, 68: 61–84.

David, C.-P. and Vallet, É. 2009. "Mirror, Mirror on the Wall – Why Is there a Wall after All? The Return of the Wall in IR". Paper delivered at the conference of the International Political Science Association, Santiago de Chile.

Davis, M. 2007. *In Praise of Barbarians: Essays against Empire*. Chicago: Haymarket Books.

Davis, M. and Akers Chacón, J. 2006. *No One Is Illegal: Fighting Racism and State Violence on the U.S.-Mexico Border*. Chicago: Haymarket Books.

Debardebelen, J. 2005. *Soft or Hard Borders?: Managing The Divide in an Enlarged Europe*. Aldershot: Ashgate.

Dryef, Z. 2008. Rueil: autour de la cité, le mur de la honte … ou du renouveau? *Rue89*, 6 August.

Duffin, J. 2009. "The Plague Wall: Health-Care Surveillance in Eighteenth Century Europe". Paper delivered at the "Walls and Fences in International Relations" conference, Raoul-Dandurand Chair of Strategic and Diplomatic Studies, UQAM, Montreal, October 29–30, 2009.

Economist, The. 2006. Walls and Fences from Sea to Shining Sea, January 12, 2006.

El Maslouhi, A. 2009. "Murs et reterritorialisation des relations internationales post-Guerre froide". Paper delivered at the "Border Walls in International Relations" conference, Raoul-Dandurand Chair of Strategic and Diplomatic Studies, UQAM, Montreal, April 1, 2009.

Foucault, M. 1999. *Les Anormaux*. Paris: Gallimard.

Foucher, M. 2004. *Fronts et frontières, un tour du monde géopolitique*. Paris: Fayard [1st edition 1989].

Foucher, M. 2007. *L'Obsession des frontiers*. Paris: Librairie Académique Perrin.

Galli, C. 2001. *Spazi politici – L'età moderna e l'età globale*. Bologna: Il Mulino.

Gonzalez, S. 2012. Muro fronterizo infinito: http://www.ipernity.com/blog/occupyusa/40 2373 [November 12, 2012].

Gottmann, J. 1952. *La politique des États et leur géographie*. Paris: Armand Colin.

Hassner, R. and Wittenberg, J. 2009. "Barriers to Entry: Who Builds Fortified Boundaries and Are They Likely to Work?" Conference, Raoul-Dandurand Chair of Strategic and Diplomatic Studies, Fences and Walls in International Relations conference, UQAM, October: http://polisci.berkeley.edu/people/faculty/WittenbergJ/Barriers%20to%20Entry%20UQAM.pdf [May 25, 2013].

International Court of Justice (IJC). 2004. Public sitting held on Monday 23 February 2004, at 10 a.m., at the Peace Palace, President Shi presiding, on the Legal Consequences of the Construction of a Wall in the Occupied Palestinian Territory (Request for advisory opinion submitted by the General Assembly of the United Nations). Verbatim Record, online.

Israel Ministry of Defence. 2003. *Israel's Security Fence*: http://www.seamzone.mod.gov.il/pages/eng/default.htm [July 24, 2007].

Jones, R. 2009. Geopolitical Boundary Narratives, the Global War on Terror, and Border Fencing in India. *Transactions of the Institute of British Geographers*, 34(3): 290–304.

Jones, R. 2010. The Border Enclaves of India and Bangladesh: The Forgotten Lands, in Diener, A.C. and Hagen, J., *BorderLines and Borderlands – Political Oddities at the Edge of the Nation-State*. Lanham: Rowman & Littlefield, 15–32.

Kahan, R. 2004. Building a Protective Wall Around Terrorists – How the International Court of Justice's Ruling in the Legal Consequences of the Construction of a Wall in the Occupied Palestinian Territory Made the World Safer for Terrorists and More Dangerous for Member States of the United Nations. *Fordham International Journal of Law*, 28(2004–2005): 827–878.

Karlin, M. 2012. The Border Wall: The Last Stand at Making the US a White Gated Community, Truthout, March 11: http://truth-out.org/news/item/7147:the-border-wall-the-last-stand-at-making-the-us-a-white-gated-community [May 10, 2013].

Konrad, V. and Nicol, H. 2008. *Beyond Walls: Re-inventing the Canada-United States Borderlands*. Aldershot: Ashgate.

Lasky, J.R., Jetz, W. and Keitt, T.H. 2011. Conservation Biogeography of the US–Mexico border: A Transcontinental Risk Assessment of Barriers to Animal Dispersal. *Diversity and Distributions*, 17: 673–687.

Latte Abdallah, S. and Parizot, C. (eds). 2011. *À l'ombre du mur –Israéliens et Palestiniens entre separation et occupation*. Arles: Actes Sud/MMSH.

Le Boedec, G. 2007. Le détroit de Gibraltar. *EchoGéo*, Numéro 2 [En ligne], mis en ligne le 22 February 2008: http://echogeo.revues.org/index1488.html [July 30, 2010].

Lecumberri, B. 2006. Los muros, una estrategia geopolítica que alimenta la violencia – Entrevista: Yves Lacoste, Geopolítico Frances. *La Republica*, October 28, 2006.

Lévy, A. 2005. Des murs, remparts contre la réalité. *Libération*, October 20, 2005.

Martinez, O. 2009. Border Conflict, Border Fences, and the "Tortilla Curtain" Incident of 1978–1979. *Journal of the Southwest*, July 30, 2009.

Medina, I. 2007. At the Border: What Tres Mujeres Tell Us About Walls and Fences. *Journal of Gender, Race & Justice*, 10: 245.

Newman, D. 2006. The Lines that Continue to Separate Us: Borders in our Borderless World. *Progress in Human Geography*, 30: 1–19.

Newman, D. and Paasi, A. 1998. Fences and Neighbours in the Postmodern World: Boundary Narratives in Political Geography. *Progress in Human Geography*, 22(2): 186–207.

Novosseloff, A. and Neisse, F. 2007. *Des murs entre les homes*. Paris: La Documentation française.

Ohmae, K. 1990. *The Borderless World*. New York: Harper Business.

Paasi, A. 1998. Boundaries as Social Processes: Territoriality in the World of Flows. *Geopolitics*, 3(1): 69–88.

Paasi, A. 2009. Bounded Spaces in a "Borderless World": Border Studies, Power and the Anatomy of Territory. *Journal of Power*, 2(2): 213–234.

Pallister-Wilkins, P. 2012. "Fences don't make us safe": http://www.politics.co.uk/comment-analysis/2012/02/14/comment-fences-don-t-make-us-safe [May 19, 2013].

Rekacewicz, P. 2009. Vers la sanctuarisation des pays riches. Un monde interdit, in *Frontières, migrants et réfugiés*, Cartographier le présent, Études cartographiques, décembre, p. 11: http://www.cartografareilpresente.org/article418.html [September 15, 2010].

Ritaine, É. 2009. La barrière et le *checkpoint*: mise en politique de l'asymétrie. *Cultures & Conflits*, 73(Frontières, marquages et disputes): 13–33.

Rosière, S. 2009. "La prolifération des murs, symptôme d'une mondialisation 'fermée'?" Paper delivered at the "Walls and Fences in International Relations" conference, Raoul-Dandurand Chair of Strategic and Diplomatic Studies, UQAM, Montreal, 29–30 October.

Sajjad, A.S. 2006. Fencing the Porous Bangladesh Border: Worldpress.org, December 14, 2006.

Sanguin, A.-L. 2007. Les nouvelles perspectives frontalières de l'union européenne après l'élargissement de 2004, *L'Espace Politique* [En ligne], 1, 2007–1: http://espacepolitique.revues.org/index437.html [July 30, 2009].

Schroer, M. 2006. *Räume, Orte, GrenzenAuf dem Weg zu einer Soziologie des Raums.* Frankfurt: Suhrkamp.

Sivan, E. 2006. À propos du mur en Israël, in Michel Foucher, Henri Dorion, *Frontières – Images de vies entre les lignes*. Paris: Glénat et Muséum.

Sorel, J.-M. (ed.). 2010. *Les murs et le droit international*. Paris: Éditions Pédone.

Staniland, P. 2005. Defeating Transnational Insurgencies: The Best Offense is a Good Fence. *The Washington Quarterly*, 2005–2006: 31–34.

Sterling, B.L. 2009. *Do Good Fences Make Good Neighbors?* Washington, DC: Georgetown University Press.

Su, H., Qu, L.-J., He, K. et al. 2003. The Great Wall of China: A Physical Barrier to Gene Flow? *Heredity*, 90: 212–219.

Weizman, E. 2008. *À travers les murs – L'architecture de la nouvelle guerre urbaine*. Paris: La Fabrique éditions.

Zielonka, J. 2002. Introduction: Boundary Making by the European Union, in Zielonka, J. (ed.), *Europe Unbound – Enlarging and Reshaping the boundaries of the European Union*. London: Routledge.

Zolberg, A.R. 1989. The Next Waves: Migration Theory for a Changing World. *International Migration Review*, 23(3): 403–430.

Zolo, D. 2004. *Globalizzazione. Una mappa dei problemi*. Rome-Bari: Laterza.

PART I
Insecurity and Borders in Europe and North America

Chapter 1
The Mediterranean Sea as a European Border: Trans-Mediterranean Migration, Forced Return and Violation of Fundamental Rights

Maria Chiara Locchi

Immigration Policies in Europe and the Transformation of European Borders

European and particularly Italian immigration policies are a useful point of observation in the transformation of state borders. Many scholars, especially political scientists and legal sociologists and philosophers, have been studying this phenomenon trying to clarify the conceptual categories and the mechanisms of social control that lie underneath the legal regulations of European border control systems (Cuttitta, 2006a, 2007a, 2007b, 2009; Bigo and Guild, 2005a; Bigo and Guild, 2010). State borders can no longer be considered only as lines between spheres within which two or more political entities exercise their constitutional authority and exclude the others' sovereignty (Lombardi, 1985: 435). This notion of "border" has been inherited from the past, from the long and troubled process of formation and consolidation of territorial and national States in Europe, with the transition between the "personal State", which was based on personal ties, and the "territorial State", which was defined by spatial control as an essential feature of sovereign power (Tilly, 1993; Maczak, 1995: 125). The institution of rigid and well-controlled borders and the consequent transition from private to public control of human mobility have played a key role in facilitating the shift from feudalism to modern capitalism. In this regard, John Torpey's work (Torpey, 2000) represents a remarkable contribution, since it points out the importance of improving personal identification techniques in order to control people's movements. Using new registration systems, population census, identity and travel documents, states were more easily able to identify and distinguish between "their" members and the "others", which was an essential step to "penetrate" society and gain control over it.

Geopolitical and legal structures that were built upon the pillars of territorial and national States have been subjected to processes of deep erosion that can be labelled as "globalization" for a significant period of time. In such a framework international migration is an important causal factor and a privileged perspective for the comprehension of the erosion phenomena implied by globalization. Furthermore, in the context of immigration policies, the tensions that are shaking nation-states should not be associated too simplistically with the dissolution of the State and the superimposition of supranational political entities. In the domain of immigration policy, States continue to be the dominant players and their weight on the international scene is heavily influenced by the political and economic balance of power, with the result that among all sovereign states, which are equal on a formal level, some states are "more sovereign" than others.

With regard to the transformation of the "border", European immigration policies represent an interesting case study. The process of European integration and the consolidation of the right to free circulation within the EU has changed the notion of what constitutes a border. The 1985 Schengen Agreement established an area of free movement through the abolition of "internal" borders, or the borders of Schengen member States.[1] The Schengen Agreement and the subsequent 1992 Maastricht Treaty produced an "Europeanization" of the notion of "citizen", who is entitled to free entry and circulation, as well as of the concept of "alien". After Schengen the conceptualization of the "alien" was no longer based on an exclusively national perspective, since nationals of a State that does not join the Schengen area are considered to be "aliens".

Therefore the abolition of internal borders has not only resulted in the improvement of the freedom of movement; it has also caused the strengthening of "external" frontiers, making Europe a "fortress" to people who wish to enter it. The features of European border policy poses the question of whether the transformation of European State-borders has meant the overcoming of a "State logic" or if there has been an intensification of national paradigms in the exclusion of the "others".

An "Anticipated" European Border: The Application for a Schengen Visa

Didier Bigo and Elspeth Guild have explained the process of "anticipation" and delocalization of European borders into immigrant-sending countries, where borders "contact" individuals prior to their departures for Europe (Bigo and Guild, 2005b). An alien who wishes to enter Europe has to apply for a visa to the diplomatic representative of the European destination country if he or she is a national of a State subject to a visa requirement.[2] The application for an entry visa can be viewed as a "first European border" considering that entry visas have turned into important tools for the prevention of and fight against illegal immigration. Diplomatic officers carry out what has been defined as "policing at a distance", consisting of different forms of controls and investigations implemented through sophisticated technological devices (SIS, VIS, Interpol) and typical police procedures and means. The dominant logic is such that suspicion towards a "country" or a "nationality" makes "the granting of a visa […] an exception to the exclusion" (Bigo and Guild, 2005b: 236). Checks carried out by diplomatic representatives aim to verify whether aliens respect general and specific entry conditions to the Schengen area and to assess if he or she represents a "threat" to public policy, national security or international relations. The implementation of this activity on the part of diplomatic officers cannot be considered only from a legal and formal perspective, referring to their duty to verify sufficient means of support, medical insurance, SIS report or other risks to public order. Diplomatic authorities themselves become *de facto* immigration policy makers implementing legal rules by highly-discretionary practices

---

1   Being a European State does not automatically coincide with being a "Schengen State": "To prove that they are ready to join the Schengen area, the Member States undergo a 'Schengen evaluation' by Member States' experts (supported by the experts of the European Commission) to verify all relevant areas of the Schengen *acquis*: control of land, sea and air borders (airports); issuing of visas; police cooperation; readiness to connect to and use the Schengen Information System; and data protection" (from the site of the EU Directorate-General for Home Affairs).

2   According to the "Community Code on Visas" (Reg. EC n. 810/2009 of 13 July 2009) Schengen States can issue short-term visas (Schengen visas) for stays that do not exceed three months within a six-month period and visas for visits exceeding that period. While the first are valid for the entire Schengen area, the second remain subject to national procedures. However National visas are valid as short-term visas for a period of not more than three months.

(Infantino, 2010).[3] In checking whether the foreign citizen is reported on the SIS or is a threat to public policy, internal security or public health in any way, diplomatic officers use the concepts of "threat" and "security", which have developed by the accumulation of the different notions and criteria elaborated in European countries (Rigo, 2007: 128). Therefore, each Schengen State has to take on the responsibility of issuing of Schengen visas on behalf of the other member States.

The Countries of Origin and Transit of Migrants as "Europe Gatekeepers"

European countries and the European Union as a subject of international law actively involve North African countries in preventing and fighting against irregular immigration, even more so since 9/11. This involvement is carried out by several instruments, such as: readmission agreements, through which the countries of origin and transit of immigrants commit to the readmission of undocumented aliens pushed back by European countries;[4] police cooperation agreements, which can provide for joint surveillance to patrol the Mediterranean Sea, joint investigative and formative activities, liaison officers dispatched from one country to another in order to coordinate cooperation activities; and the construction of detention centres and the reinforcement of the deportation of illegal immigrants from North African countries. This kind of involvement in the fight against irregular immigration raises several economic and political problems for those countries, since it is the result of a cooperation that is formally bilateral but is basically dominated by European States. Europe succeeds in gaining this "assistance" by offering some "incentives", such as: financial contributions in order to buy border surveillance equipment or to build detention centres; special funds in the framework of development cooperation; reservation of shares of the yearly legal immigration quotas; and facilitations for nationals of the cooperating countries who reside in the European destination country (Cuttitta, 2006b: 116).

A key point of this cooperation is the legal adjustment of North African countries to restrictive European paradigms on immigration and the legal condition of aliens. Most North African countries have passed "Euro-style" legislation in the last 12 years, improving and strengthening legal devices which are typical of the Western and European immigration model: entry visa restrictions; the strict connection between employment contract, entry visa and residence permit; the multiplication of detention centres; and forced deportations (see Perrin, 2005: 70; Perrin, 2009: 19).[5]

---

3   F. Infantino has conducted interesting empirical research at the Italian Embassy and Consulate in Rabat and Casablanca, addressing the issue of the delocalization of the Italian (and European) border into the countries of origin and transit of immigrants.

4   The readmission policy has gained an increasing importance at the EU level. See European Council Conclusions, 2006: "Managing migration requires dialogue and close cooperation with third countries. The European Council has called for such cooperation in the context of the comprehensive policy and, in a first stage, the focus of implementation has been on Africa". The latest European institutional developments (the five-year Stockholm program and the Lisbon treaty) confirmed such importance. Readmission agreements between European Union and some North African countries are still under negotiations, such as those with Morocco and Algeria; Italy signed return and readmission agreements with Libya, Algeria, Morocco, Tunisia and Egypt.

5   The following North African countries recently passed restrictive legislative reforms on immigration: Libya (2004 and 2005); Tunisia (2003–2004); Algeria, (2002–2003); and Morocco (2003). Sociological and legal analyses of immigration policies in North Africa can be found in CARIM – *Consortium for Applied Research on International Migration*.

The hallmark of these legislative acts and related administrative practices is the consolidation of the idea of national citizenship as a "border", as a line between an "inside" and an "outside". With the rise of national States in the Arab world, Western legal institutions, such as territorial and national States as well as nationality as the right to belong to a nation State, have already been transplanted to a different legal system. This transplant had caused an irreversible change in the political and legal conceptions of "belonging" in terms of being a "legitimate member" or an "alien", in the Islamic world. In fact, in the Islamic State the conception of belonging to the political community was defined by different connection criteria. On the one hand, there was the common religious "matrix" under which non-Muslims were regarded as aliens; on the other hand, there was the mosaic of affiliations to families, tribes, and Islamic schools of thought (Lewis, 1999; Chabel, 2002; Vercellin, 2002; Parolin, 2007; Perrin, 2011). The incorporation of the Western national citizenship model into the Arab world has not definitively neutralized multiple belongings but the contact with European political and economic necessities and legal rules has been producing major transformations of social and legal categories relating to the condition of aliens, migrants, nomads and stall holders. In this regard the contemporary case of the traditional trans-Saharan migration routes is significant (see Pliez, 2006, who studied the Libyan region of Fezzan). Transit economies have been developing over centuries along ancient routes and the repressive approach of European immigration policies has had a negative impact on the configuration of trans-Saharan mobility, which is now regarded as "trans-Mediterranean" migration.

The Italian Policy of Returning "Boat People" and the Violation of Fundamental Rights

The Italian measures of readmission and forcible return of irregular migrants in the Mediterranean has to be situated within the wider context of European policy to fight illegal immigration. In addition to the increasing cooperation between Europe and transit countries, the European Agency for the Management of Operational Cooperation at the External Borders of the Member States, called Frontex, was instituted in 2004. The aim of Frontex is to improve the integrated management of the external borders of EU member States by facilitating and rendering more effectively the application of European Union measures related to the management of external borders.

Due to its geographical position, Italy is one of the southern "gates" of Europe, along with Greece and Spain. Therefore the repressive measures adopted by the Italian government have a key role in fighting against irregular immigration in Europe as they benefit other European countries. Since 2009 the Italian policy has resulted in a dramatic increase in the return and readmission of undocumented migrants, especially through intense cooperation with Libya. From a human rights and ethical perspective, the intensification of this restrictive approach raises many serious questions, particularly concerning the respect of legality and of fundamental principles and liberties. In fact, it is worth noting that since 1988 more than 19,372 migrants have died in the Mediterranean trying to reach European coasts.[6] In the last two years (2011–2013) alone more than 3,500 migrants have died along the

---

6 See Fortress Europe, an online observatory on immigration and its victims in the Mediterranean. The observatory collects all the news related to boats sinking or being lost in the Mediterranean and it support journalistic inquiries on the matter: http://fortresseurope.blogspot.com/p/fortezza-europa.html.

maritime borders of Europe, but the real number could be much larger; in fact, no one really knows how many wrecks have actually occurred in the Mediterranean.

Compliance with the Obligation of Transparency and Respect of Legality in the Italian Legal System

The Italian policy of returning boat people in the Mediterranean raises problems with regard to transparency and the respect of legality because of the way that cooperation with Libya has been implemented over the years. The relationship between the two countries has had a long history, since the Italian colonial enterprise at the beginning of the twentieth century it has been filled with violence, injustice, opportunism, diplomacy and cooperation. The cooperation achieved in recent years is highly ambiguous since it is based on the exchange of assistance in the fight against irregular migration for huge economic support which is officially presented as restitution to Libya for the Italian colonial enterprise.

The cooperation between Italy and Libya on immigration matters began in 2000 through several agreements, signed by both centre-right-wing and centre-left-wing Italian governments without full disclosure of the terms and conditions. The behaviour of Italian authorities invited criticism since it demonstrated utter disregard for the requests of civil society and the role of the parliament. In 2007, a clearer and more detailed protocol "to deal with the phenomenon of illegal immigration" was signed and in 2008 Italy and Libya established the Treaty of Friendship, Partnership and Cooperation (Ronzitti, 2009). This treaty created a partnership between the two countries and made explicit reference to the respect of fundamental human rights and liberties. This important remark was intended to appease those who had been denouncing the gross injustices and human rights violations which were occurring in Libya with regard to the treatment of sub-Saharan immigrants and have been documented in detail in reports by several important organizations (see Human Rights Watch, 2009, 2010; FIDH, 2012; Amnesty International, 2013). The reference to the respect of fundamental rights was indeed limited since it consisted of the specification that "legislations" of both countries should have observed. The chapter on immigration was also broad and vague about the Libyan obligations; neither the treaty nor the following implementation protocol provided a legal basis for intercepting boat people in international waters and returning them to North African coasts (Tondini, 2010: 4). The criticism of legal scholars focused on the implementation protocol. In particular, the protocol was considered to violate the Italian Constitution, which obliges the government to ask for a preventive parliamentary intervention in order to ratify international agreements on political matters or that provide economic burdens.[7]

The 2008 treaty – which was ratified by the Italian parliament – was then "*de facto* suspended" before the 2011 military attack on Libya due to the troubles and abuses occurring in the African country.[8]

Since the fall of the Gaddafi regime in 2011 the situation of asylum seekers, refugees and irregular migrants in Libya has worsened considerably. Human rights and the respect of legality are increasingly at risk and violence, racism and xenophobia are on the rise across the country. Despite the institutional chaos and the open violations of human rights of migrants, the collaboration between Italy and Libya on migration issues has continued.

---

7   Art. 80 Ital. Cost. See T. Di Pasquale, 2010: 5.
8   Those were the exact words of the former Italian Ministry of Defense, Ignazio La Russa, see: Libia: La Russa, Trattato con Italia di fatto sospeso, *La Repubblica*, 26 February 2011.

After a first agreement with the National Transitional Council of Libya for cooperation in the fight against illegal immigration, including the return of irregular migrants (17 June 2011), the Ministers of Interior of Italy and Libya signed a verbal agreement which set out a number of additional areas of cooperation including border surveillance and voluntary return and repatriation (3 April 2012). Amnesty International expressed serious concern about the contents of the agreement, which have not been disclosed despite repeated requests to the Ministry of the Interior, and is convinced that the operations "against illegal immigration" have not been made in accordance with international standards on human rights (Amnesty International, 2012).

In October 2013 Italy launched "Mare Nostrum", a highly controversial operation, both military and humanitarian, with the aim of improving search and rescue operations and enhancing the protection of national borders. With the new operation, which includes amphibious ships, unmanned drones and helicopters with infrared equipment, Italy is attempting to deal with the waves of refugees and migrants arriving on its coasts and the risk of further tragic incidents like the capsizing of a boat carrying migrants on 3 October 2013, near Lampedusa.[9] In November 2013 two additional "technical agreements" between Italy and Libya were signed, with the aim of strengthening the bilateral cooperation on migration; the Italian Ministry of Defense, Mario Mauro, stated that "safe and stable borders are necessary for an appropriate management of migration flows and to protect the fundamental rights of migrants".[10] Many observers have expressed their concerns about the overall sense of the recent collaboration between the two countries; with the signing of the last technical agreements the true meaning of mission "Mare Nostrum", more military and less and less humanitarian, has been unveiled (Vassallo Paleologo, 2013).

The relations between Italy and Libya are part of a wider cooperation framework put in place by the EU, which is also mostly unknown to the general public. On 22 May 2013, the Council of the European Union initiated EUBAM Libya, a civilian mission under the Common Security and Defense Policy (CSDP), to support the Libyan authorities in improving and developing the security of the country's borders.

The Infringement of the Law of the Sea

A second question concerns the infringement of maritime law conventions,[11] with particular reference to the determination of competency on international waters between North Africa and Sicily and the obligations to assist persons in distress at sea and have them disembark at a "place of safety".

---

9 On 3 October 2013, a boat carrying migrants from Libya to Italy sank off Lampedusa, a Sicilian island representing the Italian (and European) outpost in the Mediterranean. It was reported that the boat had sailed from Misrata, Libya, but that many of the migrants were originally from Eritrea, Somalia and Ghana. More than 360 people died in the shipwreck, which can be considered one of the worst disasters to occur in the Mediterranean in recent years.

10 *Italy – Libya: Cooperation Agreements*, 29 November 2013, http://www.difesa.it/EN/Primo_Piano/Pagine/20131129_Italy%E2%80%93Libyacooperationagreements.aspx. In particular, two agreements were signed: a first one on the employment of Italian remotely piloted aircraft to support Libyan authorities in border control activities in southern Libya; a second one on training activities in favour of Libyan personnel.

11 1982, United Nations Convention on the Law of the Sea (UNCLOS); 1974, International Convention for the Safety of Life at Sea (SOLAS); 1979, International Convention on Maritime Search and Rescue (SAR); 1989, International Convention on Salvage.

With regard to the first aspect, the problems arise in relation to the Italian Revenue Police (*Guardia di Finanza*) intercepting and stopping boat people in international waters and returning them to Italian–Libyan patrol boats with the assistance of Frontex. One of problematic aspects of this is the violation of those maritime international rules, which qualify international waters between North Africa and Sicily as a SAR (*Search and Rescue*) zone of Malta. In this respect a dramatic event occurred on 16 April 2010. The Turkish cargo ship *Pinar* rescued 154 immigrants whose boat was at risk of sinking in the waters of the Sicily Channel and also found a young woman's body. The *Pinar* was prevented from reaching either a Maltese or an Italian port because neither country would accept responsibility for the people rescued due to a different interpretation of international law. Immigrants were left stranded for four days with insufficient food and water and forced to sleep on the deck of the ship. They were finally allowed to disembark in Italy on 20 April (Amnesty International, 2010).

The legal treatment of Sicilian fishermen, who rescue illegal immigrants in distress at sea while working on their fishing boats in the Mediterranean, represents a clear example of the extent to which a restrictive immigration policy is able to cause flagrant violations of international human rights law. On one hand, Italian law recognizes the crime of aiding illegal immigration, even if the same law dismisses such a crime in cases of "rescue and humanitarian assistance". Regardless, judges are charged with the establishment of all the relevant circumstances of the case and sometimes fishermen have been put on trial and convicted by courts. On the other hand, from the humanitarian side of maritime law, States should provide the "most appropriate assistance available" to people in distress at sea who are rescued by fishing boats.[12] Every shipmaster has the responsibility to render assistance to people in distress anywhere at sea without any discrimination and respecting human dignity. According to these conventions illegal immigrants have the right to be disembarked at a "place of safety", which is defined as the "next port of call" of the rescue ship and does not necessarily coincide with the nearest or the most convenient port of call. It is likely that, to an Italian boat, the nearest "place of safety" is an Italian port, where it can dock and where the right to asylum and fundamental rights of immigrants are (at least in theory) granted (Vassallo Paleologo, 2009).

The Violation of the Right to Asylum

A final question concerns the violation of the right to asylum and international protection of the refugee *status*. By intercepting and returning boat people Italian authorities infringe several international, European and national legal norms, which comprise the "multi-level system" of asylum. This system is based on different legal sources: Art. 3 of ECHR (European Convention on Human Rights), which prohibits torture and inhuman or degrading treatment or punishment and provides a sort of *de facto* right to asylum and principle of non-*refoulement*; the 1951 UN convention relating to the *status* of refugees; the EU asylum directives; Art. 10, par. 3 of the Italian Constitution, which provides for an autonomous constitutional right to asylum; and the Italian immigration law, which imposes substantial and procedural guarantees in the area of push-backs of undocumented immigrants. The main problem is that the Italian returning policy prevents boat people from applying for the recognition of asylum as well as refugee *status*. Individuals who risk sinking in the Sicily Channel are considered to be "illegal immigrants", or are charged with entering Europe in

---

12 SAR Convention, Annex, Ch. 2, Art. 2.1.9.

contravention of immigration law: a "pathology" to fight against through the appropriate repressive measures.

The Strasbourg-based European Court of Human Rights certainly has a key role in defending the rights of forcibly returned aliens, even if it has developed an ambivalent case law over the years.

Strasbourg judges first addressed the issue with regard to the collective expulsions of hundreds of illegal aliens from the Assistance Centre in Lampedusa. On that occasion the European Court did not get to the heart of the matter, which concerned the alleged violation of the already mentioned Art. 3, 23 and 24 of the ECHR, which relates to the right to defence and the prohibition of collective expulsions. On the contrary, the court restricted itself to consider procedural aspects, striking out some applications of the list since the defence counsel had lost contact with applicants, which is quite paradoxical if it is considered that the applicants had been forcibly returned to Libya. The court neither addressed the crucial aspect of the State's responsibility for the identification of aliens or for the exact knowledge of their destination at the moment of the expulsion.[13]

The court had further opportunity to approach the question with the *Hirsi* decision, which "stands out as a beacon for protecting the rights of migrants who attempt to cross the sea in search of a better life elsewhere only to be confronted with measures of interdiction" (Den Heijer, 2013).[14] The applicants, 11 Somali and 13 Eritrean nationals, were part of a group of about 200 individuals who left Libya in 2009 aboard three vessels with the aim of reaching the Italian coast. On 6 May 2009, when the vessels were within the Maltese SAR of responsibility, ships from the Italian Revenue Police and the Coastguard intercepted them; the occupants of the intercepted vessels were then transferred onto Italian military ships and returned to Tripoli. The court found the Italian government violated several norms of ECHR: Art. 3, with regard to the risk of ill treatment in Libya, as well as in the applicants' country of origin; Art. 4 of Protocol No. 4, since the transfer of the applicants to Libya had been carried out without any examination of each applicant's individual situation and the removal of the applicants had been of a collective nature; and Art. 13, as the applicants had been deprived of any remedy, which would have enabled them to lodge their complaints under Article 3 of the convention and Article 4 of Protocol No. 4 with a competent authority, and to obtain a thorough and rigorous assessment of their requests before the removal measure was enforced.

Europe between a Repressive Immigration Policy and the Protection of the Freedom of Movement: The Difficult Logic of Solidarity

The Schengen regime is based on the abolition of internal borders controls and the resulting strengthening of the "external frontier", so that national authorities of the external States have to carry out their controls, on behalf of all European countries, on people who wish to enter Europe. Border checks have to be carried out according to the Schengen Borders Code (Reg. CE n. 562/2006), the community code on the rules governing the movement of persons across borders. The EU country that is the first point of entry of a third-country national has to verify several conditions of entry since the alien, once in Europe, has the

---

13   ECHR, *Hussun and others v. Italy*, 19.01.2010.
14   ECHR, *Hirsi Jamaa and others v. Italy*, 23.02.2012.

right to move freely within the Schengen area for a period not exceeding three months.[15] Border guards have to respect human dignity and fundamental rights by not discriminating against individuals on grounds of gender, racial or ethnic origin, religion or belief, disability, age or sexual orientation. The hardening of the repressive approach in migration policy and the increasing selection of "desirable" migrants are likely to produce serious infringements of those rights and principles: formal criteria which are established in legal norms are often enforced by authorities in contravention of the non-discrimination principle insofar as they run along the "color line" and lead to racial profiling (Marmo and Smith, 2010: 223).[16]

The abolition of internal borders checks within the Schengen area means that internal borders may be crossed at any point without border checks on persons "irrespective of their nationality".[17] The establishment and further consolidation of the principle of free movement of persons has been accompanied by several exceptions and derogative clauses. European States can still exercise some "police powers" in relation to "checks within the territory",[18] but these operations cannot constitute systematic border checks nor have border control as their objective, only "spot-checks" are permitted (Faure Atger, 2008: 5). Internal border checks can be re-established by national authorities only "exceptionally", when there is a serious threat to public policy or internal security and for no more than 30 days (or for the foreseeable duration of the serious threat).[19]

The basic principles ruling free circulation within European Union have been challenged by events that occurred in North Africa in 2011. In that year there was a massive displacement of populations from several North-African countries, in particular from Libya, due to political turmoil and the overthrow of political regimes, the "Arab Spring" (Sakbani, 2011: 127). During the Libyan crisis, more than one million migrants and their families exited the country to escape the conflict, finding hospitality in neighbouring countries, primarily in Tunisia and Egypt. Only 25,000 of them, mainly from Tunisia, also managed to enter Europe irregularly, reaching the shores of Italy and Malta (Fargues and Fandrich, 2012: 5).

The Italian government initially handled the situation without taking emergency measures. North-African migrants were put together in the Assistance Centre of Lampedusa, which was normally used as a place of first aid and rescue, but instead became a "detention centre" where people were restrained until it became possible to deport them to their country of origin. This practice violated many international and constitutional norms such as *habeas*

---

15 Art. 5 Schengen Borders Code. For stays not exceeding three months the entry conditions for third-country nationals are: to have a valid travel document; to have a valid visa; to justify the purpose and conditions of the intended stay and to have "sufficient means of subsistence"; not to be subject to an alert in the Schengen Information System SIS; and not to be considered a "threat to public policy, internal security, public health or the international relations of any of the member states".

16 The authors studied the practice of "virginity testing", performed by British governments on women who sought to legally enter Britain from the Indian sub-continent in the seventies. The test consisted of a gynaecological examination, which was made at the airport before the entry, or in the British embassies in the country of origin of the woman; the purpose of the test was to prevent illegal entry of fake fiancées and wives of immigrants already residing in the UK.

17 Art. 20 Schengen Borders Code, Reg. (EC) n. 562/2006.

18 Art. 21 Schengen Borders Code, Reg. (EC) n. 562/2006.

19 Art. 23 Schengen Borders Code, Reg. (EC) n. 562/2006. In the case of "foreseeable events" the national country involved should immediately inform the other member States and the European Commission, guaranteeing transparency and publicity. In those cases where considerations of public policy or internal security call for "urgent action" national States may exceptionally and immediately reintroduce border control at internal borders.

corpus and right of defence; procedural and substantive limitations to the detentions of illegal immigrants in the centres; European common standards and procedures for returning illegal immigrants; prohibition of collective *refoulements* and deportations; and prohibition of deportation of unaccompanied minors (Vassallo Paleologo, 2011). During an initial phase, Italy did not enforce the national law on emergency protection for humanitarian reasons, nor ask the European Union to apply the Directive 2001/55/EC on temporary protection; it was only requested that the EU-assisted Italian institutions repatriate and deport illegal immigrants (ASGI, 2011). This approach can be explained by considering that the former Italian Ministry of Interior, Roberto Maroni, is one of the major exponents of the *Lega Nord* (Northern League), a right-wing and xenophobic party expressing an anti-immigration ideology. The Minister was indeed in an uneasy position as he had to manage the delicate situation of thousands of migrants fleeing from violence or political uncertainty and entering Europe without documents, but he did not want to displease his constituency (see Cento Bull, 2010, on the ambiguous *Lega Nord*'s policy about immigration).

The situation was finally faced in April of 2011 and the measures adopted by the Italian government gave rise to a dispute between Italy and other EU countries, clearly illustrating the difficulty for the European Union to follow a common immigration strategy other than a repressive one. In fact, Italy decided to grant temporary, six-month, residence permits to the thousands of North-African migrants who had arrived through the Mediterranean.[20] Some European States (in particular, France) did not welcome Italian measures, since they contested the unilateral approach used by Italy to deal with a situation that was likely to affect the entire European Union. The problem appeared to be the absence of internal borders within the Schengen area: the freedom of circulation, which is one of the fundamental principles of the European Union, had become a contested issue with regard to the mobility of the "others". According to European law North-African migrants holding the Italian six-month residence permits were allowed to move to France, as well as to the other Schengen States, and stay for a period not exceeding three months. During this three-month period national authorities were only allowed to check whether immigrants held a valid travel document and had a minimum amount of money per day. However, European States had no intention to welcome thousands of people who were viewed to be "simply" irregular economic immigrants and accused Italy of undermining the mutual trust on which the Schengen agreement is based on.[21] This criticism appeared to be well-founded according to some experts, who noted that "beyond the façade of the residence permits for humanitarian protection, the primary goal pursued by the Italian authorities has been to promote the mobility of those TCNs holding the permits" (Carrera, Guild, Merlino, Parkin, 2010: 10). On the one hand, both European and national law foresaw the possibility of issuing temporary permits for humanitarian reasons to aliens who do not comply with the

---

20 DPCM 5 April 2011. On the same day the Italian government also signed a bilateral agreement with the Tunisian authorities. Even if the precise content of the agreement was not publicly available it seemed to allow for the repatriation of those migrants from Tunisia who had landed on Italian shores. Two days later a second decree was issued declaring in rather contradictory terms a "state of humanitarian emergency in the territory of North Africa in order to effectively contrast the exceptional flow of migrants in the Italian territory" (DPCM 7 April 2011).

21 During a press briefing in Luxembourg, at the end of a long debate over Mediterranean migration, the German Ministry of Interior, Hans-Peter Friedrich, said that: "What Italy is doing is using a national emergency law for temporary protection in order to politicise the whole Tunisian immigration issue so that everyone in the EU is affected by it. They've succeeded in doing that, but now we expect that they stick to the rules" (V. Pop, 2011).

conditions for legal entry but, on the other hand, the Italian government's measures were likely to violate the principle of sincere and loyal cooperation between European States.

In response to Italian measures France reintroduced internal border checks at the French–Italian border. French authorities pushed back into Italy hundreds of immigrants holding Italian temporary residence permits and blocked NGO representatives from crossing the French–Italian border (Hooper and Traynor, 2011). The national political context has also played a key role in France, since the "securitarian" discourse on immigration has hardened in recent years, and the former French government finally adopted a new restrictive immigration law that makes it easier to detain illegal immigrants.[22] The French reintroduction of internal border checks was an interesting case study about the respect of European law and the freedom of circulation as a fundamental liberty in Europe.[23] A worrying aspect of the measures adopted by French authorities at the French–Italian border was the tension with the non-discrimination principle and other fundamental rights protected by European and national law (CIMADE, 2011). In fact, since North-African citizens coming from Italy were the specific targets of the border checks, there was a danger that the behaviour of national officers turned out to be racial and ethnic profiling, which is prohibited by the European anti-discrimination law.

Dramatic events that occurred in recent times have demonstrated that Europe (and, in particular, the EU Council and Commission) continues to express a "double" policy, attempting to combine both the protection of human rights (and, *in primis*, the right to asylum) and the repression of irregular migration by sea.

The logic of solidarity is certainly the most difficult to implement. With an important resolution issued shortly after the tragic Lampedusa shipwreck in October 2013, the EU Parliament formally declared that "Lampedusa should be a turning point for Europe and that the only way of preventing another tragedy is to adopt a coordinated approach based on solidarity and responsibility, with the support of common instruments". In particular, the parliament identified "the relocation of beneficiaries of international protection and asylum seekers" as "one of the most concrete forms of solidarity and responsibility-sharing" (European Parliament, 2013).[24]

The development of a common European strategy on migration has, so far, occurred as a sign of restriction, following the logic of surveillance. The establishment of EUROSUR, which came into force on 2 December 2013, is a clear example of this trend. EUROSUR is thought of as a pan-European border surveillance system aimed at reducing the number of irregular migrants entering the EU undetected as well as the number of deaths of irregular migrants by saving more lives at sea, and, at increasing the internal security of the EU as a whole by contributing to the prevention of cross-border crime. The initiative has been

---

22 The new immigration law is the Law n. 2011–672.

23 In particular, the major legal problems concerned the compliance with the condition of "serious threat to public policy and internal security", which is required by the Schengen Borders Code to justify the reintroduction of internal border checks; the fundamental principle of proportionality, which asks for national measures to be adequate, suitable and necessary; procedural requirements with regard to the obligation to notify the other European States and the European Commission about reasons, scope, date, duration and other details of the border checks (Carrera, Guild, Merlino, Parkin, *A Race against Solidarity*, cit., 11).

24 In this context, the EU Parliament has stressed the importance of projects such as the Pilot Project for Intra-EU Relocation from Malta (EUREMA) and the extension thereof, under which beneficiaries of international protection have been relocated from Malta to other member States, and has advocated developing more initiatives of this kind.

driven by complex motivations and objectives, both securitarian and humanitarian, "with an overarching belief in surveillance technologies as the ultimate way to solve these issues" (Gabrielsen Jumbert, 2012: 35). By externalizing the effective border of the EU further out, this new surveillance system will contribute to raising tensions between a security approach to migration and the human rights of undocumented migrants.

Conclusion

Far from having disappeared due to the enforcement of human rights and the institution of a free circulation area in Europe, borders seem to have gained renewed importance in the fight against trans-Mediterranean migrations. Legal scholars are expected to observe and monitor the social and legal processes brought about by human mobility in the Mediterranean area from different perspectives.

A first approach concerns the study of borders and frontiers as social and legal constructs, whose different patterns play a key role in the transformation of European immigration policies. In fact, the current features of European borders delineate Europe as a continent that appears to be a "dam" filtrating useful immigrants, rather than an inaccessible "fortress" (Mezzadra, 2005: 11).

A second issue addressed by trans-Mediterranean migration flows is represented by the powerlessness of the European Union as it faces global challenges like international migrations and the displacement of asylum seekers. From this perspective immigration and border policies serve as tools for the analysis and interpretation of the very nature of the European Union as a political subject. Some important European institutions have expressly stressed the importance of European solidarity and better sharing of responsibility between European countries but the recent tragedies in the Mediterranean demonstrate the resistance to abandoning a national strategy in favour of a fundamental rights-based common culture.

A third perspective is connected to the infringement of fundamental rights and principles such as the right to asylum, the right of defence, the prohibition of collective expulsions and inhuman or degrading treatment and the duty to render assistance to individuals in distress at sea. The strengthening of European external border controls is justified as a way to ensure the respect of legality but it is likely to be a paradoxical claim. In fact, by violating international, European and constitutional law, repressive norms and administrative measures infringe a "higher law" which is super-ordinated and is expected to be the "the law of the weakest" (Ferrajoli, 2011: 339).

References

Amnesty International. 2010a. Libya – Report 2010. Human Rights in Socialist People's Libyan Arab Jamahiriya, http://www.amnesty.org/en/library/asset/MDE19/007/2010/en/65e2d9ca-3b76-4ea8-968f-5d76e1591b9c/mde190072010en.pdf (accessed on 15/05/13).

Amnesty International. 2010b. Human Rights in Republic of Malta, Report 2010, http://www.amnesty.org/en/region/malta/report-2010 (accessed on 15/05/13).

ASGI. 2011. Istituire la protezione temporanea è la sola via razionale per governare oggi l'esodo dalla Tunisia, 31 March, www.asgi.it (accessed on 15/11/12).

Bigo, D. and Guild. E. (eds). 2005a. *Controlling Frontiers. Free Movement Into and Within Europe*. Aldershot: Ashgate.

Bigo, D. and Guild, E. 2005b. Policing at a Distance: Schengen Visa Policies, in Bigo, D. and Guild, E. (eds), *Controlling Frontiers. Free Movement Into and Within Europe*. Aldershot: Ashgate.

Bigo, D. and E. Guild. 2010. The Transformation of European Border Controls, in Ryan, B. and Mitsilegas, V. (eds), *Extraterritorial Immigration Control. Legal Challenges*. Leiden: Brill.

Carrera, S., Guild, E., Merlino, M. and Parkin, J. 2010. "A Race against Solidarity. The Schengen Regime and the Franco-Italian Affair". CEPS Paper.

Cento Bull, A. 2010. Addressing Contradictory Needs. The Lega Nord and Italian Immigration Policy. *Patterns of Prejudice* (5).

Chabel, M. 2002. *Le sujet en islam*. Paris: Seuil.

CIMADE. 2011. *Appel Urgence pour la solidarité*, 2 Mai 2011, www.cimade.org.

Cuttitta, P. 2006a. Points and Lines. A Topography of Borders in the Global Space. *Ephemera* (1).

Cuttitta, P. 2006b. I confini d'Europa a Sud del Mediterraneo. Strumenti e incentivi per l'esternalizzazione dei controlli, in Cuttitta, P. and Vassallo Paleologo, F. (eds), *Migrazioni, Frontiere, Diritti*. Napoli: ESI.

Cuttitta, P. 2007a. Le monde-frontière. Le contrôle de l'immigration dans l'espace globalisé. *Cultures & Conflits* (68).

Cuttitta, P. 2007b. *Segnali di confine. Il controllo dell'immigrazione nel mondo frontiera*. Milano: Mimesis.

Cuttitta, P. 2009. Il controllo dell'immigrazione nel mondo frontier. *Ragion Pratica* (33).

Di Pasquale, T. 2010. La protezione dello straniero e il rimpatrio di migranti intercettati in alto mare tra ordinamento europeo ed ordinamento interno. *Federalismi.it* (15).

European Commission. 2005. Technical Mission to Libya on Illegal Immigration 27 Nov–6 Dec 2004. Report, 7753/05.

European Commission. 2011. *Communication from the Commission to the European Parliament, the Council, the Economic and Social Committee and the Committee of the Regions on Migration*, COM(2011) 248 final.

European Council. 2006. *A Comprehensive European Migration Policy*, MEMO/07/188.

Faure Atger, A. 2008. The Abolition of Internal Border Checks in an Enlarged Schengen Area. Freedom of Movement or a Web of Scattered Security Checks? *Challenge Liberty Security*. Paper no. 8.

Ferrajoli, L. 2011. Diritti fondamentali. Un dibattito teorico, in Vitale, E. and Roma-Bari, L. 2011. *Frattini Says Migrant Repatriation Agreement to be Signed Tomorrow with Libyan National Transitional Council*, 16 June, migrantsatsea.wordpress.com (accessed on 15/11/12).

Hooper, J. and Traynor, I. 2011. Sarkozy and Berlusconi to Call for Return of Border Controls in Europe. *The Guardian*, 25 April.

Human Rights Watch. 2006. Stemming the Flow: Abuses Against Migrants, Asylum Seekers and Refugees, http://www.hrw.org/reports/2006/libya0906/libya0906webwcover.pdf (accessed on 15/05/13).

Human Rights Watch. 2009. Pushed Back, Pushed Around. Italy's Forced Return of Boat Migrants and Asylum Seekers, Libya's Mistreatment of Migrants and Asylum Seekers,

http://www.hrw.org/sites/default/files/reports/italy0909webwcover_0.pdf (accessed on 15/05/13).
Human Rights Watch. 2010. Rights on the Line. Human Rights Watch Work on Abuses Against Migrants in 2010, http://www.hrw.org/sites/default/files/reports/wrd1210web wcover.pdf (accessed on 15/05/13).
Infantino, F. 2010. La frontière au guichet. Politiques et pratiques des visas Schengen à l'Ambassade et au Consulat d'Italie au Maroc. *Champ Pénal* (7).
Lewis, B. 1999. *The Multiple Identities of the Middle East*. New York: Schocken Books.
Libia: La Russa, Trattato con Italia di fatto sopseso. *La Repubblica*, 26 February 2011.
Lombardi, G. 1985. Spazio e frontiera tra eguaglianza e privilegio: problemi costituzionali tra storia e diritto, in *Scritti in onore di Vezio Crisafulli*, II, CEDAM, Padova.
Maçzak, A. 1995. Lo Stato come protagonista e come impresa: tecniche, strumenti, linguaggio, in M. Aymard (ed.), *Storia d'Europa*, vol. 4, *L'età moderna. Sec. XVI–XVIII*. Torino: Einaudi.
Marmo, M. and Smith, E.B. 2010. Is There a Desirable Migrant? The Case of "Virginity Testing". *Alternative Law Journal* (4).
Mezzadra, S. 2005. Confini, migrazioni, cittadinanza, in Salvatici, S. (ed.), *Confini. Costruzioni, attraversamenti, rappresentazioni*. Bolzano: Rubbettino.
Parolin, G.P. 2007. *Dimensioni dell'appartenenza e cittadinanza nel mondo arabo*. Napoli: Jovene.
Perrin, D. 2005. Le Maghreb sous influence: le nouveau cadre juridique des migrations transsahariennes. *Maghreb-Machrek* (185).
Perrin, D. 2009. Sémantique et faux-semblants juridiques de la problématique migratoire au Maghreb. *Migr. Soc.*, 123–124.
Pliez, O. 2006. La frontiera tra la Libia e il Sahel, Uno spazio migratorio rimesso in discussione, in Cuttitta, P. and Vassallo Paleologo, F. (eds), *Migrazioni, Frontiere, Diritti*. Napoli: ESI.
Pop, V. 2011. Italian minister questions value of EU membership, 11 April 2011, euobserver. com (accessed on 15/11/11).
Rigo, E. 2007. *Europa di confine. Trasformazioni della cittadinanza nell'Europa allargata*. Roma: Meltemi.
Ronzitti, N. 2009. "The Treaty on Friendship, Partnership and Cooperation between Italy and Libya: New Prospects for Cooperation in the Mediterranean?" Paper presented at the Mediterranean Strategy Group Conference "Is regional cooperation in Maghreb possible? Implications for the Region and External Actors", in cooperation with German Marshall Fundo of the United States, Genoa, 11–12 May, IAI 909.
Sakbani, S. 2011. The Revolutions of the Arab Spring: Are Democracy, Development and Modernity at the Gates? *Contemporary Arab Affairs* (2).
Tilly, C. 1993. *Le rivoluzioni europee. 1492–1992*, Coll. *Fare l'Europa*, Laterza, in Roma-Bari (ed.), *European Revolutions, 1492–1992*. Oxford: Blackwell Publishers.
Tondini, M. 2010. *Fishers of Men? The Interception of Migrants in the Mediterranean Sea and Their Forced Return to Libya*, INEX paper, http://www.inexproject.eu/index.php?option=com_docman&task=doc_download&gid=51&&Itemid=72 (accessed on 30/12/12).
Torpey, J. 2000. *The Invention of the Passport. Surveillance, Citizenship and the State*. Cambridge: Cambridge University Press.

Vassallo Paleologo, F. 2009. *La strage. Omissione di soccorso come pena di morte per i migranti nel Canale di Sicilia*, 21 August 2009, www.globalproject.info (accessed on 30/12/12).

Vassallo Paleologo, F. 2011. Dall'emergenza umanitaria allo stato d'eccezione, 4 May 2011, www.asgi.it (accessed 29/12/12).

Vercellin G. 2002. *Instituzioni del mondo musulmano*, Torino, Einaudi.

Chapter 2
The Canary Islands' "Maritime Wall": Migration Pressure, Security Measures and Economic Crisis in the Mid-Atlantic

Josefina Domínguez-Mujica, Ramón Díaz-Hernández and Juan Parreno-Castellano

Global capitalism, the technological revolution and the security crisis make up the context within which the Canary Islands have reinforced their geostrategic position as Europe's southern border. As part of the Kingdom of Spain, they have historically been linked to the European continent, and these ties have been strengthened by the islands' specialization in tourism and their statute as an ultraperipheric and insular region of the European Union. Their income is thus typical of highly developed countries, which contrasts sharply with their proximity to the shores of Africa, where per capita income is four times lower than in Spain – a circumstance that strongly favours an intense irregular immigration flow by sea. Both Spain and the European Union have undertaken political and military measures to try and stop a flow that acquired great intensity towards the middle of the first decade of the twenty-first century, when many migrants lost their lives at sea while trying to pursue their dream of reaching European Union territory. The fall in immigration pressure on European Union borders that has taken place from 2008 until 2010, has been interpreted as a success of EU policies based on the implementation of new security measures and the signing of certain agreements with African migration sender and transit countries.

Without underestimating the importance of these measures, in this chapter we explain our view that the drop in irregular migration flows between Africa and Europe would not have reached the same extent if we had not found ourselves immersed in a phase of deep economic crisis, especially in Spain, where this situation stands in stark contrast to the marked low-productivity growth that favoured economic activity and immigration until 2007. It must not be forgotten, consequently, that borders are porous to the aspirations and dreams of human beings who wish to improve their circumstances, and that this is dependent on their perception of economic situations and opportunities. This forces us to take into account economic cycles and transnational contact and information networks, which regulate human mobility beyond security policies and border controls. In this sense the Canary Islands have become a privileged vantage point from which to analyse mobility within those socioeconomically fractured spaces which delimit wealth and poverty, as well as to study the political and military policies developed by the European Union to put the brakes on irregular immigration, and to examine the strategies for survival adopted by citizens from African countries hoping to improve their living conditions, even if it involves risking their lives or that of their children.

Conceptual Framework

The Literature on Migration and Border Control

Human mobility is one of the phenomena that have generated the most interest among social researchers throughout history. Examining the bibliographical production of the first few years of the twenty-first century will bring to light the fact that there is not only a vast number of publications whose subject is migration, but that there is also a wealth of conceptual approaches underpinning multiple analyses. However, this wide-ranging conceptual kaleidoscope narrows down severely when the object of study deals with irregular migration in border regions, and even more so when the migration pressure studied is not related to the US–Mexican border.

An example of the first theoretic focus corresponds to the special number of *Geopolitics* entitled: "Borderline Contradictions: Neoliberalism, Unauthorised Migration, and Intensifying Immigration Policing" (Varsanyi and Nevins, 2007). As far as unauthorized immigration in Europe is concerned, many of the works published relate migration to the issues of security, sovereignty and mobility within the Union. As Martín-Pérez (2010) has stated, the historic process of incorporating immigration-related issues into the sphere of European Union policies has proven to be extremely complex, since it has brought about a confrontation between the individual member states' reluctance to lose control over a question rooted in the very concept of national sovereignty on the one hand, and, on the other, the need to cope with international challenges, such as migratory pressure and security in a global world.

As a result, in the most recent works, the entity of the Union's borders and the new process of the externalization of borders appear inextricably linked to sovereignty and human mobility within the context of neoliberalism. Nowadays "it is possible to recognize a contradictory process which encourages economic flows across international borders, while at the same time maintaining nationalistic political-geographic closure across those same borders via expanding boundary enforcement and militarization" (Carter and Merrill, 2007). Thus, for instance, "the interstate system and sovereignty have been restructured in such a way that it has essentially erased borders. Debordering is a selective process and it is often paralleled by a rebordering, or border creation at new locations to guard against 'undesirable' elements" (Kimball, 2007). Likewise, Clochard and Duyperon (2007) have stated that "it is becoming difficult to know where the borders of the European Union are located". Hollifield, 2004; Lavenex, 2006; Rijpma and Cremona, 2007; van Houtum and Pijpers, 2007; Kaufmann, 2007; Ferrer-Gallardo, 2008; Dover, 2008; Rohrmoser, 2008; Illamola, 2008; and Casey, 2010, have authored some of the research undertaken on this process of the restructuring of European borders. In all of these works migration is analysed as an integral component of the actions and policies that, while favouring the free circulation of people between member states (early Schengen Agreement, 1985), have also contributed to the construction of "fortress Europe". Consequently, according to them all, the blurring of internal borders has been accompanied by the reinforcement of the Union's external borders, as the management of migration has been deferred to non-Union countries. This has meant, in the case of southern Europe, that the containment of African emigration has been left in the hands of Libya, Morocco, Mauritania and Senegal, among other countries.

These same premises coincide with the analyses performed by other researchers from a juridical perspective, some of them somewhat descriptive in character, as in the cases of Fernández Sánchez, 2006, or Triandafyllidou, 2010, and others more critical in their approach, as those who highlight the need to ensure that the process of securitization of the Union's external borders is not undertaken at the expense of the rule of law or human rights (especially as far as refugees, asylum seekers and minors are concerned). In fact, the predicated existence of new "dangers" – international terrorism and organized crime – is the perfect alibi to justify the restrictive legislation and measures brought about by the expansion of a security-focused culture of military origin. As stated by Kaufmann (2007), "in such a mode, governmental security measures operate in a manner analogous to the networks of terrorism, of organised crime and human trafficking – the very networks it pretends or purports to protect again". For this reason, the works of Soddu, 2006; Baldwin-Edwards, 2006; Fernández, Manvella, Rijpma and Cremona, 2007; Spijkerboer, 2007; Gebrewold, 2008; and Ceriani, 2009, make, according to Adepoju, van Noorloos and Zoomers "a critical assessment of the way the EU – and individual countries such as Spain, France and Italy – have played active roles in reshaping old and developing new strategies for keeping migration under control" (2010).

The process of externalizing the EU borders has also led to a shift in the focus of research that has been gaining in importance over the last few years, as a result of the European Union signing border control agreements with third countries and as a consequence of the bilateral agreements between some member states and third countries. Transit migrations have become a new object of interest, in as much as they are an issue of great importance within the process of the externalization of borders, and they have been studied, among others, by van Moppes, 2006; Collyer, 2006; Schapendonk and van Moppes, 2007; Sadiqi, 2007; Kimball, 2007; Schapendonk, 2008 etc.; in all the cases mentioned Morocco has been the main area of study.

The focus on security, the externalization of borders and respect for human rights, as far as non-authorized migration is concerned, has tended to obscure the relationship that has developed between economic factors, transnational processes and irregular human mobility in border regions. The number of researchers who have shown an interest in these issues is small (Arango and Martin, 2005; Sandell, 2005; Lacomba and Boni, 2008; Gielis, 2009; de Haas, 2010; etc.), despite the fact that in December 2005 the European Council adopted the *Global Approach to Migration* road map and that the European Union has organized a number of conferences (Rabat, 2006 and Tripoli, 2006) with the specific aim of linking migration and development. These guidelines, however, have not been economically supported and that might explain why scientific debate has been largely lacking as regards the consequences of partnerships and other initiatives that establish a relationship between migration, economic development and the job market. Some of the few authors who have tackled this issue are the following: Martin, Martin and Cross, 2007; Bosch and Haddad, 2007; Lavenex and Kunz, 2008; Chou, 2009; Chou and Gibert, 2010; and Serrano, 2010.

The Study of Unauthorized Migration in Europe's Southern Maritime Borders

There are numerous documents available on the different actions of control and vigilance undertaken to prevent unauthorized immigration across the European Union's southern borders, especially in the case of Spain. The Spanish Ministry of the Interior, in particular, has released a large number of reports and working papers describing these actions and measures in detail. From a strategic and geopolitical perspective, the articles published by the Real Instituto Elcano are worth highlighting; it is a Spanish private foundation that serves as a forum for analysis and discussion of international relations and it has recently focused its interest on the role Spain is playing as Europe's southernmost border. Arteaga, 2007; Alvear, 2008; Díaz and Abad, 2008; Vélez, 2008; Ilies, 2009; García, 2010; and Ripjma, 2010, have published works on this issue.

As far as the Canary Islands are concerned, as the flow of irregular immigration by sea gained in intensity, a number of scientific papers were published that went beyond a mere description of events or a listing of control mechanisms. Nevertheless, the attention paid by social researchers to these matters has been hardly comparable to the attention paid to them by the media and human rights organizations. Thus, some of the better known works have been authored by journalists, such as Naranjo, 2006. As Jorgen Carling stated in 2007: "while there are numerous studies about the dynamics of migration and border control on the US–Mexican border, academic research on irregular migration in southern Europe has by and large concentrated on the situation of undocumented residents after arrival, and not on the unauthorized itself. The European media, by contrast, report on unauthorized migration from Africa almost daily, and measures to contain this flow stand very high on the European policy agenda" (Carling, 2007: 316).

Among the most representative scientific papers we have those by the already cited Carling (2007a, 2007b) and Ferrer-Gallardo (2008),[1] as well as those by Domínguez, Díaz and Parreño, 2001; Parkes, 2006; Carrera, 2007a, 2007b; Godenau and Zapata, 2008; and Fargues, 2009. The works authored by Carling, Godenau and Zapata and Fargues are especially complete, providing a detailed and lengthy analysis of the said unauthorized immigration, the changes it has undergone (routes, types of boats, different strategies of human smuggling), the sequence of arrivals and the fatalities associated to them, as well as an assessment of the measures of control adopted and a critical examination of the management itself of unauthorized flows. However, the analysis of these processes from a short term perspective has meant that insufficient attention has been paid to their economic context, which is an important dimension that we feel contributes to a greater understanding of the complexities of this kind of migration flows.

Migrations and Security in a Globalized World

The Construction of the European Fortress

In 1897 Friedrich Ratzel described a border as "the skin of the living state",[2] a poetic definition that contrasts with the less literary but more widespread notion of the border as a fixed line that delimits the territory over which a state is sovereign. Sovereignty is a key concept in international law, for it refers to the legitimacy of a state to exercise its power within its territory. However, international coexistence and the strategies of capitalist development have increasingly led towards the configuration of regional integration processes that go beyond the traditional concept of the sovereign state, with the result that borders have become more flexible. The firm boundaries that followed the historical consolidation of nation states have gradually succumbed to a trend towards greater accessibility, which facilitates the sharing of the benefits of the free circulation of goods, capital and services, while preserving control over the labour market and security.

---

  1 The latter touches on the Canary Islands migration pressure only in passing, as the main focus of his work lies in the cities of Ceuta and Melilla.
  2 "Die Haut des lebendigen Zustand".

This process, which has already taken place at a regional level, is also beginning to expand worldwide, and globalization is giving rise to a growing opening of borders or, at least, to their greater permeability.

On the other hand, the use of technological developments in the management of borders has led to remarkable changes. The preoccupation with security against terrorism, fanaticism, arm and drug smuggling, transborder crime and unauthorized immigration has resulted in the creation of standardized databases, information networks and, especially, in the incorporation of new technologies (biometrics, sensitive radars, crewless aeroplanes, satellite surveillance systems, etc.) that have led to the strengthening of "technological borders". As a consequence, "the use of these technologies, in combination with the widespread reliance on risk management, contributes to the re-imagination of borders and the bodies that cross them" (Muller, 2011).

As has been said, in the case of Europe, border management forms part of the European Union's policies against illegal immigration and it ranks among its highest political priorities, involving a range of costly economic, commercial and diplomatic measures. The Schengen Agreement, in 1985, laid the foundations of the current EU border control system. Later, in 2002, a border policy plan of action was approved that led to the creation of Frontex in 2004, the European Agency for the Management of Operational Cooperation at the External Borders of the Member States of the European Union, whose function was further regulated in 2007. Frontex coordinates operational cooperation between Member States in the field of management of external borders; assists Member States in the training of national border guards, including the establishment of common training standards; carries out risk analyses; follows up the development of research relevant for the control and surveillance of external borders; assists Member States in circumstances requiring increased technical and operational assistance at external borders; and provides Member States with the necessary support in organizing joint return operations.

These functions of Frontex highlight the complexities of managing immigration not only from an operational point of view, but also from the perspective of diplomatic relations, since borders constitute a pivot of complex bilateral relations at different levels: between Spain and Morocco, between southern Europe and the Maghreb, and between the European Union and Africa. In this sense, "migration concerns are central to the agenda of all these relationships, and are invariably entangled with other issues" (Carling, 2007). In fact, the diplomatic effort undertaken by the European Union has resulted in important changes in terms of material resources and public services in the African countries with whom joint border vigilance agreements have been signed.

Shortly after the greatest process of regularization of immigrants ever undertaken in Spain (2005) had been brought to completion, the impact on public opinion of the assaults on the border fences of Ceuta and Melilla in September and October 2005, and their tragic consequences, brought about a change in the Spanish government's migration policies. Another contributing factor was the humanitarian alarm raised on account of what came to be known as the "boat crisis", when in summer and autumn 2006 many fishing boats arrived in the Canary Islands carrying youths and children from coastal countries south of the Sahara (Mauritania, Senegal, Gambia ...) (Figure 2.1).

The crossing was long and dangerous and many boats sunk. The social alarm generated by the arrival of a large number of immigrants (only in 2006, 31,678 immigrants arrived this way in the Canary Islands) and the difficulties to cope with them (police resources and sea rescue and humanitarian assistance services were overwhelmed) drove the government to

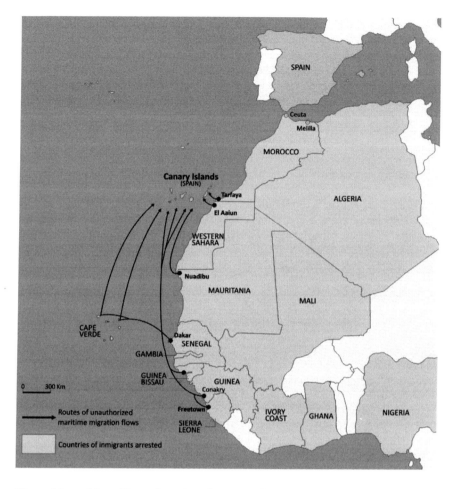

Figure 2.1   Map of irregular migration routes from Africa to the Canary Islands (2006)

Source: Ministry of the Interior (Spain): www.mir.es/DGRIS/Balance/Balance_2008/pdf/bal_lucha_inmigración_ilegal_2008.pdf (accessed 27/12/2010), adapted by the authors.

reinforce border controls and redouble its efforts to reach agreements with sender countries in order to prevent the crossings and facilitate repatriations (Table 2.1).

The Canary Islands: Policing Europe's Ultraperipheral Regions

Maritime border control involves certain difficulties that do not affect land borders, such as patrolling and guarding vast extensions, as well as further obligations derived from international legislation on maritime search and rescue (Godenau and Zapata Hernández, 2008). Thus, when the arrival of precarious crafts is detected, with undocumented people in appalling conditions (wounded or injured, suffering from hypothermia or

Table 2.1 Landmarks in the management of unauthorized migration flows in the EU and in Spain (1985–2010)

Date	European Union — Treaties/Summits/Agreements	European Union — Communications/Conferences/Others	Spain and Other Countries
1985 (June)	The Schengen (Germany) agreements, abolishing internal controls and creating a joint external border among France, Germany, Belgium, the Netherlands and Luxembourg.		
1997 (October)	The Treaty of Amsterdam (The Netherlands) established an area "freedom, security and justice", which brought immigration policy under EU jurisdiction.		Bilateral agreement with Morocco to facilitate the readmission of Moroccan nationals as well as transit migrants.
1999 (September)			
1999 (October)	In the Tampere (Finland) Summit, the European Council agreed to set up a Common European Asylum system and partnerships with countries of origin as proposed by Ministers of Justice and Home Affairs.		
2002 (June)	In Seville (Spain) the European Council established that all EU agreements with non-EU states are to: "include a clause on joint management of migration flows and on compulsory readmission in the event of illegal immigration".		
2002 (August)			Development of SIVE (System of Integrated External Surveillance). A prototype station is set up in Algeciras.
2002 (December)		Communication from the Commission to the Council on Integrating migration issues in the European Union's relations with third countries.	

Date	European Union — Treaties/Summits/Agreements	European Union — Communications/Conferences/Others	Spain and Other Countries
2003 (June)			First revision of the Cotonou Agreements between African, Caribbean and Pacific countries (ACP) and EU on the readmission clause (Art. 13).
2003 (November)			Passage of a Law in Morocco (Loi, 02/03) regulating the entry and stay of foreign national in the Kingdom of Morocco and dealing with irregular immigration.
2003 (December)			Memorandum signed with Morocco regarding the issue of unaccompanied children (readmission).
2003 (December)			The first SIVE radar station is set up in the Canary Islands (Fuerteventura).
2004 (October)		(EC) 2007/2004 Frontex regulation. Creation of the Agency for the Management of Operational Cooperation at the External Borders.	
2005 (January)		Communication from the Commission to the Council and the European Parliament: The Hague Programme: The Partnership for European renewal in the field of Freedom, Security and Justice.	
2005 (May)			"Guanarteme" Maritime Joint Operations in the Canary I.
2005 (December)		The European Council adopted the Global Approach to Migration: Priority actions focusing on Africa and the Mediterranean.	

Date	European Union - Treaties/Summits/Agreements	European Union - Communications/Conferences/Others	Spain and Other Countries
2005 (December)			Contract signed with AENEAS in order to carry out the SEAHORSE Programme (2006) a plan of cooperation with Morocco, Mauritania, Cape Verde and Senegal for the prevention of illegal maritime migration.
2006 (January)		Communication from the Commission to the Council and the European Parliament State of the AENEAS thematic programme for the cooperation with third countries in the areas of migration and asylum.	
2006 (March)		Council Regulation establishing a Community Code on the rules governing the movement of persons across borders (Schengen Borders Code).	
2006 (April)			Beginning of the "Atlantis" programme of cooperation with Mauritania, aimed at fighting irregular immigration by means of a joint maritime patrol by Spain's Civil Guard and Mauritania's Gendarmerie.
2006 (May and July)		Euro–African conference on Migration and Development in Rabat (Morocco). Regional approach to create partnerships and adopt an Action Plan to link migration and development.	
2006 (July)			Different European countries send experts to support the Spanish National Police Brigade with the identification of irregular immigrants arriving in the Canary Islands: "HERA I y HERA II" operations.

Date	European Union		Spain and Other Countries
	Treaties/Summits/Agreements	Communications/Conferences/Others	
2006 (July)			Spain's Royal Decree N° 845/2006, of 7 July, which regulated the concession of an extraordinary subsidy to the Kingdom of Morocco for the reinforcement of its border control and for its struggle against illegal immigration.
2006 (August)		Creation of a special group of Commissioners dealing with migration.	
2006 (September)	Agreement between EU and Mali on migration control in exchange for development aid.		
2006 (different months)		Two short-term cooperation projects between EU and Senegal to contribute to surveillance operations, repatriation and rehabilitation, and to provide local support for activities of non-State actors engaged in migration.	
2006 (October)			Creation of the Regional Coordination Centre of the Canary Islands (CCRC), to deal with illegal migration into the Canary Islands, and the establishment of regulations to develop its functions (BOE 11/10/2006).
2006 (November)		Euro–African conference on Migration and Development in Tripoli (Libya).	
2006 (November)		Communication suggestion plans for the control of maritime borders.	
2006 (December)		JHA Council meeting on Integrated Approach to Borders and Migration (IBM).	

Date	European Union		Spain and Other Countries
	Treaties/Summits/Agreements	Communications/Conferences/Others	
2006 (different months and following years)			Bilateral readmission agreements with Morocco, Algeria, Nigeria, Ghana, Mali, Cape Verde, Guinea, Guinea-Bissau and Pakistan.
2006 (June)			"African Plan" (strategy document on Spanish foreign policy towards Africa 2006-2008). Reissue (2009-2012).
2006 (different months)			Bilateral migration cooperation agreements with Gambia, Guinea, Senegal, Conakry, Mali and Cape Verde.
2007			Development of the SEAHORSE programme by means of the SEAHORSE NETWORK. Spain issues 700 labour migration visas to Senegalese fishermen.
2007 (January)			
2007 (February)		Decision taken to establish a Migration Information and Management Centre to coordinate job offers in the EU with job seekers in Bamako (Mali).	
2007 (February)			Different European countries send experts to support the Spanish National Police Brigade with the identification of irregular immigrants arriving in the Canary Islands: "HERA III" operations.
2007 (March)			Bilateral agreement with Morocco to cooperate in the prevention of "illegal" emigration of unaccompanied children.

Date	European Union		Spain and Other Countries
	Treaties/Summits/Agreements	Communications/Conferences/Others	
2007 (July)		Regulation (EC) No 863/2007 of the European Parliament and the Council establishing a mechanism for the creation of Rapid Border Intervention Team ("RABITs Regulation").	
2007 (December)	Lisbon 2nd Africa–EU Summit to launch Africa–EU Migration, Mobility and Employment Partnership.		
2008 (May)			The Ministry of the Interior (Spain) awarded Indra the contract to set up the Sea Horse Network system (satellite surveillance) for the control of illegal immigration and drug trafficking between Spain, Portugal and North African countries.
2008 (June)		Beginning of the mobility partnership with Cape Verde to facilitate circular migration (Council document).	
2008 (July)			The Cooperation Framework Agreement between the Kingdom of Spain and the Republic of Senegal of 10 October 2006 came into force.
2009			Development of the "Seahorse Cooperation Centers" project by means of the transformation of the "Seahorse network" project contact points (Mauritania, Cape Verde, Senegal and Portugal) into Vigilance Coordination Centres and the reinforcement of the South Atlantic Border Cooperation Centre in the Canary Islands.

Date	European Union - Treaties/Summits/Agreements	European Union - Communications/Conferences/Others	Spain and Other Countries
2009 (April)			Modification of Mauritanian legislation to include crimes related to irregular immigration and setting up a Ship Registry.
2009 (September)			Formal agreement between Spain and Senegal for the prevention of illegal migration and readmission of irregular Senegalese nationals.
2009 (different months)			Bilateral agreements with Morocco, Senegal and Gambia.
2009 (December)			Modification of the Spanish Residents Law.
2009 (December)	The Treaty of Lisbon came into force, with new provisions regulating the common space of freedom, security and justice that opened the door to the development of a common immigration policy (the treaty guarantees the free movement of people across the Union, with no internal borders, together with a measure regarding external border control, asylum, immigration and prevention of and fight against crime).		
2010 (June)		The Stockholm Programme sets out the European Union's (EU) priorities in the area of justice, freedom and security for the period 2010–14. European citizenship and its rights.	
2010 (November)		EU Communication or the Joint Africa–EU strategy.	
2010 (November)	3rd Africa–EU Summit in Libya.		

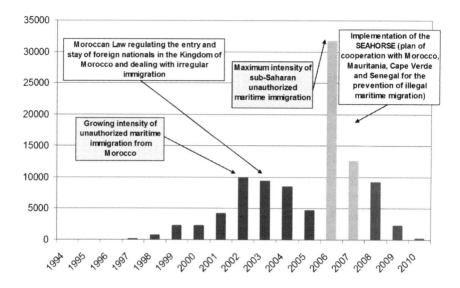

Figure 2.2   Links between migration stages and policing measures
Source: Ministry of the Interior (Spain): http://www.la-moncloa.es/ServiciosdePrensa/NotasPrensa/MIR/_2010/ntpr20100116_Inmigracion.htm (accessed 27/12/2010).

dehydration …) on board, maritime border control requires a range of actions that combine detection, deterrence, and intercepting and dismantling human smuggling rings with search and rescue operations and humanitarian assistance to immigrants.

This frame of reference invests the illegal maritime immigration flow across Europe's Atlantic border with a characteristic dynamic, which can be divided into three distinct stages of different dimension: a) from 1994 to 2005, years of growing intensity during which no action protocol had been developed yet to deal with unauthorized flows; b) from 2006 to 2008, a period of maximum intensity during which multiple measures were taken and initiatives developed at all levels in the fields of diplomacy, policing and humanitarian assistance; c) from 2008 to 2010, a stage of decreasing intensity and loss of prominence for this type of migration processes (Figure 2.2).

   a. Until 2005, irregular migration flows out of sub-Saharan Africa tended to travel by land towards Ceuta and Melilla, and also by sea from other locations in the north of Morocco, across towards the southern coast of Spain. In the case of the Canary Islands, during this period irregular immigrants generally made use of what was known as "slave ships", fishing boats and, to a lesser extent, inflatable rafts. The former were mostly old ships, generally unfit to sail, under flags of convenience, and which tended to come from West African coastal countries. Inspections in the docks of the islands or water leaks that forced them to moor in the ports of the islands on their way to Europe often led to the discovery of their "cargo", generally a considerable number of people packed in their hold in subhuman conditions. The fishing boats used – essentially, large canoes – are fragile crafts that can easily capsize and sink in the open sea or when they approach a craggy coastline. They used to set sail from Morocco's southern coast, Western Sahara or Mauritania, and sought to arrive in the eastern islands of the Canarian Archipelago. The first one arrived in 1994, and from that year on their numbers gradually increased until the first years of the twenty-first century – 2003, 2004 and 2005 – when a greater cooperation between Spain and Morocco regarding the prevention of departures led to a drop in the immigration flow and to a displacement of the points of departure further south, as human smugglers were forced to reorganize their activities.

b. From 2005 on, as a consequence of greater Moroccan vigilance, irregular migrant smugglers and departure points shifted south towards the coast of central West Africa, areas that are further removed from the Canary Islands, and as a result the crossings became longer, more difficult, costly and dangerous (Kimball, 2007). The type of vessel used changed as well, and the immigrants replaced the *pateras* (small fishing crafts) with *cayucos*, larger fishing boats with greater range. Departure points tended now to be located along the coasts of Mauritania, Senegal, Gambia, Guinea Bissau, Guinea Conakry or Sierra Leone, and consequently passengers, in this second stage, were mostly sub-Saharan nationals who usually disembarked on the coast of the western islands of the archipelago as a consequence of the new sailing patterns. During this period human smuggling developed so successfully that, for instance, in 2006, crossings in *cayucos* were offered online (senegalaisement.com), very much in the style of a standard travel agency (Merino, 2010).

These crossings were undertaken by young adults, mostly men, and some minors who, like their fellow travellers, came from sub-Saharan countries, especially Senegal and Mali. Whereas, in 1999, 83.9 per cent of unaccompanied minors came from Morocco, in 2006 and 2007 this figure changed and 71 per cent of the children placed under the protection of the government of the Canary Islands came from countries south of the Sahara. The management of this flow has required a special protective measures by the government of the Canary Islands in order to safeguard their rights and well-being, as required by international (Convention on the Rights of the Child) and domestic law (Basic Law for the Legal Protection of Minors and Civil Code), with the entailing obligations to implement special reception and training programmes.

c. In the last few years, from 2008 to 2010, there has been a gradual drop in irregular maritime immigration flows across Europe's southern Atlantic border. Many analysts believe that the measures of vigilance and control adopted by the European Union and by Spain, as well as the agreements signed with sender countries, might have contributed to deter irregular immigration. In fact, the centres for minors that had been set up (CAME) are largely under used at present. According to 2009 figures, the number of arrests for unauthorized maritime arrivals in Spain dropped that year down to 7,285, of which 2,246 arrived in the Canary Islands, among them only 192 minors (82.2 per cent less than in 2006).

There is no doubt that the trend described above is to some extent the result of the fact that potential African emigrants and their relatives have come to understand that even if they are successful in reaching Europe, they are very likely to be confined in a detention centre while their deportation is arranged, which in turn has brought about a decline in human smuggling. However, without denying the importance of these measures, it should be borne in mind that immigration is a very complex phenomenon which is not only conditioned by police vigilance and control actions, but also by the migrants' collective imagination, shaped under the influence of diverse information, the support offered by their networks of contacts and their personal assessment of the risk rewards ratio. Consequently, the role played by the evolution of the economy should not be underestimated, as it directly affects the migrants' perception of their chances to improve their situation and, thus, it indirectly links migration processes to productive cycles.

Economic Activity and Human Mobility

As is well known, immigration has been one of the pillars supporting the evolution of developed economies. The availability of immigrant labour has played an essential role in sustaining the productive system and in controlling salary levels in countries with higher national incomes. At the same time, emigration and its effects cannot be separated from the economic evolution of developing countries. During the expansion cycle of the post-Fordist stage, especially in the case of certain European countries such as Spain, Italy and Ireland, the increase in the demand for labour was met by immigration, as their economic development was based on a low-productivity labour-intensive model dependant on highly flexible employment. However, during a contraction cycle, the drop in demand for labour has affected immigrants severely, particularly in the case of those activities in the secondary labour market segment. This drop in demand and immigrants' unemployment rates has had deep effects on the evolution, dimension and characteristics of the migrant labour supply and, more generally, on international migrations as a whole.

Consequently, it is necessary to examine the different productive cycles and the role played by the transnational information networks developed by immigrants, in order to establish the relationship between them and the different unauthorized maritime immigration rates described above.

Economic Growth during the Cycle of Expansion and Migration 1995–2007

The 1980s saw the beginning of a new phase of capitalist development characterized mostly by technological innovation and fast circulation of capital, accompanied by a restructuring of socio-spatial relationships among the world's different geographical areas. From the point of view of population mobility, this phase of global capitalism has contributed to a greater complexity of migration processes, as revolutionary developments in transport and means of communication and new channels of information have given rise to what might be termed a world perspective, which makes it possible for any country to potentially become a destination for emigrants and for migration flows to take place anywhere in the world. For this reason some authors regard migration flows as a characteristic feature of a globalized economic system. According to UN data, in 2005 over 195 million people lived outside their home country, 60 per cent of them in developed countries, especially in the EU and the USA. These migrants represented 3.1 per cent of the world population and made up the "fifth largest country" in terms of population (UN, 2008).

This rise in migrant population was accompanied by a more noticeable visibility than in the past, and it became, given the growing presence of clandestine migrants, one of the main worries of the native population in western countries. The dimension of irregular flows has generated legal and economic insecurity for emigrants and political and social uncertainties for recipient states which, as a result of the process of globalization, have had their capacity to freely take measures restricted. In fact, migration circuits and mobility trends are now the result of complex processes based on economic and political decisions, on family, ethnic or religious networks and on individual or group aspirations derived from the migrants' collective imagination, which together structure the new geography of migration flows (Sassen, 2008).

In Spain, the rise in foreign immigration over the last 15 years has been unprecedented and it has transformed the country into an emerging destination in the context of international labour mobility (Domínguez-Mujica et al., 2008). From 1986 on, both Spain's incorporation into the European Union and the process of convergence the country underwent with its most developed neighbouring countries, favoured the arrival of a new type of immigrant closely linked to the socioeconomic dynamic that coincided with the onset of a post-Fordist economic phase. Later, from the mid-1990s on, the consolidation of an economic model characterized by low productivity and rapid growth contributed to intensify migration flows into Spain. For that reason, until 2007, as the foreign population increased there was also a parallel rise in the number of irregular immigrants and a more intense immigration pressure on the border.

The government tried to solve the problem of unauthorized immigration without altering the productive model. Among other measures, three important regularization processes were undertaken, in 2000, 2001 (regularization on the strength of community ties) and in 2005 (known as normalization process). The first two processes were linked to the length of time migrants had resided in Spain and the last one to the participation of migrants in the labour market. At this point it is worth considering whether unauthorized maritime immigration was also conditioned by the appeal of the Spanish productive model and by the "pull effect" generated by the regularization processes. In both cases the answer would be in the affirmative. Regarding the first issue, a survey performed in the Canary Islands during the 2000 regularization process confirmed that many African immigrants had arrived in Spain irregularly by sea and that they had benefited from the support of fellow countrymen who had previously settled in Spain. Regarding the second question, in the case of the Canary Islands, the highest figures in the number of immigrants detained after their arrival by sea were recorded in the years following the immigrant regularization processes, in other words, in 2001, 2002 and 2006 (Figure 2.3).

The Global Economic Crisis of 2008–2010 and Migrations

The circumstances that favoured the growth of the world economy up until the year 2007 have not changed in the context of the current economic crisis. Furthermore, some of the structural elements on which globalization has been based, such as the fast circulation of capital beyond the control of state regulations, lie at the heart of the economic recession that started in 2008, when the worst cyclical crisis of the capitalist system since 1929 broke out, affecting almost all countries in the world. Among the consequences of this crisis there is the drop in demand for goods and services and, consequently, for labour. As a result, the ILO predicted an increase in unemployment figures for 2009 of between 18 and 30 million workers compared to 2007, or even of 50 million workers if the situation continued to deteriorate (ILO, 2009).

As it has been pointed out, during the period of economic expansion the influx of workers from abroad contributed to maximizing growth and controlling salaries in recipient countries. As opposed to this, in a situation of economic recession, migrant workers are the first to lose their jobs. If at times of growth unemployment rates are higher among migrant workers than among their native counterparts, at times of crisis the difference grows. Thus,

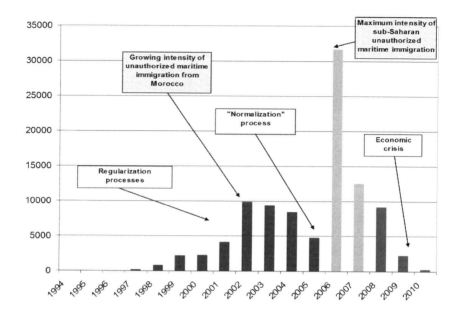

Figure 2.3   Links between migration stages and the labour market regulation
Source: Ministry of the Interior (Spain): http://www.la-moncloa.es/ServiciosdePrensa/NotasPrensa/MIR/_2010/ntpr20100116_Inmigracion.htm (accessed 27/12/2010).

the impact of the global crisis on migrant workers has been very severe. Unemployment rates among migrant workers have shot up, and are substantially higher than those affecting native workers, while there has been an increase in irregular employment.

As far as those who have not emigrated are concerned, the situation varies. When a change in the country of residence is considered, the crisis is seen through the filter of the migrant's own perception of the crisis potential duration and intensity. The longer the situation prolongs itself, the more pessimistic the migrants tend to become (Domínguez and Godenau, 2010). Migrants might also be affected by the hostile social environment generated by the crisis in recipient countries. For that reason, the medium and long term consequences of the slowdown in economic activity may lead to more limited and selected immigration flows, subjected to greater adjustments and controls in the case of those countries, such as Spain, that have received massive waves of immigrants in their recent past (Papademetriou and Terrazas, 2009).

In the specific case of unauthorized migration, according to SOPEMI (2009: 30–33), in 2008 there had already been a drop in the number of border crossings in the case of the USA. In the European Union, irregular migration into Spain, Italy the United Kingdom and Ireland slowed down as well, which confirms that there is a link between the fall in the number of immigrants arriving and the evolution of the economy and of the rates of unemployment among immigrants; there is also a positive correlation between the number of irregular immigrants detained on their arrival by sea and the evolution of GDP, and a negative correlation between the number of detentions and unemployment rates among immigrants (Table 2.2). Thus, unauthorized immigration flows weaken at times of economic

Table 2.2   Spain's economic indicators and immigration

	Number of detentions for unauthorized maritime arrival	Unemployment rates among the foreign population	GDP average growth
2005	17,347	11.4	3.6
2006	41,180	11.8	4.0
2007	19,610	12.2	3.6
2008	14,634	17.5	0.9
2009	7,285	28.4	-3.6
2010	196	30.4	0.8
Unemployment rate – GDP average growth (PEARSON)			-0.8
Number of detentions – Unemployment rate (PEARSON)			-0.8
Number of detentions – GDP average growth (PEARSON)			0.6

Source: Ministry of the Interior and National Statistics Institute: http://www.la-moncloa.es/ServiciosdePrensa/NotasPrensa/MIR/_2010/ntpr20100116_Inmigracion.htm; http://www.ine.es/jaxi/menu.do?type=pcaxis&path=%2Ft22/c308_inmu&file=inebase&L=0; http://www.ine.es/jaxi/menu.do?type=pcaxis&path=%2Ft35/p009&file=inebase&L=0 (accessed 27/12/2010).

crisis, for the same risks that seemed worthwhile during a period of economic expansion now seem increasingly purposeless.

Furthermore, the recession and the situation of economic paralysis Spain is immersed in is divulged not just by the media, but also by the networks of contacts established among Africans who reside in Spain and their relatives and friends in their countries of origin, which are as effective or more than any securitization measures. It should not be forgotten that precarious employment at times of crisis reduces the assistance that immigrants might offer to potential migrants back home, a fact that also contributes to slowing migration flows down. This has been pointed out in the media which, as we have mentioned above, have examined this issue well ahead of the specialized literature. At the beginning of February 2010, for instance, an obsolete cargo ship which was supposed to take illegal immigrants to the Canary Islands failed to set sail from Sierra Leone, as the organizers did not manage to find travellers in Mauritania, Mali, Senegal, Guinea Bissau, Conakry or Sierra Leone able or willing to pay the €1,500 per head they were demanding; only a few years before, potential migrants would have been able to pay that sum with help from relatives already settled in the Canary Islands or other points in Europe.

However, the drop in unauthorized migration flows cannot in any case be linked to initiatives that aim at complementing migration policies of vigilance and repatriation with the incentives to economic development the European Union has established in its Global Approach to Migration road map. In other words, from an economic perspective, the lessening flows of unauthorized immigrants are the consequence of the severe economic crisis affecting the world, and Spain in particular, and not of development initiatives. In fact, it is evident from top-level meetings, communiqués, reports and so on, that the EU is still in the initial stages of developing the initiatives mentioned, and that statements of purpose are still more common than specific measures. For example, the Communication on the Joint Africa–EU strategy (published in November 2010) took political stock of partnerships and progress since 2007 and included political guidance and impetus for further work. This suggests that the EU is aware of the need to move towards a genuine partnership based not only on development cooperation but on aid as a catalyst for inclusive and sustainable growth.

In a stricter sense of the term, linking them exclusively to circular migration, partnerships have not been tried extensively. The Cape Verde–EU partnership agreement is the only one to have had some success, while the partnership with Senegal seems to be on hold (Lavenex and Kunz, 2008; Chou, 2009; Chou and Gibert, 2010). The former's success is likely to be due to geopolitical and economic reasons that exceed the scope of this chapter, among them the fact that over the last few years Cape Verde has been a strategic destination for Spanish private investors, especially in the tourist sector, which has probably led to the archipelago receiving greater attention. Additionally, the Cape Verdean diaspora is to be found mainly in the USA, which lessens the impact of the migratory pressure that the contact networks of the nationals of this country can exercise in Europe, which in turn simplifies the management of these flows.

As far as the Centre for Migration Information and Management (CIGEM) is concerned, which started to work in Bamako (Mali), in October 2008, we have not been able to assess its actions, as is the case with the agreements to facilitate the authorized immigration of small groups of third-country nationals (for example, by means of bilateral agreements between Spain and Senegal, the authorization for women to be employed in the agricultural sector, or the authorization to employ a number of fishermen) which have had varying results and whose renewal seems to have been placed on hold. As has been stated by Bosch and Haddad (2007), "politics is a volatile domain. What may be a political priority at the top of the agenda one day, may be overtaken by a different issue just some days later, often due to a new event making the headlines. Thus the focus on implementing the Global Approach to Migration and the continued emphasis on partnership and comprehensiveness may not last forever".

Conclusion

Border regions have acquired a greater importance in a globalized world where the circulation of goods, services and capital has not kept up with free human mobility. The construction of new security borders with advanced technological devices, even in marine environments, has contributed to slowing down the flow of irregular immigration. But, beyond acknowledging the effectiveness of this initiative from a geopolitical perspective, border regions should be analysed from the point of view of the socio-economic imbalances, productive cycles and transnational networks of contacts and information which regulate human mobility. That is the working hypothesis this chapter is based on.

Sealing borders is not possible if no measures are taken simultaneously to reduce the differences in national income between countries and if statements of purpose and road maps, such as the Global Approach to Migration, stay in the realm of good intentions. A few and isolated examples of partnerships do not make up for the impact of other economic factors of greater weight, such as productive cycles and the labour markets associated with them. These are the factors that make any border permeable, for they are the material that rouses the collective imagination of potential immigrants, eventually imposing its own reality, as an analysis of the sequence of migration flows shows, and as is borne out by the evolution of irregular maritime migration into the Canary Islands, one of the world's most important geo-economically fractured areas.

References

Adepoju, A., Van Noorloos, F. and Zoomers, A. 2010. Europe's Migration Agreements with Migrant-Sending Countries in the Global South: A Critical Review, *International Migration*, 48 (3), 42–75.

Arango, J. and Martin, P. 2005. Best Practices to Manage Migration: Morocco-Spain, *International Migration Review*, 39 (1), 258–69.

Arteaga, F. 2007, Las operaciones de última generación. el Centro de Coordinación Regional de Canarias, *Real Instituto Elcano ARI*, 54, available at: http://www.realinstitutoelcano.org/wps/portal/rielcano/contenido?WCM_GLOBAL_CONTEXT=/elcano/elcano_es/zonas_es/defensa+y+seguridad/ari+54-2007 (accessed 27/12/2010).

Baldwin-Edwards, M. 2006. Between a Rock and a Hard Place: North Africa as a Region of Emigration, Immigration and Transit Migration, *Review of African Political Economy*, 33 (108), 311–24.

Bosch, P. and Haddad, E. 2007. Migration and Asylum: An Integral Part of the EU's External Policies. Paper presented in Forum natolinskie at Centrum Europejskie Natolin on June 1, available at: www.natolin.edu.pl/pdf/FN/FN_3_2007_bosh_haddad.pdf (accessed 27/12/2010).

Carling, J. 2007. Migration Control and Migrant Fatalities at the Spanish African Borders, *International Migration Review*, 41 (2), 316–43.

Carling, J. 2007. Unauthorized Migration from Africa to Spain, *International Migration*, 45 (4), 3–37.

Carrera, S. 2007. The EU Border Management Strategy: FRONTEX and the Challenges of Irregular Immigration in the Canary Islands, CEPS Working Document No. 261. Centre for European Policy Studies.

Carrera, S. and Geyer, F. 2007. Terrorism, Borders and Migration: The Commission's 2008 Policy Strategy in the Area of Freedom, Security and Justice. CEPS Policy Brief, 131, available at: http://ssrn.com/abstract=1334194 (accessed 27/12/2010).

Carter, D. and Merrill, H. 2007. Bordering Humanism: Life and Death on the Margins of Europe, *Geopolitics*, 12, 248–64.

Casey, J.P. 2010. Open Borders: Absurd Chimera or Inevitable Future Policy? *International Migration*, 48 (5), 14–62.

Ceriani, P. 2009. European Migration Control in the African Territory: The Omission of the Extraterritorial Character of Human Rights Obligations, *Sur. Revista Internacional de Direitos Humanos*, 6 (10).

Chou, M.-H. 2009. European Union Migration Strategy towards West Africa: The Origin and Outlook of "Mobility Partnerships" with Cape Verde and Senegal. Paper for EUSA Biennial International Conference "Information and Ideas on the European Union". Los Angeles, 23–25 April. Available at: http://www.unc.edu/euce/eusa2009/papers/chou_08C.pdf (accessed 27/12/2010).

Chou, M.-H. and Gibert, M. 2010. From Cotonou to Circular Migration: The EU, Senegal and the "Agreement Duplicity", Paper for "Migration: A World in Motion", Maastricht, 18–20 February. Available at: https://www.appam.org/conferences/international/maastricht2010/sessions/downloads/296.1.pdf (accessed 27/12/2010).

Clochard, O. and Dupeyron, B. 2007. The Maritime Borders of Europe: Upstream Migratory Controls, in *Borderlands: Comparing Border Security in North America and Europe*, edited by E. Brunet-Jailly. Ottawa: University of Ottawa Press, 19–40.

Collyer, M. 2006. States of Insecurity: Consequences of Saharan Transit Migration. Working Paper No 31, University of Oxford. Available at: http://www.compas.ox.ac.uk/fileadmin/files/pdfs/WP0631-Collyer.pdf (accessed 27/12/2010).

De Haas, H. 2010. Migration and Development: A Theoretical Perspective, *International Migration Review*, 44 (1).

Diaz, G. and Abad, G. 2008. Migración y seguridad en España: seguridad humana y el control de fronteras. El caso FRONTEX, *UNISCI Discussion Papers*, 17, May, 135–50.

Dominguez-Mujica, J. et al. 2008. La population étrangère en Espagne: quelques éléments d'une géographie changeante, *Revue Sud-Ouest Européen. Revue Géographique des Pyrénées et du Sud-Ouest*, 26, 71–88.

Dominguez-Mujica, J. and Godenau, D. 2010. Las migraciones internacionales en el siglo XXI, in *Migraciones laborales. Acción de la OIT y política europea*, ed. Bomarzo. Albacete.

Dover, R. 2008. Towards a Common EU Immigration Policy: A Securitization Too Far, *Journal of European Integration*, 30 (1), 113–30.

Fargues, P. 2009. Work, Refuge, Transit: An Emerging Pattern of Irregular Immigration South and East of the Mediterranean, *International Migration Review*, 43 (3), 544–77.

Fernandez-Sanchez, P. 2006. *Derecho comunitario de la inmigración*, ed. Atelier. Barcelona, 341.

Ferrer-Gallardo, X. 2008. The Spanish-Moroccan Border Complex: Processes of Geopolitical, Functional and Symbolic Rebordering, *Political Geography*, 27, 301–21.

Garcia Andrade, P. 2010. Extraterritorial Strategies to Tackle Irregular Immigration by Sea from a Spanish Perspective, *Extraterritorial Immigration Control. Legal Challenges*, edited by Ryan, B. and Mitsilegas, V. Martinus Nijhoff Publishers, The Hague.

Gebrewold, B. 2008. The Impact of African Illegal Migration to Europe on Euro-African Relations, in *Rethinking Global Migration: Practices, Policies and Discourses in the European Neighbourhood*, KPRA – Center for Black Sea and Central Asia. METU – Middle East Technical University, 115–43.

Gielis, R. 2009. Borders Make the Difference: Migrant Transnationalism as a Border Experience, *Tijdschrift voor Economische en Sociale Geografie*, 100 (5), 598–609.

Godenau, D. and Zapata, V. 2008. Immigration Flows and the Management of the EU's Southern Maritime Borders, *Documentos CIDOB*, no 17. Migraciones, Barcelona.

Hollifield, J.F. 2004. The Emerging Migration State, *International Migration Review*, 38 (3), 885–912.

Illamola Dausà, M. 2008. La emergencia del concepto de frontera exterior en la Unión Europea. El nuevo Código de Fronteras Schengen, *Documentos CIDOB. Migraciones*, 15.

Ilies, M. 2009. La política de la Comunidad Europea sobre inmigración irregular: medidas para combatir la inmigración irregular en todas sus fases, *Real Instituto Elcano ARI*, 38, available at: http://www.realinstitutoelcano.org/wps/portal/rielcano/contenido?WCM_GLOBAL_CONTEXT=/elcano/elcano_es/zonas_es/demografia+y+poblacion/dt38-2009 (accessed 27/12/2010).

ILO-OIT. 2009. *Global Employment Trends*, ILO, Geneva, January.

Kaufmann, S. 2006. Border Regimes in the Age of Global Networks. On the Politics of Technologies of Monitoring Borders. Second Plenary Conference of the Tensions of Europe Network and Launch of the Tensions of Europe Research Programme. Lappeenranta, Finland, May 24–28. Available at: http://www.histech.nl/tensphase2/Meetings/FinlandCD/Papers/Session%2012/RS%2012%20Kaufmann.pdf (accessed 27/12/2010).

Kimball, A. 2007. The Transit States: A Comparative Analysis of Mexican and Moroccan Immigration Policies. Working Paper 150. The Center for Comparative Immigration Studies, University of California.

Lacomba, J. and Boni, A. 2008. The Role of Emigration in Foreign Aid Policies: The Case of Spain and Morocco, *International Migration*, 46 (1).

Lavenex, S. 2006. Shifting Up and Out: The Foreign Policy of European Immigration Control, *West European Politics*, 29 (2), 329–50.

Lavenex, S. and Kunz, R. 2008. The Migration–Development Nexus in the External Relations, *Journal of European Integration*, 30 (3), 439–57.

Martin, P., Martin, S. and Cross, S. 2007. High-level Dialogue on Migration and Development, *International Migration*, 45 (1), 7–25.

Martin-Perez, J. 2010. Las competencias de la Unión Europea en materia de inmigración: nuevas potencialidades tras la entrada en vigor del tratado de Lisboa, in *Migraciones laborales. Acción de la OIT y política europea*, ed. Bomarzo. Albacete.

Merino, D. 2010. Trayectoria del fenómeno migratorio por vía marítima desde África hasta Canarias (1999–2009), *Actas II Congreso Internacional Latino de Comunicación Social*. Universidad La Laguna.

Muller, B.J. 2011. Risking it all at the Biometric Border: Mobility, Limits, and the Persistence of Securitisation, *Geopolitics*, 16, 91–106.

Naranjo-Noble, J. 2006. *Cayucos*, Madrid, Editorial Debate.

Papademetriu, D.G. and Terrazas, A. 2009. *Immigrants and the Current Economic Crisis: Research Evidence, Policy Changes, and Implications*, Washington, Migration Policy Institute.

Parkes, R. 2006. "Joint Patrols at the EU's Southern Border. Security and Development in the Control of African Migration", *Stiftung Wissenschaft und Politik*, German Institute for International and Security Affairs, SWP Research. Comments 21.

Ratzel, F. 1897. *Politische Geographie*, Munich et Leipzig, Verlag von R. Oldenbourg.

Rijpma, J.J. and Cremona, M. 2007. The Extra-Territorialisation of EU Migration Policies and the Rule of Law, *EUI Working Papers*, 2007/01. European University Institute, Department of Law.

Rohrmoser, F. 2008. Migration at the Southern Borders of European Union: The EU's Migration Policy Towards the Mediterranean and the Case of Spain. Doctoral thesis. Institut Européen des Hautes Études Internationales. Available at: http://www.iehei.org/bibliotheque/memoires2008/ROHRMOSER.pdf (accessed 27/12/2010).

Sadiqi, F. 2007. Morocco: The Political and Social Dimension of Migration. CARIM Mediterranean Migration Report 2006–2007. European University Institute-RSCAS, http://www.carim.org/publications/CARIM-AR2007_Part1.pdf (accessed 27/12/2010).

Sandell. R. 2005. Were They Pushed or Did They Jump? The Rise in Sub-Saharan Immigration, *Instituto Elcano ARI*, 133, available at: http:/www.realinstitutoelcano.org/analisis/835/Sandell835.pdf (accessed 27/12/2010).

Sassen, S. 2008. *Territory, Authority, Rights: From Medieval to Global Assemblages*. Princeton: Princeton University Press.

Schapendonk, J. and Van Moppes, D. 2007. Migration and Information: Images of Europe, Migration Encouraging Factors and En Route Information Sharing, Working Papers Migration and Development Series, Report No. 16, Nijmegen.

Schapendonk, J. 2008. Stuck between the Desert and the Sea: The Immobility of Sub-Saharan African "Transit Migrants" in Morocco, *Rethinking Global Migration:*

Practices, Policies and Discourses in the European Neighbourhood, KORA – Center for Black Sea and Central Asia. METU – Middle East Technical University, 129–43.
Serrano-Argüello, N. 2010. Labour Migration in the European Union: About a New European Union Policy: Common Immigration Policy, Working paper 2010–17. Institute for Research on Labor and Employment. University of California, available at: http://escholarship.org/uc/item/47x6w3gh;jsessionid=8D7B86A6A67BFE41C0504 5704058F8B0#page-8 (accessed 27/12/2010).
Soddu, P. 2006. Ceuta and Melilla: Security, Human Rights and Frontier Control, *Culture and Society/Migrations*, Institut Europeu de la Mediterrània, 212–14.
SOPEMI. 2009. *International Migration Outlook 2009*, Paris, OECD.
Spijkerboer, T. 2007. The Human Costs of Border Control, *European Journal of Migration and Law*, 9, 127–39.
Triandafyllidou, A. 2010. Control de la inmigración en el sur de Europa (1ª parte): estrategias de "cerco" (fencing). *Real Instituto Elcano ARI*, 7, available at: http://www.realinstituto elcano.org/wps/portal/rielcano/contenido?WCM_GLOBAL_CONTEXT=/elcano/ elcano_es/zonas_es/demografia+y+poblacion/ari7-2010 (accessed 27/12/2010).
UN. 2008. United Nations' Trends in Total Migrant Stock: The 2008 Revision, available at: http://esa.un.org/migration (accessed 27/12/2010).
Van Houtum, H. and Pijpers, R. 2007. The European Union as a Gated Community: The Two-faced Border and Immigration Regime of the EU, *Antipode*, 39 (2), 291–309.
Van Moppes, D. 2006. The African Migration Movement: Routes to Europe. Working papers. Migration and Development series, Report No. 5.
Varsanyi, M.W. and Nevins, J. 2007. Introduction: Borderline Contradictions: Neoliberalism, Unauthorised Migration, and Intensifying Immigration Policing, *Geopolitics*, 12, 223–7.
Vélez-Alcade, F.J. 2008. Pateras, cayucos y mafias transfronterizas en África: el negocio de las rutas atlánticas hacia las Islas Canarias, *Real Instituto Elcano ARI*, 14, available at: http://www.realinstitutoelcano.org/wps/portal/rielcano/contenido?WCM_GLOBAL _CONTEXT=/elcano/elcano_es/zonas_es/ari14-2008 (accessed 27/12/2010).

Chapter 3
A Community of Borders, Borders of the Community: The EU's Integrated Border Management Strategy

Denis Duez

The construction of a political community is often explained by a process founded on the emergence of feelings of solidarity between individuals. Such solidarity is the result of a common history, of a culture, of a language or even of a political project or of values shared by all components of the social body. It is often the result of deepening relationships between people and of the discovery of *the Other* and of its status as an *alter ego*. Collective identity, where it exists, is above all a question of affectivity, even of friendship, between fellow citizens. At the European level, the transition of multiple *demoi* to a single European *demos* could also be seen as a double process. Firstly, it would be a vertical process of attachment to the European project, to its values and symbols. Secondly, it would be a horizontal process in which sentiments of friendship between European citizens are strengthened. The narrative that Europe has chosen to promote in recounting its own history is a narrative of friendship between peoples and of bridges successfully crossed. It is a narrative of reconciliation, solidarity and recognition of *the Other* and of differences.

However, political history as well as the history of political ideas teaches us that the formation of a unified social body is not always founded on positive sentiments and love between compatriots, and even that is quite rare. The body politic is also the product of historical turmoil, wars and armed combats of all kinds. It is built on hostilities, even hatreds, as much as upon friendship. It is a defence mechanism leading men to join together and unite, not necessarily because they have any mutual regard but because they are attempting to jointly protect what is dear to them. Indeed, since Thomas Hobbes and theories of the Social Contract, a number of writers have underlined the crucial role played by insecurity and fear in the emergence of feelings of belonging (Duez 2008a, 97–119).

This reasoning, often used to explain the formation of national identities and the structuring of modern States, appears to us to be equally useful when applied to the European Union (EU). The progressive application of Community projects for internal security and integrated management of external borders provides a new context for such questions. On the basis of this suggestion, we analyse in the following pages the impact of Community policies directed against illegal immigration on the emergence of a "community of Europeans". In fact, it seems to us that in posing the question of controlling the Union's external borders, illegal immigration also poses the question of symbolic and mental borders defining the conditions for belonging to a particular political order. It provides an identification principle for defining the contours of the body politic.

In the pages that follow, we explore the hypothesis that the European integrated management project for the Union's external borders cannot be entirely reduced to a policy for managing migratory flows, but that it must also be seen as a politically constructed discourse on the dangers weighing on Europe. This policy encourages a distinction between «them» and «us» which contributes to the process of forging a European political community on the basis of an emotion, namely anxiety concerning, or even fear of, *the Other.* In a situation in which a culturally or politically homogeneous whole has not been created, Europeans thus find themselves united and sharing a sense of solidarity as a consequence of a shared feeling of collective insecurity.

Unfolding the IBM: Towards Common Controls at the External European Border

Launched in the post-September 11 context, the IBM project has become one of the priorities of the EU's Justice and Home Affairs. This project, very directly inspired by policies developed in the United States, is characterized by the implementation of a surveillance of external borders strategy revealing two major trends, namely the militarization of border controls and an extensive use of new technology.

Integrated Management of External Borders: A Priority for the European Union

On 13 February 2008, the European Commission tabled what can be called, in Community jargon, a "Border Package". This package included three communications relating to integrated management of European external borders. It can be seen that the Commission thus took an important step in a process that had begun several years previously at the Laeken European Council in December 2001. Following the 11 September 2001 terrorist attacks, European governments and heads of State had made a solemn declaration that "Better management of the Union's external border controls will help in the fight against terrorism, illegal immigration networks and the traffic in human beings" (European Council 2001: 42). Border management was thus put very high in the political priorities of the Union. This political initiative accelerated intergovernmental cooperation that had started in the mid-eighties within the framework of the Schengen Agreements, and amplified in the nineties on the basis of the 1992 Maastricht Treaty, within the third pillar of the Union and as part of the implementation of the area of freedom, security and justice (AFSJ) (Duez 2008b: ch. 2). The 2008 "Borders Package" did not therefore emerge from a vacuum. It brought together and extended the principles and practices applied since at least 2001 with regard to integrated management of Union external borders.

Of the three communications made public by the Commission, two suggest important changes with regard to the role played by the European Agency for the Management of Operational Co-operation at the External Borders of the Member States of the European Union (Frontex): the communication on the evaluation and future development of the Frontex agency (European Commission 2008: 67) and the communication on examining the creation of a European Border Surveillance System (EUROSUR) (European Commission 2008: 68). The third more programmatic document proposed various ways to prepare for the next steps in European Union border management (European Commission 2008: 69).

A little less than three years after the Frontex agency began work in May 2005, and in accordance with an injunction appearing in the Hague Programme, the Commission undertook an initial assessment of its operational agency. At the same time, the whole European Integrated Border Management project was re-examined. In spite of the absence of any objective overview of the activities of Frontex, the Commission gave a good overall grade to the agency (Jeandesboz 2008: 5). In addition, it recommended a widening of

Frontex's remit to the degree required by specific needs, in order to enable it to occupy a central role in the strategy for integrated management of Union borders (European Commission 2008: 67).

In fact, Frontex's role was already being strengthened before the Commission's positive assessment was given. Whilst the initial agency budget amounted to 6.2 million Euros in 2005, by 2006 it had already reached 19.2 million. By 2007, the figure had risen to 41.9 million, and by 2008, the year in which the "Borders Package" was adopted, it had reached 71.2 million. For the year 2011, this budget amounted to some 92.8 million Euros, or 13 times the sum allocated in 2005 and four times the sum granted in 2006, the first full year of the agency's activities.[1]

This confidence in the future development of the agency raises several questions. On reading the Commission documents, one cannot fail to notice that they contain no critical assessment of Frontex activities for the period 2005–2007. Based upon an essentially quantitative approach, the evaluation stresses mainly the growth in the number of joint operations carried out at land, sea and air borders of the European Union; the number of people arrested or refused entry at borders during such operations; or the number of ships, planes, helicopters and other surveillance equipment (radar, vehicles, thermal cameras and mobile detectors) recorded in the Centralized Record of Available Technical Equipment (CRATE).

This purely statistical interpretation – which is also the kind of interpretation to be found in the annual agency activity reports – gives only a very restricted picture of the work carried out by Frontex. It says nothing about difficulties encountered on the ground. The difficulties experienced by the agency in mobilizing the human and material resources made theoretically available to it by the Member States in the context of joint operations are ignored. However, it will be remembered that, for example, the NAUTILUS patrol operation in the central Mediterranean was interrupted for several weeks during the summer of 2007 as a result of insufficient resources contributed by the Member States (Duez 2008b: 136). In reality, solidarity and commitment, subscribed to in public, are sometimes undermined by the unwillingness of Member States to fully participate. The agency's operations can stumble, in particular over the delicate question of how financial costs linked to joint operations are to be allocated. The responsibilities of the States in terms of reception of migrants intercepted at sea is another obstacle, as shown by the tensions surrounding responsibility for Tunisian migrants fleeing their country in the wake of the democratic risings in Spring 2011 (European Commission 2010a).

Militarization and Technology as Models for IBM Strategy

Looking beyond this particular example of the Frontex agency and its evaluation we see that the 2008 Border Package displays certain marked trends in border control strategy. These trends resurface a little later in the 2009 Stockholm Programme (European Council 2009) and the 2010 Internal Security Strategy for the European Union (European Council 2010). Firstly, the Community approach confirms a trend towards quasi-militarization in external border control. Although there is no talk, as in the United States, of "*prevention through deterrence*" (Ritaine 2009: 24), European Commission policies, the discourse of Member States and the strategy of the Frontex agency all converge to give the impression of a

---

1 Details of the Frontex budget are available on the agency's site at: http://www.frontex.europa.eu/budget_and_finance/.

vigorous policy, requiring exceptional methods, and committed to the "front line" in the struggle against illegal immigration. The lexical field used to describe Frontex coordination activities makes marked use of terms drawn from the world of defence. There is talk of "joint operations", of a "European Patrol Network" (EPN) and of deploying "Rapid Border Intervention Teams" (the so called RABIT teams).[2] The use of the term "intelligence" for describing Frontex "risk analysis" missions, instead of more neutral terminology such as "information processing" or "data analysis" should also be highlighted. In a similar vein, the recurrent use of a visual display showing helicopters, planes and ships included in the Centralized Record of Available Technical Equipment (CRATE) is reminiscent of a display showing forces engaged in a military combat. Finally the use of spatial maps and cartographic codes reminiscent of battle plans accentuates a symbolic connection with warfare (Frontex 2010–2011).

Secondly, the European Union IBM programme emphasized the essential role of new communication and information technologies. Lacking operational resources of its own, the Union chose to go down the road of an "electronic border", somewhat reminiscent of the North American "*smart border initiative*" (Le Texier 2010: 759–62). The common factor in the new tools that the European Union proposes implementing is reliance on intensive use of electronic monitoring technologies, IT data exchange networks, and automation of control procedures. This use of so called smart technologies for detecting, identifying and monitoring individuals is the consequence of a desire to adapt to their increasing mobility. The aim is to monitor these individuals and trace their itineraries without interrupting their journeys, at least in cases of movement considered as legitimate (Ceyhan 2010: 133–4). What is being (or attempted at being) constructed is a globalized world in which mobility is fluid but nevertheless perfectly controlled.

Among the three strategic strands identified in the IBM program, two are technology-driven: 1) an enhanced use of new technology for border checks (the SIS II, VIS, entry/exit system and registered traveller programme); 2) an enhanced use of new technology for border surveillance (European Border Surveillance System, EUROSUR).[3]

Regarding the first strands, the 2008 Border Package proposes setting up an exit/entry registration system for third-country nationals. Inspired by the US-VISIT programme,[4] this system should enable electronic registration of information on dates and places of entry of third-country nationals and of the dates notified for exit from the Schengen area. It would replace the current system of stamping passports. For third-country nationals requiring a short stay visa, this control would eventually be combined with an obligation to provide biometric information for the Visa Information System (VIS). If the period for authorized stay is exceeded, the data of the person in question would be automatically

---

2 RABIT resources were first deployed on 25 October 2010 on the border between Greece and Turkey. This deployment followed an aid request from the Greek government when confronted with serious difficulties in controlling its land border with its Turkish neighbour. During the first three months of 2010, no less than 45,000 irregular migrants crossed the Greek border illegally. According to the Agency, in the Orestiada region alone some 350 people were trying to cross the border illegally every day, along a border zone of 12.5 kilometres in length (Frontex 2010).

3 The third strand is an enhanced coordination of Member States through Frontex.

4 US-VISIT (United States Visitor and Immigrant Status Indicator Technology) is a United States Department of Homeland Security immigration and border management system. The system involves the collection and analysis of biometric data (fingerprints, etc.), which are checked against a database to track individuals deemed by the United States to be terrorists, criminals, or illegal immigrants. More details available on the DHS website: http://www.dhs.gov/files/programs/usv.shtm.

communicated to the relevant authorities. In the same vein, the IBM strategy includes a registered travellers programme (RTP) to facilitate border crossings for frequent, pre-vetted and pre-screened third-country travellers. It would make use of new technologies such as automatic border gates, which can provide automated border control for personal and/ or biometric data thanks to electronic passports.[5] According to the Commission, the RTP would give the Member States tools to manage their passenger flows efficiently and release human resources needed at the external border in order to check riskier travellers or serve other travellers.[6] Finally, the Union is examining the possibility of setting up an electronic travel authorization system – once again inspired by the US Electronic System for Travel Authorization, or ESTA.[7] In the long term, this system could be considered as an alternative to the visa obligation for some categories of non-EU member country nationals or could be imposed on those of the latter who are not currently subject to such obligation.

To an even greater extent than the entry/exit system, the second strands of the IBM program, namely the development of the European Border Surveillance System (EUROSUR), is revealing with regard to the trend towards the increasing dominance of technology in border control. The aim of this project is to support the Member States in reaching full situational awareness on the situation at their external borders and to increase the reaction capability of their law enforcement authorities.[8] Based upon the principle of interconnecting already existing monitoring systems in the various Member States, the goal of EUROSUR is to eventually provide a shared technical environment enabling rationalization of cooperation and communication between the relevant national authorities. The main aim of this "system of systems" is to facilitate use of advanced technology in border monitoring. As in the of the entry–exit system, the EUROSUR is inspired by the United States' SBInet programme.

In terms of political aims, EUROSUR is a response to three goals in particular.[9] Firstly, to reduce the number of illegal immigrants who enter the European Union undetected. Secondly, to increase the internal security of the EU as a whole by contributing to the prevention of cross-border crime. Finally, to reduce the number of deaths of illegal immigrants by saving more lives at sea. Although regularly emphasized, the question of saving migrants who find themselves in difficulties really appears to be no more than an accessory to machinery whose main purpose has been thought to be an instrument of migration control.

Whether in the context of the EUROSUR project or of other existing arrangements, recourse to technology makes new kinds of walls and barriers socially and politically acceptable. These walls and electronic barriers are less visible and, in appearance at least, less "violent" than their equivalents in concrete and steel (Neisse, Novosseloff 2010: 736). Here again, the American experience can be seen as a model for the European strategy.

---

5   European Commission 2008. Preparing the Next Steps in Border Management in the European Union, Communication from the Commission, COM 69 final: 6–7. Such electronic gates are already in operation in several European airports, notably in Finland, in France, and in the UK.

6   European Commission, Background Information on Smart Border Initiative, Directorate-General Home Affairs, n.l., n.d., p. 2; document available on Statewatch website: www.statewatch.org/news/2011/jul/eu-com-smart%20borders-note.pdf.

7   European Commission, Preparing the Next Steps in Border Management in the European Union, Communication of the Commission, op. cit.: 11.

8   European Commission 2008. Examining the Creation of a European Border Surveillance System (EUROSUR), MEMO/08/86: 4–5.

9   Ibid., pp. 3–4.

The argument as put forward in Europe shares certain theses developed across the Atlantic, in particular by the former Democrat Governor of Arizona and the current Secretary of State for Homeland Security Janet Napolitano. In fact, her attack on barriers, summed up in the well-known formula "Show me a 50-foot wall and I'll show you a 51-foot ladder" should not be understood as a defence of open borders. Her argument is accompanied by an alternative project, that of a barrier at the border between the United States and Mexico which is no longer physical, but virtual:

> Here are some of the key elements of a real border plan: The first is the development of innovative, technology-driven border control between the ports of entry. Boots on the ground definitely help, but we can shore up our border gaps with ground-based sensors, radar, and unmanned aerial vehicles for wide-area intrusive-detection. Any combination of the above will work far better than any 10 or 20 or 50 miles of wall. The Department of Homeland Security is now installing this kind of technology. They need increased funding to sustain their efforts. (Napolitano 2007)

This faith in the potential of new technology, however, ignores its exorbitant cost as well as its relative efficiency. According to an evaluation report by the Department of Homeland Security, the American project for a SBInet virtual border developed by Boeing[10] has cost the American taxpayer almost a billion dollars for equipping a mere 53 miles of border. It was eventually abandoned in January 2011, the DHS considering that "the SBInet program, as originally proposed, does not meet current standards for viability and cost-effectiveness" (Department of Homeland Security 2011).

Despite their failure, current discourse on a technology-driven monitoring of border zones gives sustenance to a narrative: exits and entries from and to the European Union can be completely and efficiently controlled. Therefore such discourse gives support to the idea that it is possible to promote legitimate mobility whilst at the same time effectively preventing mobility thought to be illegitimate, in other words movement by migrants from Southern and Eastern countries in search, whatever the conditions and cost may be, of the chance of a better life in Europe. This progressively drawn distinction between legitimate and illegitimate types of mobility in turn feeds an *insider/outsider* type opposition. The barrier or wall, even if virtual, becomes, in the public imagination, a demarcation between an inside and an outside, between "us" and "them".

Shared Borders and Political Community

Sustained by an unbreakable faith in the potential of information and communication technology, the European project for integrated border management is only a partial response to the phenomenon of irregular migration. In fact, this approach tends to reduce policy on immigration to no more than a struggle against illegal immigration, a struggle making use of just one strategy, border monitoring. However, the majority of irregular migrants do not reach Schengen territory illegally. According to the European Commission, a high proportion of illegal immigrants are "overstayers" that enter the European Union

---

10 The abandonment of the project was announced in January 2011 by Janet Napolitano, the very person who had called for it, as a result of its failure to meet "current standards for viability and cost effectiveness" (Greenhouse 2011).

holding a valid travel document. Many only become "illegal" once the document has expired or once they infringe the terms of their stay, for example by carrying out an activity in return for remuneration (European Commission 2011: 7). By focusing on the border and border control, countries within Europe approach irregular immigration from only one restricted angle. It can be seen from the design of these European arrangements that the machinery is either incomplete or incapable of relative success.

In addition, the experience of Europe in managing migratory flows has shown that the efficiency of arrangements for monitoring flows at local level has been accompanied by relative failure at a more global level. On the one hand, each reinforcement of border surveillance tends to lead not to a drying up of irregular flows but to smugglers redirecting their attempts towards less intensively monitored routes (Duez 2008b: 194–8). On the other hand, although applying electronic monitoring along the entire borders of the Union may be technically feasible, the setting up of a patrol network on the same scale is almost certainly far less feasible, both as a result of financial and political costs that such a decision would entail.

Taking into account these limitations, how can the Union's focus on securing its external borders be explained? Various possible replies can be given to this question. Many commentators, particularly those associated with the Copenhagen School and Critical Security Studies underline the identity role played by borders. Identifying lines of demarcation and control of these borders is equivalent to a process of "marking out" which is both active and reactive (Bigo, Bocco, Piermay 2009: 12). It enables differentiation of social groups and creates a space in which tension concerned with protection of identities can be played out. This logic of defending identities – whether it stems from the deliberately provocative approach of Samuel Huntington or from the more subtle approach of the Copenhagen school – nevertheless does not help us to understand the process by which immigration in the context of the European Union is being securitized. Applied to Europe, such an approach assumes that a European identity, threatened by illegal immigration, already exists (McSweeney 1996: 85). However, there is no such identity. There is no such thing as "European society". Even the most optimistic or those most in favour of Europe would say "not yet". In a revealing fashion, the work carried out by Ole Waever is more useful in explaining how national identities resist European integration than the resistance shown by a European identity to apparent dangers generated by migratory flows (Wæver 1998: 91–138; 1996: 103–32).

In order to overcome the impasse encountered by analysis of European security in terms of defence of a shared identity, in the second part we shall develop an alternative hypothesis to those suggested by S. Huntingdon and the supporters of the Copenhagen school. On the basis of a critical interpretation of the work of Carl Schmitt on the friend–enemy distinction, we believe that far from being an expression of an involuntary response to protect identity, Community policy on illegal immigration creates links between Europeans where they did not exist previously or only weakly. From this point of view, this policy is not directed at defending a previously established identity. Rather, it may be performative. It may take an active part in the construction of a sense of belonging and of a symbolic territory which is truly European.

Europe and Undocumented Migrants: A Reactivation of the Friend–Enemy Distinction

The invocation of an existential menace is, according to Carl Schmitt, constitutive of a sense of belonging. The friend–enemy distinction provides a principle of identification which enables definition of the contours of the body politic (Schmitt 2007: 25–7). It creates a distinction between "them" and "us" which makes it possible to create or strengthen the links indispensable for the cohesion and survival of a community. If one interprets the policy of the Union towards illegal immigration in terms of Schmitt's principles, the irregular migrant would represent a figure of alterity contributing to forging a shared "community of Europeans". It is the presence of a common "enemy" which could help the European Union to develop as a politically and emotionally unified body politic. In posing the question of management and control of European Union external borders, the European policy on illegal immigration would also lay down symbolic and mental borders defining the conditions for belonging to a European political order. The strategy of rejecting undesirable foreigners would then be in response to a double pragmatic and ontological imperative. On the one hand, it would correspond to a managerial logic – often emphasized – of controlling and selecting non-EU member country nationals authorized to access the territory of Member States. On the other, it would be a factor in the construction of a figure of *Otherness* providing a foundation for a collective European identity. We should point out that this identity imperative has been followed by the European Commission at least to a degree. In its communication "Towards Integrated Border Management of the External Border of the European Union" dated 2002, the latter in effect emphasizes that "The European Union's external borders are also a place where a common security identity is asserted" (European Commission 2002: 5).

This process of defining a social group by reference to the Other is a classic mechanism (see Badie, Sadoun 1996). The works of Gérard Noiriel in particular have shown how the "identity revolution" driven by European States during the nineteenth century allowed a clear distinction to be made between nationals, who benefit from certain privileges, and foreigners, whose movements can be reasonably monitored with the goal of preventing any risk of disorder (Noiriel 2001: 448 ff.; 1998: 155–80; Torpey 2000). By reinforcing the national/non-national distinction, the setting up of administrative and technological arrangements for identifying individuals helped to consolidate the foundations of the nation State. These mechanisms have helped to define its limits ever more precisely at the social and geographic level (Schnapper 1993: 89–96). More generally, the foreigner has always been the incarnation of the perfect "figure of alterity" (Lochak 1985: 14; Fisbach 1993: 65–88). By definition, he or she is a person belonging to a different community. The foreigner is always defined negatively. He or she is a mirror reflecting our own image back to us: and classifying the person as a foreigner fixes, at the same time, the limits of the reference group, since in order to say that he or she is the Other, it is necessary for us to say who "we" are. This dynamic of defining Self and Other is accentuated even more by the fear which the latter generally inspires. For if the foreigner is outside the group, he or she is also a source of disturbance and anxiety. Dutch (*vreemdeling-vreemd*), German (*fremde-fremd*), Spanish (*extranjero-extraño*) and French (*étranger-étrange*) all suggest (Carlier 2002: 151) that the "foreigner " (i.e., stranger) is "strange". You must beware of him.

The logic of the friend–enemy distinction suggested by Carl Schmitt, however, goes much further than this conventional distinction between *insiders* and *outsiders*. The friend–enemy distinction is the "most intense and extreme antagonism" (Schmitt 2007: 29). It presupposes the possibility of a physical struggle that could even undermine the survival of a political entity. It is this radical nature of the friend–enemy distinction that can provide political authority. The strength of political enmity can help disguise all other divisions in the social body, whether they are cultural, moral, religious, aesthetic or even economic. By feeding hopes for an existential combat against a shared adversary, it is a powerful factor in unifying a community.

In this struggle for survival, the border marks out in spatial terms the line of demarcation between friends and enemies. The frontier (in other words, the border) becomes once again the "front" to which it is etymologically related. It draws a line that marks both a geographical and legal distinction constructed by political authority. The border appears in particular as the territory in which order from within is confronted by the threat of disorder from without. But, even more crucially, disorder from without can be a condition of order within. According to Étienne Balibar, the border in Carl Schmitt's thinking is both a geographical and an ethical limit:

> The border is above all a place in which the controls provided by the 'normal' legal order are suspended [...], the place in which the 'monopoly on legitimate violence' takes the form of preventive counter-violence. The nomos of the planet is no more than 'border-order': violence which is expected to domesticate violence by placing it at the service of reasons of state. (Balibar 2000: 56)

This concept of the border as a violent territory and as a space beyond the reach of the normal legal order is a reflection of the human experience of how borders have actually been managed in Europe. The reinforcement of migratory controls at borders and the definition of a specific European territory are not in fact without consequences. These factors make access to the territories of Member States ever more difficult. In fact, they indirectly contribute to the deaths of several hundreds of irregular migrants every year, mainly when ships hired by gangs of "people smugglers" get into difficulty in the Mediterranean and in the Atlantic. They also lead to frequent human rights violations, in particular violations of the non-refoulement principle (Goodwin-Gill 2011). Finally, they encourage growing frustration amongst populations of some non-member countries with a Europe thought to be selfish and even hostile.

However, the sense of urgency and the social preoccupations which make possible this European machinery at the origin of such human rights violations are exacerbated by continually increasing pressure from the media and politicians. One of the discourse registers most frequently used to evoke illegal immigration is in fact one of combat. The events occurring close to the Spanish enclaves of Ceuta and Melilla, in autumn 2005, were presented as "conflicts" resulting from "massive assaults" led by an "army of illegal immigrants".[11] The arrival of migrants on the coasts of Italy, Malta, Cyprus, or, some years ago, on the Canary Islands, are regularly compared to "invasions" or "landings". These landings are said to be the results of "waves" of migrants. Beyond these terms of discourse, it is the very nature of the European response to the phenomenon of illegal immigration which tends to reinforce the narrative of a struggle between Europeans and illegal migrants. Contrary to political declarations, EU immigration policy does not assign much importance to prevention strategies, development aid or even to opening legal avenues for economic immigration. On the contrary: it strengthens security arrangements: securitization of travel documents, development of data bases and information exchange systems, deployment of

---

11 The press has used and abused such metaphors. As an example, an article published on the *Le Monde* website in October 2005 talks repeatedly of "attempts at massive infiltration", "massive assaults" and "coordinated assaults". These terms appear seven times in an article of barely 15 sentences, "350 immigrants se sont infiltrés dans l'enclave de Melilla, lors d'un nouvel assaut groupé".

tools for border monitoring, and even, as we have seen, the quasi militarization of the combat against illegal immigrants as part of joint maritime operations led by the Frontex agency in the Mediterranean (Coda 2005: 385–7).

There is a trend for this militarization of the struggle against irregular migrants to create in collective representations the idea of combat and of a specific conceptual framework, that of war. Just as, since the attacks of 11 September 2001 there has been a "war" against terrorism (Corten 2004: 3–13), so there is also now a war to be waged against "floods" of irregular migrants. The latter are not stigmatized as individuals, but are presented collectively as a peril for European societies. This war, however, is not war as envisaged by Clausewitz, in other words, as a military confrontation. It is a "metaphorical war". To use an expression taken from Ole Waever, it is *"a test of will and strength"* in which a political entity resists a danger in order to impose recognition of its existence and identity (Waever 1995: 53).

An examination of the European policy of combating illegal immigration in the light of the friend–enemy distinction therefore makes it possible to perceive the formation of the body politic as a discursive practice resulting from the actions of a political authority. Applied to the case under discussion, this idea can help us to conceptualize the formation of a European body politic independently of any reference to a pre-existing community. In addition, this idea can be separated from perspectives putting an emphasis upon a will to live together based upon adhesion to ethical or political principles. In the work of Schmitt, the figure of the enemy does not correspond to any predefined social group, whether based on biology, culture, ethnicity or religion. The enemy is essentially political. Consequently, such an enemy is not necessarily bad morally or ugly aesthetically. It is simply that

> [...] the political enemy need not to be morally evil or aesthetically ugly; he need not appear as an economic competitor, and it may even be advantageous to engage with him in business transactions. But he is, nevertheless, the other, the stranger; it is sufficient for his nature that he is, in a specially intense way, existentially something different and alien, so that in the extreme case conflicts with him are possible. These can be neither be decided by a previously determined general norm nor by the judgement of a disinterested and therefore neutral third party. (Schmitt 2007: 27)

In short, the alterity of this Other does not stem from characteristics proper to it. It is the Other because it has been named as such by an authority which, in doing so, creates itself.

The relevance of Carl Schmitt's work therefore lies in the fact that he proposes an exclusively political definition of the community. This definition is particularly relevant to the case of the "European political model" in which the meaning of Europe is translated into legal principles and institutional mechanisms, and never into ethno-cultural givens or value choices (Heine, Magnette 2007). Schmitt does not explain the formation and legitimization of political authority by reference to a cultural conception of the community. His position is at the other end of the spectrum from the "essentialist" conception of the nation, constructed on the basis of the theses of Johann Gottfried Herder, Johann Gottlieb Fichte or Théodore Mommsen. For Schmitt, the community is not founded on language, history, geography or culture (Herder 1992; Mommsen 1985). Nor does it resemble the "volontarist" conception, stemming from the French Revolution and developed by Ernest Renan. Although the political community genuinely results from a "decision", it does not follow that it is the result of a regular act of commitment on the part of free and enlightened citizens. Schmitt's political community is not, in Renan's words, "a plebiscite renewed every day" (Renan 1882). It is not founded on positive values. It is built upon and is consolidated *in opposition to* another community. It is essentially an entity for defence, even survival.[12]

Carl Schmitt's thinking is marked by the historical context in which it arose. It was developed in the troubled period between the wars with the aim of justifying a new kind of State destined to replace the weakened Weimar Republic (Hummel 2005: 51–75). Carl Schmitt, then, attempts to formalize the conditions for legitimizing an authoritarian power. Clearly, the Member States of the European Union are not authoritarian regimes. Moreover, the figure of the enemy implies reference to an organized social group. The friend–enemy distinction is an opposition between entities of the same type (Barker 2007: 25–8). Irregular migrants do not represent an organized political force conscious of its own existence. Clearly, Schmitt's thinking cannot be considered as a theoretical model for European integration and its project for management of its external borders. Its interest lies elsewhere. Above all, it is heuristic. The German jurist's thinking can provide an analytical grid for interpreting the processes by which the body politic is formed, independently of any reference to identity or ethics. What seems decisive in Schmitt's interpretation is not the question of war but the question of the place assigned to the otherness and to the border as demarcation line. Equally important is the possibility it opens of adapting certain historically distant categories to contemporary politics. For behind the friend–enemy distinction, we can in fact discern the political anthropology of Thomas Hobbes and the universal and atemporal scope of his theories (Duez 2008a). The friend–enemy distinction as a motor for political unity has in fact no meaning other than in relation to the fundamental human characteristics of fear of danger and the desire to free oneself of it.

Fear of the Other or Policy of Fear?

Underlining the role of fear, or at least of uncertainty, in the formation of the European social body inevitably leads us to question ourselves on the political use to which it can be put. In other words, is European policy against illegal immigration an example of a policy exploiting fear which has been deliberately undertaken by the European political elites? Is the branding of the disquieting figure of the irregular migrant a result of a deliberate effort to create sentiments of fear in the public, in order to encourage the formation of a community to which people feel they belong?

Suggestions that there is a strategic intention by politicians to exploit insecurity are frequent. From Albert Hirschman to Zygmut Bauman, and from Giorgio Agamben to Michel Foucault, several writers have seen a technique of government in policies for (in)security. For example, Murray Edelman emphasizes that:

> when the enemy can be seen to be objectively harmful, there is a powerful tendency to eliminate it in order to suppress the threat; but an opposite tendency comes into play when the enemy is an aggregate of groups behind a regime or a cause; in this case, those who are constructing the figure of the enemy have every reason to perpetuate and exaggerate the danger it represents. (Edelman 1991: 130)

---

12 On this point, Carl Schmitt's ideas and those of Norbert Elias are to some extent similar. The "law of monopoly" proposed by Elias leads to the formation of "offensive and defensive survival units" which do not necessarily reflect clear social identities (Elias 1997: 274).

A rapid overview of contemporary history leads us to believe that such theories cannot simply be brushed aside. Nevertheless, it seems that such analyses do not fit very easily with the case of the European policy against illegal immigration. Often guided by hostility in principle to political authority, these approaches, when applied to processes of European integration, generally overestimate the ability of Member States to agree to a coherent plan. It is true that the 1999 Tampere Scoreboard, the 2004 Hague Programme and various other specific plans have sketched out a path for a common policy on illegal immigration and management of external borders, but the application of these policies is never carried out in a consistent way. Progress has been made in a disorderly, even unwilling, manner.[13] Steps taken have often been carried out under pressure from day to day events, not following a precise plan. Securitization of travel documents and development of information exchange systems are a heritage of cooperation under the Schengen Agreement. Recent strengthening of these elements can be explained largely by the political dynamic created by the 11 September attacks and by pressure exerted by the United States on European States (Lodge 2004: 267–72). Deepening cooperation in the field of trafficking and exploitation of human beings can be seen as occurring in an environment marked by random cases highlighting such problems. We need only think of the case in which 58 irregular Chinese migrants were found dead in the port of Dover in June 2002. Finally, the setting up of the Frontex agency can be seen as being related to anxieties linked to the enlargement process of the Union to Eastern Europe and the development of a humanitarian crisis on Europe's southern borders.

More prosaically, European cooperation in the field of illegal immigration is closely linked to a logic of political opportunism. There is no European project for securitizing immigration which could have been defined in advance and then applied. Rather, national strategies have come together in a fairly haphazard manner and have led to political agreements on specific matters, the final nature of such agreements often being in response to the difficulties experienced in European negotiations. The upgrading in importance of the question of illegal immigration, firstly at the European Council, and later, in the Council of Ministers, has taken place following the "principle" of the highest common denominator. In contrast with the image of the terrorist, which is much more polemical than appears at first sight, there is a high degree of consensus on the issue of irregular migration. It is relatively vague and anonymous, whilst at the same time being fairly evocative. It is a symbol of otherness which can give tangible support to the uncertainties and fears of the majority of Europeans. These fears are not necessarily related to the same realities in different countries in the Union. In some cases, it is fear of the irregular working migrant who threatens jobs. In others, the concern is rather with the "ethnic" criminal, terrorist or "foreign exploiter" who abuses European social welfare systems (Huysmans 2006). Each Member State, and within each Member State, each social group, can provide the irregular migrant with a face adapted to its own preoccupations. In all cases, the polymorphous image of the irregular migrant encourages Europeans to unite around a political project defined in negative terms: the protection of acquired privileges and rights, and the preservation, not of a single European identity, but of European identities, in the plural. The manipulability, not to say the lack of definition, in the image of the Other appears here as an advantage. It

---

13 This unwillingness was also in evidence from the European Parliament in the name of defending the individual rights of European citizens and protecting human rights of migrants, as well as from certain Member States who saw the measures as infringing their sovereignty (Lodge 2004: 254; Apap, Carrera 2004: 399–416).

enables Member States to agree on a common European project, politically exploitable at the national level and meaningful for the majority of Europeans.

Following a mechanism reminiscent of the "self-fulfilling prophecies" discussed by Robert Merton (Merton 1998), this concentration on illegal migratory flows reinforces stereotypes and negative social representations. An increasingly closer link is drawn between irregular migrants and security issues. Far from calming social anxieties over migratory phenomena, the arrangements made for dealing with illegal immigration contribute to the tendency for illegal immigration to be dramatized in the media. They nourish new fears calling for new security measures (Huysmans 1995: 64). As so often, once the dynamics of an increasing sense of insecurity are unleashed, the latter discovers in its own development the very conditions of its reproduction. *Rapprochement* between Europeans therefore grows stronger as anxieties increase.

Conclusion

A product of the violent rifts between European countries in the twentieth century, Europe was consciously constructed in response to the risk of a hobbesian "war of all against all" (*bellum omnium contra omnes*). In the context of the cold war, it became a "survival unit" – in the words of N. Elias – in resistance to the threat from the Soviet Union. Fear is therefore at the heart of the European project, and was so from the beginning. Is that equivalent to saying that it is fear that has constructed Europe, and that fear is the foundation of European identity? Certainly not. Nevertheless, it contributed to it and continues to contribute to it. Committed since the beginning of the 1990s to a common internal security policy, the European Union has over the last few years developed its own security narrative in which the image of the border has come to play a central role. The Union has begun to identify and point out dangers confronting it. It has constructed a coherent discourse concerning the threats weighing on it. In this context, European discourse on the management of external borders has become a "unifying discourse" between Europeans. More consensual than the discourse on terrorism or drug trafficking, and politically more useful than organized transnational crime, the discourse on illegal immigration is received favourably by the populations of all the Member States. These discourses are liable to evoke the most universal experience of all, that of fear of otherness.

Whether deliberately or otherwise, IBM strategy feeds the syndrome of a "besieged citadel". That does not imply that Europe has become "Fortress Europe", even if that is sometimes claimed to be the case. It simply means that all the material, normative and discursive resources mobilized as part of external border management helps to create an image of a Europe confronted by the danger of illegal immigration. The migrant is not perceived as belligerent or openly hostile. But none the less he represents a threat to the security and well-being of Europeans. In developing this figure of alterity, in encouraging it to become anchored in collective representations, the Union is providing itself with a powerful instrument for integration and unification. But building a political community on the dynamics of a definition of *Self* and *the Other* necessarily implies that symbolic and material borders be constructed. In that case, integration is achieved at the cost of rejecting the outsider. From that moment onwards, Europe, by discovering its *Other*, may discover its *demos*. However, is that really the true essence of the European project?

References

Apap, J. and Carrera, S. 2004. Maintaining Security Within Borders: Toward a Permanent State of Emergency in the EU? *Alternatives*, 29 (4), August–October, 399–416.
Badie, B. 1998. *Réfugiés et sans-papiers. La République face au droit d'asile. XIXe–XXe siècle*, Paris, Hachette.
Badie, B. and Sadoun, M. (eds). 1996. *L'Autre. Études réunies pour Alfred Grosser*, Paris, Presses de Science Po.
Balibar, E. 2000. Prolégomènes à la souveraineté : la frontière, l'État, le peuple, *Les Temps Modernes*, 61, septembre–novembre.
Barker, R. 2007. *Making Enemies*, Basingstoke, Palgrave Macmillan, 25–8.
Bigo, D., Bocco, R. and Piermay, J.-L. 2009. Logiques de marquage: murs et disputes frontalières, *Cultures et conflits*, 73.
Carlier, J.Y. 2002. L'étranger: de l'ennemi au citoyen, *Les cahiers internationaux de symbolisme*, 101–103, 151.
Ceyhan, A. 2010. Les technologies européennes de contrôle de l'immigration. Vers une gestion électronique des "personnes à risque", *Réseaux*, 159, 133–4.
Coda, P. 2005. L'Agence européenne pour la gestion de la coopération opérationnelle aux frontières extérieures des États membres de l'Union européenne, *Revue du Marché commun et de l'Union européenne*, 489, June, 385–7.
Corten, O. 2004. La "guerre antiterroriste", un discours de pouvoir, *Contradictions*, no. 105, 2004, 3–13.
Department of Homeland Security. 2011. Report on the Assessment of the Secure Border Initiative-Network (SBInet) Program, 14 January.
Duez, D. 2008a. L'Europe et les clandestins: la peur de l'Autre comme facteur d'intégration? *Politique européenne*, 26, 97–119.
Duez, D. 2008b. *L'Union européenne et l'immigration clandestine. De la sécurité intérieure à la construction de la communauté politique*, Bruxelles, Éditions de l'Université de Bruxelles, coll. Études européennes.
Edelman, M. 1991. *Pièces et règles du jeu politique*, Paris, Seuil.
Elias, N. 1997. La transformation de l'équilibre "nous-je", in *La société des individus*, edited by N. Elias, Paris, Fayard.
European Commission. 2001. Communication from the Commission to the Council and the European Parliament on a Common Policy on Illegal Immigration, COM (2001) 672 final, 15 November.
European Commission. 2002. Towards Integrated Border Management of the External Border of the European Union, Communication of the Commission to the Council and the European Parliament, COM (2002) 233 final, 7 May.
European Commission. 2008. Report on the Evaluation and Future Development of the FRONTEX Agency, Communication of the Commission, 13 February, COM (2008).
European Commission. 2010a. Commission Proposes Better Management of Migration to the EU, Press release IP/11/532, 4 May.
European Commission. 2010b. Delivering an Area of Freedom, Security and Justice for Europe's Citizens. Action Plan Implementing the Stockholm Programme, COM (2010) 171, 20 April.
European Commission. 2010c. Background Information on Smart Border Initiative, Directorate-General Home Affairs, 1, available at: www.statewatch.org/news/2011/jul/eu-com-smart%20borders-note.pdf (accessed 12/11/11).

European Commission. 2011. A Better Management of Migration to the EU Press Conference on Communication on Migration Brussels by Cecilia Malmström, Commissioner responsible for Home Affairs, SPEECH/11/310, 4 May.
European Council. 2001. Presidency Conclusions, Laeken, 14–15 Decembre.
European Council. 2009. The Stockholm Programme – An Open and Secure Europe Serving and Protecting Citizens, doc. 17024/09, Brussels, 2 December 2009.
European Council. 2010. Internal Security Strategy for the European Union Towards a European Security Model, March.
Fichte, J. 1992. *Discours à la nation allemande*, Paris, Imprimerie Nationale.
Fisbach, F. 1993. L'Autre et l'Étranger: les enjeux de la reconnaissance et les stratégies de l'exclusion, *Revue internationale de philosophie politique*, 3, June, 65–88.
Foucher, M. 1991. *Fronts et frontières: un tour du monde géopolitique*, Paris, Fayard.
Frontex. 2010. Frontex Deploys Rapid Border Intervention Teams to Greece, *News Release*, 25 October.
Frontex. 2010–2011. Frontex Press Pack, available at: http://www.frontex.europa.eu/newsroom/press_pack/ (accessed 24/12/2012).
Goodwin-Gill, G.S. 2011. The Right to Seek Asylum: Interception at Sea and the Principle of *Non-Refoulement*, Fondation Philippe Wiener – Maurice Anspach, Chaire W.J. Ganshof van der Meersch Inaugural Lecture given at the Palais des Académies, Bruxelles, 16 February.
Greenhouse, L. 2011. Legacy of a Fence, *The New York Times*, 22 January.
Heine, S. and Magnette, P. 2007. Europe, les identités troubles, *Politique étrangère*, 3.
Herder, J.G. 1962. *Idées sur la philosophie de l'histoire de l'humanité*, Paris, Aubier.
Hummel, J. 2005. *Carl Schmitt. L'irréductible réalité du politique*, Paris, Michalon, 51–75.
Huysmans, J. 1995. Migrants as a Security Problem: Dangers of "Securitizing" Societal Issues, in *Migration and European Integration: The Dynamics of Inclusion and Exclusion*, edited by Miles, R. and Thränhardt, D., London, Pinter.
Huysmans, J. 2006. *The Politics of Insecurity. Fear Migration and Asylum in the EU*, London and New York, Routledge.
Jeandesboz, J. 2008. Reinforcing the Surveillance of EU Borders: The Future Development of FRONTEX and EUROSUR, CHALLENGE papers, August.
Le Texier, E. 2010. Mexique/Etats-Unis: de la frontière intelligente au mur intérieur, *Politique étrangère*, 4, 759–62.
Lochak, D. 1985. *Étranger: de quel droit?* Paris, Presses Universitaires de France.
Lodge, J. 2004. EU Homeland Security: Citizens or Suspects? *European Integration*, 26 (3), September.
McSweeney, B. 1996. Identity and Security: Buzan and the Copenhagen School, *Review of International Studies*, 22.
Merton, R. 1998. *Éléments de théorie et de méthode sociologique*, Paris, Armand Colin.
Mommsen, Th. 1985. *Histoire romaine*, Paris, Laffont.
Napolitano, J. 2007. Address to the National Press Club.
Neisse, F., and Novosseloff, A. 2010. L'expansion des murs: le reflet d'un monde fragmenté? *Politique étrangère*, 4, 2010.
Noiriel, G. 2001. *État, nation et immigration. Vers une histoire du pouvoir*, Paris, Gallimard.
Renan, E. 1882. *What is a Nation?* Conference delivered at the Sorbonne, Paris, 11 March.
Ritaine, E. 2009. La barrière et le checkpoint – Mise en politique de l'asymétrie, *Cultures et Conflits*, 1.

Schmitt, C. 2007. *The Concept of the Political*, Chicago and London, University Press of Chicago.

Schnapper, D. 1993. La nation et l'étranger, *Revue internationale de philosophie politique*, 3, June, 89–96.

Torpey, J. 2000. *L'invention du passeport. États, citoyenneté et surveillance*, Belin, Paris.

Waever, O. 1996. *European Security Identities*, 34 (1) March, 103–32.

Wæver, O. 1998. Insécurité, identité: une dialectique sans fin, in *Entre Union et nations: l'État en Europe*, edited by A.-M. Le Gloannec, Paris, Presses de Sciences Po, 91–138.

Chapter 4
Border Games: From Duel to Russian Roulette at the Border

Markus Heiskanen

Border security has undergone dramatic changes as a result of globalization and the proliferation of cross-border crime. State frontiers have expanded both outwards and inwards. The burden of their growing importance has been paid for both by states and people crossing the borders. States have to secure more permeable borders, just as travellers will be subject to more intensified border control measures. This chapter examines how the state border has been transformed from its visible, temporal and spatially defined settings into invisible, continuous and omnipresent surveillance of *the human body*. By analysing this quantitative and qualitative shift in border security in Europe, North America and Australia I will suggest that the frontier as a fixed borderline has been replaced by *mobile* and *speculative bioborders* – the human body and its virtual representative, the data subject. The "smart" shift to expedite cross-border movement of trusted travellers through biometrics may have catastrophic consequences for the non-trusted, the "others". This fuzzy embodiment may exclude them not only from the Promised Land of West, but even from their own selves, as their data subjects travel without any impediments in a borderless world. In addition to the post-911 climate of "fear and insecurity", *everybody* has been made a suspect. It is not only criminals, illegal migrants or "global outcasts" from the third world who have been put under the microscope, but even ordinary citizens, promoters of western ideas and values, who through risk analysis and data mining have been "profiled" as potential terrorists.

Borders are places of demarcation, state performance and social interaction. Borders are places of power relations. Borders are places of political, legal and administrative *games* between state and people. Every game has its rules, as with the duel and Russian roulette, where a death is a probable outcome for some players. In some games, such as gambling, speculation, manipulation and cheating are possible. One cannot rely on the rules of fair play being followed. This should not be the case at state borders where people move and pass across the outer edges or limits of *legal* entities (i.e. states). But I will argue here that, in some sense, border "performance" in contemporary borders resembles places of "border games", where nobody can be sure about the outcome of one's move. Borders can emerge out of state frontiers, in the territory of third states, or even within a state e.g. in a railway station, unexpectedly like a trump card a player pulls from up his sleeve in poker. Taking into account these observations, I have made four paradoxical propositions which I will deal with in my chapter. These are as follows:

- Borders are everywhere;
- Borders are nowhere;
- Everybody is a suspect;
- Everybody is nobody.

Borders are Everywhere: The Transition from the Borderline to Global and Fuzzy Border Spaces

Borders have undergone dramatic changes during the last few decades. Some argue that borders have lost their meaning due to the multiple processes of globalization, such as increased movement of people, better means of transportation, compression of time and space, global media penetration, new technologies in telecommunication and computing. Then there are those who underline the importance of the evolution of politics in nation states as a major actor in international relations. For example the collapse of communism generated around 20,000 kilometres of new territorial borders in Europe that have to be managed by EU member states.

Some scholars (Rumford 2006; Torpey 2000; Zolberg 2003) have analysed these new borders and spaces as emerging from the "spatial turn" in territoriality. Until the second half of the nineteenth century dealing with unwanted aliens in Europe was basically a local issue. Only after the First World War did the implementation of border control become increasingly centralized into national agencies. State frontiers and their control must be understood as an element of the invention and evolution of the nation state (Zolberg 2003). Control over the movement of people is part of the *stateness* of modern state (Tholen 2010). And now, when European integration has real momentum and consists of 27 member states, it is suggested that development of post-national regional communities (EU, NAFTA), or more generally, the shift from modern states towards *post-modern* forms of governance, will bring us beyond territorial control.

One of the most illustrative analyses as regards borders and border control is by Berry Tholen (2010). In his article he has analysed and compared the old "classical border control" to the "new border control". The shift towards the new border control seems to entail a number of multiplications. In this new system of control, the focus is less on the physical crossing of territorial borders than the process as a whole, from visa application and ticket reservation up to monitoring the travellers through their journey and passage from country of origin to the country of destination. This new mode of border control has resulted in a multiplication of borders, a multiplication of actors and a multiplication of data and technology.

Multiplication of borders means that travellers have to pass numerous checks during border control procedures. "The border" – instead of being a single borderline – can be illustrated by a model of concentric circles. This model is widely used for border management in the West. The EU has presented a four-tier border security model in the Schengen Catalogue (2002). The tiers are: 1) measures at the third countries; 2) cross-border cooperation with relevant authorities and institutions; 3) border checks and border surveillance at the EU external border; and 4) measures inside the EU. The US applies a similar approach, putting the emphasis on pre-frontier measures in countries of origin. The American approach is much more integrated, in the sense that Department of Homeland Security (DHS) was established soon after and in response to the terrorist attacks of September 2001, merging 22 law enforcement institutions (FBI, CIA, The Coast Guard, The Customs, The Border Police, Immigration and Nationalization Service etc.) under a common command.

Deterritorialization of spaces and a layered approach to border control can also be seen in politics. Neighbouring states can be seen as buffer zones or as a remote control of threats to mitigate security challenges at EU external borders. The candidate countries have to introduce Schengen standards and EU migration policy priorities years before full membership of the EU. The EU has also pushed forward its border control through neighbourhood policy with would-be members and other states contributing to EU border security. The European border agency Frontex has made "working arrangements" with many African and former Soviet states to cooperate on issues like migration and cross-border crime. The issues such as to what extent these agreements fall under the mandate of Frontex or their operational implementation under the international law of the sea during joint operations have been circumvented through political imagination. According to the COWI-report (2009) "The Working Agreements shall not be considered as an international treaty and as such are not legally binding. They are letters of intent and as such only work when such intent is present".

In this section, I have analysed some of the shifts that have happened in border control. These shifts can be called multiplications – citing Tholen. The term multiplication reveals something of their nature. In recent decades border control has been intensified: larger budgets, more staff, more actors involved, more data gathered and more technologies. By elaborating the "classical" and "new" border control models presented by Tholen the transformation of borders can be characterized in Table 4.1.

The evolution of border control from protection of state borders to governance of cyberspace can be divided in three periods. These periods are not sharply delimited. The end of Cold War was the kick-off for new security thinking. The same can be said of the terrorist attacks of 11 September, which turned the focus from migration to terrorism overnight. Transformation from border guard to border security or Integrated Border Management (IBM) has happened in stages but evolution in various countries has not occurred evenly. Especially in third countries where western countries have assisted in setting up modern border management systems, this evolution may have advanced rapidly.

Transformation has taken place simultaneously in North America, Europe and Australia (Andreas and Snyders 2000; Cornelius 2004; Torpey 2000). As Tholen has described, not all elements were new in every region. For instance, in the US private actors have been involved since the nineteenth century and in Europe special technologies for identification were tested and used in the late 1930s (Tholen 2010). There is also divergence between the states as regards the actors and involvement of "third" or "fourth" sectors within IBM. In the United States the third sector is much more widely used in border control than in the EU. Certainly, there is wide consensus as regards threats for border security, but their regional focus may differ. Border security in the US is much more terrorism-orientated than in the EU, which is more concerned about the management of illegal migration.

The evolution of border security or Integrated Border Management (IBM) through the *governance turn*, *spatial turn* and other multiplications has raised a number of concerns. It has been widely recognized that there has been a discrepancy between politics and practice. As Wolff (2010), Hills (2006), and many others have proven, integrated border management is at odds with the reality of different member states' interests and priorities and there is also the multiplication of grey areas. The multiplication of bilateral agreements between the EU, its member states and third countries to control immigration and co-operate on border management has opened a Pandora's Box of uncertainties regarding the legal, political and humanitarian aspects of those relationships (Wolff 2008, 29). In the next section, I will review the multiplication of legal loopholes, the purpose of which is not to make the borders porous, obscure or even questionable *but to make them disappear*.

Table 4.1   Transformation of borders

	Border guard	Border control	Border security/IBM
Modus operandi	Reaction	Pre-action	Prevention
Location	Border line	Border zone	Cyberspace
Focus of control	Territory	Flows/people	Data subject
Moment of control	Single	Multiple	Continuous
Actors	Military	Law enforcement	Security apparatus
Technology	Surveillance	Identity/biometrics	Data management
Threat	Military	Migration	Terrorism
Idea of government	Guard/segregation	Surveillance	Governance
	End of Cold War		**911**

Border is Nowhere: Legal Manipulation on the Border

Previously, I argued that borders have spread out from their territorial and national boundaries both inwards and outwards. They are everywhere. Now I will make a counter-argument and claim that borders have disappeared. I argue, like many academics, that borders are paradoxical entities by their nature (e.g. Marenin 2010; Diez 2006; Browning 2003). Borders are dividing lines not only in geography, culture, language, ethnics or politics but also in a social sense, in the construction of our identity and refining who belongs to "us" and who are "the others". New *smart* borders, where security threats are blocked at the very same time when *trusted* travellers pass the border without any impediments, contain concepts which are difficult to reconcile with each other. The basic policy issue at borders is how to balance the need for mobility with the need to control. In other words, how to adapt security concerns with those of freedom.

Manipulation has a negative image, suggesting scheming and intrigue, tampering in state affairs such as law and politics. What I mean when speaking about legal manipulation is exactly that: International law and state responsibilities are circumvented by "evolutionary" interpretation of law, annulling state sovereignty and integrity, removing some parts of state territory temporarily out of its jurisdiction, or pushing border control beyond the state border, operating in international waters and territories of foreign states preventing illegal migrants and would-be asylum seekers to reach the continent of Europe, Australia or the US. As Carrington (2006) has put it, in an era of heightened tension fuelled by global terrorism, western states in the neo-colonial antipodes have embarked on an aggressive policy of interventionism into the internal affairs of their neighbours to restore "law and order on the border".

Not only in legal or political terms, but also in a moral sense this is the most serious form of misuse of power. The Western world has been a champion of human rights and has made great efforts to establish them as a part of international law. The West has also exported western values through politics (e.g. the European Neighbourhood Policy) and practice when constructing border management in third countries. Rhetoric in politics to establish modern border management in third countries via different aid programs to promote regional stability has been justified by the weakness of state institutions, absence of rule of law, human rights violations and widespread corruption in state institutions. In the light of legal manipulation and "law and order on the border", western standard-setting can be seen as remote control of migration and construction through "buffer zones" – pushing the border forward "from our doorstep".

The most flagrant example of the intensification of politicization of border control, the "border games", can be found in the "Pacific solution" where a package of border protection measures was introduced in Australia two weeks after the September 11 terrorist attacks in the United States. Following the politicization of border control issues during the 2001 election, new laws were passed. The Migration Amendment (Excision from Migration Zone) Act 2001 allowed for certain parts of Australian territory to be excised from the migration zone. What this means is that asylum seekers landing on any excised part of Australia are unable to invoke protection under the United Nations Refugee Convention, for they have not *technically* (or in a *legal* sense) arrived in an Australian migration territory (Carrington 2006, 184). In some cases the decision of excision was made retrospectively since the asylum seekers had already come ashore and been apprehended for mandatory detention. Importantly, Australia still claims sovereignty over zones excised from Australian territory, but treats these zones as extra-territorial for migration purposes. This unconventional thinking disrupts the nexus between territory and sovereignty in trying to establish a sort of legal vacuum where international law has been nullified as in Guantánamo or in CIA secret jails in European soil.

The European Union has almost been as innovative as the US "deputy" in the Pacific Ocean when implementing new generation of Integrated Border Management. Following the lead of the United States in linking aid for the developing world to "worthy" states engaged in democratic reform and economic freedom, the European Union's aid to its neighbours (like Australian aid to Pacific islands) has been linked to a series of similar conditions (von Strockirch 2004, 376). In parallel to Australian new interventionism in foreign policy, the EU has taken similar steps with its Mediterranean and Atlantic neighbours. In June 2003, the European Union rejected the United Kingdom's proposal (supported by both the Dutch and Danish governments) to establish regional protection zones and detention centres in North Africa (Green 2006). But Italy, which suffers constant migration pressure from Libya, enacted an "Anti Landing Decree" (2003), which grants the Italian police special powers to intercept and turn back boats *before* they enter Italian waters (Green 2006). This legal manoeuvre resembles the Australian migration zone where a state uses its (illegal) powers outside of the state's territory.

The EU has been successful in operational cooperation organized and coordinated by its External Border Agency, Frontex. Frontex has negotiated Working Agreements (WA) and many other agreements are in progress to cooperate with its neighbours in border management. Cooperation has been tied to economic support and construction of border management systems. This "*European solution*" includes repatriation agreements and (joint) patrolling of international waters as well as in the territorial waters of the contracting parties. Even though this policing is not as intrusive as the Australian solution to deploy hundreds of police officers and other state officials across the South Pacific to stabilize law and order in the island nations (Dinnen 2004), this new "interventionism" in the policing of "weak and failed states" is, according to Carrington (2006), a "strategy of illiberal governance under the familiar guise of protecting our security". The "law and order on the border" approach has given a strong impetus to the law that has been made a servant of security needs and high politics motivated by a culture of fear and suspicion.

In the following section I will review how the expansionist security regime has put not only migrants, but even EU citizens, under suspicion in the "war against terrorism".

Border control is seen as one of the major means to prevent terrorism. This should not go unchallenged. What is terrorism? Or who is a terrorist? How to distinguish a "bad guy" from a trusted traveller at the border? These and other relevant questions will be studied in the following section, to shed light on the discourse about border security as a means of counterterrorism. I will argue that an even bigger challenge than terrorism *per se* is to protect our society against the "war on terrorism".

Everybody is a Suspect: From "Facts of Acts" to "Invention of Intention"

Now I will study and question current border security tools such as profiling and risk analysis when we are waging *war* against terrorism. In these "border games" everybody is made a suspect and put under scrutiny. This *may* be justified *if* measures taken to protect our security are *necessary*, *effective* and *proportional* compared to other means available and valued against other rights rooted in a state governed by law. If not, there is a danger that our constitutional rights and fundamental freedoms will be compromised unnecessarily in the name of security, which instead of protecting us from external threats, invades our privacy more thoroughly, generating more serious internal threats to our informational self-determination. In the worst-case scenario the relationship between our human body and informational e-body will be cut off and we are debordered from our data subjects.

Terrorism is by no means a new security challenge. As Bailes (2005) has suggested, terrorist acts are probably as old as mankind and have been frequently used in conflict situations. What was different on 11 September and since is the dimension and international aspects of the attacks and how they have changed the agenda of the United States of America, which later on became a global agenda. Terrorism became an issue of "high" politics and the securitization of borders. This is not to say we should underestimate the need and necessity of state action to curb terrorism or to undervalue human suffering and losses in attacks all over the world. Instead, policy actions and legal measures taken in the name of border security to catch criminals need to be questioned. The 11 September attacks and manipulation of the attendant fear of the "other" serve as an opportunity for states to respond with a control-oriented security strategy which has the goal of controlling potentially problematic populations who have been increasingly marginalized in the global economy. After September 2001, the states engaged a war on terror that involved significantly tightening immigration procedures and border controls, and loosening legal standards related to surveillance and detention (Danner 2006).

The events of 11 September led to a knee-jerk reaction against terrorism. For the first time in the history of the UN, article 51 of the UN Charter was invoked after a terrorist incident. But what is terrorism? The international community has taken concrete measures against it since at least 1937, when the League of Nations adopted a Convention for the Prevention and Punishment of Terrorism. Nevertheless, a legal definition of terrorism that can be universally agreed upon, and universally applied, is missing (Bailes 2005). To surmount this dilemma states have resorted to define terrorism through "terrorist acts" in their criminal codes. The same approach is used in international conventions and policy papers.

A lack of definition – or competing definitions – was only one part of the problem. Broadening the definition of terrorism to cover even normal criminal acts can cause trouble in several ways. Even more challenging for the prevention of terrorism is the function creep from criminal acts to judgment of intention to commit such acts. Transformation from "facts of acts" to "invention of intention" means a shift from objective elements of crime to subjective elements, not only of criminal minds, but also law enforcement's perception of, intentions towards and speculation about alleged criminals and their future orientation. This may lead to the manipulation of the law for security purposes and the erosion of privacy rights of those suspected. At the same time the purview of terrorist acts have expanded to cope with support of terrorism by providing information or material resources, or by funding its activities by any way. In addition, inciting, aiding or abetting, and attempting an offence labelled as "terrorism" is made punishable. Terrorization of criminal codes is part of the securitization manoeuvre in progress. Offenders guilty of petty crimes such as the theft of mobile phones, 10 chickens, or even a bowl of cherries (Scheinin et al. 2010) have been recorded on European Arrest Warrant, a tool that has been used to pursue terrorists and other serious criminals.

One major challenge for risk management at the border is the question of profiling. Risk analysis and profiling are modern tools of border agents to detect security threats within the stream of border traffic. They are based on data mining that can be defined as "the application of database technology and techniques – such as statistical analysis and modelling – to uncover hidden patterns and subtle relationships in data and to infer rules that allow for the prediction of future results".[1] Thus data mining consists of not only the collection and managing of data, but includes analysis and prediction, too. Analysis can be subject-based or pattern-based. Subject-based data analysis seeks to trace links from known individuals or things to others. In pattern-based analysis, investigators use statistical probabilities to seek predicates in large data sets.

Academics (Jonas and Harper 2006; Kessler and Daase 2008) have questioned the *state-of-the-art* of modern border security tools to pursue terrorists. Jonas and Harper have claimed that the possible benefits of predictive data mining for finding planning or preparation for terrorism are minimal. Instead the financial costs, wasted efforts, and the threats to privacy and civil liberties are potentially vast. Those costs outstrip any conceivable benefits of using predictive data mining for this purpose. What is also noteworthy is that "attempting to use predictive data mining to ferret out terrorists before they strike would be a subtle but important misdirection of national security resources".

Why is terrorist profiling a mission impossible? Predictive data mining has been applied most heavily in the area of consumer direct marketing. Companies have spent hundreds of millions if not billions of dollars, and studied consumer behaviour based on millions of patterns to draw up a profile of the typical or "ideal" consumer. Despite all of this information collection and statistical analysis, the false positive[a] rates in marketers' searches for new customers are typically in excess of 90 per cent.[3] According to Jonas

---

1 Government Accountability Office, Data Mining: Federal Efforts Cover a Wide Range of Uses, GAO-04-548, May 2004.

2 A false positive is when system identifies a terrorist plot that really is not one. A false negative (known also "black number" problem) is when the system misses an actual terrorist suspect or plot. Depending on how detection algorithms are set up, one can err on one side or the other: increase the number of false positives to ensure one is less likely to miss an actual terrorist plot, or reduce the number of false positives at the expense of missing terrorist plots.

3 The statistics on effectiveness for data mining programmes are less impressive. Bruce Schreier (2006) conducted calculations on the accuracy of data mining systems in the US. According to Schreier, a data mining system with an assumed accuracy rate of 99 per cent false positive (one in 100 is false positive) and 99.9 per cent false negative (one in 1,000 is false negative), and 1 trillion possible indicators (being 10 communications, per person, per day) will generate 1 billion false alarms for every

and Harper there are at least two reasons why predictive data mining is not useful for counterterrorism. First, the absence of terrorism patterns means that it would be impossible to develop useful algorithms. Terrorism does not occur with enough frequency to enable the creation of valid predictive models. Second, the corresponding statistical likelihood of false positives is so high that predictive data mining will inevitably waste resources and threaten civil liberties.

In practice, there is little evidence that profiling is an effective approach to combating crime. On the contrary many research findings suggest that profiling reduces the effectiveness of law enforcement. An operation known as *Rasterfahndung* in Germany provides an illustrative example. Between 2001 and early 2003 German state police collected sensitive personal data from approximately 8.3 million people since it was discovered that several of the perpetrators of the 11 September terrorist attacks had lived and studied in Hamburg. The German federal government tasked the state governments to collect and process personal data in a massive data mining operation to identify other potential terrorist cells. Despite the collection and trawling of the data of several million people, the operation failed to identify a single terrorist (Moeckli and Thurman 2009).

There is some evidence that efficacy has improved when law enforcement changed their profiling practices by removing race and ethnicity from a criminal profile. For example, in 1998, the US Customs Service changed its stop and search procedures by removing race and ethnicity from the search profiles. At that time, 43 per cent of searches were of African-Americans and Latino/as. By 2000, the racial disparities in Customs searches had nearly disappeared. Customs conducted 75 per cent fewer searches and their hit rate improved from under five per cent to over 13 per cent. In addition the hit rate for all ethnic groups became almost even. Using intelligence-based, race neutral criteria allowed Customs to improve its effectiveness tenfold while stopping fewer innocent people, the vast majority of whom were people of colour. More recently, a "STEPPS" project (Strategies for Effective Police Stop and Search) in Bulgaria, Hungary and Spain achieved similar results (Ethnic Profiling 2009). As we will see now, not only third-country nationals, but even citizens may be bordered out of territory and spaces, and even themselves.

Everybody is Nobody: Nobodization of the New Digital World (B)order

Above I have examined how everybody is under suspicion in the name of terrorism. Here I will briefly address the issues about how our personhood may be questioned in "border games". We are *nobodies* for the state. This may happen in multiple ways. Our presence in certain spaces may be questioned. One may be present in a physical sense through his/her bodily manifestation at the border, but in legal terms (s)he has not entered the country. Transit passengers are typical examples of people in these "in-between" spaces, where people are at the same time present and non-present. Our identity may be questioned at the border, if there are some problems in our travel documents. Identification is based on information on numerous databases, which were cross-checked during entry/exit procedures. Our bodily integrity may be intruded against not only in informational sense but physically, too. CCTV, heart beat detectors and body scanners are only few examples of the technology used during border checks. And finally, as in dangerous games like Russian roulette, many lose their

---

real terrorist plot in uncovers. In practise this means that police will have to investigate 27 million potential plots every day, in order to find one real terrorist plot per month.

lives. Border security measures taken by states to protect their citizens create real victims when thousands of people lose their lives every year on their way to the Promised Land of West.

Establishing the identity of its citizens has been one of the key concerns of the modern nation-state (Higgs 2001; Torpey 2000). Moreover, states have deliberately sought this power in order to define who may move within and across their borders. The desire of nation-states to maintain greater surveillance over populations is evidenced by the spread of biometric identification technologies – automated systems that use biological or behavioural characteristics to identify individuals. Biometric technology offers the possibility of rapid flows of capital and global elites through borders while simultaneously fortifying the border against unwanted intrusion from "deviant" outsiders (Wilson 2006). Biometric border control systems thus serve to exacerbate the trend identified by Bauman (2000, 221) as "the extraterritoriality of the new global elite and the forced territoriality of the rest".

The issuing of smart entitlement cards and the coding of "illegal" migrants with biometric technologies serves to merge discourses of mobility with those of terrorism and transnational organized crime. The integration of biometric technologies into the international passport and visa system has renewed the capacity of states to police their boundaries. Biometric technologies are seen as both symbolic and constitutive of new expressions of state sovereignty. The particular focus upon asylum seekers in biometric deployment is intertwined with the securitization of migration and the criminalization of persons seeking to move from the global south to the global north (Wilson 2006, 101). The act of seeking asylum is itself constructed as a "crime of arrival" (Weber and Landman 2002, citing Webber 1996).

In order to exclude these "folk devils" (Cohen 2002) and "global outcasts" (Carrington 2006) from society, states must be able to determine their identity and country of origin. According to information provided by Frontex, a total number of 18,987 irregular immigrants landed in the Canary Islands during HERA I operation in 2006. Only in 100 cases could the country of origin be determined (Carrera 2007). This is one of the reasons that have led the western states to strive for a global identity system (Policy Laundering Project 2005). Expanding databases and the incorporation of biometric identifiers in international passports facilitate new and powerful forms of cataloguing, coding and filing individual identities (Wilson 2006, 98).

Borders are not watertight. Some people who have entered lawfully then remain after their permission to stay expires. In fact overstay when the visa has expired, is the most common form of illegal migration in the European Union. In addition deportation procedures are expensive and time-consuming and reach only a minimal share of illegal migration. In the name of security, states have to be firm "ensuring that unauthorised arrivals do not enter the *community* until their claims have been properly assessed; ensuring that unauthorised arrivals do not enter the community until after essential identity and health checks are conducted and assessments of character and security issues can be made", as claimed by the Australian government (Carrington 2006, 189). These outlaws are not only out of law, but out of the state. They are nobodies within the state territory but without any legal status. This parallels the punitive treatment of lepers some centuries ago described by Foucault (2007).

The rise of "law and order" politics, "governing through crime" (Simon 1997), "militarization of policing" (McCulloch 2004) and "governing through counterterrorism" (Virta 2011) are manifestations of the progressive securitization and *militarization of societies* in the affluent global north (Wilson 2006). As argued by Bigo (2002) and Lyon

(2004), heightened concerns surrounding borders and mobility post-11 September have been coterminous with an increased securitization of societies *within* the boundaries of the nation-state. The use of biometric technologies, initially introduced in relation to specific categories of people such as travellers, welfare recipients, and asylum seekers, is expanding to encompass whole national populations. Moreover, as the net of suspicion appears to widen, so the category of ideal suspects is more broadly applied and normalized as the routine identity of the nation-state. Citizens are being reconfigured as ideal suspects, too (Wilson 2006). Examples from the US, Australia and member states of the EU show that even citizens of so-called post-modern western states have met expulsion like traitors in ancient times (Carrington 2006; Bennett 2005; Lewis 2005).

Besides the biometrics there is another issue in border control that is challenging our privacy. Looking at the Greek roots of the word privacy, it refers to being deprived of something essential, which according to ancient Greeks was taking part in society. In modern times, privacy means the ability to seclude oneself or information about oneself selectively. It describes a sphere in which a person can decide about the matters he does not want to share with others, where one determines a way of life that reflects one's own attitudes, values, tastes and preferences. Privacy has also been termed "the right to be left alone". A newer dimension, or concept of privacy, is "informational privacy". According to Westin (1967) it can be described as the "claim of individuals as to determine for themselves when, how and to what extent information about them is communicated to others". Miller (1971) understands informational privacy as the individual's ability to control the circulation of information about them (as quoted in Ploeg 2005).

Modern border control is based on information management and risk analysis. An increasing number of operational agreements have been developed to facilitate law enforcement cooperation and automated access to law enforcement information between member states in order to fight terrorism and serious crime. Furthermore, the EU (and the US) are rapidly building vast databases for immigration and border control and allowing law enforcement access to these resources to assist in fighting terrorism and crime. Vaguely formulated legal instruments such as regulations on SIS II and VIS allow the risk of *function creep*. By authorizing "designated authorities" and "coordinating authorities" on information exchange they carry the risk of granting access to the data by every agency or authority member states wish to include (Ahumada-Jaidi 2010). It also makes possible to transfer data to countries outside the EU and to international organizations.

Trends towards interoperability between EU-operated databases and information exchanges across borders should be accompanied by the establishment of a comprehensive, specific and legally binding data protection framework with adequate safeguards to cover risks related to large scale storage and use of personal data. Unfortunately transnational operational capacity and cooperation is being developed at a pace that far outstrips the development of accountability standards and oversight mechanisms. This is even more regrettable when one takes into account the liability of the security community to indulge in mission creep and use information for other purposes than those authorized by law. This is evidenced by numerous data mining programs which have been terminated after they came under increased public scrutiny.[4] In addition to possible misuse, leaks and loss

---

4 For instance the following programmes have been terminated according to DETECTER Report: Survey of Counter-Terrorism Data Mining and Related Programmes D08.1, 30 November 2009: Multi-State Anti Terrorism Information Exchange (MATRIX), USA; Analysis, Dissemination, Visualization,

of data will increase the more authorities have access to sensitive personal information (Ahumada-Jaidi 2010).

Modern border security places high confidence in technology. Technology has a seductive appeal – presenting pretty pictures or easy solutions – to which decision makers may too often surrender. The EU Integrated Border Management (IBM) strategy has been characterized as one that relies on management of risk and threat together with the exchange of information and the use of technology "as the most efficient 'solution' to guarantee a secured European border" (Carrera 2007). But technology is far from perfect, without errors and malfunctions. The EU's own Data Protection Supervisor, Peter Hustinx, has pointed out that in two or three per cent of the passports there is something wrong with the biometric data (van der Hilst 2009). One may assess, how many errors in data is possible in the 20 million visa applications processed every year in Europe in the light of spelling, transliteration, transcription of date of birth and other linguistic and numerical practices endogenous to each state. And in case of contradiction, the onus of correctness of data is put on the person under control, who does not know, and is not allowed to know, what kind of data is collected and used to evaluate his or her eligibility to enter or leave a country in question.

In addition to informational privacy, border control intrudes into our private sphere by subjecting our bodies to control. CCTV, body scanners, substance detectors and hidden cameras are used for screening passengers. Biometric technology is a subset of sensors and uses body parts and features to identify and authenticate people in order to be sure that they are who they say they are. Biometric passports in EU use RFID-chips that contain, besides regular personal data, a picture and fingerprints of both index fingers. A passenger can be scanned and millimetre waves are beamed to create a virtual three-dimensional image from the reflected energy. The scanner essentially creates a "naked" image of the passenger, which makes it easy to detect weapons or other items prohibited by law. The full body scan also shows breast enlargements, body piercing and a clear black-and-white outline of the passengers' genitals. The image taken can in some cases be very identifiable. The data sought by this technology can therefore be considered personal data (van der Hilst 2009).

Our personhood may be questioned at the "border games" in multiple ways. The most serious form of this "nobodization" is to disvalue humanity, disregarding harmful consequences of border control. It is estimated that around 4,000 asylum seekers or irregular migrants drown at sea every year as they attempt to flee conflict, persecution and poverty. Around 2,000 of these drowning are estimated to occur in the Mediterranean Sea (Moorehead 2005; Pugh 2005). According to Pugh, around a third of those who begin these perilous voyages die en route. They depart from Libya, Tunisia or Morocco, having already journeyed thousands of miles from sub-Saharan Africa, or countries such as Iraq, Bangladesh and Palestine. According to a report in the *European Race Bulletin*, those attempting to reach Europe as irregular migrants almost always rely on the services of traffickers or smugglers for at least some part of their journey (Fekete 2003a, 3; Morrison 2000; cited in Green 2006).

Attempts to make borders impenetrable have forced would-be border crossers into more irregular and dangerous modes of travel. Cornelius (2005) estimates that the fortified border between the United States and Mexico has been 10 times deadlier over the last nine years for those attempting to enter United States without permission, than was the Berlin

---

Insight and Semantic Enhancement (ADVISE), USA; Able Danger (USA), Threat and Local Observation Notice (TALON), USA, and Terrorist Rasterfahndung, Germany.

wall to those attempting to leave East Germany during the entire 28 years of its existence. Not only this, but the United States border strategy has manifestly failed in its objective to curb unauthorized border crossing, and has, according to Cornelius (2005, 782), "been more effective in bottling up unauthorized migrants inside the US than deterring them from coming in the first place" (cited in Pickering and Weber 2006, 10).

Conclusion

Mobility has shaken the traditional understanding of borders. Some authors have identified the changing and dynamic nature of borders in Europe from territoriality towards a hugely disperse and complex web of non-physical lines which move every time a person exercises mobility (Guild 2003). Borders have become portable, not only in the sense, as Lyon has described them, as being embedded with the plastic cards (2005, 66) but through their fixation to the human body. It is just how Amoore puts is, bodies become "sites of encoded boundaries", and individuals can actually carry the border within them, forever standing on it but never actually crossing it, never free from suspicion (2006, 347–8). The physical and fixed borderline has been replaced by *speculative* and *movable bioborders*.

How is this shift from physical frontier line to the management of flows of people and risk seen in politics? In fact actual policy strategies at EU level still present the strengthening of the principle of territoriality, and its securitization, as one of the more important European responses and values for dealing with the dilemmas posed by globalization and modernity (Carrera 2007). But this "new territoriality" can be described as "extraterritoriality" and "interventionism" (Carrington 2006). The borders of the United States of America, European Union and Australia are pushed away from their geographical settings and "forced" into the high seas and territories of third states. This is possible through "weak state" strategies (Smith 2005) and a political imaginary that is based on the manipulation of both international and national law. At the same time, and using the same line of argument, the western states can extend their executive powers beyond the state territory, even inside the third states, and exclude their international obligations because of extraterritorial action. This revolutionary state practice is supported by wide policy convergence. Policies of development, immigration, and good neighbourhood are tied up with economical support and construction of border management in the third states.

All these "solutions" – Pacific, Caribbean or European – have questionable reputation in the immediate past because they include not only violations of international law but also unjust treatment of "the others". Perhaps we "Westerners" have, intentionally, very short institutional memory forgetting how our ancestors have, in the hope of better life, conquered foreign continents like New Europe (America) and Australia exterminating Aboriginals and destroying their culture. We do not see these poor people from the third world as adventurers but as "global outcasts" and "folk devils" to be segregated and prevented from leaving their country of origin. At the same time mobile elites enjoy free movement through smart border technology and trusted traveller programs, and more remote places on Earth have been made reachable for them. Why it is impossible for us to review the borders *not only* as dividing lines, barriers, more closely policed, more violent "sharp edges" (Gready 2004, 352) of territory, but at the same time bridges, places of exclusion *and* inclusion, manifestations of sovereignty *and* identity, and cursors of security *and* freedom. It is this biased approach by states, dazzled by the neurotic pursuit of security in the climate of the fear of terror confused with the suspicion of the other that has made borders paradoxical sites of passage through implementation of questionable practices and suspicious "rites of passage" (Salter 2005).

Creation of a legal vacuum at the border is ever more striking when one takes into account our western values such as democracy, respect of human rights, and state governed by law. In addition to border control is the law enforcement function by its very nature. The rule of law, good governance, the principle of proportionality and other legal, professional and ethical standards ought to be followed during the daily performance at the border. The European Union is eager to export democratic and human norms and values to the third world, too. Paradoxically these ideals have not been followed in modern border management. Moving the border outside Europe and delegating the responsibility over the third-country nationals to the hands of a third state – often known to be authoritarian regimes, whose record on human rights and respect of the rule of law are weak – reveals the discrepancy of high politics and low practice.

It is not then a surprise why "border games" are far from an even match, a duel between equals. On the one side we have a suspect who is usually black, male, from Africa or a Muslim-looking person from anywhere on the other side we have neither a state, nor the EU or the United States but the whole West and their ring of friends, who share common concern on terrorism. The suspect is subjected to border control procedures that are based solely on his or her intention to cross the border. Basically in theory, in a legal sense, it is an administrative procedure to be followed without any prior view of one's culpability. In practice (through risk analysis and profiling) the border-crossers are treated as suspicious, would-be terrorists, illegal migrants, bogus refugees or other "global outcast". Traditional presumption of one's innocence rooted in western criminal codes is ignored. A border-crosser is "guilty" if not proved "not guilty".

What about the weaponry between the rivals in these "border games"? A traveller, besides his travel documents and belongings, has only his words. In a duel, each of the fencers has a sword. On the other side, states have access to a whole weaponry of international databases (SIS, VIS, Eurodac, Interpol, Europol etc.) as well as national databases. In one state this may include tens of databanks from police, border guard, intelligence, security service, customs and military. In many countries border guard officers also have access to other state administered databases like foreign affairs, social service, traffic administration, and ministries or authorities such as finance, labour and taxation. The evolution of the "principle of availability" in EU law has also opened up access to information in other EU member states for the prevention of terrorism and other serious crime. Thus the game at the border reminds us more of Russian roulette than a duel. It is only a question of time when "the other" will be lost – drowned, deported, e-bodily stigmatized and "injured", disgraced by "shaming by naming" etc. – if not lucky enough to pass the digitalized electric fence of West.

This uneven trait hides one of the biggest peculiarities and paradoxes of European border security. Border security tools – legal instruments, policy papers, law enforcement practices (risk analysis, profiling) and technological innovations (biometrics), have been developed on the verge of a political "nervous breakdown" since 11 September. Terrorism, and especially Islamic fanaticism, has been widely cited as the biggest threat to the EU when "putting humans under the microscope". In Europe, the most common form of terrorism is political or religious and occurs only in a few countries. European extremism is mainly locally limited, ethno-historically orientated, politically motivated and has nothing to do with borders or border security. Nevertheless, the limitation of political and human rights (e.g. freedom of movement, informational privacy, bodily integrity), increased information exchange within and across borders between law enforcement, and the mushrooming of data mining techniques has been promoted to secure the EU at the borders. Securitization of border security has occurred in the leading strings of the US. How far is the EU ready to follow its overseas ally? When the first preventive attack on European soil is compared with the attacks against alleged terrorist targets in Afghanistan, where more civilians had been killed compared to the malefactors?

Post-11 September securitization has led to state of "hypersecurity". It is a kind of extremism, and thus as dangerous as other forms of extremism in generating more insecurity than security. In border security this security nervousness has led to an intensive rebordering process where borders have been, not only pushed but more forced on to third countries through extra-territorialization. Intense pursuit of risk analysis and management has led to *de*territorialization, and when this "solution", through experimentations in the Pacific, Caribbean, Mediterranean and Atlantic, has proven to be ineffective, to hyperterritorialization, following the analogy of hyperterrorism. Within this policy the inclusion of e-bodies of third-country nationals (TCN) on law enforcement data banks means their physical presence can be excluded from European "banks" and society. Humanity has been reduced to bare figures in statistics or human bar codes in databases. Agamben (2004) has warned that humanity *per se* becomes the dangerous class. This encourages me to ask whether we are waging the right war when striving to maximize security at the borders. Or should we be more concerned about the war against terrorism that has produced great restrictions on our privacy, caused human suffering and been a waste of money without proven efficiency to catch the wrongdoers. Are we not on the way to dystopia, which can be characterized as Burgess and Rodin (2008, 57) have suggested as "*bad security and no privacy!*"

References

Ahumada-Jaidi, A. (2010). Border Control and Internal Security in the European Union – Information, Technology and Human Rights Implications for Third-country Nationals. *DETECTER Collaborative Project*, No. 14.1, 1 March 2010.

Agamben, G. (2004). No to Bio-political Tattooing. *Le Monde*, 10 January 2004.

Amoore, L. (2006). Biometric Borders: Governing Mobilities in the War on Terror. *Political Geography*, 25(3): 336–51.

Andreas, P. and Snyders, T. (eds). (2000). *The Wall around The West: State Borders and Immigration Controls in North America and Europe*. Langham, MD: Rowman & Littlefield.

Bailes, A. (2005). Terrorism and the International Security Agenda Since 2001. In Winkler, T.D., Ebnöther, A.H. and Hansson, M.B. (eds), *Combatting Terrorism and its Implications for the Security Sector*, Swedish National Defence College, Stockholm: 12–25.

Bauman, Z. (2000). Social Issues of Law and Order. *British Journal of Criminology*, 40(2): 205–21.

Bennett, C.J. (2005). What Happens When You Book an Airline Ticket? The Collection and Processing of Passenger Data Post-9/11. In Elia Zureik and Mark B. Salter (eds), *Global Surveillance and Policing*. Portland, Oregon: Willan Publishing: 133–8.

Bigo, D. (2002). To Reassure and Protect after September 11th. *Social Science Research Council Essays*, available at: http://www.ssrc.org/sept11/essays/bigo.htm (accessed 15/05/13).

Browning, C.S. (2003). The Internal/External Security Paradox and the Reconstruction of Boundaries in the Baltic: The Case of Kaliningrad. *Alternatives*, 28: 545–81.

Burgess, J.P. and Rodin, D. (eds). (2008). The Role of Law, Ethics and Justice in Security Practices. Conference report. International Peace Research Institute, Oslo (PRIO), Prio Papers.

Carrera, S. (2007). *The EU Border Management Strategy. Frontex and the Challenges of Irregular Immigration in the Canary Islands*. CEPS Working Document No. 261.

Carrington, K. (2006). Law and Order on the Border in the Neo-colonial Antipodes. In Pickering, S. and Weber, L. (eds), *Borders, Mobility and Technologies of Control*. A.A. Dordrecht, Springer: 179–206.

Cohen, S. (2002). *Folk Devils and Moral Panics: The Creation of the Mods and the Rockers*, 3rd edn. London: Routledge.

Cornelius, W.A. (ed.). (2004). *Controlling Immigration: A Global Perspective*, 2nd edn. Stanford, CA: Stanford University Press.

COWI Final Report 2009. External Evaluation of the European Agency for the Management of the Operational Cooperation at the External Borders of the Member States of the European Union.

Danner, M.J.E. (2006). Borders, Belonging and Homeland (In)security. In Pickering, S. and Weber, L. (eds), *Borders, Mobility and Technologies of Control*. A.A. Dordrecht, Springer 111–22.

Diez, T. (2006). The Paradoxes of Europe's Borders. *Comparative European Politics*, 4, 235–52.

Dinnen, S. (2004). Lending a Fist? Australia's New Interventionism in the Southwest Pacific. *State Society and Governance in Melanesia Discussion Paper*, Discussion Paper 5, Research School of Pacific and Asian Studies. Canberra: ANU.

Ethnic Profiling 2009. ENAR Fact Sheet 40. Available at: http://cms.horus.be/files/99935/MediaArchive/pdf/FS40%20-%20ethnic%20profiling.pdf (accessed 15.03.2011).

EU Schengen Catalogue (2002). External Borders Control, Removal and Readmission: Recommendations and Best Practices. Council of the European Union.

Foucault, M. (2007). *Security, Territory, Population: Lectures at the Collège de France, 1977–1978*, translated by Burrchell, G. New York: Palgrave Macmillan.

Gready, P. (2004). Conceptualizing Globalisation and Human Rights: Boomerangs and Borders. *International Journal of Human Rights*, 8: 345–54.

Green, P. (2006). State Crime Beyond Borders. In Pickering, S. and Weber, L. (eds), *Borders, Mobility and Technologies of Control*. A.A. Dordrecht, Springer: 149–66.

Guild, E. (2003). The Border Abroad – Visas and Border Controls. In Groenendijk, K., Guild, E. and Minderhoud, P. (eds), *In Search of Europe's Borders*. Hague: Kluwer International Law.

Higgs, E. (2001). The Rise of the Information State: The Development of Central State Surveillance of the Citizens in England 1500–2000. *Journal of Historical Sociology*, 14(2): 175–97.

Hills, A. (2006) Control, Protection and Negligence. In Pickering, S. and Weber, L. (eds), *Borders, Mobility and Technologies of Control*. A.A. Dordrecht, Springer: 123–48.

Jonas, J. and Harper, J. (2006). Effective Counterterrorism and Limited Role of Predictive Data Mining. *Policy Analysis*, 584: 1–12.

Kessler, O. and Daase, C. (2008). From Insecurity to Uncertainty: Risk and the Paradox of Security Politics. *Alternatives*, 33: 211–32.

Lewis, N. (2005). Expanding Surveillance: Connecting Biometric Information Systems to International Police Cooperation. In Zureik, E. and Salter, M.B. (eds), *Global Surveillance and Policing: Borders, Security, Identity*. Portland, Oregon: Willan Publishing: 97–112.

Lyon, D. (2004). Identity Cards: Social Sorting by Database. *Internet Issue Brief*, No. 3, Oxford Internet Institute, University of Oxford.

Lyon, D. (2005). The Border is Everywhere: ID Cards, Surveillance and the Other. In Zureik, E. and Salter, M.B. (eds), *Global Surveillance and Policing: Borders, Security, Identity*. Portland, Oregon: Willan Publishing: 66–82.

Marenin, O. (2010). Challenges for Integrated Border Management in the European Union. DCAF Occasional Paper, No. 17.

McCulloch, J. (2004). Blue Armies, Khaki Police and the Cavalry on the New American frontier. *Critical Criminology*, 12: 309–26.

Miller, A. (1971). *The Assault on Privacy*. Cambridge: Harvard University Press. As quoted in van der Ploeg, I. 2005. *The Machine Readable Body, Essays on Biometrics and the Informatization of the Body*. Shaker Publishing.

Moeckli, D. and Thurman, J. (2009). Survey of Counter Terrorism Data Mining and Related Programmes, D08.1. Detection Technologies, Terrorism, Ethics and Human Rights. EU 7th Framework Programme, DETECTER, FP7-SEC-2007-217862.

Pickering, S. and Weber, L. (2006). Borders, Mobility and Technologies of Control. In Pickering, S. and Weber, L. (eds), *Borders, Mobility and Technologies of Control*. A.A. Dordrecht, Springer: 1–19.

Rumford, C. (2006). Rethinking European Spaces: Territory, Borders, Governance. *Comparative European Politics*, 4: 127–40.

Salter, M. (2005). At the Threshold of Security: A Theory of International Borders. In Zureik, E. and Salter, M.B. (eds), *Global Surveillance and Policing: Borders, Security, Identity*. Portland, Oregon: Willan Publishing: 36–50.

Scheinin, M., Vermeulen, M. and Tzanou, M. (2010). EU Law and Policy Approaches to the Applicapility of Human Rights Norms in the Fight Against Terrorism. DETECTER Collaborative Project, D06 No. 2, 31 May 2010.

Schreier, B. (2006). Why Data Mining Won't Stop Terror, 3 September 2006, available at: http://www.schreier.com/blog/Bruce Schreier is the CTO of Counterpane Internet Security.

Simon, J. (1997). Governing Through Crime. In L. Friedman and G. Fisher (eds), *The Crime Conundrum: Essays on Criminal Justice*. Boulder, CO: Westview Press.

Smith, P.J. (2005). Policy Convergence or Divergence in Canadian–American Legislative Responses to 9/11 and the US–Canada Border. Paper prepared for European Union and North American Border Security Policies in Comparative Perspective Conference, University of Victoria, 2–3 December 2005.

Tholen, B. (2010). The Changing Border: Developments and Risks in Border Control Management of Western Countries. *International Review of Administrative Sciences*, 76(2): 259–78.

Torpey, J. (2000). *The Invention of the Passport: Surveillance, Citizenship and the State*. Cambridge: Cambridge University Press.

van der Hilst, R. (2009). Human Rights Risks of Selected Detection Technologies. Sample Uses by Governments of Selected Detection Technologies. DETECTER Collaborative Project, No. 17.1, Draft V.0.5 FINAL, 11 December 2009.

Virta, S. (2011). Re/Building the European Union. Governing through Counterterrorism. In Bajc, V. and de Lint, W. (eds), *Security and Everyday Life*, New York and London: Routledge: 185–211.

von Strockirch, K. (2004). The Region in Review: International Issues and Events 2003. *The Contemporary Pacific*, Fall, 370–82.

Webber, F. (1996). *Crimes of Arrival: Immigrants and Asylum seekers in the New Europe*. London: Statewatch Publishing.

Weber, L. and Landman, T. (2002). *Deciding to Detain. The Organisational Context for Decisions to Detain Asylum Seekers at UK Ports*. Human Rights Centre, University of Essex, Colchester.

Westin, A.F. (1967). *Privacy and Freedom*. New York: Atheneum. As quoted in van der Ploeg, I. 2005. *The Machine Readable Body, Essays on Biometrics and the Informatization of the Body*. Shaker Publishing.

Wilson, D. (2006). Biometrics, Borders and the Ideal Suspect. In Pickering, S. and Weber, L. (eds), *Borders, Mobility and Technologies of Control*. A.A. Dordrecht, Springer: 87–109.

Wolff, S. (2008). Border Management in the Mediterranean: Internal, External and Ethical Challenges. *Cambridge Review of International Affairs*, 21(2): 253–71.

Wolff, S. (2010). *EU Integrated Border Management Beyond Lisbon: Contrasting Policies and Practise*. Available at: http://kms1.isn.ethz.ch/service-engine/Files/ISN/122303/...0b07.../ch_1.pdf (accessed 10.11.2010).

Zolberg, A.R. (2003). The Archeology of "Remote Control". In A. Fahrmeir (ed.), *Migrtion Control in the North Atlantic World: The Evolution of State Practices in Europe and the US from the French Revolution to the Inter-war Period*. Oxford: Berghahn: 195–222.

Chapter 5
Borders, Bordered Lands and Borderlands: Geographical States of Insecurity between Canada and the United States and the Impacts of Security Primacy

Victor Konrad

On January 9, 2011, *The Chronicle of Higher Education* featured a story about the penetration of US Border Patrol agents and activity "Far From the Border" between the United States and Canada, and the detention of foreign students enrolled at US universities as they returned to school after the holiday break in Canada. The article suggested that aggressive US border patrols were expanding efforts to snag foreign students (Woodard 2011). This story, and many others like it portrayed by the media over the last decade, reveals that security has become a part of every border crossing function, and that pervasive security has expanded and re-shaped the borderlands of interaction. The infusion of more security to make the border more definitive and incisive has in fact created a broader borderland of border-related interaction, most of it aligned with and impacted by enhanced security. This anachronism suggests an important revelation about how borders work or do not work in a globalizing world: the higher the wall that is created, the greater the shadow that it casts. Also, as more attention, human resources, money, and activity are concentrated spatially in an effort to enhance security, there will in fact be spillover that dissipates spatially to expand and complicate the security zone. This spillover effect is related to the "breaking points" that occur with the spatial and temporal concentration of security (Konrad 2010a). The overall effect may be approaching the chaotic, as delivery systems are taxed beyond capacity, enhanced security procedures and products are not tested adequately or explained effectively, and the border-crossing firms and public (customers) are not apprized sufficiently about the impacts. This overall effect also conveys the states of insecurity that continue to prevail fully a decade after the events of 9/11 in both the United States and Canada. Security and insecurity have become inseparable, pervasive and invasive in the lives of Americans and Canadians. Nowhere is this situation more evident than along the border and in the borderlands.

This condition would be acceptable if Americans and Canadians would welcome and tolerate the visible, expanded border security zone, but they do not. Indeed, Americans and Canadians want to feel secure, yet they do not want the invasion of pervasive security in their daily lives, or in the borderland interaction zone where they go about their daily activities. Border security is but one additional dimension of security in the dialectical struggle between inherent freedoms in our societies, and the assault on these freedoms by forces both inside and outside Canada and the United States (Konrad 2010b). The creep of security into borderland society and the establishment of security primacy in the borderlands of interaction are unwelcome forces, even for the security agencies which now are more visible and will need to be more accountable. More and more evident is the need to explore the impact of security on other aspects of border-related activity, to theorize about what is happening and how it works, and to develop policy solutions acceptable to Canadians and Americans.

Americans and Canadians are not alone in dealing with the dilemma of heightened borders and intensified securitization in a world that is becoming, in many other ways, borderless. The forces of globalization, re-territorialization and identity shifts have rendered a new geographical order, have obscured, initially, and then revealed emphatically, that borders do matter. Borders are not only problematic in a "borderless" world but also borders figure prominently in the economic, environmental, cultural, and geopolitical debates about this world (Diener and Hagen 2009: 1196–216). Bordering process is now viewed by theorists as spatial and social practice as well as physical and symbolic marking of difference. Borders shape and are shaped by what they contain, and borders grow in significance in a world of increasingly asymmetric relationships based on wealth and power (Konrad 2009).

> We need to change the way in which we think about borders to openly acknowledge their equivocal character. In other words, we need to see a border not as that which is either fixed or that as such must be overcome, but as an evolving construction that has both practical merits and demerits that must be constantly reweighed.

"Borders matter, then, because they have real effects *and* because they trap thinking about and acting in the world in territorial terms" (Agnew 2008: 175–91). All of these insights may be applied in the case of the Canada–US border, where both Americans and Canadians have been trapped indeed into thinking too territorially with the advent of an era of securitization concurring with advanced globalization. How do we conceptualize borders that straddle these powerful forces? This challenge has led to the conceptualization of a general theory of borderlands that envisions interaction of policy activities of multiple levels of government with local cross-border culture, local cross-border clout, and market forces and trade flows (Brunet-Jailly 2005: 145). A related conceptualization defines power as the operative force in the momentum of the relationships between the policy activities of multiple levels of government, market forces and trade flows, cross-border political clout, socially constructed and reconstructed identities, and multiple levels of cross-border culture (Konrad, Nicol 2008: 55). At the very least, the theoretical advances have enabled researchers to isolate, and, to a degree, articulate the forces at work in bordering and re-bordering.

Theorizing about borders has revealed the powerful and pervasive role of culture in defining and mediating borders (Konrad and Nicol 2011: 70–90).

> Borders and Cultures are both diminished, ostensibly, through globalization, yet both concepts have re-emerged as more evident, real and powerful social constructs in the 21st century. Combined as one concept, as borderlands culture, the constructions of more emphatic division, on the one hand, merge with the more strained, intense and anxious threads of connection, on the other hand, to display a new cultural geography in the borderlands. This geography, at and near the border, exhibits greater and more defined spatiality: the boundary line is more evident, flows across the border are channeled, connections are managed, communities on the line are at once differentiated and aligned

selectively, and cross-border culture is seeking a new spatial order in an era of security primacy. (Konrad 2010b)

This chapter explores both the states of insecurity and the related impacts of security on the borderlands between the United States and Canada. The perspective is geographical, and so the dimensions of insecurity and the impacts identified for consideration are those that relate to territory, environment, and community. The states of insecurity are grounded in the geographical asymmetry of the United States and Canada and the sustained regionalization of both countries. Added to this framework of insecurity is another geographical and social contributor to insecurity: the differentiation of community along the border. A fourth state of insecurity is found in the reticence of systems and structures to prevail across the boundary. Two related states of insecurity round out the set: the anchor and impact of culture and identity, and the institutionalization of borders, bordered lands and borderlands. Six related impacts arising from the states of insecurity are discussed in this chapter, although these are by no means considered to be definitive due to the incipient nature of this research. Spatial re-ordering is the first and the most apparent impact. The escalation to security primacy has not been evident at the borderline alone, nor has it been an even, consistent and non-resisted force in the borderlands. Security primacy has differential spatial qualities, and the spatial result of applying more security, and making security paramount, has been to change and define more sharply the hierarchy of border crossing points, to stretch the securitized zone between these points, to funnel expedited corridors through this zone, and extend, differentially, the security zone throughout the borderlands. As a result of this extension a new definition of borderlands is apparent, and a new geography of security borderlands begins to emerge. Another impact of heightened security is the detrimental effect on the environment of the borderlands. This operates in various ways from direct pollution concentration from idling vehicles waiting for inspection, to sudden security operations impacts on protected lands and waters. Elsewhere in the borderlands, the social fabric is being stretched and torn with the barriers, regulation changes, wait times, and restrictions of the heightened security border. Communities near the border are impacted socially and economically with enhanced security, whereas communities across the border are severely strained to the point of dissolution. In these communities, and among the business, cultural and social groups who live there, a heightened sense of uncertainty prevails because security primacy impacts most activity in the borderlands, and it does so in an unpredictable way. Due to this heightened uncertainty, and the other dimensions of change outlined, pervasive security polarizes secured and non-secured spaces, places and people to create a segregated spatial dynamic in the borderlands that rivals the division enforced by the border itself.

Geography, Security and States of Insecurity

After the events of 9/11, the security and insecurity border between the United States and Canada grew immensely on the land and in the perceptions of Canadians and Americans. Yet, the insecurity of the relationship between Canada and the United States has been revealed in the border regions and along the boundary since the line was drawn. The geographical states of insecurity are well documented and acknowledged if not defined explicitly as a set of underlying conditions that both contribute to and align impacts of the enhancement of security in the bordered lands and borderlands of Canada and the United States.

Two related geographical forces have formed a framework for insecurity. One is the asymmetry between the more populated, more powerful United States and Canada.[1] The other is the extensive and sustained regionalization of both countries.[2] The asymmetry slants the playing field of bilateral relations and enhances the insecurity of the Canadian position. With the security concerns of Americans aggravated by the events of 9/11, the asymmetry became more exaggerated as the border became incised and flows were impeded across the boundary. This exaggerated asymmetry has prevailed since 9/11. Border regions have been sustained as defined geographical entities along and to a lesser extent across the borderline even though the "top down" federal presence has become more evident along the boundary. The resulting national-regional tensions regarding border enforcement have produced another dimension in the insecurity framework.

Contained and operating within this insecurity framework is an even greater reticence of systems and structures to prevail across the boundary after 9/11 than before the massive security breach occurred. Advances made in trade cooperation with the NAFTA, and in various other facets of integration, were either lost or scaled back after 9/11. The discourse of cooperation is now a discourse focused on the search for heightened security. To this end, the systems and structures that are growing rapidly across the border are those designed to facilitate enhanced security and the reduction of risk through advanced technologies.

The border has always differentiated communities located on or near the line. This differentiation has enabled economic and social engagement during periods of intense interaction, prosperity, and mutual interdependence. Yet, in periods of insecurity, particularly in the United States, the differentiated communities have become front line places in the effort to build security. The same places that epitomized cooperation, even integration, have now become the staging locations of security infrastructure, operations and discourse. This reversal has in effect created more insecurity through the expression of enhanced security.

The reversal is possible in part due to the anchor of national identity that is planted firmly at the boundary. Borderlands culture is at once capable of cross-border expression and firm national identification. This schizophrenic condition, in its own right, imparts an element of insecurity, which becomes a strong component in the expression of the geographical states of insecurity between the United States and Canada. Add to this the institutionalization of the border, the differentiation of bordered lands, and the vacillating expression of borderlands, and the base for constructing and re-constructing geographical states of insecurity becomes evident beneath the veneer of the ostensible "longest undefended border in the world".

New and Expanded Spatial Dimensions of Security and Insecurity

Border analysts have characterized the post-9/11 border between the United States and Canada as thick, and the process of security enhancement as thickening (Ackelson 2009: 336–51). The boundary has not been expanded; it remains the same line with the same dimensions maintained by the International Boundary Commission. The process of securing the border, however, has changed, and it is this process and our views and discourse about this process that have changed the spatiality of the border and the adjacent borderlands. During

---

1   This asymmetry is the subject of considerable discussion among social scientists concerned with Canada–US relations. A geographical overview is offered in Konrad and Nicol, *Beyond Walls*, chs 2, 3 and 4.
2   Ibid., ch. 4.

most of the twentieth century, when Canada and the United States shared the so-called "longest undefended border in the world", border security was conducted and concentrated at *points* along the boundary. These points or *ports* gathered flows and were the sites of security and other forms of compliance screening. Airports and seaports offered similar border compliance functions and facilities, and they were points as well in a spatial system that was essentially disaggregated. As security became more of a concern for Canadians, and particularly Americans, a new spatial system emerged in which points/ports were superseded by corridors and zones to form a continuous security space along the boundary (Konrad and Nicol 2004).

In the contemporary Pacific Northwest border region, for example, the core of the border region is a primary corridor comprised of four associated land border crossings, combined with water, rail and air crossings (Loucky, Alper and Day 2007). This Cascade Gateway now funnels most of the cross-border traffic in the region to the extent that flow enhancements to both land and air traffic are concentrated at the ports in the corridor and at both primary and secondary international airports in the corridor borderlands (Figure 5.1). The corridor, with world cities Seattle and Vancouver at both ends, is evolving and expanding to serve a growing population in the entire international region, as well as a substantial number of visitors.

The Cascade Gateway has grown in several significant ways. Each of these dimensions of growth has a border effect, and each of these border effects is expressed spatially in the borderlands. Most evident is the expansion of security infrastructure at and around the ports-of-entry (POEs), and particularly the two major POEs at the Peace Arch and Pacific Highway crossings situated almost adjacent to each other. The Pacific Highway crossing, also referred to as the truck crossing, has experienced substantial expansion of infrastructure during the last two decades. It serves commercial, bus and passenger car traffic, whereas the Peace Arch crossing is restricted to cars. With the recent modernization, expansion and reconstruction of border facilities on both sides of the border at both the Peace Arch and Pacific Highway, these two crossings have all but merged to create a border security zone along the border from the coast more than a mile inland. The few remaining private properties are in a web of sensors and surveillance along the border. The spatial impact is an integration of security functions and facilities along the border, and the destabilization and removal of other land use in the border zone, unless it conforms with or benefits from the security primacy. In order to enable expansion of the security zone, some residences were purchased by the governments and demolished. This appropriation, and the expansion of security facilities and functions, has, according to residents and local community officials, reduced the value of properties in the security zone. The result has been a variant of residential "blockbusting", in this instance authorized by the governments. Land uses consistent with security, brokerage firms for example, have expanded in the security zone where regulations have permitted. These functions, as well as additional security facilities not required at the immediate border, are now located within several blocks of the boundary. These include Border Patrol, express delivery services, secure storage facilities, and other services linked to maintaining the secured border. These facilities have been situated in the borderland rather than immediately adjacent to the border due to land price considerations, zoning, and anonymity concerns. The overall spatial impact has been to expand the security zone both along the border and back from the border.

If security land use was consistent with residential, commercial, farm and other traditional land uses in the Cascade Gateway, this expansion of the security zone might be welcomed, but security primacy dictates a form of secured spatial segregation marked

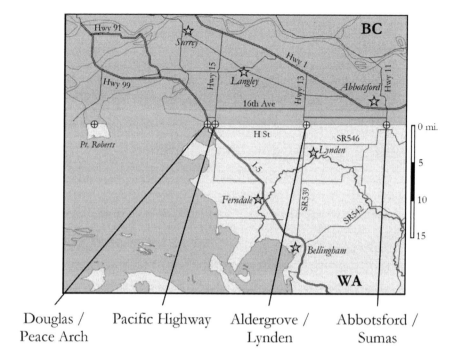

Figure 5.1   Map of the Cascade Gateway
Source: Permission of the Border Policy Research Institute, 2013.

by walled and fenced perimeters around secured facilities both along the border and in the borderlands. In Blaine, WA, the once small, isolated, and softly landscaped border crossing facilities have grown into a massive security installation and complex of secured institutional structures that dominates the landscape and pervades the borderlands. The Peace Arch and surrounding international peace park, constructed in the twentieth century, look strangely out of place in this new border landscape. Local officials acknowledge that the new federal jobs and cash infusion in the local economy are good for a town that has lost much of its "border business" of retail facilities dependent on a border that was easy to cross. Yet, they are concerned that Blaine's "security enforcement identity" is inconsistent with the coastal retirement image that the community wishes to promote.[3]

The security enforcement presence is not restricted to Blaine and the other border crossing points in the Cascade Gateway. Although less evident between the smaller, eastern crossings in the Gateway, the sensors and other barriers stretch along the border to Lynden and Sumas and beyond. Border Patrol surveillance is evident all along this boundary zone, and this surveillance now extends as well into the borderlands to the south as far as Bellingham and beyond into the Skagit Valley.

The expansion and enhancement of security at, between and beyond the ports-of-entry of the Cascade Gateway illustrate spatial extension, concentration and linkage of security

---

3   Interviews in Blaine, WA, 2009 (see Konrad 2010a).

in the borderlands. Also apparent is the differentiation and even segregation of security-related land uses from other land uses at and near the border. Overall, security functions now command space along the boundary and well into the borderlands to establish a secured zone or at least a zone under surveillance. This zonal extension of security is graded or scaled back from the border with greater emphasis placed on surveillance of major routes and communities in the borderlands. Security has developed a new spatial signature and this is decidedly zonal rather than point oriented. Point or port orientation, however, remains predominant as the main security focus thus conveying a dual strategy for security enforcement. People who cross the border and also live in the borderlands are now even more likely to encounter security wherever they go. Furthermore, borderland residents have yet to acknowledge and accept that the point orientation of border security that prevailed previously, and did less to impact their spatial behavior and lives, has given way now to a more prevalent and invasive spatial reach of multi-faceted security.

Environmental Impacts of Security: Extending the Insecurity Border into Protected Lands

Immediately to the east of Sumas, WA, the easternmost POE in the Cascade Gateway, the Cascade mountain range rises quickly astride the border and the landscape changes dramatically from flat farmland in the Nooksack-Fraser Valley to steep ridges surrounding volcanic Mount Baker. Here the land on both sides of the border is under the stewardship of state/province and federal authorities bound by conservation and preservation legislation. These environmental regulations, claim Republican members of the US House Natural Resources Committee, impede the US Border Patrol in the accomplishment of its duties along the border. For example, environmental regulations prohibit motorized vehicles in ranges of the endangered grizzly bear thus impeding the mobility of the US Border Patrol (Lengell 2010) Although these regulations still remain intact, there is mounting pressure from Republicans to repeal these environmental constraints to consistent security implementation along the entire Canada–US border, or to transfer control over the public border lands from the Department of the Interior, the National Parks Service and the National Forest Service to the Department of Homeland Security (Margetta 2011).

This Republican initiative is driven in large part by events and debates originating along the border between Mexico and the US where environmentalists and enhanced border security advocates argue about the negative ecological effects of security installations, fences, and patrols, and the environmental regulations as obstacles to border securitization. Along the southern border, the security imperative is more advanced and linked to the more immediate, more apparent and more constant double threats of large scale illegal immigration and drug smuggling. As such, the impacts on environment, and specifically on the fragile Sonoran Desert environment, are more evident. Yet, the arguments for greater militarization of the border and the release of public lands from conservation covenants are equally compelling for ranchers and anti-immigration advocates. This level of polarization and controversy does not yet exist with regard to the northern border environment, although there has been an uneasy truce for almost a century between ranchers, stockmen, and large private land owners, on the one hand, and the National Forest Service and the Bureau of Land Management on the other hand (Konrad 2010a).

The danger of course is the possibility that legislation ostensibly aimed at the southern border will impact cross-border environmental rules and standards established by Canada and the United States for maintaining boundary water quality, protecting endangered species, assuring air quality, and many more aspects of the shared environment. Canada and the United States have not always agreed on how this shared environment should be managed, but most of these differences have been mediated successfully with the result of stronger, binding environmental regulation on both sides of the border. This record does not exist to the same extent at the southern border.

Consequently, any efforts to draw parallels between the borders with regard to environmental issues are necessarily strained. In a recent survey of border stakeholders in the northwestern border region, few statements posed in the survey elicited the almost complete, and substantially emphatic agreement that "The border between Canada and the United States is fundamentally different than the border between Mexico and the United States". The more specific statement "The United States Department of Homeland Security needs to establish and operate a common border policy for U.S. boundaries with Mexico, Canada and the Caribbean" also evoked substantial disagreement and some uncertainty, particularly among US respondents. The responses are consistent with the substantial reaction against DHS "common outlook" approaches to dealing with all borders of the US. When interviewed about this "one border" perspective, most stakeholders, including retired US enforcement officials, who were willing to speak to the subject, dismissed the notion as uninformed, unworkable and politically motivated (Konrad 1995: 194–223).

The imperative to enhance security on the southern border by de-regulating environment may gain some traction in the southern border regions of the US, but the same strategy attempted on the northern border may find considerably less support. In part this is due to the variable environments from northwest to east along a 5,000-mile boundary bisecting six distinctive cross-border regions, and the fact that all of these environments have strong independent, constituencies. Furthermore, the web of international agreements and protocols for environment between Canada and the US is extensive and daunting to unravel.

Meanwhile, there have been enhancements to border security in protected lands. The Border Patrol uses horses to survey the borderline on the ground whereas air surveillance, sensors at and near the boundary line, enhanced satellite photography, and special patrols along highways through protected areas, are among the security enhancements used to accommodate the special requirements of working within protected environments.

Yet, the limited impact of security enhancement in protected lands stands in sharp contrast to the extensive impact on the land at or near cross-border corridors and in populated areas along the boundary. This contrast questions the efficacy of securitization, and underlines the value of maintaining lands where not only is the environment protected but also the area is protected from unbridled security infrastructure development occasioned by one political interest in one particular era.

There is an argument as well for solidifying environmental protection through international agreements such as World Heritage designations. This has worked for Canada and the United States in the isolated wilderness surrounding Mount Elias on the Alaska–Yukon–British Columbia border. This area marks the northern extent of a region designated the Crown of the Continent which encompasses areas above 10,000 feet in the Rocky Mountain cordillera south to Colorado. At a similar scale, a loop around Lake Superior defines a cross-border ecological region around the world's largest fresh water lake. Smaller scale loops across the border mark drainage systems and core waterways of environmental significance.

Returning to the Cascade Gateway, those border residents concerned about environmental protection in the area, have noted that the security enhancements have hampered grass-roots participation across the boundary (Norman and Bakker 2008: 1–19). Stakeholders in environmental organizations and in government point to a thicker border which blocks integrated action across the border with the result that these stakeholders are working in "silos" on common environmental problems and cross-border environmental issues (Konrad 2010a). Connections and committees do not filter down, and community does not filter up. "Something has happened to cross-border environmental conscience". "We don't galvanize around environmental issues across the border the way we used to" This problem is ameliorated in the boundary waters realm where the International Joint Commission remains a cross-border force with 100 years of experience and political clout (Nijnatten and Boardman 2009).

Some stakeholders do feel, however, that advancements in cross-border cooperation are being achieved despite the enhanced security border and its negative impact on easy and spontaneous collaboration. One advance is in the area of cross-border air quality alignment where standards may be invoked and agencies, both governmental and non-governmental, have strong legacies of cross-border cooperation. A second advance is in the area of collaboration on dealing with the flooding of the Nooksack River with its cross-border impacts in the Abbotsford area. A third area of advance is with regard to cross-border protection of the Sumas Aquifer (Konrad 2010a).

Changing Social Fabric in the Borderlands: Insecurity across the Border

Security primacy is the prevailing construct in the post-9/11 Canada–US borderlands. A mantra of vigilance has sustained this primacy. Yet, vigilance is not really in question, nor is the value of effective security. The difficulty lies in the overwhelming weight and presence of the security imperative and the articulation of this imperative at the border and in the borderlands. Security enforcement is viewed in isolation: security is the primary consideration and all other considerations become secondary. Security primacy quite simply overshadows and obscures other functions of the border, and security primacy becomes like a magnet that draws other border functions and re-shapes them as security-related priorities. This makes it difficult to clarify and understand issues surrounding tourism, immigration, transportation, and trade, for example, because they all need to pass through security filters first. All border functions have become transfigured as security functions.

The border Americans and Canadians have come to imagine is an insecure border. For Americans, the border is insecure because even the investment of billions of dollars, the deployment of an extensive military presence, the immense application of new technologies, and the substantial enhancement of border zone infrastructure, cannot guarantee total security. For Canadians the border is insecure because Canadian prosperity depends on an efficient, predictable and rapid-crossing system, a border that is essentially porous, interactive and integrative. This imagined border has yet to evolve. As long as the construct of the insecurity border prevails between the US and Canada, the social reconstruction of an integrated border space, shared between neighbors, allies and friends, remains hollow rhetoric. After 9/11, as Americans suddenly and rapidly turned their attention to the border with Canada, they imagined a porous and penetrable boundary, and they constructed a thickened border in response. This imagined boundary has become the operational border. In a sense, we get the border that we imagine.

Americans used to say that Canadians are "just like us". Canadians were indignant and disagreed, but it was comforting for Canadians to know that American neighbors, allies and trading partners also felt an affinity for Canadians. Affinity is complicated, questioned and even lost when identities change, and if one identity prevails over another or reduces the other. Affinity is affected as well when it is not affirmed in periods of crisis and change. In the immediate wake of 9/11, faced with uncertainties and security concerns, US policy makers initially affirmed friendship and collaboration through the partnership forged by Deputy Prime Minister John Manley and Homeland Security Chief Tom Ridge. Yet, this affinity was diminished as Canada did not join the alliance against Iraq, and the affinity was abrogated with continued references to terrorists from Canada, and the deportation of Canadian Mayer Harar to Syria where he was tortured.

One of the major concerns of borderlands stakeholders interviewed in the Pacific Northwest was that the trust so vital to the sustainability of a vibrant and enabling borderlands culture, had deteriorated with the securitization of the border (Konrad 2010a). Border stakeholders agree with media pundits and the public at large, particularly in Canada, that a "trust deficit" has emerged or become more apparent between the US and Canada. It is at the border and in the borderlands where this lack of trust is evident and articulated. Stakeholders feel the problem needs to be addressed. One stakeholder, among the 98 interviewed in the Washington–British Columbia boundary region, made the bold statement: "trust is local. It cannot be mandated by DC". Community and society at the border are in transition, and ostensibly threatened by substantial security enhancements at the border. "We don't bowl anymore" states a resident of Blaine, lamenting the previous engagements with neighbors in White Rock, BC.

For some cross-border societies like the Dutch in the Fraser and Nooksack Valleys, there has been recognizable social breakdown in the cross-border community as a direct result of the security enhancements. People do not cross regularly anymore for social and cultural events. Gone is the "church rush" across the border when you picked up some groceries as well and stopped at the dairy north of Lynden for ice cream and inexpensive milk. Young Dutch Reform community members no longer participate as actively in cross-border socialization with the result that cross-border marriages within the church have dropped off. The Dutch are not alone in suffering the social impact of a thicker border. East Indian communities across the border feel the impact as well through enhanced profiling, delays due to wait times, and additional regulation that complicate their agricultural and family connections across the border.

A discontinuity emerges, according to one stakeholder, because transnationals are seen as an asset in Canada and a problem in the United States. In addition, border problems and breaking points have created a negative discourse which in turn extends the impact of the difficulties and leads to greater distance between "thin" and "thick" border positions and advocates. "Thin" border advocates assert surprise at border treatment and assert their right to "customer service", emphasizing that "Customers have rights. We have a right to cross the border". Others decry the lack of civility among border authorities, and call for a return to the "Peace Arch celebration". Stakeholders in the smaller cross-border communities in interior BC/WA claim that cross-border society still works, and point to the symbolic elements like the "six pack border" which continues to allow Canadians to cross casually for purchases in the US. But, "communities at smaller crossings don't interact as easily and spontaneously as they once did before 9/11". Sports teams do not cross as often and there are fewer joint events. All of these seemingly small changes are part of a larger and potentially debilitating alteration of borderlands culture (Sadowski-Smith 2002).

Affinity is being challenged in another sense as well by the increasing number of Americans immigrating to Canada, and Canadian residents of the US returning to Canada from the United States. Americans are coming to Canada and staying because it feels and is different according to migrants interviewed in a British Columbia study (Hardwick, Mansfield, 2009: 383–405). "They are attracted by their perceptions of Canada's more liberal political system, multicultural policies, support of gay and lesbian rights, prosperous real estate market, and universal health care". Canadians are returning to Canada from the US for most of the same reasons, and according to a doctor from Westport, Ontario, who recently returned to his ancestral Canadian home:

> We feel as if we have finally come home. We have made more friends here in a few months than we had in the U.S. after years of living there and raising a family. I feel that I am appreciated here for what I do in the health care system.[4]

Yet, the doctor from Westport, and numerous US immigrants to Canada do not regret their experience or sever ties to the United States, including US citizenship. In this sense the migrants and returnees are both potentially contributors to a new realization of affinity in the borderlands in which the abrogation fueled by post-9/11 insecurity re-bordering, US identity over-determination, and ultimately American exceptionalism, all are recognized for what they are, and repudiated in favor of positive and productive linkage and integration in the borderlands.

Insecurity in Community at the Border and Community across the Border

Whereas the imposition of security primacy has impacted the social fabric of the borderlands in negative ways, the ultimate result has been a reshaping of society and social connections across the border and in the borderlands. This result has reinforced an over determination of American identity and it has reinforced the line between communities at the border, and contributed a discontinuity to community across the border. The new, robust American identity displayed at the border with Canada operates at several levels but with negative effects for the borderlands at all of these scales. In twentieth-century border communities, where the simple display of the flag was deemed confirmation of American or Canadian identity, verification is now required, even between neighbors in daily contact. Up the scale of contact, between regions and nations, identity verification is required by statute.

Although the process of human identity construction remains an issue of considerable theoretical debate, there is consensus that identity construction emerges from either or both ego formation and/or oppositional processes. Identity is realized in one sense as the result of struggle or quest, and in the other through self-realization which is then communicated into collective identity and by constructing "others". Imaginary and historical identities as evolved through world views and altruism play a role also in shaping individual and group identities. Identity constructs are shaped as well by interests and causes, and identities in turn align these directions.

National (nation-state) identities are institutionalized and expressed as citizenship. Citizenship documentation is required to cross the boundaries of most nation states, and certainly to cross boundaries between blocs of aligned states (EU for example) emerging on the globalized map. In a globalizing world, the concept of global citizenship remains an abstraction for everyone because statist alignment remains mandatory for identity

---
4 Anonymous interview with Victor Konrad, July 24, 2009.

verification. Dual and multiple citizenship, in one sense an acknowledgement of emerging globalization, also becomes a complication and constraint in identity verification. What citizenship is required at the border? In cosmopolitan identity construction there are several difficulties that remain to be resolved before global identity construction may proceed as envisioned by Homi Bhabha (Bhabha 1994). Among these are the disentangling of the concepts of citizen and subject, and the privileging of certain citizens and the "othering" of those deemed less worthy of full rights. The institutionalization of othering in nation states in transition toward a global common humanity remains a glaring paradox. In the United States for example, othering takes the forms of identity differentiation, extension of oppositional processes, delineating differences, and an array of re-bordering practices, of which actual border "thickening" is evident between the US and Canada as well as the striking re-bordering of the US and Mexico.

The thickened border between the US and Canada has many dimensions involving complications in trade, transportation, tourism and other flows, yet the difficulties emerging in identity verification have become among the most unsettling problems for both countries (Salter 2003; 2008). Evolving policies initiated in the implementation of NAFTA and culminating with the Western Hemisphere Travel Initiative (WHTI) have attempted to standardize, streamline, and otherwise regulate identity verification at the borders of the US. The result, however, has to date been more complication and uncertainty, as noted by many observers and researchers (Konrad, Nicol 2008). The purpose in this chapter is not to relate how identity verification between the US and Canada has moved from a loose, imperfect system to a tighter yet complex system, but to characterize the identity constructs emergent in the borderlands.

With the implementation of the WHTI and associated policies, nationalism, transnationalism and citizenship have become complicated rather than simplified at the border because many borderlands residents hold dual and multiple identities. In the shift to a postmodern state, or states, these multiple identities actually become impediments rather than assets while collective state identities are in transition from national to transnational identity. Indeed, in the US, national identity has emerged as more strident and over-determined in the wake of terrorist incursion and perceived threats. The impact in the borderlands is that Americans resident in the border regions need to be both more American, and less Canadian or other. Canadians who intend to cross into the US need to be definitely Canadian citizens (or American citizens as well). Foreign nationals with citizenship status in Canada are scrutinized, ostensibly because Canada has more relaxed immigration policies than the US.

In the borderlands of the Pacific Northwest, over-determination of US identity is evident in the enhanced symbolic display of nation-state authority at the border, as well as in the more subtle elements of over-determination noted by border stakeholders on both sides of the boundary (Konrad 2010a). Among these are the extension of the "war on drugs" into Canada with the extensive engagement of Canadian law enforcement agencies, the well-established but expanded role of US pre-clearance authorities in Canadian airports, and the accommodation of US cruise ship passengers departing from Vancouver with expedited clearance procedures. Meanwhile, some Canadians in the region have responded to the over-determination of US identity and the enhanced restrictions and wait times at the border, by curtailing or eliminating visits to the US. Although wait times and uncertainty at the border are the major disincentives to crossing, borderlands stakeholders often refer to the intimidation of an over-determined US presence in the borderlands, including flights by unmanned drones, surveillance with Blackhawk helicopters, sensors at the border, and the militaristic stance of border officials.

Rise of Uncertainty in the Borderlands: Fueling the Insecurity Cycle

Most of the border stakeholders interviewed in the Pacific Northwest cited the rise of uncertainty in the borderlands. This uncertainty was noted predominantly in the wait times at the border, but also specifically in business transaction and transportation where regulations were changing, and in tourism where lack of proper identification was cause for entire tours being delayed or turned back. A more pervasive sense of uncertainty derives from the cumulative impacts of security enhancement noted by friends, relatives and neighbors, and verified and vilified in the media on both sides of the border. The result has been to seek remedies to these symptoms but not to confront the problem of security primacy (Konrad 2010a).

One of the remedies utilized is the electronic posting of wait time information in advance of arrival at the border POEs. This remedy has enabled some travelers to divert effectively to alternative crossings, but on heavy traffic weekends, when all of the POEs are swamped, this approach only serves to confirm the interminable three to four hour wait times experienced at all of the crossings. In some instances, posted wait times were inconsistent. In one highly publicized case, travelers were diverted to a smaller crossing only to find it closed at midnight.

Another remedy is the expedited traveler program (NEXUS) designed to move frequent travelers, who have security clearance, rapidly and efficiently through a special traffic lane. On occasion, when substantial numbers of expedited travelers all crowd the NEXUS lane, the lanes for ordinary travelers are under-utilized and available, yet the NEXUS travelers cannot change lanes because they are committed. In such instances the remedy actually results in more uncertainty.

The NEXUS card is now one of the growing number of alternative documents acceptable under the terms of the WHTI. In addition to passports, passport cards (US only), and NEXUS trusted traveler documentation, a growing number of states and provinces are issuing enhanced driver's licenses (EDLs) as compliant identity verification documents. Identity verification has moved from a situation of uncertainty for the security services when all manner of unverified documentation was accepted prior to 9/11, to a situation where the public remains uncertain about which identity documents are acceptable.

Uncertainty among the travelling public has had a definite impact on the frequency and nature of travel across the border for both Americans and Canadians in the borderlands. In the Pacific Northwest, stakeholders and other residents interviewed underlined that many people just do not bother to cross the border due to the uncertainties of wait times, enforcement intimidation, identity verification, and concern about personal data held in security data bases on both sides of the border. "They don't bother to cross". Those who do cross the border tend to plan the trip more carefully than previously. They time their border crossing to avoid waiting. They make multi-purpose trips to shop, visit friends, pick up mail, conduct some official business, and so on. They venture further into the US or Canada, and they stay for a longer period of time. The spontaneous travel that once supported the economic well-being of border settlements has diminished as a result, thus adding the element of economic uncertainty to the list (Konrad 2010a).

Uncertainty is a direct and immediate effect of security primacy, yet the remedies have addressed the symptoms and not the cause. Both American and Canadian stakeholders underlined that the border policies over the last decade have been reactive rather than established according to strategic plans developed with extensive research and testing. In the estimation of some stakeholders it is a "constant process of catch up" to deal with border issues that emerge, and that is what drives policy making for the Canada–US border. Even the implementation of smart and well-articulated new border policies, the "no idle" program at Peace Arch for example, are viewed among some stakeholders as "band-aid" solutions. The fact that the policy only holds for southbound traffic supports this view. The initial reaction of course was the swift security enhancement that occurred after 9/11. Some stakeholders interviewed commented that the reactive process occasioned by 9/11 has become a "model" or "template" for dealing with border issues. In a sense policy makers have been spared the time, effort and money to evaluate a potential issue before initiating a response. Also, the veils of "national security" have facilitated rapid response, and reduced the requirements of transparency and accountability (Konrad 2010a). These observations and opinions lead to the disturbing conclusion that we are building or "re-inventing" a twenty-first-century border without the careful consideration of what really works, what works best, what is in the interests of American and Canadians, and what will last.

Pervasive Security Polarizes Secured and Non-secured Spaces, Places and People

Policy makers are uncertain at best, and polarized at worst, about what needs to be done regarding the growing impacts of security primacy. The gaps between federal, provincial and municipal policies in each country, and then across the border, are apparent in the positions and opinions of stakeholders. The multiple directions and competing interests of transportation policies intended to deal with increased traffic and border effects in the lower mainland of BC are a case in point. Federal, provincial and municipal agencies are attempting to address the growing demands of both east–west as well as north–south traffic in a set of constricted and spatially juxtaposed corridors. In addition, these policies need to mesh with US federal, state and municipal policies at the border. In addition, each transportation issue has spawned public constituency groups on both sides of the border. The wedge of security primacy has further complicated an already sensitive and complex set of negotiations and procedures.

At the border, and throughout the borderlands, the immediate impact of pervasive security is to differentiate secured and non-secured spaces, places and people. This is accomplished through a wide range of practices including fences, walls, partitions, signage, uniforms, and show of force, among others. This polarization is not conducive to communication or mediation, and, in fact, leads to human distress and trauma, as well as spatial segregation and place distinction. Although the avowed purpose of security enhancement is to differentiate security space, the actual effect on the places and the people in or near these secured spaces is excessive and disturbing. These are places to avoid. They are places of fear, concern and potential violence. One does not want to be there.

With these considerations in mind, there are signs that new planning efforts for security facilities at the border are responding to these concerns. The new US Customs and Border Protection facility at the Peace Arch features a spiral entry that diminishes the sense of long lines, and removes the secondary examination facilities from the lobby catering to customs processing the Canadian Border Services Agency facility immediately across the boundary is a bright, open structure designed to welcome travelers into security space (Konrad 2010a).

Other gaps are being addressed as well. Stakeholder consensus in the Pacific Northwest region, and specifically in the Cascade Gateway, has expanded the work of the International Mobility and Trade Corridor Project (IMTC) as security primacy has grown. "The IMTC is a U.S.–Canadian coalition of government and business entities that identifies and promotes improvements to mobility and security for the four border crossings that connect Whatcom County, Washington State and the Lower Mainland of British Columbia" (IMTC 2009). The IMTC model makes stakeholder involvement work, and more important, it makes it work through consensus group representation and engagement.

Stakeholder consensus as enabled and articulated by the IMTC clearly works to develop and adjust border policy at the scale of the Cascade Gateway. Can this model work in other corridors and gateways? Can it work "up the line" at the regional, and even at the national scale? When asked these questions, stakeholders were uncertain how to achieve the exceptional stakeholder engagement and consensus beyond the "Gateway", although they felt that the model should work in other major cross-border flow areas. The success of the IMTC suggests not only that policy makers develop parallel consensus groups in other gateways, but also that policy makers examine the potential of regional and national scale border stakeholder consensus building. Currently, the Pacific Northwest is served effectively at the regional level by PNWER, as are other cross-border regions with similar collaborative governance forums. Yet, border focused regional forums and organizations do not exist solely to evaluate and build better border policy.

From Security Primacy and States of Insecurity to the Affirmation of Borderlands Community, Place and Culture

The shift to security primacy is troubling in any border relationship, and this is certainly the case in the context of the US–Canada border where a more benign interaction was the norm during the twentieth century. The numerous references by stakeholders surveyed in and interviewed in the Pacific Northwest, to militarization and even intimidation at the border, need to be addressed. Humanizing security should be just as much of an imperative as making certain that security is effective and efficient. More civility is required. More affirmation of borderlands community, place and culture is necessary to realign the operational space that security primacy and insecurity have appropriated.

Affirmation of borderlands community, place and culture lies at the very heart of an effective border relationship that works for both the United States and Canada. Affirmation requires empowerment of border stakeholders, recognition that balanced approaches work best at the intersection of two nation-states, effective scaling of the border relationship, humanized security and the acknowledgement of diversity. This is not a new model for affirmation but rather a new perspective on how to bundle proven approaches to working borderlands. Border stakeholders need to be encouraged and supported in their efforts to help with the immense task of guiding the evolution of the border. This requires financial support, organization, facilitation and many other aspects, but foremost it requires recognition of the role and contribution of stakeholders (Alper and Hammond 2009).

Border stakeholders are realistic and pragmatic Americans and Canadians who acknowledge and understand the nature of an international boundary, and the adjacent borderlands. Unanimously, they endorse a balanced approach to border and borderlands security, management, governance, and growth and development. There are other facets of balance as well. Stakeholders surveyed in the Pacific Northwest responded overwhelmingly that "There needs to be a balance between local stakeholder (bottom up) and national stakeholder (top down) management of our border region". Clearly, stakeholders acknowledge the role of the federal government in border management, yet they maintain that this role cannot be exclusive. The underlying basis for this belief in balance is due to the fundamental understanding among stakeholders that a border serves both as a bridge and a boundary, and most effectively so in the border region. Furthermore, almost all stakeholders surveyed agree as well that the border between the US and Canada needs to balance mobility with enhanced security. A balanced approach, the engagement of "top down" and "bottom up" directions in border management, mediation of scales of governance, and, eventually, a working model for integrated border management, are all part of a growing discourse of border management in the Pacific Northwest (Konrad 2010a).

Effective scaling of the border relationship does require balance, yet it requires as well the acknowledgement that certain border functions and specific borderlands characteristics and activities are aligned most appropriately with community, place or region. Scaling the border is aligned with scaling the Canada–US relationship, and lessons learned in either context may be affirming in the other.

How do we affirm the borderlands culture that has emerged over several centuries? And, how do we explain the cross-border community, latent if not resurgent, along most of the boundary between the US and Canada? Finally, where does security fit in integrated borderlands space? Compared to Europe where the EU, nation-states and euro-regions exhibit compressed integration space, compelled integration and extensive social cohesion, North American, and specifically Canada–US borderlands, show expansive integration space, selective or elective integration, and isolated or localized social cohesion (Brunet-Jailly 2010). Expansive integration space has both advantages and disadvantages for borderlands integration. On the one hand, integration may prove more difficult if populations are separated by unoccupied space, yet this same expansive quality also nurtures cooperation as evidenced in the isolated communities along the Alaska–Yukon boundary. Expansive integration space requires a carefully defined security approach which promotes balance, as already emphasized, and combines this with an acknowledgement and engagement of community within regional context. This is particularly important where integration is selective or elective, and social cohesion is isolated or localized, as expressed emphatically along the very extensive and regionally differentiated US–Canada border.

Can security enhancement be accomplished in a borderlands context if it threatens the very culture that enables and sustains the equally important goal of integration? It may not be possible if security primacy is maintained. Yet, if security enhancement is sensitive to community, region, place, and ultimately, borderlands culture, it could become part of the integration process as opposed to being diametrically opposed to it. This is the very lesson that security forces in urban places have learned about policing all across the United States and Canada. Furthermore, the extended transitions emergent in the borderlands to accommodate security spillover may only expand to a certain "breaking point" before the geography of the borderlands crosses the threshold between an enabling landscape of transition and a restrictive landscape of partition. Once Americans and Canadians are caught in the trap of expanded enforcement, re-integration of the borderlands may prove difficult if not impossible.

References

Ackleson, J. 2009. From "Thin" to "Thick" (and Back Again?): The Politics and Policies of the Contemporary US–Canada Border, *American Review of Canadian Studies* 39 (4), 336–51.
Agnew, J. 2008. Borders on the Mind: Re-framing Border Thinking, *Ethics and Global Politics* 1 (4), 175–91.
Alper, D. and Hammond, B. 2009. Stakeholder Views on Improving Border Management, Border Policy Research Institute, Research Report 8.
Bhabha, H. 1994. *The Location of Culture*. New York: Routledge.
Brunet-Jailly, E. 2005. Theorizing Borders, *Geopolitics* 10, 645.
Brunet-Jailly, E. 2010. *Understanding Borders*, presentation and manuscript of chapter for discussion at ABS, Reno, April 14–17. Commentary by Victor Konrad.
Diener, A. and Hagen, J. 2009. Theorizing Borders in a "Borderless World": Globalization, Territory and Identity, *Geography Compass* 3 (3), 1196–216.
Hardwick, S. and Mansfield, G. 2009. Discourse, Identity, and "Homeland as Other" at the Borderlands, *Annals of the American Association of Geographers* 99 (2), 383–405.
International Mobility and Trade Corridor Project. 2009. *IMTC Resource Manual*. Bellingham: Whatcom County Council of Governments.
Konrad, V. 1995. Homesteading the Pryor Mountains of Montana, in *The Mountainous West: Explorations in Historical Geography*, edited by Wyckoff, W. and Dilsaver, L.M. Lincoln: University of Nebraska Press, 194–223.
Konrad, V. 2009. Commentary on "Theorizing Borders in a 'Borderless World': Globalization, Territory and Identity", *Geography Compass* 3 (3).
Konrad, V. 2010a. "Breaking Points", but no "Broken" Border: Stakeholders Evaluate Border Issues in the Pacific Northwest Region, *Border Policy Research Institute Research Report* 10, July, 75.
Konrad, V. 2010b. Imagination, Identity, Affinity, and the Social Construction of Borderlands Culture. Paper presented at the Symposium on Borderlines/Borderlands: Culture and the Canadian–U.S. International Boundary, Library of congress, Washington, DC, June 15–16.
Konrad, V. and Nicol, H. 2004. Boundaries and Corridors: Rethinking the Canada–United States Borderlands in the Post-9/11 Era, *Canadian–American Public Policy* 60, December, 60.
Konrad, V. and Nicol, H. 2008. Passports for All, *Canadian-American Public Policy* 74, May, 64.
Konrad, V. and Nicol, H. 2008. *Beyond Walls: Re-Inventing the Canada-United States Borderlands*. Aldershot: Ashgate, 2008.
Konrad, V. and Nicol, H. 2011. Border Culture, the Boundary Between Canada and the United States of America, and the Advancement of Borderlands Theory, *Geopolitics* 16 (1), 70–90.
Lengell, S. 2010. Border Patrol has Bear of Time Stopping Terrorists from North, *Washington Times* June 6.
Loucky, J., Alper, D. and Day, J.C. (eds). 2007. *Bio-Regions and Coastal Corridors: Transboundary Policy Challenges in the Pacific Border Regions of North America*. Calgary: University of Calgary Press.
Margetta, R. 2011. Lawmakers Clash Over Whether Environmental Laws Hurt Border Security, *CQ Homeland Security*, April 15.

Norman, E.S. and Bakker, K. 2008. Transgressing Scales: Water Governance Across the Canada–U.S. Borderland, *Annals of the Association of American Geographers* 98 (4), 1–19.

Sadowski-Smith, C. (ed.) 2002. *Globalization on the Line: Culture, Capital and Citizenship at U.S. Borders.* New York: Palgrave.

Salter, M. 2003. *Rights of Passage: The Passport in International Relations.* Boulder: Lynne Rienner.

Salter, M. 2008. *Politics at the Airport.* Minneapolis: University of Minnesota Press.

Van Nijnatten, D. and Boardman, R. 2009. *Canadian Environmental Policy: Prospects for Leadership and Innovation.* Don Mills: Oxford.

Woodard, C. 2011. Far From Border, U.S. Detains Foreign Students, *The Chronicle of Higher Education*, January 9.

PART II
Towards a Theory of Border Walls?

Chapter 6
Walls and Borders in a Globalized World: The Paradoxical Revenge of Territorialization

Jean-Jacques Roche

Since the end of the Cold War, over 26,000 kilometres of borders have been created throughout the world. Of the 33 new entrants to the United Nations, 26 are new States, 17 emerging from the ruins of the ex-Soviet empire. These new States may themselves fall victim to autonomist claims and secessions, as was the case of Ossetia and Abkhazia in Georgia. In each of these historic experiences, a border was demanded by the independence movements to materialize their aspiration of a State, the ultimate solution available to minorities wishing for independence from the "great powers" where their status no longer guaranteed their security. "A rampart against insecurity", as Hobbes defined it, the State emerges from the drawing of borders that it must then defend.

When circumstances require and the population's feeling of insecurity increases too fast, the border can turn into a wall like that we thought we had pulled down in Berlin. We thought globalization had put paid to that, but more walls are appearing in various countries, such as those between the United States and Mexico, and Israel and the Occupied Territories. Yet more are being built between India and Pakistan in Kashmir and, further east, between India and Bangladesh. There is a wall between Botswana and Zimbabwe, and between the Sultanate of Brunei and Limbang. In the Western Sahara, the Berm, a wall of sand reinforced with minefields and barbed wire, is intended to protect Morocco from Front Polisario attacks. Elsewhere, in Asia, China has erected a fence along its border with North Korea, which, in concert with South Korea, has built the most hermetic barrier possible along the DMZ. In Central Asia, after a territorial dispute, Ouzbekistan built a continuous fence along its border with Kirghizstan, and is building another with Afghanistan to protect itself from the warfare. In the Persian Gulf, walls are sprouting up in the desert, between the UAE and Oman, and even, on the initiative of the United Nations, between Kuwait and Iraq. As for Saudi Arabia, its borders are almost entirely fortified following the creation of a first line of defence with Iraq and then with Yemen, followed by virtual and material wall on its borders with the UAE and Qatar. The total length of all these fortifications is likely to be 18,000 kilometres according to Foucher (Foucher 2007, 2011) and 41,000 according to Ballif and Rosière (2009: 193–206). For Vallet and David, the 45 walls already constructed in 2011 covered 29,000 kilometres (Vallet and David 2011).

Without even touching upon Europe, it is thus easy to see that walls did not disappear with the Cold War. Old demarcation lines, contemporaries of those separating the two Germanys, persist, such as the Green Line in Cyprus. When the final traces of the Iron Curtain disappeared, the Spanish government decided to surround Ceuta and Melilla, its enclaves in Moroccan territory, by a double fence. In December 2010, Greece also announced that it was building a wall along a bend of the river Evros, which separates Turkey from Greek Thrace over a distance of 11 kilometres. Until then, 100,000 illegal migrants poured through this gap every year.

The proliferation and militarization of borders thus appear to contradict liberal globalization which, on the Common Market model, recommends the four freedoms of movement for workers, capital, services and goods, it being understood that the free movement of workers leads to free movement of ideas. United against this resurgence of the old order, liberals and libertarians, altermondialists and financiers all denounce this parcelling up of a planet that is now too small to be organized on the basis of the old territorial partitioning. The already stringent criticism of developed nations that are unwilling to welcome "the world's poor" is even worse when levelled against Europe, which would replace a wall of shame by an equally ignoble iron curtain. Deliberately ignoring that the same causes (political, economic or social) will cause the same reactions on all the other continents, these critics recommend a new postmodern era, where, in a post-Westphalian world, man would reorganize society on a recomposed territorial base totally divorced from the old State order. This Utopian ideal of an "end of all territory" has not completely disappeared, but borders have somewhat returned to favour in the wake of the 9/11 attacks and the 2008 financial crisis (Senarclens 2009; Debray 2011). This is not so much due to the fact that the old territorial order is supreme as to the fact that we are incapable of reaching the same level of security by other methods.

Liberal and Libertarian Proponents of No Borders

When he published *La fin des territoires* in 1995, Bertrand Badie attacked the principle of centralized organization of modern societies that has long been presented as nature's answer to society and has thus imposed itself on politics (Badie 1995). In the years following the Cold War, people were expected to jettison the references of the bi-polar past for a new order, and the optimism common to all post-war periods combined with the prevailing postmodernism to produce visions of a future that would form a unique experience in the history of humanity, and politics would be reinvented. These approaches, common in political science, ranged from the post-Clausewitzian (Maurice Bertrand), to the post-national or the post-strategic, and described a universe in flux characterized by "the transient, the arbitrary and the disjointed". Thus virtual existence, networks and trans-nationalism would triumph over the heritage of the past, which in fact had never prevented ideas, goods and workers from moving around with or without the permission of the authorities.

These visions, ignoring the fourth wave of creation of nation States, argued that the territorial State was in decline. In total defiance of common sense, the initiators of the new model did not merely list the preliminary plans for this new, de-territorialized world to justify their construction, but went further, caricaturing the old representation so that it would appear less credible.

The Postmodernist Avant-garde

This vision is in fact recurrent. It is particularly popular in the aftermath of big conflicts. The hopes for a peaceful future gave rise to the condemnation of war in the Briand-Kellog Pact in 1928, and to the Preamble of the UN Charter, the purpose of which was to "combat the scourge of war". In 1972, at the height of the détente period, it took the form of two major works, one on *World [human] Society* by John Burton, and the other *Transnational Relations and World Politics*, by Robert Keohane and Joseph Nye, on the "transnational relationships" that naturally crossed borders, not necessarily "in the shadow of war". The visions change from one period to another (Valéry's "monde fini", McLuhan's "planetary village"), but the main thrust of the demonstration is the same, repeating the same themes: management of a common habitat, development of transnational solidarity, growing networks, predominance of civil society over the State, and so on.

In each of these variations, the two arguments become tautological, since the State must be challenged by something above (because the international community has come into existence) and by something below itself (because man's natural rights are now recognized), but on the other hand, failure of the State is acknowledged at the same time as the increasing power of supranational governance.

If we take the case for obsolescent borders, their opponents and the heralds of the global economy condemn the classic territorial order on the ground of the paradox of globalization and relocation of identities, and also on the ground that a world too small for six billion humans cannot be parcelled up.

Undoubtedly, the paradox of globalization and relocation of identities is the commonest argument against the State's claim to remain the basis of political representations. Revealed by Norbert Elias in *La Société des Individus* and James Rosenau in *Turbulence in World Politics*, this paradox is constituted of the contradictory forces working towards globalization yet at the same time fostering rediscovery of local identities, as if the new world citizen, lost in a boundless universe, needed to feel the clay of his own village under his feet to maintain a concrete link with an environment on his own scale. In the case of the migrant, his vaunted freedom of movement becomes a twofold challenge to the State since, as pointed out by Bertrand Badie and Catherine Wihtol de Wenden, he both refuses the poverty of his own country and ignores the laws of his adopted country (Badie, Wihtol de Wenden 1994). However, his first reflex will be to rejoin his countrymen in a classic, first-generation impulse to form a ghetto. The two contrasting spaces – the open world and the ghetto – cause national identity to melt, since the ghetto works on regional and ethnic bases as strongly as on national ones.

The idea that the world is now too small a space to be partitioned off is the second recurring argument, not by any means new. In *L'Émile*, Rousseau noted that there were "hundreds more links [...] between Europe and Asia than between Gaul and Spain in the past; Europe alone was more piecemeal than the entire world is today". In 1931, after the First World War and then the 1929 crisis had broken up the effective globalization of the early twentieth century, Paul Valéry noted that "the time of the end of the world has begun". More recently, the appearance of a "unified strategic field" due to ballistic weapons and peripheral conflicts during the Cold War revealed a world closed in upon itself which generated a feeling of common destiny throughout mankind. "The Earth in danger", personality of the year 1989 for *Time Magazine*, is the current masthead of this theme, illustrated by the financial markets that are both global (unified financial, monetary and bond markets) and dematerialized. The new perception of a unified space and experience also arises from our management of common goods that are over-exploited by raging consumption (but also by population growth), accelerated propagation of epidemics and epizootics – also in part due to accelerated communications – and transnational crime, benefiting from global networks. Because there are "no borders for threats", the national stage is no longer adequate to provide solutions adapted to these globalized perils. Altermondialists and traders in the global economy thus find themselves allying to denounce the former political geography now subverted by network geography.

Unjust Borders

The old territorial borders are not only blamed because they are ill-adapted to the challenges of globalization: they are also criticized because the old Westphalian order was a form of exploitation of borders. The parallel often drawn between borders and prison is also one between borders and poverty.

The "border-prison" criticism represents the border as a circle of barbed wire around prison States, with border posts imagined as the sandbagged casemates with machine guns, controlling the opening of a red and white barrier between Syldavia and Borduria, seen in Hergé's Tintin adventures. This border fences in populations often held against their will in artificial States. Thus it is not so much the State itself that is criticized by the proponents of this thesis as the fact that it is too often an artificial structure resulting from Westernization of the world. *Uti possidetis juris*, the guiding maxim for those setting African borders, must in this context be viewed as the primary cause of the political crisis in sub-Saharan Africa. Forcibly grouping populations incapable of living together, these same borders have, elsewhere, separated communities reduced to the status of minorities in States that were not their own. The Kurds, divided up between Iraq, Iran, Turkey and Syria, symbolize these populations victims of border drawing that ignores human realities. Thus, borders were held up as universal institutions when in fact they were merely the result of European public law (Postel-Vinay 2011). The idea of exporting a territorial sovereignty which made the King of France an "Emperor in his Kingdom" then led to the principle of "territorial exclusivity" which prevented neighbouring countries from intervening in the other's domestic affairs. This principle of non-intervention, consecrated in Article 2 §4 of the United Nations Charter, was based on the desire to reduce the causes of war between States. It also led the international community to ignore anything happening in these artificial States, often failed ones, where violence remained the way to resolve the many political crises. From Stalin to Mao, from Pol Pot to Idi Amin Dada, from Suharto to Saddam Hussein, the list of tyrants massacring minorities and opponents with impunity should also include lawful States that have invoked the domestic character of de-colonization wars to deny other States the right to oversee their "pacification" techniques. Borders in this case were viewed as opaque "iron curtains" – which therefore meant that the corollary of non-intervention was non-assistance.

The parallel between borders and poverty is not a recent one. The nineteenth-century liberals developed their ideas based on the hypothesis that international trade was a source of mutual wealth. It was in the interest of English people to buy wine from Portugal and in that of the Portuguese to buy their broadloom from England. Even if Ricardo's model required restrictions to work at its best (such as an equal level of economic development, and no competitive use of currency), belief in the virtues of free trade governed nineteenth-century thinking and organized economic and financial governance after the Second World War when the condition for sustainable peace was said to be free exchanges among economies. Thus the border, and everything preventing free circulation, was considered to be the primary cause of poverty and war. The widening choice of products to be traded – agriculture, services, culture – also struck a blow against the border, which was palpable not only in geographical but also in material terms. The ongoing pressure from business to encourage immigration – despite often high rates of unemployment – is one among many components of this free trade, since migrants will accept salaries that nationals would refuse for unqualified work that is often the hardest. They are also sometimes foreign experts in areas where the domestic educational system cannot supply enough qualified staff. The fact that the altermondialists regularly complain about the restrictions to immigration and contest the hardening of the right to asylum demonstrates that the altermondialists of the past have also become partisans of globalization. They may disagree with the liberals as to the nature of the globalization we should implement, but at least they agree in denouncing protectionism or withdrawal, which would go against peoples' interests. Thus the most high-minded of liberals and the most anarchistic of libertarians both agree on the free movement of workers, goods or capital, and are united in denouncing every form of hindrance to these vital flows.

A Glowing Future for Borders

The tens of thousands of kilometres of borders built since the end of the Cold War confirm the realistic adage that says that you only destroy what you replace, and foreshadow a great future for this much-decried demarcation. Many of the criticisms of borders are actually worth listening to. The universal model of the State and the border, resulting from the historical experience of the Old World, has often produced monstrous copies in which the State was the primary threat to the security of populations imprisoned within hermetically sealed borders. Conversely, the border, and its corollary, non-intervention, have often served to justify passiveness in the face of exactions reproved by anyone with common sense, but impossible to condemn for reasons of State. The idea of un-crossable *lines* disappeared with Rome, and the Maginot line has taught caution as to the efficacy of bunkers and barbed wire. That was incapable of stopping armies, and borders are also useless against individuals ready to risk their lives to change existences. Indeed, the many obstacles have led mafias to join the fray, and they are prospering on the backs of the thousands of illegal migrants. However, none of the obvious drawbacks of these borders that we seek to abolish is so serious as those that would arise from no borders at all. Without paraphrasing Régis Debray, we can draft a "eulogy to the border" that will toll the death knell of any postmodernist illusions.

In Praise of the Border

Despite all the elaborate arguments in favour of an end to all territory, dyed-in-the-wool independentists continue, to claim – even at their own peril – the right to control a border, because in fact it gives them irreplaceable protection.

First of all, a border provides security, and therefore freedom. Israel is still seeking a "secure" border; Palestinians also aspire to a State within the borders of which they would be guaranteed the right to self-government, the first of Human Rights according to the Pact on civil and political rights of 1966. A border does not hold danger at bay and it is as vulnerable to threats as it is to the other flows of globalization. Moreover, overly protective walls can cause some nations to lose their dynamism and initiative because too much effort is spent on defence. We all know that sales of armoured doors increase when people feel insecure, and nations as well as individuals are prepared to put great effort into ensuring this security, which is the first of their rights according to the original Social Pact. It is therefore paradoxical to observe that the mainstream international relations theory is now based on inter-subjectivity – that is to say, crossed perceptions – yet at the same time it denies people the right to define the degree of protection they deem necessary for their protection, because it would be irrational. That being said, even if wars to conquer territory are now an unpalatable memory for the Western nations, it should be recalled that space has always been a major cause of war, and that by basing international life on the principle that borders are inviolable, now replacing the notion of intangibility, we have afforded the peoples living in States the borders of which are undisputed, an era of lasting peace.

The second irreplaceable feature of the border is to mark out the territory inside which citizens benefit from the same rights. Citizenship can only exist within a border surrounding the public space regulated by the same laws. Citizens exercise the same political rights within this space. Economic and social rights are not linked just to citizenship, but the territory of the State remains the only area in which the social compromises organizing the distribution of wealth can be made. The failure of the Luxembourg Summit of December 1997, during which the EU Member States attempted to draw up criteria for social convergence equivalent to the financial criteria of Maastricht, shows how indispensable – albeit unexplained – the border is for marking out the territory within which political choices are made to share the rights and duties of the economic and social players of the nation.

The border is also essential in determining the identity of the group living within it. Of course, there are other identities that do not fall within this logic, but nevertheless, the nationalistic fervour that is evinced in great sporting events, even in developed nations, shows how much this identity predominates over the others. A border is not merely a way of grouping together populations united by the same wish to live together. By defining the Other, it plays a negative, but equally effective, central role in constituting a national identity that remains predominant.

The fourth irreplaceable characteristic of the border is its capacity to create wealth. Even though the idea may seem doubtful for the adepts of de-territorialized globalization, the border is a source of wealth. The recent film *Rien à declarer* tells the story of the closing of a border post between Belgium and France, which resulted in ruin for the shopkeepers on either side of the customs barrier because the disparity in prices and thus demand were swept away. In this regard, it should be recalled that the border cities such as Reims, Troyes, Cologne, Leipzig and Geneva enjoyed great prosperity in the Middle Ages because of their trade fairs. Returning to more recent times, it may also be observed that with the exception of the financial markets, there is no global market, and globalization is still based on territory. It is disparate prices and legislation that spark international trade, and national genius should not be forgotten in the specializations inherent in free trade.

Borders, which appeared with nation States, also seem to afford indispensable protection against imperialist ambitions and the crossed invasions inherent in the *Imperium Mundi* and *Aeclesia Universalis* of the Middle Ages. As Jean-Christophe Romer pointed out, the notion of borders is incompatible with that of empire, with its talk of "limits" and "marches" (Romer 2004). Now that economies are facing supranational governance and interventionism has come back into favour, the border must be considered as a rampart protecting the most defenceless from the demands of globalization. Territory remains a controlled space on a human scale, despite the enormous flows, accelerated exchanges and virtual living. It is the final refuge for those excluded and denied by globalization. The fact that new walls are being built shows this fear of the outside on the part of a considerable proportion of the population, who prefer to preserve what they have rather than risk opening up to the unknown. The thousands of kilometres of wall built along borders deemed too porous also indicate egoism as well as fear on the part of nations ill-adapted to globalization. These far from altruistic feelings cannot be a basis for policy-making. On the other hand, it is hardly ethical to come to the aid of populations in emergency situations via an intervention that is often barely legal in international terms, while at the same time refusing to address the problems of populations nearer to home using defensive means that are in compliance with international law.

Finally, the border remains the safest instrument by which to cross it. There has never been a lack of transnational ideologies. During the Cold War, the international proletariat, Afro-Asian relations, Pan-Arabic relations, and Pan-African relations mobilized energies but never fulfilled their promise. Conversely, the construction of Europe, which is probably the most accomplished model of a supranational structure, is as much the product of the market as of political will. Although the economy played a leading role – very well described by the spillover effect of neo-functionalism – State intervention was required to give it impetus and stimulate the mechanism of regionalization when it seized up. In light of the many attempts at integration in the African continent, it has to be said that the only recent historical case of internal borders being removed successfully has been in Europe, via the cooperation of stable States whose survival was guaranteed by the existence of recognized borders inside which a process of regional integration could be contemplated without them losing their identities.

Europe, or the End of the Postmodernist Illusion

The building of Europe resulted in the disappearance of internal borders in the course of a process still governed by States as evinced by Denmark's decision to re-introduce border controls on 11 May 2011 tends to confirm. However, this is also the best example of the postmodernist illusion of a de-territorialized world without borders.

In fact, for many years, Europe was seen as a unique postmodernist object. Jacques Delors's "Unidentified Political Object" was neither a federation of nation-States, nor a simple international organization for cooperation, since it combined cooperation (intergovernmental) and integration (supranational), liberalism (the Single Market) and interventionism (the common policies). This "upside-down federation", the central organizations of which merely possess technical powers and which has built an internal judicial order via international treaties, also claims postmodernity in its symbols: a flag, the stars on which represent concord and not its members, a hymn with no words, a passport and a currency with two references. In terms of territory, Europe has also renounced the classic representations, but it has a "market" (internal), a "space" (Schengen), a "zone" (of free trade in the framework of the European Economic Area) limited by tariff barriers and a common external tariff. The external limits of the European Union remained the segments of the external borders of the Member States, because the EU itself, with no legal personality, could not have its own. This "isobar" border, as Jacques Ancel put it, a victim of unstable, constantly changing pressures (Ancel 1938), was justified for two reasons. First, Europe denied the notion of border intangibility, which would have hampered its expansion.[1] Second, the promoters of a unified Europe refused to envisage a new identity based, like the old Europe, not only on the wish to live together but also on the rejection of the Other. The argument about the origins of Europe and the wish, during the negotiations for a Constitutional Treaty in 2005, to exclude any reference to Europe's Christian and

---

1 In this regard it is interesting to recall that it was the CSCE that negotiated the abolition of the notion of "intangibility" desired by the Soviet Union, and its replacement by "inviolability" which suggested possible changes of borders as long as they complied with one of the first common positions taken by the European States as recommended by the Declaration of European Identity of 1972.

Jewish roots, demonstrated this desire to present the European Union as a completely original political construction unlike previous political experiments.

The situation has changed considerably today. The attribution of a legal personality to the EU in Article 47 of the Lisbon Treaty first of all put a stop to the paradox of legal personality for the Communities, but not for the Union that was created by Maastricht in 1992. Although the EU officiously gave itself legal personality and took the right to sign international undertakings with the WEU in 2001, the United States in 2003 (an extradition and legal assistance agreement), and Switzerland in 2004 (participation in the Schengen area), it was clearly in an uncomfortable position, with high international visibility but no legal existence. Conscious of this problem, Europe very early on asked the question of how it could enter the international stage in terms of its identity (Declaration of European Identity in 1973, Solemn Declaration of European Identity in 1983, European Security and Defence Identity etc.). Secondly, the negotiation for Turkish membership, led by France and Germany as of 2007, caused a setback for the postmodernists because it reiterated the medieval idea that the southern borders of Europe were located in the Bosphorus and the Dardanelles, at a time when the Ottoman Empire was considered as an invader. The new political orientation, which sets aside the possibility of an imminent Turkish entry into the EU, thus favours geography rather than history since, although it may be desirable to forget the Turkish imperial conquests and extend European *Soft Power* to the Islamic countries, it is nevertheless difficult to imagine that Europe could have common borders with Iran, Iraq and Syria.[2] Finally, the creation of Frontex in 2004 and the transfer of immigration policy from the third to the first pillar, have accelerated the process of placing the EU borders in common, even though Frontex's only mission for the moment is to coordinate the operational cooperation between the Member States and assist them in training, research and risk analysis. However, carefully hidden in the underbrush of the many EU undertakings, there is a 1.7 billion euro envelope appropriated for "security research" set up by the 7th Programme for Research and Development, to fund research projects that will mainly be designed to reinforce this common border. This shows that people realize that a more efficient, closer-knit external border must be constructed to replace the current, purely symbolic signposting around Europe. Of course, this movement is not linear. By declaring their opposition to a wall between Greece and Turkey, criticising opponents to the Schengen area who would, if allowed, turn Europe into a fortress, and working towards dismantling of the Green Line in Cyprus, the European authorities – mainly the Commission and the Parliament – have not completely abandoned the idea of reinventing politics and its instruments. However, vigilant States in the Council have reminded them that Europe cannot claim both legal personality – thus benefiting from the classical attributes of political action – and the right to act in different spheres with totally new references. Europe has long cultivated ambiguity as to its own nature; by claiming legal personality, it has clearly opted for a more classical framework, no doubt to cease being "a political dwarf and a military worm" in Mark Eysken's pithy language.

---

2   However, it should also be noted that if we agree with Paul Valéry's idea that the European cultural area extends to countries where the triple influence of Greece, Rome and Christianity is felt equally, then Armenia and Georgia, located on the north-eastern border of Turkey, would naturally fall within the European family.

Conclusion

With the advent of globalization, borders have become a particularly attractive research topic. Based on the observation that in the contemporary world they have become characterized by the dialectic of border claims and border crossing, the Centre d'Études des Relations Internationales (Paris) devoted the first issue of its new online magazine, Ceriscope, to this subject in February 2011. Two years earlier, the Raoul Dandurand Chair for Strategic Studies at the University of Quebec in Montreal had launched a vast pluri-disciplinary programme on the topic of "Walls and Borders", funded by the Canadian Council for Research in the Human Sciences. The title of the programme is significant and its association of terms – also used by Ceriscope with its association of "walls" and "fences" – implies condemnation. Rejecting the distinction between "same and inside" and "different and outside", most of the criticism is levelled at xenophobia and inward-looking civil societies, and it denounces the counterproductive nature of security-oriented policies that encourage illegal settlement whereas free movement would enable more fluidity. These may be current issues, but it is fairly easy to detect the old arguments dating back to the liberal criticisms of the first half of the nineteenth century, and the various versions of the anarchist movement of the second half (Proudhon, Elysée Reclus etc. – see Pelletier 2008). As then, critics of borders still come from intellectual or economic elites who use their social and cultural capital to promote the conception of the world that is theirs. Members of the academic world, or people used to travelling for business, speaking several languages or at least able to speak a little English, bankers and intellectuals, merchants and artists are all the more tempted to promote a world without borders as it corresponds to their interests and their vision. However, the overwhelming majority of the world population has no opportunity to travel or even to exchange with a foreign country which, even though it may be nearby, remains unknown. It is worth consulting the annual statistics of the International Union of Telecommunications to discover that the planetary village is not so influential as all that, and realize that the conclusions of the Maitland report on the gap between the "over-communicators" of the North and the "under communicators" of the South remain true. Without seeking to compare with Third World populations, for whom the border question is expressed in radically different terms, it can be observed that even in developed countries, "abroad" remains *terra incognita* for a majority of people who have never had the opportunity or the means to leave the national territory. Consultation of the annual survey on French tourist demand (STD), which includes both tourism and business travel, reveals that only 23 per cent of French people travel abroad each year (French Tourist Travel 2008). This figure should be interpreted taking into account the fact that French overseas territories are included in the statistics, and that it is often the same people that travel several times during the year (the average number of journeys per individual in 2008 was 3.8 for short trips and 2.6 for long stays). When it is realized that most French tourism abroad is in Spain and Italy, it becomes clear that "abroad" is in fact very near at hand, and that the Orient begins, as in the Quai d'Orsay entrance examinations, on the other bank of the Rhine.

Thus the debate on making borders more secure opposes "active minorities" with considerable influence, and the sedentary majority of the population, much more conservative in its relations with foreign countries. Elected governments must thus constantly duck and dive between the twin rocks of "tyranny of the majority" and denial of that same majority. The populist surge currently observed in Europe must not be the only criterion by which to set border policy, and it is essential for democratic governments to find social artefacts to explain and render acceptable a controlled opening of the borders. However, it would be politically dangerous for these same governments to ignore popular fear of permeable borders merely on the grounds of economic interests and because humanist values are put forward by the active minorities who, as John Plamenatz once said, exercise "uncontrolled power and as a result, form a leading class or, if you prefer, a controlling elite" (Plamenatz 1965: 28–39). Because every time the border issue is raised it is denounced on the ground that there is exclusion, it is important to avoid excluding the voices raised against the *doxa* of no borders, bearing in mind that if good borders are not enough to create a good neighbourhood, bad ones will necessarily raise social problems which democratic governments have shown they are powerless to resolve.

References

Ancel, J. 1938. *La Géographie des Frontières*, Paris, Gallimard.
Badie, B. 1995. *La Fin des Territoires*, Paris, Fayard.
Badie, B., Withol de Wenden, C. 1994. *Le Défi Migratoire*, Paris, Presses de Sciences Po.
Ballif, F. and Rosière, S. 2009. Le Défi des Teichopolitiques. Analyser la Fermeture Contemporaine des Territoires, in *L'Espace Géographique*, 38, 3, 193–206.
Burton, J.W. 1972. *World [human] Society*. Cambridge University Press.
de Senarclens, P. (ed.). 2009. *Les Frontières dans tous leurs États, Les Relations Internationales au Défi de la Mondialisation*, Bruxelles, Bruylant.
Debray, R. 2011. *Éloge de la Frontière*, Paris, Gallimard.
Delors, J. September 9, 1985. President of the European Commission, speech. Luxembourg: Office des publications officielles des Communautés européennes, available at: http://www.cvce.eu/obj/intervention_de_jacques_delors_luxembourg_9_septembre_1985-fr-423d6913-b4e2-4395-9157-fe70b3ca8521.html (accessed 12/05/14).
Elias, N. 1991. *La société des individus*, Paris, Fayard.
Foucher, M. 2007. *L'Obsession des Frontières*, Paris, Perrin.
Foucher, M. 2011. Chronique de la Scène Frontalière Contemporaine, in *Ceriscope*, March, available at: http://ceriscope.sciences-po.fr/content/part1/chroniques-de-la-scene-front aliere-contemporaine?page=2 (accessed 21/12/12).
French Tourist Travel. 2008. Available at: www.veilleinfotourisme.fr/…/com.univ.collabor atif.utils.LectureFichiergw?… (accessed 10/10/12).
Keohane, R.O. and Nye, J.S. 1972. *Transnational Relations and World Politics*. Harvard University. Center for International Affairs, Harvard University Press.
Pelletier, P. 2008. Indigènes de l'Univers – Des Anarchistes et le Territoire, in *Refractions*, Autumn, available at: http://refractions.plusloin.org/spip.php?article303 (accessed 12/10/12).
Plamenatz, J. 1965. La Classe Dirigeante, in *Revue Française de Science Politique*, 15, 1, 28–39.
Postel-Vinay, K. 2011. La Frontière ou l'Invention des Relations Internationales, in *Ceriscope*, March 2011, available at: http://ceriscope.sciences-po.fr/content/part1/la-frontiere-ou-linvention-des-relations-internationales (accessed 12/10/12).
Romer, J.-C. 2004. (ed.) *Face aux Barbares – Marches et Confins d'Empire*, Paris, Taillandier.
Rosenau, J. 1990. *Turbulence in World Politics: A Theory of Change and Continuity*, Princeton, Princeton University Press.

Rosière, S. 2009. *La Prolifération des Murs, Symptôme d'une Mondialisation "Fermée"?* "Walls in International Relations", conference, Chaire Raoul-Dandurand en etudes stratégiques et diplomatiques, UQAM, Montréal, 29–30 October 2009.

Vallet, É. and David, C.-P. 2011. *The (Re)building of the Wall in International Relations*, Introduction, Borders, Fences and Walls International Conference, Raoul Dandurand Chair of Strategic and Diplomatic Studies, UQAM, 17 and 18 May.

Chapter 7
Border Fences in the Globalizing World: Beyond Traditional Geopolitics and Post-Positivist Approaches

Serghei Golunov

Although some national borders have become increasingly permeable in the age of globalization, there are a growing number of countries who try to fence themselves off from their neighbours with impressive artificial barriers that may evoke associations with the Great Wall of China or medieval fortresses. What does this increasing popularity of border fences mean? Does it signal a powerful counteroffensive of some national states against the challenges of globalization, their vain efforts to postpone the inevitable agony, or neither of these trends? What ways can border fencing issues be conceptualized and solved?

In an attempt to contribute to the conceptual understanding of the phenomenon, I will start not with theories, but with some practical regularities showing how border fences usually work, and what their advantages and vulnerabilities are. After this, taking into account these considerations, I will try to estimate the potential possibilities and problems of conceptualizing border fences with the help of both traditional geopolitical representations and post-positivist Border Studies theories, including ideas related to post-modernist, constructivist, and critical approaches. While it is not easy to generate concrete and realistic practical solutions on the basis of such approaches, I suggest that the application of dialogism can help to make research on border fences more practically oriented.

Why is There a Need for Border Fences?

Fencing and other similar methods have been utilized for territorial protection for a very long time. Among contemporary border fences, those of the US–Mexican and Israeli–Palestinian borders (both Israel–Gaza Strip, and Israel–West Bank) attract special attention from the global mass-media. Apart from this, there are fences that India has at its borders with Pakistan, Bangladesh, and Myanmar; Spain – at the outer limits of its exclaves Ceuta and Melilla neighbouring Morocco; Botswana – with Zimbabwe; Saudi Arabia – with Yemen; Malaysia – with Thailand; Kuwait – with Iraq. This list is far from exhaustive.

A "physical" border fence is just a part of a barrier protection system together with other engineering construction objects and sensors; special border protection practices designed to contend, detain, or even destroy an adversary. Indeed, the fence itself can be relatively easily left behind by climbing over, damaging, or tunnelling, let alone the possibility to cross a border (or bring in prohibited items) legally or illegally (e.g. in hiding places made in vehicles) via checkpoints, eluding the vigilance of border guards or customs officers. Thus more or less efficient border fences are supplemented by ditches, barbed wire, surveillance cameras, sensors, patrolling vehicles, aircraft, sometimes even mine fields, and also by rigid control at checkpoints.

Each of these border fence protection systems is virtually unique and unmatched. This specificity is caused by many factors, such as the political system and foreign policy of a protected state, its financial capability, attitude to human rights issues, and of course by the challenges to be dealt with. While the vast majority of current border barriers are not serving as defence lines against hostile armies (though border fortifications of the Korean Demilitarized Zone are still serving this purpose) or a prison enclosure for the country's own citizens (as socialist states did at the time of the Cold War), protection against illegal immigration or penetration by terrorists/militant groups are their most typical functions. These functions can be combined with each other and with some purposes not mentioned. Moreover, the main priorities of fencing can change over time: for example, before the first decade of 2000s the Indian–Bangladeshi barrier was mainly anti-immigration, it has later turned into an anti-terrorist blockade.

The most often mentioned anti-immigration border fence separates the USA and Mexico; though the barriers of Ceuta and Melilla separating Spain from Morocco, fences between Saudi Arabia and Yemen, and some other fences serve the same purpose. None of the corresponding governments in any of these cases seem to be so naive as to hope that fences can be a panacea against illegal immigration; rather they aim to use it as one of several means (together with tightening legislation and internal control) to reduce it. This kind of fence is designed not to destroy but impede and delay trespassers; that is why evidently inhumane supplements, such as minefields, high-voltage electrification, or mutilating fixtures[1] are typically not used. Nevertheless, for trespassers surmounting such border protection systems this is still a very dangerous undertaking that may end with injuries, enslavement by criminal groups, being shot or abused by border guards or the military, or perishing without help in the inaccessible areas that are often chosen for illegal crossings.

Even from the governmental perspective, the efficiency of border fences as a means to reduce illegal immigration is rather controversial. Here are typical advantages and disadvantages of this method of border protection.

On the one hand, facing public anxiety about the scale of illegal immigration, a government often has to undertake visible and rapid measures demonstrating its capability to cope with the problem in order not to lose electoral support. Building a fence is one of the most visible measures possible, overtly signifying that something has been done. In this case, demonstration of vigorous efforts can be of more importance for politicians than the efficiency of the barrier itself. As Bhagwatti noticed of Indira Ghandi's government decision to build a fence at the Indian–Bangladeshi border in 1980s, it was "the least disruptive way of doing nothing while appearing to be doing something" (Bhagwati, 1986: 124).

Building a fence often allows the achievement of impressive statistical results. For example, in the 2010 fiscal year the number of apprehensions at the US–Mexico border (447,700) was four times smaller in comparison with the 2000 financial year (United States Border Patrol, n.d.). It should, however, be taken into account that the apprehension statistics

---

[1] An incident of this kind took place in 1978 when the US government planned to develop existing border fences in the areas of San Diego and El Paso. The information that the new fence will be designed to cut fingers and toes of trespassers (McGreal, 2011) gave rise to a US–Mexico diplomatic scandal. It was settled when the parties came to the agreement that the new fence should be designed in a way that minimizes the odds of injuring climbing infringers. See McGreal, 2011; Stoddard, 2002: 72).

usually reflect not the actual number of arrested illegal entrants but the number of detected attempts.[2] Apart from this it should also be borne in mind that the decrease in number of apprehensions can be caused not so much by the construction of a border fence but by some other factors such as improvement of the economic situation in a migration-sending country (or, on the contrary, by the worsening economic situation and decline in demand for labour in a recipient country), change of the tactics used by unwanted entrants,[3] toughening of penalties for habitual offenders, etc. Taking all of this into account, it is no wonder that statistical indices can be easily manipulated: in particular, success (as well as the need for more resources for border protection) can be claimed, both if the number of apprehensions is increasing, and if, on the contrary, it is decreasing (Andreas, 1999: 218–19). More broadly speaking, "successful border management depends on successful image management, and this does not necessarily correspond with levels of actual deterrence" (Andreas, 2009: 9).

Deterrence is another effect of the construction of a fence to potential infringers. Some of them can be scared off (either by difficulty of the obstacle or by increasing fees charged by clandestine experts in illicit border crossings) and give up their intentions to enter a protected country unlawfully.

On the other hand, fences as a method of border protection have a lot of serious disadvantages. Again, infringers have a lot of options to overcome these obstacles: some of them climb over them with or even without help of ladders or other equipment, use tunnels dug under the barrier, penetrate the protected territory through checkpoints by hiding in vehicles or using forged documents, or bribe border guards and other officials. Meanwhile, multilayered barriers (that should delay infringers and simultaneously not kill or injure them) with their surveillance cameras and sensors, and also with ground and air patrolling, typically costs huge amounts of money. It can be an excessive burden for the budget, especially if a country is trying to protect extensive territory. Not surprisingly, even the US government in 2010 decided to halt the multibillion SBInet programme aimed to equip the fenced border with the latest technologies (Hsu, 2010).

Finally, as the US experience also shows, enclosing a border can bring results somewhat opposite to those that were expected: in particular, to cause an increase in the number of long-term illegal residents and indirectly stimulate cross-border criminal groups. According to the Pew Hispanic Center, between 1995 and 2004 the number of illegal Mexican immigrants residing in the USA grew almost threefold from 2.2 to 6.2 million (Passel, 2006). This dramatic increase can be explained by the fact that many immigrants, instead of returning home after finishing their temporary work, now preferred to reside in the USA in order to avoid the risks of subsequent illicit border crossing (Andreas, 2009: 214). Mexican criminal groups have also evidently gained from the toughening of the US border policy in the 1990s and the first decade of 2000s, as both the majority of people who wanted to enter US territory illegally, and also South American drug-traffickers, increasingly had to rely on the service of "professionals" for finding vulnerabilities in the US border protection system (McCaul, 2007: 11–12). The growth in strength and financial power of borderland-based drug cartels has contributed to the dramatic criminalization of the northern Mexican

---

2   Many illegal entrants are deported to Mexican territory after apprehension and attempt to cross the border with the USA again and again, even during the same day or night.

3   For example, a part of them can switch to applying for legal entrance using forged documents of the purposes of their visits.

borderland,[4] which could have a profoundly negative impact on the adjacent areas of the USA itself.

Thus, attempts to fence off demand-driven cross-border flows can be fraught by escalation and increasing criminalization of confrontation between "gatekeepers" and trespassers, similar to the armour vs. shell competition. Such escalation can be endless (though theoretically one of the sides can find ways to gain evident advantages) while it is extremely difficult to reverse it and get out of this vicious circle.

Another kind of fence, which can be found for example at Israeli borders with Palestinian territories and the Indian border with Pakistan, is designed mainly for detaining terrorists and militants. This kind of barrier is more ruthless and less sensitive to human rights issues than anti-immigration ones: minefields, electrification, and other similar methods can be used for its protection, even if it causes numerous fatalities and injuries not only among malefactors but also civilians. In many cases the interests of property-owners in the expropriation zone are also damaged, as authorities building an anti-terrorist barrier tend not to respect their rights (Bennet, 2003; Sengupta, 2002).

As practice shows, construction of fences facilitates a reduction of the number of terrorist attacks (Gilani, 2005; Israel Diplomatic Network, n.d.) but by no means eliminates the problem completely: adversaries can try to break through by way of digging (as it was in June 2006 when intruders from Gaza took Israeli soldier Gilad Shalit as a hostage), or to enter the targeted country legally using their accomplices in this country, or other methods (for example Palestinian extremists shell Israel by Qassam rockets). Construction of fences provokes the escalation of tension between an enclosed country and its neighbours, thus delaying peaceful settlement that would make a fence needless. However, if prospects to achieve such a settlement seem to be bad, fencing off a border can seem to be a rather tempting solution. It can increase hardline politicians' popularity while some part of the population may subjectively feel itself more protected from the dangerous and aggressive "Other".

Though an intention to reduce large-scale drug-trafficking can be put forward as one of the reasons for border fence construction, it is doubtful if this kind of barrier can effectively serve this purpose and justify the huge amount of money spent on it.[5] As a matter of fact, the efficacy of fences against narcotics smuggling is questionable: illicit drugs can be brought via checkpoints, thrown over a wall, delivered across a border with the help of carrier pigeons, and so on. Not surprisingly, the efficiency of the US–Mexico separation barrier against drug-trafficking is estimated to be very low: according to one official assessment just 1.5–3 per cent of cocaine smuggled through the border is seized by border guards and customs officers (McCaul, 2007: 4).

On the whole, construction of border fences is a bad strategy of border protection, which is criticized by experts, activists, and the mass media for a good reason. Due to being very expensive, provoking numerous violations of human rights and causing the escalation of confrontation with the separated country and community, a barrier can hardly be an ultimate solution to a targeted problem, being able, at best, to somewhat diminish its scale and partially transform its character. It should, however, be taken into account that fencing

---

4 It is especially shocking that Ciudad Huarez has the highest murder rate of any city in the world. See Heiser, 2011.

5 Of course, ideas to build anti-narcotic border fences are sometimes set forth. For example, in 2006 several Russian parliamentarians proposed to apply the US–Mexico border protection system to the 7,500-kilometer border between Russia and Kazakhstan. This proposal was suggested due to the huge volume of Afghan heroin brought to Russia from Central Asia. See: Pavlova, 2006. Fortunately, this idea was not put into practice.

off a country from troublesome adjacent territories is often a bad choice from a set of bad available options, when doing nothing would likely have unfortunate domestic political consequences for a government. In choosing the construction of a fence, at least such a government demonstrates to the public that "something is being done" and makes a large part of the public feel subjectively more secure when a dangerous "Other" is separated off by a visible barrier.

Fences in the Light of Border Studies Theories

For a long time borders were predominantly conceptualized by scholars as some sort of objective reality and/or strictly localized limit of a national state's sovereign power: a barrier and filter regulating communication between a state and its external environment (House, 1982), specific landscapes (Prescott, 1978: 192–3), projection of some institutions' power to a state's outer limits (Prescott, 1965: 76) etc. From the outset of Border Studies (Lord Curzon, 1907; Holdich, 1916; Lyde, 1915) and during the rise of classical geopolitics, borders have been regarded as an instrument of territorial control, that is why before World War II the issue of optimal delimitation (sometimes assuming seizure of adjacent territories) was the focus of scholarly attention. After World War II and the collapse of the European colonial empires, the "theory of natural borders" lost its popularity. To some extent this was also the fate of Border Studies in their entirety, as mainstream international relations theories of the post-war period (especially realism) regarded border issues to be of little importance for many decades, since borderline fortifications proved to be of little help against modern weapons (Herz, 1957: 482), flows of information, transnational movements (Aron, 1984: 290, 392), and so on.

Despite the fact that traditional geopolitical representations, and "the theory of natural borders" in particular, look outdated now, they may still have some potential for conceptualization of the considered phenomenon. In the spirit of "natural borders", fences can be conceptualized as an attempt to create artificial substitutions for landscape barriers in the period when desirable territorial seizures are much more difficult than before (though a more powerful country, as practice shows, can construct a fence on disputed territory in order to improve its functionality). However, when it is not possible to satisfy territorial claims, a separation barrier can also be moved inside the country's own territory that, at the same time, does not mean abandoning control over the strip between this barrier and a legitimate borderline.[6]

Contrary to the assumption of realists about the insignificance of modern boundaries as protection shells, fences do still matter as traditional adversaries are replaced by non-traditional ones. The latter have no weapon that can easily make a fence irrelevant, but are very inventive, persistent, and resistant to measures of political pressure and paramilitary intimidation. The outcome of confrontation between a fenced-off state and trespassers is almost always difficult to predict.

---

6   This option, however, can damage the interests of the own country's inhabitants whose property can remain virtually unprotected by fence from cross-border criminals. Such a problem can cause serious conflicts between the government and unprotected inhabitants of an out-of-fence borderland strip as it was in the case of Indian borderland residents living outside the barrier between their country and Bangladesh (Buerk, 2006; Donaldson, 2005: 186).

In relevant contemporary theories (in particular, within the complex inter-tangled ideas of post-modernism, constructivism, and critical studies) borders are conceptualized, not as some physical reality, but rather as a product of subjectivity. In many such theories, as Prozorov notices, there is "hostility of contemporary political discourse toward boundaries" and the trends to "denigrate" them (Prozorov, 2008: 26) are salient. Logically, border fences should look like a red rag for such theories; thus they have to be deconstructed and labelled as anachronisms.

For radical post-modernism, which proclaims the death of national borders because of intensifying global flows of goods, information, and people (Ohmae, 1989; Lash and Urry, 1994: 28), border fences can probably be associated with something like the carapaces of dinosaurs that desperately but unsuccessfully try to save themselves from extinction. Statements of this kind can easily be supported by numerous examples showing that fence-based border protection systems are ostensibly inefficient, being somehow vulnerable. The problem is, however, that selection of opposite examples, showing that border fences help to significantly reduce the number of illegal crossings, may seem to be no less persuasive for a wide range of competing theories, starting with traditional geopolitics and ending with Beck's "second modernity", allowing national states to adjust themselves to the contemporary challenges of globalization, can be flexible, and even blurring to some extent (for instance, many fenced-off countries do their best at increasing and maintaining their control over outside territories adjacent to a fence – S.G.) but rigid in other respects (Beck, 2005: 48). Specifically, if not to consider the "up-to-dateness" of post-modernism against the "obsolescence" of traditional geopolitics (Bigo, 2008: 105; Vaughan-Williams, 2009: 165) as some kind of *ultima ratio* for choosing an appropriate Border Studies theory, it is not even easy to find persuasive arguments why the first approach is better for conceptualizing fortified borders than the second one.

According to a moderate version of post-modernist Border Studies, borders in the globalizing world are not vanishing but are instead reshaping, multiplying, and becoming functionally more complex (Albert, 1998: 62). For adequate comprehension of the phenomenon of border fences, it can be important indeed to bear in mind that fortified borders are not the sole defence line against illegal entrants,[7] that they often do not coincide with the legal boundaries of a protected state, and, ultimately, that a fence is just one of many physical and virtual borders separating an enclosed group from the "Other".

The problem with innumerable "alternative" borders is that they are not equally important, and some of them should be preferred to others in order not to diffuse excessively the focus of any research. As virtual borders are now more fashionable objects of study than "traditional" geographical ones, there is a danger that border barriers, shaping the behaviour of the huge number of people dealing with them in the capacity of "hard facts", will be neglected by academic fashion in favour of small nuances of intergroup communication.

From the constructivist point of view, a physical border is naught if taken apart from its meaning. In this context borders are "metaphorical spatializations of difference" and "rules of differentiation" (Morehouse, 2006: 19; Newman, 2010: 774) that give "shape to the ordering of society". So, changing meaning can transform the functional importance of a separation barrier: for example, the Berlin wall in 1989 virtually lost its previous significance even before the time it was destroyed.

---

7 Specifically, border barriers are typically complemented with special security regime zones and with a protected state's sphere of informal influence in the neighbour state's adjacent borderland area, as well as with rigid virtual border between "us" and the "Other" supported by rigid migration policy.

It is also important that a rigid and extremely expensive border policy, resting upon physical barriers and numerous personnel vested by wide powers, can be considered as a result of successful securitization – meaning the construction of a problem (e.g. migration or smuggling of some illicit items) as a security issue that should be dealt with by extraordinary methods, if such presentation of a problem is accepted by a significant audience (Buzan, Waever, de Wilde, 1998: 25–32). By the analogy with securitization, it is also possible to speak about the borderization of security issues. This means that a significant audience should be persuaded that a security issues should be dealt with mainly at the border and by agencies specializing in its protection (Golunov, 2008: 23–4; Golunov, 2011: 11–21). For example, the issue of illegal migration can be managed by stricter regulation of a labour market and not necessarily by construction of a fence.

As in the case of moderate post-modernism, the challenge that constructivist Border Studies scholars should bear in mind is the potential risk of losing sight of "material" problems related to border fences. It should be taken into account that while, from the strategic point of view (the perspective of decision-makers or theorists observing borders from "God's-eye view") the meaning of a border fence may seem to be primary in respect to its physical essence, but for people having to deal with such a border, the barrier is primarily not so much a set of norms and perceptions as a hard and quite tangible reality, narrowing the range of options available. To neglect such a perspective would mean to make the theory irrelevant to reality. It seems to be likely indeed that the removing or weakening of invisible mental barriers can be crucially important since this can cause the elimination of physical ones, but it is extremely difficult to achieve this purpose in the foreseeable future. Thus, focusing on those "hard facts", that create so many problems for "gatekeepers" and border-crossers aiming to systematically target these mundane problems, seems to be at least as important as deconstructing the norms and perceptions that underlie border barriers.

According to critical studies' perspectives, border fences are used for the exclusion of suspicious outsiders on ethnic, racial, and social grounds. With this in mind, such border barriers are denounced as unfair, inhumane, and contradicting principles of liberal democracy (Abizadeh, 2008; Lomasky, 2001). In as much as border and visa barriers are allegedly designed to separate rich countries from deprived labour immigrants typically belonging to ethnic and racial minorities, some scholars label these countries' enhanced control as global apartheid (Dalby, 1998; Balibar, 2004; van Houtum, 2010), while EU counties and the USA are deemed to be "gated communities" (van Houtum and Pijpers, 2007). From this viewpoint, a large number of border fences can probably be conceptualized as striking examples of the exclusion of ethnic, racial and poor "Others" from the aforementioned rich "gated communities". It is not obvious, however, if disadvantaged citizens of enclosed states support the fencing any less than their more prosperous compatriots.

Unfortunately, the alternatives to the existing unfair order, proposed by critical Border Studies (in cases where alternative solutions are even proposed at all), are usually unrealistic and, hence, persuasive. The ideas to abolish entry restrictions for labour immigrants (Steiner, 2001: 80) or to establish democratic control over border policies with participation of such immigrants (Balibar, 2004: 117), that are sometimes put forward, are typically not based on any serious analysis of possible side effects and do not take into account the need for dialogue with numerous and influential supporters of strict migration policy (Golunov, 2012: 26). Once again, construction of a border fence is usually not considered by advocates of such a measure as an optimal solution, allowing the perfect balance between national security and respect for human rights, but that it is not the worst option among bad ones. Moreover, the dilemma about constructing or maintaining a fence, in many cases, can be considered by them as a "wicked problem" when "you don't understand a problem until you have developed a solution" and tried it, but every solution offered is "not right or wrong" and "exposes new aspects of the problem that requires further adjustment of the potential solutions" (Conclin, 2006: 14–15), and hence a pretext not to react to a destructive criticism (Golunov, 2012: 6).

As can be seen from the above critique, from a traditional geopolitical perspective border fences may be conceptualized as one of the possible responses of national states to non-traditional challenges in the age of globalization. While such an explanation can be regarded as a possible way to explain the increasing popularity of this method of border protection, it fails to contain any clear suggestion as to how it can be possible to prevent or reduce escalation between an enclosed state and numerous infringers, or how to settle the situation which may be damaging the interests of people living on both sides of a fence. In their turn, post-positivist theories pay attention to such important dimensions of separation barriers as their temporality, and their vulnerability to intensify trans-border flows; the special significance of meanings and norms in the fencing-off process; and the role of such barriers in the context of domination, ordering, and exclusion of the "Other". At the same time, post-positivist approaches are rarely able to propose concrete and realistic alternatives to border fences and they also pay no special attention to concerns of the great number of people feeling insecure and therefore supporting rigid border and migration policies. The next part of the chapter will propose some ways, taking into account some of these challenges, and suggest a conceptual basis for generating practical solutions.

A Way to Combine Theory with Practice

Of course, the criticism of the previously mentioned traditional and new approaches does not mean that all of them should be considered irrelevant. These approaches can be useful for comparing current border fences with the fortified lines of the past, trying to predict the fate of modern separation barriers using both theoretical arguments and historical analogies, revealing and examining ideas and institutions that underpin physical walls, criticizing social injustices produced by exclusionist border and migration policies, or trying to foresee probable consequences of these fences' disappearance. Theoretical pluralism should be welcomed, in as much as no existing theories have sufficient ground to claim evident superiority over competing ways of conceptualization.

While applying one or another approach to study border fences, the three following issues need to be taken into account. Firstly, even if this phenomenon is considered to be somewhat obsolete and doomed to disappear in historical perspective, one should not wait passively until separation barriers die off. On the contrary, researchers should try to make their contribution to solving the problems of people who have to deal with "hard" borders now, and probably will have to deal with them for a very long time despite the border-breaking trends of globalization. Secondly, no criticisms of fences as a kind of border policy, however harsh or just, can by themselves subvert it: concrete, realistic and viable alternatives should instead be proposed. Thirdly, it must not be forgotten that border fences are not just the product of unilateral decisions undertaken by policy-makers of an enclosed country: they are a result of interaction between several parties, including the public of the mentioned country, a neighbour state, and undesirable entrants. The latter actors are often not passive objects of the process of bordering, ordering, and othering – they can be regarded as its fully-fledged co-authors. Public opinion, too, is not an innocent and abiding victim of manipulation by politicians and security professionals, as it can appear from the argumentation of some scholars employing the critical studies' paradigm (Tsoukala, 2005: 167–8; van Houtum, 2010: 965) that it can actually be strongly in favour of rigid border policy and even pressurize governments demanding its implementation.

Taking into account these considerations, cautious dismantling of border fences – aiming to minimize its possible negative side-effects – can be a slow process. As some scholars argue, in cases of ethnic conflicts borders should be opened gradually. While attempts to carry out the entire process immediately can be perceived as a threat to collective identities, It may be better to let the conflicting groups feel secure, gradually intensifying cross-border interaction between them (Diez, 2003: 131–4). In such cases, as Henrikson argues, a consociative model with a semi-permeable border and dosed (depending on the situation) trans-border communication can prove to be more advantageous than the associative (when a border is open) or dissociative (when it is closed) models (Henrikson, 2000: 128–9).

In as much as the interaction between "gatekeepers" and people crossing the border (or who are potentially interested in crossing it) is an especially important subject for practically oriented Border Studies, the application of the dialogic approach looks rather promising. In this respect, dialogue may be understood in two ways: in a broad sense as cognitive and communicative actions in interaction with others and contexts (Linell, 2009: xvii) and in the narrow sense as "ideal" symmetrical, sincere, and cooperative communication (Habermas, 2001: 97–9).

In the first case, a border fence with relevant protection is the result of the interaction between gatekeepers and trespassers. This interaction often takes the form of escalating confrontation. In response to the construction of a fence, trespassers improve tactics to overcome it which causes "gatekeepers" to strengthen the barrier by more and more advanced equipment, or even to introduce more severe punishment for certain methods of border crossing.[8] In order to find a response to these kinds of measures, trespassers have to be more organized, to know more about vulnerabilities in the border protection system, and to have connections with corrupted officials at the border service. Such a competition between trespassers and border guards can be virtually endless. Hypothetically, however, the invention of highly sophisticated and advanced control technologies or alternatively redirecting trespassers' activity to other routes of illicit crossing[9] or other types of activities,[10] can turn the balance in the gatekeepers' favour, while some crises in a "fortress country" can, on the contrary, lead to the collapse of border control. As was mentioned above, it is relatively easy to launch the escalation of border protection, but it can be quite difficult to stop this process without giving up the initiative to trespassers.

From the point of view of Habermasian-style dialogism, a border fence can mean the absence of appropriate dialogue between adjacent countries (in case of an "alienation border" according to the typology of Martinez (1994: 7)) or an incompatibility between

---

    8 According to Border Tunnel Prevention Act, adopted in the USA in 2006, "Any person who uses a tunnel or passage ... to unlawfully smuggle an alien, ... goods ..., controlled substances, weapons of mass destruction ... or a member of a terrorist organization ... shall be subject to twice the penalty that would have otherwise been imposed had the unlawful activity not made use of such a tunnel or passage". See: H.R. 4830, 109th Cong. (2005–2006).

    9 For example, a large number of illegal immigrants or smugglers can change the direction of their activities if they find routes passing via some other borders which are more vulnerable.

    10 Some potential illegal immigrants can stop their attempts of illicit border crossings if they find satisfactory legal job, such as smugglers if they switch to some other, more profitable activity (be it legal or illegal).

national policy and the interests of numerous trespassers. It is very difficult to organize dialogue towards de-escalation with illegal border crossers, because this entity is not coherent. Taking this difficulty into account, communities who provide a large number of trespassers should be involved in negotiations. On the other hand, people who want to be protected by a barrier and who support fence construction also have the right to be respected and to be heard.

It should be taken into account that in such a dialogue (if it could be organized) there is a huge disparity of resources available to participants: gatekeepers evidently have more resources and possibilities to manipulate the dialogic process. Thus, the Habermasian ideal of openness and equality can hardly be achieved (Golunov, 2012: 45–6). A more realistic task would be the transparency of information about arguments put forward by both sides, and about problems highlighted by such arguments: excessive restrictions of border regime for people who come into the country, negative influence of the border on the life of neighbouring communities, possibilities of mutual concessions (e.g. effective cross-border co-operation in the struggle with organized crime in exchange for facilitation of an entrance regime) etc.

In order to stimulate as wide a representation of different voices as possible, freedom to join the dialogue (at least in some formats) should be ensured. The forms of the dialogue may be different, including feedback, forums, consultations between governmental and non-governmental actors of corresponding countries, participation of activists defending the interests of border crossers in activities of border protection agencies, and academic–practical discussions etc. In this context, the academic community can contribute both to improving the mechanisms of such dialogue, and to searching for new ways of solving border crossing issues to be revealed during the dialogue process.

It should be stressed once more that dialogism is not the only correct and probably not the most productive approach for conceptualizing border fences, it is also not a one-size-fits-all way of solving the problems related to them. It may be understood simply as potentially useful conceptual guidance for gradual improvement of the situation at such borders, even if such improvement is slower and less considerable than advocates of radical solutions would like to have.

Conclusion

Border fences are far from being the optimal way to prevent illegal immigration and terrorism; they are an even less effective remedy against drug trafficking and other kinds of smuggling. For their proper functioning, very expensive equipment is necessary in order to have highly effective border management, with a low level of corruption within border guards and customs services. It is no wonder that this method of border protection is a very easy target for severe criticism. However, the decision to construct a fence is usually a choice, not between good and bad, but only between bad options, a choice made under severe pressure from external circumstances and domestic public opinion.

The efficiency of fencing as a method of border protection can be estimated differently, often depending on the conceptual viewpoint shared by one or another researcher. Supporters of the traditional geopolitical approach can see in fencing, something like the revival of quasi-natural borders as a response of national states to non-traditional challenges. In their turn, radical postmodernists depict the situation as vain attempts of these states to resist all-conquering transnational flows. These and other representations can be easily confirmed by sets of numerous arguments, especially if alternative points are neglected. Meanwhile, disputes concerning the viability or inevitable death of border fences, about primacy of their material or ideal components, and about the justice or injustice of such a rigid method of territorial protection are of little help in solving the problems currently faced by people who either cannot cross a border normally, or who feel insecure because of cross-border crime.

It seems, therefore, that research on border fences could be focused on searching for practical solutions. Such extreme options as the immediate demolition of barriers does not look like the best choice, as this may lead to escalation of current conflicts and the emergence of new physical and virtual borders, which can cause even more undesirable consequences. Therefore, the solution can probably be found in gradual alleviation of border policy through arranging dialogue between neighbour states, between the state, which tries to safeguard itself and the communities from which the bulk of trespassers come. Even if the results of such dialogue initially look insignificant, it can at least contribute to the gradual softening of immigration policy for an enclosed country and lay the foundation for further, more considerable steps towards the "softening" of a border barrier.

References

Abizadeh, A. 2008. Democratic Theory and Border Coercion: No Right to Unilaterally Control Your Own Borders, *Political Theory* 36 (1): 37–66.

Albert, M. 1998. On Boundaries, Territory and Postmodernity: An International Relations Perspective, *Geopolitics* 3 (1): 53–68.

Andreas, P. 1999. *Sovereigns and Smugglers: Enforcing the U.S.–Mexico Border in the Age of Economic Integration*. PhD dissertation, Ithaca: Cornell University.

Andreas, P. 2009. *Border Games: Policing the U.S.-Mexico Divide*. 2nd edition, Ithaca: Cornell University Press.

Aron, R. 1984. *Paix et guerre entre les nations*, Paris: Calman-Levy.

Balibar, É. 2004. *We, the People of Europe? Reflections on Transnational Citizenship*, trans. J. Swenson, Princeton: Princeton University Press.

Beck, U. 2005. *Power in the Global Age: A New Global Political Economy*, trans. K. Cross, Cambridge: Polity Press.

Bennet, J. 2003. Israel Destroys Arabs' Shops In West Bank, *The New York Times*, 22 January.

Bhagwati, J. 1986. U.S. Immigration Policy: What Next, in *Essays on Legal and Illegal Immigration*, edited by S. Pozo, Kalamazoo: W.E. Upjohn Institute for Employment Research.

Bigo, D. 2008. EU Police Cooperation: National Sovereignty Framed by European Security? in *Security versus Justice? Police and Judicial Cooperation in the European Union*, edited by E. Guild and F. Geyer, Ashgate: Aldershot.

Buerk, R. 2006. Villagers left in limbo by border fence, *BBC News* 28 January. Online. Available at: http://news.bbc.co.uk/2/hi/programmes/from_our_own_correspondent/4653810.stm (accessed 11 April 2011).

Buzan, B., Waever, O. and de Wilde, J. 1998. *Security. A New Framework for Analysis*. Boulder: Lynne Rienner Publishers.

Castells, M. 2000. *The Information Age: Economy, Society and Culture. Vol. 1. The Rise of the Network Society*. Oxford: Blackwell Publishers.

Conklin, J. 2006. *Dialogue Mapping. Building Shared Understanding of Wicked Problems*. Hoboken: John Wiley & Sons.

Dalby, S. 1998. Globalisation or Global Apartheid? Boundaries and Knowledge in Postmodern Times, in *Boundaries, Territory and Postmodernity*, edited by D. Newman, London: Frank Cass.

Diez, T. 2003. Borders: From Maintaining Order to Subversion, in *New Frontiers of Europe: Opportunities and Challenges*, edited by I. Busygina, Moscow: MGIMO University.

Donaldson, J. 2005. Fencing the Line: Analysis of the Recent Rise in Secuirty Measures along Disputed and Undisputed Boundaries, in *Policing, Borders, Security, Identity*, edited by E. Zureik and M.B. Salter, Portland: Willan Publishing.

Gilani, I. 2005. Harsh weather likely to damage LoC fencing, *The Daily Times*, 4 March. Online. Available at: http://www.dailytimes.com.pk/default.asp?page=story_4-3-2005_pg7_41 (accessed 9 April 2011).

Golunov, S. 2008. *The Factor of Security in Russian and Kazakhstani Policies towards their Common Border*. Doctor of Political Science's dissertation, Nizhny Novgorod: Nizhny Novgorod State University.

Golunov, S. 2010. Border Security: Problem of Conceptualization, *International Research Society. Politics. Economics* 1: 11–21.

Golunov, S. 2012. *EU–Russian Border Security: Challenges, (Mis)perceptions, and Responses*, London: Routledge.

Habermas, J. 2001. *On the Pragmatics of Social Interaction: Preliminary Studies in the Theory of Communicative Action*, trans. B. Fultner, Cambridge: Polity.

Heiser, J. 2011. Juarez, Mexico Murder Rate Up 40 per cent, *New American*, 3.03.2011. Available at: http://www.thenewamerican.com/world-mainmenu-26/north-america-mainmenu-36/6543-juarez-mexico-murder-rate-up-40-per cent (accessed 5 April 2011).

Henrikson, A.K. 2000. Facing Across Borders: The Diplomacy of Bon Voisinage, *International Political Science Review* 21 (2): 121–47.

Herz, J. 1957. Rise and Demise of the Territorial State, *World Politics* 9 (4): 473–93.

Holdich, T.H. 1916. *Political Frontiers and Boundary-Making*, London: Macmillan and Co.

House, J. 1982. *Frontier on the Rio Grande. A Political Geography of Development and Social Deprivation*, Oxford: Clarendon Press.

Hsu, S. 2010. Work to cease on "virtual fence" along U.S.–Mexico border, *Washington Post*, 16 March.

Israel Diplomatic Network (n.d.). "The Anti-Terrorist Fence – An Overview". Available at: http://securityfence.mfa.gov.il/mfm/web/main/missionhome.asp?MissionID=45187& (accessed 9 April 2011).

Lash, S. and Urry, J. 1994. *Economies of Signs and Space*, London: Sage.

Linell, P. 2009. *Rethinking Language, Mind, and World Dialogically: Interactional and Contextual Theories of Human Sense-Making*, Charlotte: Information Age Publishing.

Lomasky, L. 2001. Toward a Liberal Theory of National Boundaries, in *Boundaries and Justice: Diverse Ethical Perspectives*, edited by D. Miller and S.H. Hashmi, Princeton: Princeton University Press.

Lord Curzon. 1907. *Lecture on the Subject of FRONTIERS by Lord Curzon of Kedleston Viceroy of India (1898–1905) and British Foreign Secretary 1919–24)*. Available at: http://www.dur.ac.uk/resources/ibru/resources/links/curzon.pdf (accessed 17 February 2011).

Lyde, L.W. 1915. Types of Political Frontiers in Europe, *Geographical Journal* 45: 126–45.

Martinez, O.J. 1994. *Border People: Life and Society in the U.S.–Mexico Borderlands*, Tuscon: University of Arizona Press.

McCaul, M. 2007. *Line in the Sand: Confronting the Threat at the Southwest Border*, US Representative Michael McCaul. Available at: http://www.house.gov/sites/members/tx10_mccaul/pdf/Investigaions-Border-Report.pdf (accessed 22 February 2011).

McGreal, Ch. 2011. The battle of the US–Mexico frontier, *Guardian* 20 February. Available at: http://www.guardian.co.uk/world/2011/feb/20/us-mexico-border-fence-immigration (accessed 9 April 2011).

Morehouse, B. 2006. Theoretical Approaches to Border Spaces and Identities, in *Challenged Borderlands: Transcending Political and Cultural Boundaries*, edited by V. Pavlakovich-Kochi, B. Morehouse, D. Wastl-Walter, Aldershot: Ashgate.

Newman, D. 2010. Territory, Compartments and Borders: Avoiding the Trap of the Territorial Trap, *Geopolitics* 15 (4): 773–8.

Ohmae, K. 1989. Managing in a Borderless World, *Harvard Business Review* May–June. Available at: http://hbr.org/1989/05/managing-in-a-borderless-world/ar/1 (accessed 22 February 2010).

Passel, J. 2006. The Size and Characteristics of the Unauthorized Migrant Population in the US, Estimates Based on the March 2005 Current Population Survey, *Pew Hispanic Center*. Available at: http://pewhispanic.org/reports/report.php?ReportID=61#Other Title (accessed 22 February 2011).

Pavlova, N. 2006. State Duma Deputies will Check the State of Affairs at the South Ural Border, *Noviy Region-Cheliabinsk*, 13 September. Online. Available at: http://www.nr2.ru/chel/82700.html (accessed 9 April 2011).

Prescott, J.R.V. 1965. *The Geography of Frontiers and Boundaries*. London: Hutchinson and Co.

Prescott, J.R.V. 1978. *Boundaries and Frontiers*. Totowa: Rowman and Littlefield.

Prozorov, S. 2008. De-Limitation: The Denigration of Boundaries in the Political Thought of Late Modernity, in *The Geopolitics of Europe's Identity: Centers, Boundaries, and Margins*, edited by N. Parker, Basingstoke: Palgrave Macmillan.

Sengupta, S. 2002. The India–Pakistan Tension, *New York Times*, 2 February.

Steiner, H. 2001. Hard Borders, Compensation, and Classical Liberalism, in *Boundaries and Justice: Diverse Ethical Perspectives*, edited by D. Miller and S.H. Hashmi, Princeton: Princeton University Press.

Stoddard, E.R. 2002. *U.S.–Mexico Borderlands Studies: Multidisciplinary Perspectives and Concepts*. El Paso: The Promontory.

Tsoukala, A. 2005. Looking at Migrants as Enemies, in *Controlling Frontiers: Free Movement Into and Within Europe*, edited by D. Bigo and E. Guild, Aldershot: Ashgate.

United States Border Patrol. 2011. Total Illegal Alien Apprehensions By Fiscal Year. Available at: http://www.cbp.gov/linkhandler/cgov/border_security/border_patrol/apps.ctt/apps.pdf (accessed 5 April 2011).

Van Houtum, H. 2010. Human Blacklisting: The Global Apartheid of the EU's External Border Regime, *Environment and Planning D: Society and Space* 28: 957–76.

Van Houtum, H. and Pijpers, R. 2007. The European Union as a Gated Community: The Two-faced Border and Immigration Regime of the EU, *Antipode* 39 (2): 291–309.

Van Houtum, H., Kramsch, O. and Zierhofer, W. 2003. Bordering Space, in *Bordering Space*, edited by H. van Houtum, O. Kramsh, W. Zierhofer, Aldershot: Ashgate.

Vaughan-Williams, N. 2009. *Border Politics: The Limits of Sovereign Power*. Edinburgh: Edinburgh University Press.

Chapter 8
Is the Wall Soluble into International Law?

Jean-Marc Sorel

If the wall, in its generic sense, catches the attention of the community of internationalist lawyers because of its ambiguity as well as because of the interest given to this question by the Advisory Opinion on the wall in Palestine before the International Court of Justice in July 2004; it remains hardly definable and hardly approachable by the law. This does not, in itself, constitute an isolated phenomenon since there are several notions that are not defined, but that are, nonetheless, the object of sustained legal attention, especially because of the many legal consequences that can be drawn. This is the case of the notion of "people" which has been debated at length; but is also true for more recent notions such as that of "terrorism", which even though being reprehended does not have a definition accepted by all (Sorel 2002); or even the economic notion of "investment" whose polymorphic character is hardly masked by the long illustrative lists found in bilateral agreements (Gilles 2010). However, contrary to these acts or notions, the wall is precisely neither a notion nor an act but an object. The difficulty therefore reaches a different level: it is not the idea, the concept or the notion that cannot be seized; it is the legal significance of an object considered as such, its status as an object.

However, the difficulty to capture the wall legally constitutes in itself a legal interrogation and, as we all know, the law reveals itself just as much by its gaps or lacunae than by its entireties. Therefore, it does not seem incongruous to wonder about a certain legal emptiness that the wall would expose, as well as about its meaning. With this objective, the problem is pictured in a more general and abstract way, even if concrete walls will not be forgotten.[1] In the same manner, the point of this chapter is not to make yet another commentary on the Advisory Opinion of the International Court of Justice of 9 July 2004 concerning the wall in Palestine (on this point see notably Rivier 2004; Wedgehood 2005). However, the meeting point between international law and the phenomenon of walls is recent. Strictly speaking, it is the Advisory Opinion of the International Court of Justice of July 2004 on the consequences of the construction of a wall in the occupied Palestinian territory which for the first time tackled the legal consequences of the existence of a wall on a particular territory from the point of view of international law. It is not the first "remarkable" wall in

---

[1] For memory, this notably concerns: the Berlin wall (historical but yet close enough in the history to include it), the wall in Palestine, the wall at the border between the United States and Mexico, the "European" walls including the one in Cyprus and those of Ceuta and Melilla, without forgetting the more general problematic of protections external to the Schengen space, or even the one considered between Greece and Turkey, the wall between the two Koreas, the sand wall ("Berm") of Western Sahara, the Kashmir wall; and the walls of Bagdad (at the same time protections of foreign forces, embassies, and separation between the Sunnite and Shiite populations). There remain projects of walls that seem to be abundant throughout the world without it being always possible to assess their credibility or outcome (Botswana–Zimbabwe; Pakistan–Afghanistan; Saudi Arabia–Yemen and Iraq; India–Bangladesh; Uzbekistan–Kirghizstan; Thailand–Malaysia, etc.), even if some are starting to be constructed, along with some walls that we could have forgotten.

history, but it is nonetheless the first one that is the object of such a treatment; which is the reason why every single discussion in international law on the issue of walls steers without fail towards the Palestinian wall. This appropriation is logical but is also deceptive: in practice all walls are presented in territorial, historical and political situations in a different way, and no situation is truly comparable to another. The fact that the territory on which the wall of Palestine is located is an "occupied" territory is essential to the consequences drawn by the Court. Before this Opinion, walls were legally left to themselves, either because international law is non-existent or jabbering, or because the political question at the origin of the wall is considered in its whole; whereas the wall would seem to be only the symptom or the outcome of such a situation. It remains that the wall in itself sometimes could not have been ignored by international law. The presence of the UN and the long conflict in Cyprus gave rise to multiple negotiations where the question of the wall could have been mentioned. The same goes for the Berm of Western Sahara constructed after the Advisory Opinion of the International Court of Justice of 1975 by Morocco; and which is practically ignored by the legal process that has tried, painfully, ever since to free this territory from its dead end (Sorel 2010: 19–20).

The Wall as a Simple Object Subject to International Law

Variety, Banality and Neutrality of Walls

There are a baffling variety of types of walls to consider when talking about walls and international law: border wall, security barrier, simple limit, fortification, rampart or even virtual wall. None of them can really be distinguished by their form but all are interesting from an international point of view as soon as an element of extraneity is found; the "border wall" being the most obvious example. In the same manner, their functions are not the same and can correspond, alternatively or cumulatively, to the freeze of a conflict (Israel/Palestine, Kashmir wall, Berm of Western Sahara), to the separation of a population that used to be unified or to live in the same territory (Berlin wall, Korean wall), to the willingness to build a barrier against terrorism and/or organized crime (Bagdad walls), or even to the willingness to build a barrier against clandestine immigration (the wall between the United States and Mexico, the wall between India and Bangladesh).

This variety is coupled with an observation: the wall is banal. A wall can indeed have a legal destination as an object when used in a standard way such as for example, a party wall, without it being remarkable. The object is therefore not unusual; it is its use that can become peculiar or its destination. Whatever the form and the function of these walls, the wall is in itself a trite object and every legal system reveals its banality.

This is the case of the French Civil Code as regards party walls and neighbouring walls. Article 653 of the French Civil Code provides that:

> In cities and in the country, any wall serving as separation between buildings up to the point of disjunction, or between courtyards and gardens, and even between enclosures in fields, is deemed to be a party wall, unless there is an instrument of title or an indication to the contrary.[2]

---

2 Translation from http://www.legifrance.gouv.fr/.

Furthermore, the Civil Code dedicates several other Articles to this question.[3] The characteristic of a party wall is precisely that it belongs to two neighbours. There is a kind of joint ownership of the wall. The neighbouring wall is a wall that is built unilaterally, but that cannot be built on the limit or even less on the side of the neighbour. A neighbouring wall can be built, but to do so on its own land would be imperious.

This is stating that the essential question for international law is to know exactly where the wall is located (Marcelo Kohen 2010: 131ff.). The question asked to the Court in 2004 relates to this issue from a certain angle: the wall crossed the occupied Palestinian territory. Would such a wall have been admissible had it been built solely on Israeli territory? Would it then have been a simple neighbouring wall? Nothing is certain, because, in a first place, it would have still isolated an occupied territory; and, in a second place, the dividing line (the "green line") following the conflicts between the Israeli territory and the Palestinian territory has not been acknowledged by an agreement and is even the initial division is disputable. Simply, this green line became year after year the starting point of all negotiations on the division of the two territories. Moreover, this wall is not only built on the "side of" Palestinian territory, it is built on several parts "inside" this territory, encroaching upon numerous plots. On the contrary, the Berlin wall was entirely built on the eastern part of the city in other words in the uncontested territory of the GDR. It was in this sense, truly a "neighbouring wall" (Cohen 2010).

In any case, the wall is indeed a neutral object, as all objects are in themselves. As perfectly highlighted by Olivier Razac concerning barbwire: "The barbwire is an instrument. It is only an instrument in the sense that it does not create a function but carries out in a specific way a pre-existing function, the delimitation of space"[4] (Razac 2000: 66). This remark can easily be transposed to walls, if only because they sometimes consist exclusively of barbwire; and it can be observed that the wall is nothing in itself, and that it relies solely on its location and/or its intended purpose to acquire a significance, particularly a legal one.

Walls and Status of the Territory

The wall can first be considered as a public construction located on a territory enjoying a defined status. At first sight, the wall is first and foremost a public construction, which has been confirmed by the ICJ in its Advisory Opinion of 2004 which agreed on the quality of "construction" of the separation wall between Israel and Palestine.[5] In this sense, it remains perfectly neutral on the inside – or at the edge – of a State that possesses *ab initio* the right to organize its own sphere. It is therefore the location of the wall that matters, and not the wall itself, because it then has

> great chances to raise the question of the legal statuses of the territories where [it is constructed], by affecting the possession (if the Wall is intended to consolidate a territorial claim) or by troubling the regime (if the Wall leads, by setting up an enclave, to submit a

---

3 Articles 653 to 663. It is interesting to note that Articles 653 to 662 are devoted to the regime of party walls, whereas Article 663 mentions "enclosures" separating houses, before using the hallowed expression "dividing walls between neighbours".

4 Unless stated otherwise, quotations will be translated by the translator.

5 Legal Consequences of the Construction of a Wall in the Occupied Palestinian Territory, Advisory Opinion, I. C.J. Reports 2004, p. 164, par. 67, and p. 170, par. 82.

territory to the jurisdiction of a State other than the one possessing the title of sovereignty).
(Forteau 2010: 91)

The wall, in itself, is not distinguished from the territory where it is located as an object benefiting from its own legal regime. Everything will depend on its positioning. In itself, it is nothing more than a construction among others, whose forms differ enormously. If it is constructed entirely on the territory of a State, it will abide by the status of this territory; if it is constructed on an occupied territory, as it is the case for the Palestinian wall, it will abide by the rules of occupation, which in this case, derive from the law of war. All legal consequences deriving from these walls hence depend on its positioning and not on its simple existence as a wall. As rightly noted by Mathias Forteau: "After all, if the Walls abide indeed by *a* legal regime, dictated by the legal status of the territory where they are located, it is not *their* legal regime. International law does not give them any particular treatment; it does not regulate them as such" (Forteau 2010: 92–3). He then adds: "[…] international law does apply to Walls, but it does not say anything about the Walls" (Forteau 2010: 93).

The Advisory Opinion of the International Court of Justice of 2004, even though of great importance, neither solves the question of walls in general nor implies any legal regime particular to this object; and clearly indicates that only the status of the territory matters when judging the consequences of a public construction. It only addresses the question of the wall in Palestine in its consequences regarding principles and rules of international law. Could it have been otherwise? The Court was limited by the precise wording of the question, and the relative authority stemming from its decisions (even if in this case, it is an Advisory Opinion, and not a Judgment) does not allow it to go beyond this frame. Nonetheless, in the same way as the drawing of borders; if the Court does not use a law that is uniform – which means it cannot consider the disparity in real situations – it has experimented with the method used to consider the case of the wall in Palestine; with the consideration that it could be reproduced should another wall situation arise. It is undeniable that the study of the status of the territory where the wall is located should always precede the potential rights at issue.

Hence it can be said that the International Court of Justice isolated the wall object in order to apply a method of analysis, in the same way that it does when it has to decide upon a question related to borders. We know that it will then look for the existence of a title, then for potential effectivities if the title does not exist or is unclear; the whole process unfolding in light of certain principles such as *uti possidetis juris*. It is the same for the wall, as for the border, there is no "law of the walls" or a uniform law of territorial delimitations, at least terrestrial.

Hence, the construction does not change anything in regard to the legal regime of the territory where it is located. Palestine was occupied before the wall and it remains so after its construction. The wall, as it is the case here, only accentuates or modifies some elements of the occupation regime, such as the question of settlements or the rights of the nationals of the occupied territory to circulate or to benefit from certain services. As such, it often constitutes a threat to the status of the territory, but it remains implicit with the absence of a confirmation. As duly noted by the Court in its Advisory Opinion of 2004: "The Court considers that the construction of the wall and its associated regime create a 'fait accompli' on the ground that it could well become permanent, in which case, and notwithstanding the formal characterization of the wall by Israel, it would be tantamount to *de facto* annexation".[6] The wall does not change anything about the status, and the Court in this way recalls that it would be pointless to rely on this argument to establish *de facto* and unilaterally a future border. The construction of a wall therefore does not enable the modification of the status of the territory where it is located by moving the border or by creating a new division of the territory, even if this is the intention in some of the builders' minds. In that sense, the wall creates a threatening situation.

However, certain walls – one can think of the border wall between Mexico and the United States – even if located on the territory of a State, generate consequences that can be of interest to international law. In that case, the wall will be more than a simple construction without any possibility of contesting its locations within a State's territory.

As perfectly summarized by Christian Tomuschat:

> This means at the same time that, in principle, a wall is nothing more or less than a factual phenomenon. To appreciate its lawfulness, one needs to resort to the norms that regulate its location on the ground as well as the consequences sought or induced by its construction. It is also the administrative organisation of the passage, determined by the 'master' of the wall, that is likely to have a decisive impact on the legal consideration of the wall at issue. (Tomuschat 2010: 174)

We are starting to better define our wall "object": everything will thus depend on the status of the territory where it is located, on the modalities of its construction under this status (does it prevent, for example, a crossing?) as well as on its intended purpose that generates consequences that can be seen as threats. Among these consequences is the freedom of circulation as well as the respect of certain elementary rights.

Legal Consequences Attributed to Walls

To locate a wall in a certain place (strategic *a priori*) is to question certain possibilities, starting with the freedom of circulation. Very often, the wall includes crossing points that are check points for people or goods wishing to go from one point to another on each side of the wall. The wall is quite simply a physical obstacle but is not only characterized in this manner; placing an armed cordon is tantamount to an obstacle to crossing, even if it is not a wall.

In the same way, constructing a wall does not necessarily change the legal regime of the passage. It will change it if, up to this point, this way was free or subject to minor constraints. However, it will not change the legal regime of the right of way if this way was already subject to strict rules. It can simply accentuate it and make it more dense. This is precisely what happened in Palestine. The passage was already heavily controlled, but it became nightmarish with the construction of the wall, the crossing points becoming rarer and narrower. Its main objective was to prevent crossing outside of designed and controlled places; and relates in this sense to the wall between the United States and Mexico, which does not change the regime of the border but strongly constrains it; the difference between the two cases being once more the status of the territory since it can seem surprising to construct a wall in a territory that we are also occupying and therefore supposed to control, which is obviously not the case for Mexican territory and the United States.

---

6 ICJ Report 2004, p. 184, par. 121.

As noted by Hélène Ruiz Fabri: "For the lawyer, as soon as the wall merely concretises or supports a rule which object is to forbid circulation, it is only a device aiming at increasing the efficiency of this legal rule. Can we blame a material device for increasing the efficiency of a legal rule?" (Ruiz Fabri 2010: 155).

In a nutshell, for the device to be reprehensible, one has to detect a discrimination that would not have existed without the existence of this wall. However, in this field, everything will depend on the question of proportionality, which we know is difficult it is to handle.

The wall will finally strike a chord when confronted with extreme situations; that is humanitarian situations where populations should not be deprived of essential goods. It is indeed the issue of humanitarian rights and human rights that conveyed the essence of the Advisory Opinion given by the Court in 2004. But, once again, consequences were mainly deduced from Israel's occupation regime on these territories, thus from the status of the territory where the wall was located. Against this backdrop, as recalled by Monique Chemillier-Gendreau, the list is long: right to personal security, right to life, right to normal family relationships, right to health and education, right to property, gross violations of economic rights and even more of labour law (Chemillier-Gendreau 2010: 161ff).

Beyond the sociological or political aspects, the wall also engages the lawyer because it allows for recalling some fundamentals regarding international law, without the wall altering its essential parameters. If the wall is constructed on a border, we will find the classic questions of the limits of the border, border zone, party zone, neighbouring zone, etc. Indeed, the wall "disturbs" legal categories, it pushes them around and questions those we thought well-established; but, fundamentally, the wall does not modify these legal categories.

One can ask therefore whether it is not, ultimately, the expression of an extreme legal situation symbolized by the wall that would enable the isolation of walls from other kinds of limitations. The wall is an object, but it is also more of a symbol than an object. In other words, beyond what is at stake from a strictly legal point of view, it symbolizes circumstances able to create particular constraints and is able to push to the extreme some rights or obligations used until then "normally" or proportionally.

The Wall as a Representation of Extreme Situations Revealing the Possibilities of International Law

Particularisms and Perverse Effects of the Wall

The necessary distinction between the materiality of a wall (highly variable), and the projection that we make of it needs to be discussed. Whatever its form, it is meant as impenetrable, even if, in practice, that is not always the case. The wall therefore presents a particular dimension if we are willing to go beyond its apparent banality. Besides, if the earlier analysis proved disappointing in that it revealed that international law does not pay specific attention to it, in other words is not interested in it; the wall is however particularly indicative of the relationship between the legal frame and the territory of the builder. The wall poses questions to the lawyer sometimes too prone to behave, to quote a classic (even clichéd) image, like a chicken in front of a fork: once curiosity is gone, and after having understood that it will be useless to it, the chicken loses interest in the fork (Virally 1974). Does the lawyer not have the same attitude towards the wall? Very often, the object will be seen as without interest, but not its projection or symbol. Now, if the wall is banal, its projection allows the revisiting of a certain number of legal notions that we had thought established or completely circumscribed.

Even if the statement is not legal, a psychological aspect also needs to be stressed. If the "builder" believes that the wall only sanctions an irreversible break, immured he considers that this wall creates or reinforces the existing break. The feeling *vis-à-vis* the wall is hence different, and the wall constructed by those who have the power *a priori* (and thus capacity) to do so often appears as a confession of weakness and powerlessness, which is of course paradoxical. It is Israel that constructed the wall, the United States that constructed the border fence, it was the GDR supported by the Soviet Union that constructed the Berlin wall, a town enclaved within its territory, etc.

On another hand, the wall, whatever it is, creates a (or several) fixed point(s). Moreover, studies on the wall prove that we can have a "fixation" on walls. As objects, would we have organized a colloquium on chairs, tables, or – to take something similar – fences between fields? Perhaps yes, but it is not likely. If we take an interest in walls, whereas they do not distinguish themselves as passive objects, it is because they reveal and provoke. If two States have common borders, terrestrial and/or maritime, the crossing points will be known. If one of those States constructs a wall to control these crossing points, this will reveal a particular attitude, often extreme, symptomatic of certain uneasiness, of certain powerlessness that merits questioning. In short: *walls are always extreme cases.* They are more often a permanent justification to exceptions of national security and thus create particular problems. Hence the International Court observes that a simple wall can have significant consequences – and, in the case at issue, highly damaging – in international law. In Palestine, it became a permanent justification to circumstances desired as exceptional. Whatever is said, this simple statement is not insignificant.

It is clear that the wall intrigues. And it is without a doubt the main reason why it raises interest, including in international law. If the wall is nothing, it can become a lot. And if it puzzles, it is because it is a sort of fixing point, both for the mind and physically: it would appear "a-natural". Nonetheless, once settled, it seems to become alive and to behave almost biologically: it is born, it lives, it dies, and can sometimes be reborn. Indeed, contrary to a living body, its aspect can remain unchanged, but it may also collapse if not maintained, in the same way that it can be reborn if the man turns it into a historical or artistic object, or rebuilds it. Most of all, if it appears to be alive, it is in that it generates a *movement* because its construction would be a sign of the beginning of the end, often the beginning of a decline. In that sense, every wall implies a form of *thrust* from its construction to its destruction. We could even dare a sort of Archimedes' principle concerning walls: any construction of a wall seems to reversely thrust from the outside and towards the one that constructs it. There is indeed a dynamic of the wall that pushes it away from the banality of being a simple object (Sorel 2010: 23).

It is therefore possible to consider our earlier discussion on the banality of the wall to detect, on the contrary, its exceptional character.

Classic Concepts Revisited Because of the Disproportions Implied by Walls

The concept we need to consider when examining the issues raised by walls concerning humanitarian law and human rights is proportionality. As noted by Monique Chemiller-Gendreau: "walls are, by nature and intention, defensive projects that are militarily guarded" (Chemiller-Gendreau 2010: 161). However, as we know, all current walls are the objects of strenuous campaigns of justification in the name of security. And, since the bombings of 11 September 2001, the always-delicate dialectic between security and liberty is challenged in a manner that is not in favour of liberty at all. It is for example notable that the Court, in its Advisory Opinion of 2004, concluded that this construction was not in line with the obligations incumbent upon Israel under international humanitarian law, human rights instruments, and the right of peoples to self-determination, especially because of the issue of the disproportion between the consequences of the construction of this wall and its objectives. The argument of self-defence was notably dismissed. It is what the Court expresses in a crystal clear manner in the Advisory Opinion of 2004. It is not convinced "that the specific course Israel has chosen for the wall was necessary to attain its security objectives". Because this, it carries on, "gravely infringe(s) a number of rights of Palestinians [...] and the infringements resulting from that route cannot be justified by military exigencies or by the requirements of national security or public order" (par. 137).

Let us add moreover, and for the precise case of the wall in Palestine, that the route of the wall can notably be explained by Israel's desire to protect the Israeli colonies established in violation of humanitarian law (Article 49(6) of the Fourth Geneva Convention 1949), which was besides validated by the Supreme Court of Israel; hence consolidating an illegal situation.[7] The result is that the wall is seeking to consolidate an illegal situation (Dubuisson 2007). As such, the wall is not neutral anymore.

In the same way, if the walls are relatively neutral as a factual device, and if it is difficult to raise legal criticisms towards them, what is not neutral, is the legal rule that expresses the choice not to authorize movement or on the contrary to authorize it. And the wall is disposed to hinder the free movement that is legally recognized only if it makes the exercise excessively difficult. As noted by Hélène Ruiz Fabri: "In other words, from a legal point of view, the problematic unfolds in the question of the proportionality of the breaches of the freedom of movement" (Ruiz Fabri 2010: 157). It is therefore always proportionality that underpins this topic. For the Indian tribes whose territory is in both the United States and Mexico, and through which the construction of the American wall, as a consequence, hinders free movement, although endorsed by a US–Mexico agreement of 1848; things are clear: these Indians "do not wish to cross any border – [it's] the international border [which] crosses them"[8] (quoted by Forteau 2010: 113).

Why? Because the wall's role is to *absolutely* prevent the passage where it could have been admitted that it was to *simply* prevent the passage. Matthias Forteau summarizes this as follows:

> *As opposed to Walls*, borders and other ordinary dividing lines seem to imply an inherent porosity, a certain degree of free movement that is beyond the control of States, which has been little highlighted by the classic theory of borders. As such, Walls enable us to realise that the power of the State to control the access to its territory or its exit is perhaps not as much as we usually thought an absolute prerogative of the State's sovereignty. The Westphalian conception of the international order would not have been sufficient to annihilate the old *jus comunicationis.* (Forteau 2010: 113)

---

7 In its Judgment of 30 June 2004, the Supreme Court of Israel does not mention Article 49(6) of the Fourth Geneva Convention. Instead of confronting this provision, the Court engages in an extended discussion on the principle of proportionality, implicitly assuming that the occupying power is under the obligation to protect by all appropriate means the life and physical integrity of the inhabitants of the settlements.

8 Report of Amnesty International of 20 Mai 1998, *United States of America: Human Rights Concerns in the Border Region with Mexico*, p. 6. Available at: www.amnesty.org (accessed 14/11/11).

Once more, it is proportionality that is in motion: the proclivity to prevent passage is a lot stronger with a wall than without. In other words, walls call for the return to a rigid and absolute conception of sovereignty, at least in its territorial aspect; whereas the current tendency accustomed us to see more porosity in this territorial sovereignty, notably through the European example, if we consider the internal borders of the European Union and not the external ones that are prone to shut down. In that sense, the wall is also a historical anachronism that, paradoxically, enables the revelation of the primacy of the human, the human finality that has to intertwine with phenomena as sensitive as the border or territorial limits. Whereas we became concerned with the human consequences of the walls principally after their construction, as in with the Berlin wall,[9] the construction of new walls allows for the projection, *a priori*, of their consequences.

The wall therefore leads to a more humanist reflection on the question of limits in international law. The territory and the border have long been envisaged as objects of study in international law, but too often from the sole point of view of the rights and obligations of States. However, if the wall does not change the status of the territory or of the border, it leads to a delineation in a different manner, as the aim is quite often to directly constrain people, seen here as individuals, and not to abstractly prevent the passage of persons or goods. The wall thus raises problems as a wall, and not only as a limit or simple object.

This purpose, to prevent people from passing, creates a phenomenon qualified by some as "densification" (Bardonner 1984), a sort of paroxysm beyond the delimitation, demarcation or even marking of the border. The wall does not allow any interstice. It is the ultimate step in confinement and in the – almost – impossibility of passing. Here again, this seems disproportionate and anachronistic at the time of globalization and virtual communications. Until the nineteenth century, a wall prevented anything to pass, men, goods or information. Nowadays it does not prevent much but still constitutes for some the ultimate rampart. This gives the impression that fewer borders imply more walls, and that the wall would be a sort of substitute, or a (worse) replacement of the border. Besides, for Régis Debray 2010, the reinforcement of the border would allow for, paradoxically, the prevention of building new walls.

As a brief (non-exhaustive) summary, one has to note that the "wall" object can create potential or real threats, infringe proportionality in the obligations it imposes, by notably individualizing and making more dense the obstacles with an absolute preclusion of passage, or even by consolidating illegal situations as it is the case in Palestine. We are therefore far from the supposed neutrality of the wall and its absence of interest in law.

The wall is therefore "soluble" into international law but does not constitute a particular and identifiable legal object. There is thus no "international law applicable to the walls", in the sense of particular norms adapted to the wall, as exists, for example, in the law of the sea; but there are international law norms that do apply to the walls when they are identifiable as legal objects that can be reached by international law.

The wall is even doubly soluble. First, because it constitutes an ordinary object, which as any ordinary object, can be submitted to a legal regime depending on its location and its induced consequences. Second, because it symbolizes a situation perceived as extreme and because it more often than not challenges proportionality in every situation. This does not mean that international law is "effective" *vis-à-vis* the walls, as it in no way prevents

---

9 *Streletz, Kessler And Krenz v Germany*, Applications nos. 34044/96, 35532/97 and 44801/98, Judgement of 22 March 2001, notably pars. 72–73, 96, 100 and 102.

them from existing,[10] but they are at least present. This can lead, as it does for Serge Sur to a disillusioned outlook on the walls: "At heart, international law has certain difficulty to grasp the walls. They are for it a legal fact and not a legal act. It does not create them, it acknowledges and sometimes contests them" (Sur 2010: 197).

One can also note, in a more pragmatic fashion, the necessity to contest the wall before an *a priori* international tribunal to draw out all the consequences. Indeed, litigation only can expose the legal perversity of the wall, even if it is present, as well as obvious. In the end, a big banality for a few trivial bricks with disproportioned consequences.

But is it not the very essence of the law to frame trite objects, except if they result in a remarkable situation? It is always the occurrence of an extreme situation that exposes the potentialities of the legal content of an object, as trite as it can be; and which legal regime usually remains unnoticed. This is also the case for walls. By the status of the territory where it is constructed, by the constraints it entails in terms of free movement of people and goods, or by the consequences it induces with respect to human rights and humanitarian law; the wall can go from the shadow to the light, from banality to scandal, and more importantly from lawfulness to unlawfulness.

No, definitely, the wall is not ordinary when it has an international function or destination. This then becomes an anachronism in international law and this is the reason why it raises questions and justifies being the object of a colloquium.

References

Bardonnet, D. 1984. De la "densification" des frontières terrestres en Amérique Latine. Droit et libertés à la fin du XXe siècle. Influence des données économiques et technologiques. Etudes offertes à Claude-Albert Colliard, Paris, Pedone, 3–44.

Chemillier-Gendreau, M. 2010. Les murs, quelles conséquences en matière de droit humanitaire en matière de droit humanitaire et de droits de l'homme, in Les murs et le droit international, edited by Sorel, J-M., Paris, Pedone, 161–70.

Debray, R. 2010. Eloge de la frontière, Gallimard, Paris.

Dubuisson, F. 2007. La construction du mur en territoire palestinien occupé devant la Cour suprême d'Israël: Analyse d'un processus judiciaire de légitimation, Droit du pouvoir – pouvoir du droit. Mélanges offerts à Jean Salmon, Bruxelles, Bruylant.

Forteau, M. 2010. Le statut des territoires sur lesquels se trouvent les murs, in Les murs et le droit international, edited by Sorel, J-M., Paris, Pedone, 91–117.

Gilles, A. 2010. La définition de l'investissement international: Essai sur un concept juridique incertain, PhD Thesis, Université Paris 1 Panthéon-Sorbonne.

Kohen, M. 2010. Murs, souveraineté et frontières, in Les murs et le droit international, edited by Sorel, J-M., Paris, Pedone, 127–36.

Razac, O. 2000. Histoire politique du Barbelé, la prairie, la tranchée, le camp, La Fabrique éditions, Paris.

---

10   We would event be tempted to state the opposite. Concerning the wall in Palestine, Israel only corrected the route of the wall as indicated by its Supreme Tribunal in the two Judgments of 30 June 2004 and 15 September 2005 applying mainly its domestic law. Concerning the other walls, they continue to thrive without any responsibility in international law being raised against their builder.

Rivier, R. 2004. Conséquence juridique de l'édification d'un mur dans le territoire palestinien occupé. Cour internationale de Justice, avis consultatif du 9 juillet 2004, AFDI, 292–336.
Ruiz Fabri, H. 2010. Murs accessibilité et libre circulation, in Sorel, J-M (ed.) 2010. Les murs et le droit international, Paris, Pedone, 153–60.
Sorel, J-M. 2002. Existe-t-il une définition universelle du terrorisme? Le droit international face au terrorisme, Paris, CEDIN, Pedone, 35–68.
Sorel, J-M. (ed.) 2010. Les murs et le droit international, Paris, Pedone.
Sur, S. 2010. Vie, mort et resurrection des murs, in Les murs et le droit international, edited by Sorel, J-M., Paris, Pedone, 195 ff.
Tomuschat, C. 2010. Murs et responsabilité des États, in Les murs et le droit international, edited by Sorel, J-M., Paris, Pedone, 171–84.
Virally, M. 1974. Conclusions of the SFDI Colloquium: Pays en voie de développement et transformation du droit international, Paris, Pedone.
Wedgwood, R. 2005. The ICJ Advisory Opinion on the Israeli Security Fence and the Limits of Self-Defence, AJIL, 99.

Chapter 9
Walls of Money: Securitization of Border Discourse and Militarization of Markets

Elisabeth Vallet and Charles-Philippe David

The walls many believed had disappeared forever from the post-Cold War landscape are back with a vengeance. Walls have become a standard State response to perceived insecurity: today, they stud borderlines the world over, transforming porous, inclusive soft borders into sealed, exclusionary hard borders (DeBardeleben, 2005: 11 and 23; Zielonka, 2002: 11–12). Walls are symbols of identity reaffirmation, markers (Foucher, 2009) of State sovereignty (Brown, 2009; Parizot, 2009: 53; Parizot and Latte Abdallah, 2011), but also instruments of dissociation (Davis, 2007), the physical expression of the Other's foreignness.

There is a paradox here: even as globalization is blurring borders (Andreas, 2003: 82), walls accentuate them. Walls reassure the public, which sees them as a way to control the flow of people, goods and services (Ritaine, 2010; Addiechi, 2005; Rekacewicz, 2009) and believes its security to be thereby enhanced (Cienfuegos and Jiménez, 2006). In a risk-averse world (Beck, 2003), the wall, with its various functions (protection, pacification, separation and even segregation) and accompanying security mechanisms (El Maslouhi, 2009: 6), seems to enable the State to eliminate risk on its own. Walls are built when a State believes it can address a security issue only by itself:[1] the wall is "a unilateral, asymmetrical response to an equally asymmetrical perception of danger" (Ritaine, 2009a: 157), an illustration of social relationships "in which relations of domination delineate the social treatment of space" (Guillot, 2009: 358).

A wall therefore reflects a State's need to fully insulate its territory (striking examples include India, Saudi Arabia and China, which are literally walling themselves in) or to redefine its sovereignty (Brown, 2009). The border becomes a line that must be fortified: it is armoured, cemented, monitored, filmed. In this new environment, walls, obstacles, knife-points, sensors, captors, barriers and drones have become the accessories of hard borders in an open world.

Border barriers are demanding increasingly elaborate and complex technology, spawning a new industry and new international markets in which the private sector is playing a prominent role. Our thesis is that the post-9/11 environment has given rise to a *securitization* of border discourses that supports militarization of the borderline. The process is accelerating the fortification of the border (Vallet and David, 2012) and is serving the interests of the military–industrial complex, which has changed its shape since the late 1980s (Hébert, 2000; Fontanel, 1995). In the context of the securitization of border discourse, the relentless evolution of the military–industrial complex has continued; it is morphing into a "security–industrial" complex that enlists the same mechanisms as

---

[1] Since it is a unilateral initiative, a wall is built inside the building State's territory, not on the demarcation line.

its precursor (Saada, 2010) and, in a feedback loop, helps drive the militarization and fortification of borders.

Securitization of Border Discourse

In a globalized world in which interdependence is viewed as a necessity and the norm (Keohane and Nye, 2001), border walls appear to be things of the past, obsolete manifestations of the institution of State (Badie and Smouts, 1992). Nevertheless, walls have been spreading steadily since the end of the Cold War (Vallet and David, 2012a and b). And the boom in wall-building after the attack on the World Trade Center actually has its roots, at least attitudinally, in the pre-9/11 period, for the walls derive not from a specific fear of terrorism but rather from the global insecurity bred by globalization (Vallet and David 2014). Paradoxically (Castells, 1998; Jouve and Roche, 2006; Jones, 2012; Di Cinto, 2012; Audoin-Rouzeau, 2008), in a security-conscious world, globalization has led not to the elimination of borders but rather to the recomposition of territory and the erection of new "ramparts" (Lévy, 2005; Weber, 2008: 48; Andreas and Snyder, 2000). The wall has become a solution to the quest for security of the State, the boundaries of which never truly disappeared (Newman, 2010), a solution sublimated through an increasingly security-centric discourse in the wake of 9/11.

The Quest for Security

When a border wall is built, it becomes a counterpoint to the border, to the demarcation line based on international agreement. It enshrines the end of dialogue (Novosseloff and Neisse, 2007: 16) and evidences a fundamentally dysfunctional relationship between the two States. A wall is symptomatic of an inability to reach negotiated solutions to the security issues the States face, or think they face (Vassort-Rousset, 2006; Vallet and David, 2013). It is at once the last alternative to open conflict between the two States and a response to sharp differences in perception about their common and individual security. In this sense, the wall symbolizes the perimeter of State sovereignty and is a cornerstone of the State's deterrence strategy. From a realist point of view, therefore, it is a commendable compromise that serves to avoid open conflict between the two States.

For example, it might be suggested that rather than running the risk of nuclear confrontation, India decided to beef up its security, limit incursions and freeze the boundary by erecting a barrier along its border with Pakistan in the Punjab, in Rajasthan, in Gujarat and finally in Kashmir. Occasional clashes still occur and they are not always minor, but in the official discourse they have been downgraded to skirmishes and the risk of escalation to atomic warfare between the two nuclear powers has been reduced. Where the costs of war appear exorbitant in advance, it may well be entirely rational for a State to regard a border wall as a way to mitigate the threat; at the same time, the wall may also suit the other State, which may see it as a way to buttress its control over its own territory (Waldman, 2004).

The establishment of a buffer zone between the two parts of Cyprus reflects the international community's desire to avert open war between Greece and Turkey. The green line has been fortified in order to pause the conflict in its current state, with no solution in sight other than preserving the status quo and ultimately, perhaps, establishing a legal border by freezing the demarcation line (Fontaine, 2007). An analogous situation exists on the Korean peninsula, where the extensive border fortifications create an impassable physical barrier that confirms the division of the peninsula; South Korea is considering an additional wall on its side of the DMZ (Eckohlm, 1999). It might be argued that the creation of a barrier between India and China also derives to some extent from a desire to freeze a *de facto* state of affairs and alleviate the risk of direct confrontation along that section of their disputed border (Thaindian News, 2010).

Seen through this lens, a wall is an attractive device for a State that needs to address new security challenges (Jervis, 1978) and defend its interests. A wall can also represent a solution to a difference of opinion over a security issue, when the neighbouring State shows little concern for a matter that has become critical for the other, wall-building State. Nevertheless, of the walls still standing today, only six were built to freeze a boundary into a fragile peace. All the others were built to fight migration, smuggling or terrorism. These border barriers are therefore a State response to the instability generated by the international system and to fear of other actors of the same type (Waltz, 2000: 30; Buzan and Herring, 1998: 83; Krasner, 1999; Cohen, 2003) or of asymmetrical threats (Courmont and Ribnikar, 2002). The quest for security has caused a shift in border discourses towards the rhetoric of security, a shift that was accelerated (but not triggered) by 9/11 (Jones, 2012).

Discursive Shift

The framing of border security issues depends on which side of the boundary one is on. Transit States and destination States perceive border-related issues quite differently. Transit States (and States of origin) see migrants entering their territory from third countries and attempting to cross, and also from the destination State, whence they have been expelled. For the destination State, the migratory movements through the transit State represent a threat and it will try to stem the flow. Hence the differences of opinion between Morocco and Spain, Turkey and Greece, Mexico and the US. In all three cases, the destination States, unable to control the points of entry to their territory and unable to outsource the management of their borders, have a different perception of the unwanted flow of migrants than do their neighbours.

So it is that the wall crystallizes the divide between two worlds: the "security domain" as opposed to the "risk domain" (Ritaine, 2009a: 29).[2] From a constructivist point of view, a border wall can therefore be understood in terms of "securitization" (Buzan, Waever and de Wilde, 1998: 21–4). Peter Andreas frames the issue as a dialectic between the deterritorialization of the State and the return of borders (Andreas and Snyder, 2000). In this case, the wall is a response to a classic problem (migratory pressures) that has come to be perceived as a security issue (the migratory threat). This localized threat (border violence) takes on a national scope (becoming linked to the national security implications of the border).

After 9/11 (Jones, 2009 and 2012), the twin threats of cross-border migratory movements and terrorist movements were conflated and overlaid in wall-building legitimating discourses, including – and this is a relative novelty – the discourses of democratic governments (Foucher, 2007; Ritaine and Vallet, 2011; Clochard, 2003; Le Boedec, 2007; Sanguin, 2007; Jones, 2012; Foucher, 2009). A notable example is Israel's treatment of its 240-kilometre border with Egypt (Sadeh, 2011; Sherwood, 2012); its borders with Jordan (Hartman, 2012) and Lebanon (Khraiche, 2012) since January 2012, and of course

---

2 This observation is supported by the fact that all the security-legislation passed in the US always contains at least one immigration control provision (Robbins, 2012).

the West Bank. After building a wall to separate itself from Pakistan, India is completing another around Bangladesh to stem smuggling, immigration and potential terrorism, and is beginning work on a third along its border with China. Spain is also on the list of fortified democracies: Morocco, which has been slowly building a sand wall (berm) in Western Sahara since 1981 to isolate the Polisario Front, now faces two barriers around the Spanish enclaves of Melilla and Ceuta, originally built in 1998 to stop the flood of immigrants and then expanded into a triple barrier in 2005 (Ferrer-Callardo, 2008). Meanwhile, the US is pressing ahead with construction of the barrier separating it from Mexico, which is already 930 kilometres long, although the Obama administration decided in March 2010 to suspend the overly costly "virtual fence" project. Finally, in 2013 Greece completed a security wall along its entire border with Turkey to block the flow of illegal immigrants (Jerusalem Post, 2011; Hürriyet, 2011).

So, while it is true that 9/11 ratified (rather than generated) the return of the wall as a physical object and political instrument (Jones, 2010; Vallet and David, 2012a), it also sparked not only a quantitative surge in wall-building (Vallet and David, 2012a and b) but also a qualitative break in the discourse about walls. Illegal immigration is now being cited as a justification for border walls (as in the case of the walls around Ceuta and Melilla, along the US–Mexico border, between Turkmenistan and Uzbekistan, Uzbekistan and Afghanistan, China and North Korea, the United Arab Emirates and Oman, Brunei and Malaysia, India and Bangladesh). So too are smuggling and terrorism (as in the case of Israel, the walls between Brunei and Malaysia, Thailand and Malaysia, Saudi Arabia and Yemen, Iraq and its neighbours). Sometimes the arguments are less clear-cut; for example, the fight against terrorism and the fight against trafficking (smuggling, the drug trade, human trafficking) have been used at different times to justify the same barrier, as in the case of the wall between Mexico and the US (Ganster and Lorey, 2008: 175–87). Interchangeable discourses and rhetorical amalgamation (Bigo, 1998) serve to legitimate walls by applying to the border a broadened and shifting definition of security.

A wall is not just a piece of masonry; it is at once a "process of differentiation" which, according to David Newman (2006: 177), amalgamates all the discursive elements opposing the identity of the wall-building State (the Self/us/here) to that of its neighbour (the Other/them/there) (Newman and Paasi, 1998). It is therefore the deliberate intent of the "besieged" wall-building State (Bauman, 2007) to impose its vision of territoriality (O'Tuathail, 1996: 225), while ignoring the other State, perceived as a contributor to the threat. Not only does it build a wall to seal off its territory but it also erects, around and alongside the physical structure, a series of non-physical barriers that have a lasting impact on identities on both sides of the closed border (Zolberg, 1989). The physical fragmentation of space is accompanied by an arsenal of legislative defences (right of asylum, residence permits, visas) that convert a State's territory into a protected sanctum. This process is supported by the inter-subjectivity of the policy entrepreneurs (business, politicians, citizen groups) who frame the wall-legitimating discourse.

The fortified border (Ritaine, 2009a: 23) is a response to a perception of threat that is unilaterally constructed (Hare, 2009) by the wall-building State, which seeks assurance and insurance in a supposedly scientific and objective technological solution (Ritaine, 2009b: 158; Hayes and Vermeulen, 2012). The discourse surrounding walls enshrines the precedence of domestic politics (and appearances: Foucher, 2009: 3; Brown, 2009) over foreign policy (and diplomatic necessities) (Andreas in Davis and Chacón, 2006: 206). It reflects a civilian–military convergence (Ritaine, 2009a: 24) through which the military–industrial complex has been mutating into the security industry since the end of the Cold War.

Examples include the deployment of an Air Force Corps of Engineers unit from Alaska to build a patrol road four kilometres west of the Nogales-Mariposa border crossing between the US and Mexico (and the reasons for doing it: to support the work of Homeland Security and train soldiers in terrain similar to what they would encounter in Afghanistan) (Clark, 2012) as well as the incorporation into the US–Mexico wall of metal sheets that had been used in the Gulf War, provided by the army free of charge (Powell, 2008). The intersection of the military and security spheres is particularly clear in the border zone, where they are bound together by the logic of the fortified border.

The Technological Response to the Securitization of Discourse

Border control mechanisms are becoming increasingly sophisticated. As States aspire to absolute territorial control and imagine they can achieve it by wall-building (Bennafla and Peraldi, 2008), the wall has become the centrepiece of territorial security mechanisms. While the idea of the "closed border" never disappeared from the geopolitical landscape (Newman, 2010), since 2001 new closure strategies have been developing (Cuttitta, 2007). These trends are introducing advanced technology into the world of border control (Coleman, 2005) and promoting the growth of a true security–industrial complex (Staudt, Payan and Kruszewski, 2009; Longley, 2012) in an increasingly lucrative market.

Use of Technology for Border Security

The military–industrial complex (Mills, 1956; Nincic, 1982; Fontanel, 1983; Aben, 1992: 43) has been the major beneficiary of the transformation of the security environment since the end of the Cold War. IT providers and suppliers of surveillance systems are applying dual-use technologies to defend borders, thereby promoting what Dal Lago (2005) has called the "militarization of contiguity" (quoted in Ritaine, 2009a). The border market embraces construction of infrastructures, weapons systems, intelligence, and land-based, naval and aerial components such as radar and drones, a series of goods and services that still belong to the military sphere (Anonymous, 2010). Nevertheless, we use the term "security–industrial complex" because of the close linkages among its constituent companies. The industrial complex concept, which has been adopted by the Republican Chairman of the House Appropriations Committee, Hal Rogers (Robbins, 2012), also includes the private companies that build, maintain and supply detention centres, the companies that supply border guards with food, uniforms, etc., the companies that provide the means of air and land transport to expel immigrants, and local businesses. As border areas are not necessarily the most prosperous, border industries can represent an economic lifeline for these regions (Longley, 2012).

While the military border market is highly lucrative – in 2011, it amounted to $17 billion worldwide (Visiongain, 2011) – it remains that the end of the Cold War and the expectation of a peace dividend led to a decline in military expenditures and weapons spending (which actually began in 1988 – Hébert, 2000). Some spoke of the "end of history". Defence industries therefore had to rethink their markets and their objectives (Fontanel, 2004), a process that was eased by the privatization of formerly monopolistic defence markets (Hébert, 2001).[3]

---

3   It may be no coincidence that, according to the Center for Responsive Politics, the leading arms manufacturers in the US spent $59 million on lobbying Congress in 2011.

The trend was well underway before 9/11 (Hébert, 2000) but picked up steam after the attacks, enabling wall-building States to legitimate the already discernible trend toward the fortification of borders (Vallet and David, 2012a) and to step up the conversion of arms industries to the purpose.

However, walls *per se* do not really stem the flow of people or goods (Vallet and David, 2012b); they foster a logic of transgression that subverts their stated objectives (Sterling, 2009: 328; Courau, 2004; Lecumberri, 2006; Bennafla and Peraldi, 2008; Stier, 2009; McCarthy, 2009; Rekacewicz, 2009: 12; Guillot, 2009: 280; Brown, 2009: 36; Nuñez-Neto and Viña, 2006: 26; Ramsey, 2012). It has therefore become necessary to back up the wall with a constellation of systems designed to prevent passage. As the devices installed around the Berlin wall (preventive barriers, groomed sand cover, checkpoints, towers) proved insufficient, States have sought more hi-tech solutions. The wall must therefore be understood broadly, as a political mechanism that includes barriers of all kinds, airplanes, public or private detention centres, border guards, communication systems and intelligence.

For example, Israel Aerospace Industries (IAI) and one of its subcontractors have adapted military technologies to the wall by implementing the dual-use Plug-in Optronic Payload (POP) system for border defence. POP uses high-sensitivity thermal cameras that can focus on an object several kilometres away. Elbit Systems and its subcontractors are developing a system of electronic sensors and surveillance cameras called LORROS, remote-controlled land vehicles for deployment on patrol roads along the Israeli wall, and the TORC2H remote surveillance system (BDS, 2011). The 450 Israeli companies in the industry are attacking export markets, contributing to the 22 percent increase in Israel's technology exports since 2002 (Saada, 2010). For example, Elbit's Kollsman subsidiary is part of the consortium headed by Boeing for the Mexican border and Israelis are involved in security in India, notably in drones and radar (Jansen, 2002).

Major contracts granted since the mid-2000s include the Saudi Guard Development Program, which is expected to cost Saudi Arabia up to $9 billion in all (Saada, 2010). As part of the project, EADS will build a nearly 5,000-kilometre electronic detection system including 225 radar stations connected to a command centre and 400 border posts, train 20,000 border guards, supply 20 planes, helicopters and drones, and install the Acropol communication system developed for French police (Cordesman and Obaid, 2005: 298–300). Already, a 2.5-metre high barrier is rising along the boundary with Iraq. It comprises three sections: the first consists of barbed wire, the second of sensors, and the third connects the barrier to the command centres (Al-Saheil, 2010). Similarly, the Jordan Border Security Program, equipped with a sophisticated series of sensors and barriers to protect Jordan (Saada, 2010), particularly along its border with Syria, was completed in 2011 by DRS Technologies under a contract worth approximately $400 million.

However, technology is no panacea (Ackleson, 2003 and 2005). In the US, the Secure Border Initiative has proven to be a fiasco. While plans called for a high-tech virtual barrier along the entire length of the Mexican border, nearly $1 billion was spent on just 85 kilometres before the Department of Homeland Security decided to cancel the project (Robbins, 2012). One reason was that the wiring in the electronic surveillance towers failed under the heat, a problem that had also been encountered with the Integrated Surveillance Intelligence System in 1997. The virtual wall has therefore been replaced by the Arizona Border Surveillance Technology Plan, which uses drones and mobile radar. Its cost is estimated at $1.5 billion but could easily spiral given the lack of effective controls (GAO, 2011). More technology has been the industry's typical answer to States seeking heightened security.

Evolution of the Industrial Complex

Wall construction can be costly. According to a Government Accountability Office report, the cost of building the US–Mexico barrier, counting everything from expropriation to construction, ranged between $1 million and $4.5 million per kilometre in 2008 (Powell, 2008). Around the Otay Mountain Ecological Reserve and Smuggler's Gulch, near San Diego, the price tag ran as high as $6.4 million per kilometre (Marosi, 2010; Davis, 2009). In Israel, the original estimate of $1 million per kilometre has ballooned to nearly $2 million for an expected total of $2 billion (Troudi, 2009). The European Union has contributed 250 million euros to the construction of the barbed wire fence around Ceuta, after funding 75 percent of the first barrier built between 1995 and 2000 (Saddiki, 2012). Meanwhile, Morocco was sinking approximately 40 percent of its GDP into construction of the berm in the Sahara, consisting of a 2,700-kilometre wall and four 2-metre high inner walls equipped with surveillance technology (Hassner and Wittenberg, 2009).

Maintenance costs are also high (Regan, 2011). In the US, Customs and Border Protection estimates that the existing barrier will cost $6.5 billion to operate over the next 20 years; in 2010 repair costs alone totalled $7.2 million (GAO, 2011b) as a result of damage caused in 4,037 incidents along the wall (Karlin, 2012). Similarly, in Israel, the IDF is planning repairs to the 130-kilometre barrier along the Syrian border and the installation of additional obstacles (barbed wire, trenches, prominences) and sensors. The existing wall, which dates from the Yom Kippur War and has suffered the ravages of the Golan Heights' climate, does not meet contemporary security requirements. The cost of the repairs is estimated at close to $130 million (Cohen, 2012).

The contracts are so large that small businesses are in effect shut out of the bidding, or have to join a consortium led by a major player such as Boeing (Saada, 2010) or EADS and General Dynamics in the case of the successor to the Mexican wall project, or Cassidian in the case of the Talarion border drones program (Leblanc, 2012). On the other hand, the contracting States are sometimes forced to develop joint ventures with their neighbours in order to obtain more advantageous terms (Voice of Iraq, 2012) from these huge military–security–industrial partnerships. The same names crop up consistently as the consortium leaders: EADS, BAE Systems (UK), DRS Technologies and Raytheon Corp. (USA), LG Electronics (South Korea), Thales (France). They work with a raft of international (often Israeli – Elbit, 2014) and domestic subcontractors. The involvement of domestic players serves to circumvent protectionist contracting practices and cultures.

For defence industries, border security is a lucrative new market. To serve it and take advantage of the privatization of the border and security markets, they have reorganized by recycling their Cold War expertise. Despite the economic crisis and reduced security budgets, the market remains very substantial more than 10 years after 9/11. For example, the Saudi border market is estimated at more than $20 billion over the next 10 years – more than any other border market, including the US (UPI, 2011) – and could double between now and 2015 because of the impact of the Arab Spring on the Saudi leadership's perception of security threats (Homeland Security Research, 2012).

* * *

This would appear to be a long-term trend. No return to "normalcy" on the border, to an open dynamic in which the border functions as an interface, can erase years of identity construction supported by the existence of a wall. On one side of the wall, the structure has been glorified by a security-centred discourse; on the other, it has been denounced and the rhetoric of victimization has reigned. The wall has had the effect of distancing the two neighbours, rendering them strangers to each other. The wall-building State represses a threat, concealing it behind a concrete and barbwire screen. The other State is dismayed: the behaviour of the border guards is alien to what it has known (Human Rights Watch, 2010); the border environment has been distorted by the existence of the wall and the political apparatus to which it belongs (Falcon, 2001), which have broken up what it considered a border zone, one where there is often a similar if not common identity and culture on both sides. The security dilemma is therefore deeply engraved in national cultures. However, as long as the binational relationship remains static, the original problem that led to the creation of the barrier remains whole and continues to fester; it has only been cloaked by the wall (Banerjee, 2010; Sajjad, 2006). Worse still, the failure to establish a dialogue fuels a radicalization of the security-centred discourse.

While spending on security (including border security) is being scaled back, particularly in the West, with the receding memory of 9/11 and the pressure of the economic crisis, the market remains robust. To be sure, security industries can cultivate the security dilemma only to the extent that the environment is favourable and States are receptive. That is one of the limits to the power of the military–security–industrial complex. Its drain on the economy is another. But with the centre of gravity in international relations shifting towards the BRIC countries, which have acute security concerns, possess the financial means to address those concerns, as China and India are doing, and appear to be developing a "wall complex", there is no indication that the trend will flag. However, the security–industrial complex has not been the main driver behind the spread of walls. The seeds were there even before 9/11 and the speed with which borders were sealed after 9/11 reflects longstanding State security anxieties that predate the attacks. The stars were aligned: on the one hand, States were feeling threatened by the stresses of globalization; on the other, defence industries had embarked on the process of conversion even before the end of the Cold War. All the pieces were in place for businesses and States alike to look to border fortifications as a panacea when a perceived asymmetrical threat arose. Border walls are, first and foremost, money walls. They separate rich from poor, north from south, those on the inside from those on the outside. They are also a superfluous luxury that only some States can afford, a form of national group therapy more than a defence structure in the classic sense of the term.

References

Aben, J. 1992. *Economie politique de la défense*, Paris, Cujas.
Ackelson, J. 2003. Securing through Technology? "Smart Borders" after September 11th, *Knowledge, Technology, and Policy*, 16: 56–74.
Ackelson, J. 2005. Border Security Technologies: Local and Regional Implications, *Review of Policy Research*, 22: 137–55.
Addiechi, F. 2005. En la tarea de erigir fronteras-muros: El caso de Estados Unidos, *Política y Cultura*, printemps, 23, 211–33.
Agnew, J. 1994. The Territorial Trap: The Geographical Assumptions of International Relations Theory, *Review of International Political Economy*, 1, 53–80.
Al-Saheil, T. 2010. Securing the Saudi-Iraq Border, Asharq Al-Awsat, 28 juillet.
Andreas, P. and T. Snyder (eds). 2000. *The Wall Around the West: State Borders and Immigration Controls in North America and Europe*, Lanham, Rowman and Littlefield.

Andreas, P. 2003. Redrawing the Line: Borders and Security in the Twenty-First Century, *International Security*, Vol. 28, No. 2, automne, 78–111.

Anonymous. 2010. Increased EU Spending to Drive Border Security Market, *Biometric Technology Today*, vol. 2010, 1, janvier, 4–5.

Audoin-Rouzeau, A. 2008. La tentation des Murs. Etude sur la multiplication des barrières, murs et clôtures dans l'espace contemporain. Cisjordanie, Mexique, Corée. Mémoire de relations internationales supérieures à l'IRIS, Paris, dactyl.

Badie, B. 1995. *La fin des territoires – Essai sur le désordre International et sur l'utilité sociale du respect*, Paris, Fayard, coll. L'espace du politique.

Badie, B. 2000. *La Fin des territoires – Essai sur le désordre international et sur l'utilité sociale du respect*, Paris, Fayard, 2000.

Badie, B. and M.-C. Smouts. 1992. *Le retournement du monde. Sociologie de la scène internationale*, Paris, Presses de la Fondation nationale des sciences politiques and Dalloz, 1992.

Ballif, F. and S. Rosiere. 2009. Le défi des teichopolitiques. Analyser la fermeture contemporaine des territoires, *L'Espace Géographique*, 38, 3, 193–206.

Banerjee, B. 2010. The Great Wall of India, *Slate*, 20 décembre.

Bauman, Z. 2007. *La société assiégée*, Paris, Hachette, Coll. Pluriel Sociologie.

BDS. 2011. Brazil Military Relations with Israel, Stop The Wall, mars. Available at http://www.bdsmovement.net/files/2011/03/brazilian_military_ties_with_israel.pdf (accessed 15/01/2013).

Beck, U. 2003. *La société du risque – Sur la voie d'une autre modernité*, Paris, Flammarion, Coll. Champs, 1986.

Bennafla, K. et M. Peraldi. 2008. Introduction. Frontières et logiques de passage: l'ordinaire des transgressions, *Cultures and Conflits*, 72, hiver. Available at http://www.conflits.org/index17383.html (accessed 27/07/2009).

Bigo, D. 1998. Sécurité et immigration: vers une gouvernementalité par l'inquiétude, *Cultures et Conflits*, 31–2.

Brown, W. 2009. *Murs – Les murs de séparation et le déclin de la souveraineté étatique*, Paris, Les prairies ordinaires.

Brunet-Jailly, E. 2010. Introduction – Borders, Flows and Territories in Theorizing Borders and Borderlands. *Geopolitics*, 15, 4.

Buzan, B., O. Waever and J. de Wilde. 1998. *Security: A New Framework for Analysis*, Boulder, Lynne Rienner Publishers.

Buzan, B. and E. Herring. 1998. *The Arms Dynamic in World Politics*, Boulder, Lynne Rienner.

Castells, M. 1998. L'ère de l'information. Vol. 1. La société en réseaux. Paris, Fayard.

Clark, J. 2012. Military Engineers Dig in to Support Border Patrol, *Nogales International*, 24 January.

Clochard, O. 2003. La Méditerranée: dernière frontière avant l'Europe, *Les Cahiers d'Outre-Mer*, 222, April–June. Available at http://com.revues.org/index862.html (consulté le 30 juillet 2009).

Cohen, G. 2012. IDF reinforces security along border fence with Syria, *Haaretz*, 14 September.

Cohen, S. 2003. *La résistance des Etats. Les démocraties face aux défis de la mondialisation*, Paris, Seuil, Coll. L'épreuve des faits.

Coleman, M. 2005. U.S. Statecraft and the U.S.–Mexico Border as Security/Economy Nexus, *Political Geography*, Vol. 24, 2, February: 185–209

Cordesman, A.H. and N. Obaid. 2005. *Saudi Arabia – Threats, Responses and Challenges*, Wesport, Prager et CSIS.

Córdova, A. and C. de la Parra (eds). 2007. Una barrera a nuestro ambiente compartido – El muro fronterizo entre México y Estados Unidos, Ensanada and San Diego, Secretaría de Medio Ambiente y Recursos Naturales – Instituto Nacional de Ecología – El Colegio de la Frontera Norte – Consorcio de Investigación y Política Ambiental del Suroeste.

CIJ – International Court of Justice. 2004. Compte-rendu: Audience publique tenue le mardi 24 février 2004, sur les Conséquences juridiques de l'édification d'un mur dans le Territoire palestinien occupé. Demande d'avis consultatif soumise par l'Assemblée générale des Nations Unies. Online.

Courau, C. 2004. Ces murs qui ont divisé les hommes: l'histoire montre que toutes les murailles finissent par tomber, *Historia*, 693, septembre, 12–16.

Courmont, B. and D. Ribnikar. 2002. *Les guerres asymétriques*, Paris, PUF, Coll. Enjeux stratégiques.

Cuttitta, P. 2007. Le monde-frontière. Le contrôle de l'immigration dans l'espace globalisé, *Cultures and Conflits*, 68, hiver. Available at http://www.conflits.org/index5593.html (accessed 27/08/2010).

Dal Lago, A. 2005. Note sulla militarizzazione delle contiguità, Conflitti Globali, no. 2. Available at http://www.libertysecurity.org/IMG/pdf_conflitti2.pdf (accessed 21/07/2011).

Davis, R. 2009. A Barren Promise at the Border, *Voice of San Diego*, 22 October.

Davis, M. 2007. *In Praise of Barbarians: Essays against Empire*, Chicago, Haymarket Books.

Davis, M. and J. Akers Chacón. 2006. *No One Is Illegal: Fighting Racism and State Violence on the U.S.–Mexico Border*, Chicago, Haymarket Books.

Debardeleben, J. 2005. *Soft Or Hard Borders?: Managing The Divide In An Enlarged Europe*, Aldershot, Ashgate.

Eckholm, E. 1999. Where Most See Ramparts, North Korea Imagines a Wall, *The New York Times*, 8 December.

El Maslouhi, A. 2009. Murs et reterritorialisation des relations internationales post-Guerre froide. International Conference – Border Walls in International Relations, Raoul Dandurand Chair of Strategic and Diplomatic Studies, UQAM, April 1, 2009.

Elbit Systems of America. 2014. Elbit Systems of America Awarded Contract for the U.S. Customs Border Protection Integrated Fixed Towers Project, Press release, published: March 8, 2014, available at http://markets.on.nytimes.com/research/stocks/news/press_release.asp?docTag=201403080530PR_NEWS_USPRX____enUK20140 3082591&feedID=600&press_symbol=101952 (accessed 05/05/2014).

Falcon, S. 2001. Rape as a Weapon of War: Advancing Human Rights for Women at the U.S.–Mexico Border, *Social Justice*, 28, 2: 31–50.

Ferrer-Callardo, X. 2008. The Spanish–Moroccan Border Complex: Processes of Geopolitical, Functional and Symbolic Rebordering, *Political Geography*, 27, 301–21.

Fontaine, P. 2007. Des frontières comme ligne de front: Une question d'intérieur et d'extérieur, *Cités*, 31, 3, 127–33.

Fontanel, J. 1983. *L'économie des armes*, Paris, La Découverte-Maspero.

Fontanel, J. 1995. *Les dépenses militaires et le désarmement*, Paris, Publisud.

Fontanel, J. 2004. La conversion économique du secteur militaire dans le monde, *Arès*, Vol. XXI–1, 53, July.

Foucault, M. 1999. *Les Anormaux*, Paris, Gallimard.

Foucher, M. 2009. Le retour des frontières, *Géopolitique*, Institut International de Géopolitique, 104, January, 3–9.

Foucher, M. 2007. *L'Obsession des frontières*, Paris, Librairie Académique Perrin.
Foucher, M. et H. Dorion. 2006. *Frontières – Images de vies entre les lignes*, Glénat and Muséum.
Gale, I. 2009. EADS wins Saudi border security contract, *The National*, 2 July.
Galli, C. 2001. *Spazi politici – L'età moderna e l'età globale*, Bologne, Il Mulino.
Ganster, P. and D.E. Lorey. 2008. *The U.S.–Mexican Border into the Twenty-First Century*, Lanham, Rowman and Littlefield.
GAO – United States Governement Accountability Office. 2009. Secure Border Initiative: Technology Deployment Delays Persist and the Impact of Border Fencing Has Not Been Assessed, Report to Congressional Requesters, GAO-09-896, September.
GAO – United States Governement Accountability Office. 2011a. Arizona Border Surveillance Technology – More Information on Plans and Costs is Needed before Proceeding, Report to Congressional Requesters, GAO-12-22, November.
GAO – United States Governement Accountability Office. 2011b. Border Security – DHS Progress and Challenges in Securing the US Southwest and Northern Borders, Testimony Before the Committee on Homeland Security and Governmental Affairs, US Senate, GAO-11-508T, March.
Gomez Quinterro, N. 2007. Protestan por muro de EU en lado mexicano, *El Universal*, 26 June.
Guillot, F. 2009. Les asymétries frontalières – Essai de géographie sociale et politique sur les pratiques sociales et les rapports sociaux, Doctoral Thesis, Université de Caen Basse-Normandie, dactyl.
Hare, D. 2009. Wall: A Monologue, *The New York Review of Books*, 30 April, 8–10.
Hartman, B. 2012. PM: Security fence to be built along Jordan border, *The Jerusalem Post*, January 1.
Hassner, R. and J. Wittenberg. 2009. Barriers to Entry: Who Builds Fortified Boundaries and Are They Likely to Work, Paper prepared for prestation at the conference "Fences and Walls in International Relations", The University of Quebec at Montreal, October 2009. Available at http://polisci.berkeley.edu/people/faculty/WittenbergJ/Barriers%20to%20 Entry%20UQAM.pdf.
Hayes, B. and M. Vermeulen. 2012. *Borderline – EU Border Surveillance Initiatives – An Assessement of the Costs and Its Impact on Fundamental Rights*, Berlin, Heinrich Böll Siftung, May, 77.
Hébert, J-P. 2000. Militarisation ou démilitarisation du monde? *Mondes en développement*, Tome 28.
Hébert, J P. 2001. L'Europe de l'armement émerge lentement, *Alternatives Economiques*, 198, December, 33–7.
Heyman, J. 2008. Constructing a Virtual Wall: Race and Citizenship in US–Mexico Border Policing, *Journal of the Southwest*, 50, 3, 305–34.
Homeland Security Research. 2012. Saudi Arabia Homeland Security and Law Enforcement Market 2012–2015, Washington, DC, Homeland Security Market Research.
Hürriyet Daily News. 2011. Bulgaria mulls Turkish border fence to fight foot-and-mouth, *Hürriyet Daily News*, 19 January.
Israel Ministry of Defence. Israel's Security Fence, 2003 – updated in 2007. Available at http://www.seamzone.mod.gov.il/pages/eng/default.htm (accessed 15/01/2010).
Jansen, M. 2002. Non-aligned in the Middle East – What is the precise nature of Indo-Israeli relations, wonders Michael Jansen from New Delhi, *Al-Ahram Weekly*, 574, 21–27 February.

Jerusalem Post. 2011. Greece: Wall to be built along Turkish border, *Jerusalem Post*, 1 February.
Jervis, R. 1976. *Perception and Misperception in International Politics*, Princeton, NJ, Princeton University Press, 1976.
Jones, R. 2009. Geopolitical Boundary Narratives, the Global War On Terror, and Border Fencing in India, *Transactions of the Institute of British Geographers*, 34, 3, 290–304.
Jones, R. 2010. The Border Enclaves of India and Bangladesh: The Forgotten Lands, in A.C. Diener and J. Hagen (eds), *Borderlines and Borderlands – Political Oddities at the Edge of the Nation-State*, Lanham, Rowman and Littlefield, 15–32.
Jones, R. 2012. *Border Walls: Security and the War on Terror in the United States, India and Israel*, Zed Books.
Jouve, B. and Y. Roche (eds). 2006. Des flux et des territoires. Vers un monde sans États?, Québec, Presses de l'Université du Québec, coll. *Géographie politique*.
Karlin, M. 2012. The Border Wall: The Last Stand at Making the US a White Gated Community, *The New York Times*, 11 March.
Keohane, R. and J. Nye. 2001. *Power and Interdependance*, New York, Longman, 2001.
Khraiche, D. 2012. Israel to build wall along Blue Line: reports, *The Daily Star*, Beyrouth, 3 January.
Krasner, S.D. 1999. *Sovereignty: Organized Hypocrisy*, Princeton, Princeton University Press, 1999.
Le Boedec, G. 2007. Le détroit de Gibraltar, *EchoGéo,* Issue 2. Available at http://echogeo.revues.org/index1488.html (accessed 30/07/2009).
Leblanc, B. 2012. EADS en course pour surveiller la frontière entre le Mexique et les États-Unis, *L'Usine Nouvelle*, 14 March.
Lecumberri, B. 2006. Los muros, una estrategia geopolítica que alimenta la violencia – Entrevista: Yves Lacoste, Geopolítico Frances, *La Republica*, 28 October.
Lévy, A. 2005. Des murs, remparts contre la réalité, *Libération*, 20 October.
Longley, K. 2012. Industry of Border Security Creates Extra Layer of Regional Problems, *Statesman*, 21 January.
Marosi, R. 2010. $57.7-million fence added to an already grueling illegal immigration route, *Los Angeles Times*, 15 February.
McCarthy, R. 2009. Inside the Gaza Tunnels, *The Guardian*, 10 February.
Mills, C. Wright. 1956. *The Power Elite*, New York, Oxford University Press.
Newman, D. 2006. Borders and Bordering: Towards an Interdisciplinary Dialogue, *European Journal of Social Theory*, 9, 2, 172–86.
Newman, D. 2010. The Renaissance of a Border that Never Died: The Green Line between Israel and the West Bank, in A.C. Diener and J. Hagen (eds), *Borderlines and Borderlands – Political Oddities at the Edge of the Nation-State*, Lanham, Rowman and Littlefield, 87–106.
Newman, D. and A. Paasi. 1998. Fences and Neighbours in the Postmodern World: Boundary Narratives in Political Geography, *Progress in Human Geography*, 22, 2, 186–207.
Nincic, M. 1982. *The Arms Race: The Political Economy of Military Growth*, New York, Praeger.
Novosseloff, A. and F. Neisse. 2007. *Des murs entre les hommes*, Paris, La Documentation française.
Nunez-Neto, B. and S. Vina. 2006. Border Security: Barriers Along the U.S. International Border, CRS Research Report, 21 September.
Ohmae, K. 1990. *The Borderless World*, New York, Harper Business.

O'Tuathail, G. 1996. *Critical Geopolitics*, Minneapolis, University of Minnesota Press, 1996.

Parizot, C. 2009. Après le mur: les représentations israéliennes de la séparation avec les Palestiniens, *Cultures and Conflits*, 73, printemps, 53–72.

Parizot, C. and S. Latte Abdallah (eds). 2011. À l'ombre du mur – Israéliens et palestiniens entre séparation et occupation, Paris, Actes Sud, MMSH, coll. Études méditerranéennes.

Powell, S.M. 2008. As Texas Border Fence Lags, Costs, Controversy Rise, *The Houston Chronicle*, 11 October.

Quétel, C. 2012. *Murs – Une autre histoire des hommes*, Paris, Perrin.

Ramsey, G. 2012. Border Fence Not a Solution, Insight Crime, 3 January. Available at http://www.insightcrime.org/insight-latest-news/itemlist/user/71-geoffreyramsey (accessed 03/05/2012).

Regan, M. 2011. Barrier Rebuilt, *Tucson Weekly*, 23 June.

Rekacewicz, P. 2009. Vers la sanctuarisation des pays riches. Un monde interdit, Frontières, migrants et réfugiés, Cartographier le présent, Études cartographiques, December, 11. Available at http://www.cartografareilpresente.org/article418.html (accessed 15/09/2010).

Ritaine, E. 2009a. La barrière et le checkpoint: mise en politique de l'asymétrie, *Cultures and Conflits*, 73, Frontières, marquages et disputes, 13–33.

Ritaine, E. 2009b. Des migrants face aux murs d'un monde-frontière, in C. Jaffrelot and C. Lequesne (eds), *L'enjeu mondial: les migrations*, Presses de Sciences Po-L'Express, 157–64.

Ritaine, E. and Vallet, E. 2011. Les démocraties emmurées, *Le devoir*, 17 May.

Robbins, T. 2012. U.S. Grows An Industrial Complex Along The Border, NPR, 12 September. Available at http://www.npr.org/2012/09/12/160758471/u-s-grows-an-industrial-complex-along-the-border?ft=1andf=1001 (accessed 29/12/2012).

Rosière, S. 2009. La prolifération des murs, symptôme d'une mondialisation «fermée»?, International Conference "Les murs en relations internationales", Raoul Dandurand Chair of Strategic and Diplomatic Studies – UQAM, Montréal, 29–30 October 2009.

Saada, J. 2010. L'économie du Mur: un marché en pleine expansion, *Le Banquet*, 27, May, 59–86.

Sadeh, S. 2011. A fence, but not a solution on the Israel-Egypt border, *Haaretz*, 25 November

Saddiki, S. 2012. Les clôtures de Ceuta et de Melilla: Une frontière européenne multidimensionnelle, *Études internationales*, Vol. XLIII, 1, March.

Sajjad, A.S. 2006. Fencing the Porous Bangladesh Border, Worldpress.org, 14 December 2006.

Sanguin, A.-L. 2007. Les nouvelles perspectives frontalières de l'union européenne après l'élargissement de 2004, *L'Espace Politique*, 1. Available at http://espacepolitique.revues.org/index437.html (accessed 21/01/2005).

Schroer, M. 2006. *Räume, Orte, GrenzenAuf dem Weg zu einer Soziologie des Raums*, Frankfurt, Suhrkamp.

Sherwood, H. 2012. Israel extends new border fence but critics say it is a sign of weakness, *The Guardian*, 27 March.

Sivan, E. 2006. À propos du mur en Israël, In M. Foucher and H. Dorion (eds), *Frontières – Images de vies entre les lignes*, Paris, Glénat and Muséum.

Sorel, J.-M. (ed.). 2010. Les murs et le droit international, Paris, Éditions Pédone, coll. *Cahiers Internationaux*.

Staudt, K., T. Payan and A. Kruszewski (eds). 2009. *Human Rights along the US–Mexico Border: Gendered Violence and Insecurity*, Tucson, University of Arizona Press.

Sterling, B.L. 2009. *Do Good Fences Make Good Neighbors?*, Washington DC, Georgetown University Press.

Stier, K. 2009. Underground Threat: Tunnels Pose Trouble from Mexico to Middle East, *Time*, 2 May.

Thaindian News. 2010. Fencing of India-Bangladesh border in progress, says Chidambaram, *Thaindian News*, November 1.

Troudi, M.F. 2009. Les conséquences de la construction du mur à Jérusalem, *Géostratégiques*, 15.

United Press International UPI. 2011. Security Industry – Saudis mount cleanup amid defense scandal, UPI.com, 10 juin.

Vallet, É. 2012. La tentation du mur, in *Migreurop, Atlas des migrants en Europe: géographie critique des politiques migratoires*, Paris, Armand Colin, 2nd edn.

Vallet, É. 2013. Et la frontière devint un marché prospère et miltarisé, *Visions cartographiques – le Monde Diplomatique*, November 29. Available at http://blog.mondediplo.net/2013-11-29-Et-la-frontiere-devint-un-marche-prospere-et (accessed 02/02/2014).

Vallet, É. and C.-P. David. 2012a. Introduction – Du retour des murs en relations internationales, *Études Internationales*, Special Issue, March 2012.

Vallet, É. and C-P. David (eds). 2012b. Walls and Fences in International Relations, *Journal of Borderland Studies*, Special Issue, September 2012.

Vallet, É. and C.-P. David. 2014. Do Good Fences Make Good Neighbours – States, Couples and Walls in International relations, in B. Vassort-Rousset (ed.), *State Couples in International Relations*, Palgrave (forthcoming).

Vassort-Rousset, B. 2006. Couples interétatiques: l'intérêt national revisité, *SDEDSI*, Arès XXII–2, 57, November.

Vàzquez Cienfuegos, S. and V. Martin Jiménez. 2006. La seguridad tras el Muro: Una opción defensiva o una solución política? *HAOL*, 11, Fall, 183–94.

Vishnevski, A. 1996. Migrations européennes dans le nouveau contexte politique, in M. Morokvasic and R. Hedwig (eds), *Migrants, les nouvelles mobilités en Europe*, Paris, L'Harmattan.

Visiongain. 2011. The Border Security Market 2011–2021: UAVs, UGVs and Perimeter Security Systems, *Visiongain Report*. Available at http://www.visiongain.com/Report/706/The-Border-Security-Market-2011–2021-UAVs-UGVs-Perimeter-Surveillance-Systems (accessed 21/01/2012).

Vittori, J-M. 2007. La tentation du mur, *Les Echos*, Issue 19829, January 5, 12.

Voice of Iraq / صوت العراق. 2012. السعودية تبدأ بأولى خطوات "الجدار الأمني" مع العراق وتعززه برادارات, 27 February. Available at http://www.sotaliraq.com/mobile-news.php?id=45638#ixzz1yXm6ulXd (accessed 12/06/2012).

Waltz, K. 2000. Structural Realism after the Cold War, *International Security*, 25/1/2000, 30.

Weber. D. 2008. Ces murs qui divisent, *Le Point*, Issue 1843, January 10, 48.

Zielonka, J. 2002. Introduction: Boundary Making by the European Union, *Europe Unbound – Enlarging and Reshaping the Boundaries of the European Union*, London, Routledge.

Zolberg, A.R. 1989. The Next Waves: Migration Theory for a Changing World, *International Migration Review*, 23, 2, Fall, 403–30.

Zolo, D. 2004. *Globalizzazione. Una mappa dei problemi*, Rome-Bari, Laterza.

PART III
Fenced Borders in the Twentieth and Twenty-First Centuries

Chapter 10
Walls and Access to Natural Resources

Sabine Lavorel

At a time when countless virtues are attributed to commercial, cultural and human exchanges, the construction of walls between states and nations may appear anachronistic. However, since the fall of the Berlin wall, about 30 walls have been or are being built. When completed, there could be more than 15,000 miles of fortified borders winding around the globe (Novosseloff 2007: 4).

Whatever their geographical location, most of these walls are built out of a desire for security or to restrict migratory movements or smuggling. This is notably the case for the walls erected between the United States and Mexico, between Botswana and Zimbabwe, between India and Bangladesh, around the Spanish enclaves of Ceuta and Melilla or more recently between Israel and Egypt (Mouillard 2010) or between Greece and Turkey (Stroobants, Perrier 2011). Whether brick-built, fortified, electrified or militarized, these walls have the common objective of reinforcing a territorial limitation in order to control or even prevent the circulation of people.

As far as international law is concerned, the construction of a wall is not forbidden. Each State may build a wall on its own territory by virtue of its sovereign rights. On the other hand, the international regulations may be impeded by the legal system established around the wall (Tomuschat 2010: 171–82). Thus, the ban on North Koreans leaving the territory violates Article 12 of the 1966 International Covenant on Civil and Political Rights (signed by North Korea) which states that "Everyone shall be free to leave any country, including his own". Similarly, a wall built on the territory of a state for the purpose of restricting the rights of a minority of the national population would violate international law. The question arises in a different way if the wall is erected on the territory of another state without its agreement, or on a disputed territory: such a construction is objectionable from the perspectives of territorial integrity and self-determination.

Owing to these distinctions made according to the path of the wall and the legal system attached to it, a selection will be made among the different walls and a few examples used to back up the argument. Indeed, most walls are built along a border with a view to making it more secure. Although this was not always the case in the past, it is unusual for a state to build a wall on a disputed territory and even more unusual for it to build a wall in order to enclose a minority of its population in a specific part of its own territory. Unusual indeed, but not inconceivable, as the following examples show. The 1,600-mile long sand wall built by Morocco in Western Sahara in the 1980s; the electrified, then cement-built barrier erected by Israel around the Gaza Strip during the first Intifada; the approximately 600-mile long wall also built by Israel on the West Bank in 2002 and the 450 mile electrified fence established by India in Kashmir from 2002 onwards are all situated on disputed or occupied territory. The barbed wire surrounding certain Palestinian refugee camps in the Israeli occupied territories,[1] such as the Aida camp in Bethlehem, painfully recall the enclosures which in the past encircled certain Bantu homelands in South Africa or some native reservations in various countries such as the United States, France and Canada.

Although the aim of all these walls is not to enclose a population, their mere presence restricts the exercise of certain rights. In fact the restrictions applied to the freedom of movement inevitably lead to, or even intentionally increase, restrictions on other fundamental rights, in particular rights associated with natural resources. In all the quoted examples, although with varying degrees, the existence of the wall makes it difficult, even impossible on occasions, for the local populations to have access to natural resources such as water, grazing and arable land, forests, minerals and sources of energy. This access is essential for it determines the ability of these populations to survive and develop. One example alone, the erection of walls in Gaza and on the West Bank, has largely contributed to the tragic pauperization of the Palestinian populations which happen to be "behind" the walls.

These restrictions on access to natural resources give rise to several questions with regard to international law. The first question is tied to the extent of the rights violated by the construction and the legal regime of the walls. Which rights are infringed and who holds these rights? Are these rights really binding and justiciable? Moving on from that, the second question concerns the consequences of these violations. Can the State which built the wall be sanctioned? What possibilities can be envisaged for populations which are victims of the wall to regain the full enjoyment of their rights? Furthermore, is it possible to effectively guarantee access to natural resources, or oblige States to safeguard that access?

The lack of progress in the situations in Palestine and Western Sahara as well as in Kashmir suggests that the rights of access to natural resources remain quite ineffective. For all that, the purpose of this chapter is to move beyond the common recognition of the ineffectiveness of international law to demonstrate that the current situation is the result of the lack of political will on the part of the international community, since legal means exist to put these rights into application. Thus, faced with the wall which constitutes an effective way of restricting access rights to natural resources, international law appears as a perfectible tool to guarantee those same rights.

Building Walls to Diminish Access Rights to Natural Resources

In theory, the link between the building of the wall and the restriction of access rights to natural resources may be twofold. First of all, one assumption is that the wall is erected precisely to prevent the local populations from gaining access to the resources. The construction of the wall is only one means among others to apply the legal decision to cut off access to certain resources. Another hypothesis is that the restrictions on access to resources derive from the existence of the wall. These are only an unfortunate consequence which public authorities can attempt to overcome by guaranteeing supplies to the populations which are "behind" the walls.

---

1 According to the estimations of the UNRWA (United Nations Relief and Works Agency for Palestine Refugees in the Near East), in 2010, there were more than 4.7 million Palestinian refugees, some of whom lived in one of the 61 camps established in Gaza (8 camps), in the West Bank (19), in Jordan (10), in Syria (12) and in Lebanon (12).

It must be acknowledged that all the walls built in order to restrict populations in their access to natural resources fall into the first category. They have been built with that purpose in mind, although the official line evokes other purposes, namely security ones, which may well be legitimate but can hide other disreputable ambitions.[2] Thus, the Western Sahara "berm" is intended to guarantee Morocco's control of phosphate mines, oil and gas deposits, as well as access to the coastal fishing areas. The West Bank barrier, the layout of which differs significantly from that of the Green Line set out in the 1949 Armistice Agreements,[3] allows Israel de facto to add Palestinian agricultural land to territory it controls itself. Moreover the wall erected in Kashmir underpins India's control of the Siachen Glacier, source of all the waterways in Pakistan.

These examples show the diversity covered by the expression "access rights to natural resources". This broad denomination covers the right to water, the right to food, the right to an adequate standard of living, the right to property, the rights of native people to land, the right of peoples to freely dispose, use and exploit natural resources and even the right to development. These rights, whether individual or collective, are directly violated by the erection of the walls in question.

The Violation of Individual Rights

The advisory opinion issued by the International Court of Justice (ICJ) on 9 July 2004 on the wall in Palestine[4] has a special value as it is to date, the only jurisdictional opinion on the international lawfulness of the construction of a wall in an occupied territory. Therefore, it has been a logical starting point to determine which rights linked to natural resources were indeed violated by Israel as a result of the building of the wall and by extension, which rights to access to natural resources are violated by States building walls on disputed or occupied territories.

The court thus deemed that the construction of the wall and the legal system associated with it limited the right of the Palestinian population to an adequate standard of living as recognized by Article 11 of the 1966 International Covenant on Economic, Social and Cultural Rights.[5] According to the terms of the first paragraph of this article, the right of every person to an adequate standard of living includes the right to "adequate food, clothing and housing and to the continuous improvement on living conditions;" the second paragraph adds "the fundamental right of everyone to be free from hunger". These measures set out in a restrictive manner the right to food,[6] details of which have been given by the Committee

---

2   Thus, the building of the wall in Western Sahara was justified by Morocco by the need to defend the territory against incursions by the Polisario Front. Since 2012, India's erection of a partially electrified fence in West Kashmir of more than 350 miles has been aimed at hindering the infiltration of Pakistan supported jihad fighters, but with only limited success. Lastly, the Israeli government legitimizes the building of the wall in the West Bank by the need to protect the Israeli people from Palestinian terrorist attacks.

3   The controversial layout of the wall only follows the Green Line along 20 per cent of its route (Novosseloff 2007).

4   I.C.J., 9 July 2004, Legal Consequences of the Construction of a Wall in the Occupied Palestinian Territory, Advisory Opinion, I.C.J. Reports 2004, 136.

5   I.C.J., 9 July 2004, note 4 above, para. 134.

6   This right to food was first recognized in Article 25 of the Universal Declaration of Human Rights: "Everyone has the right to a standard of living adequate for the health and well-being of

on Economic, Social and Cultural rights. "The right to adequate food is realized when every man, woman and child, alone or in community with others, have physical and economic access at all times to adequate food or means for its procurement".[7]

The right to food imposes other consequential obligations on States. Indeed, the right to food requires that States refrain from taking measures that may deprive individuals of access to productive resources on which they depend to produce their own food (obligation to respect), that they protect such access from encroachment by other private parties (obligation to protect) and that they seek to strengthen people's access to and utilization of resources and means to ensure their livelihoods, including food security (obligation to fulfil).[8] Therefore the right to food is linked to access to land. For vulnerable populations, the right to food implies "protecting existing access to land, water, grazing or fishing grounds, or forests, all of which may be productive resources essential for a decent livelihood" (De Schutter 2010a: para. 3).

In this context, the fact that the wall "cuts off Palestinians from their agricultural lands, wells and means of subsistence" (Ziegler 2003: para. 49) and that several thousand acres "of the West Bank's most fertile agricultural land, confiscated by the Israeli Occupation Forces, have been destroyed during the first phase of the wall construction, which involves the disappearance of vast amounts of property, notably private agricultural land and olive trees, wells, citrus groves and hothouses upon which tens of thousands of Palestinians rely upon for their survival"[9] clearly constitute violations of the right to food.

A similar argument can be made concerning the Gaza Strip. By setting up a 1-mile wide security zone along the wall, Israel confiscated almost 35 per cent of the Gazan land suitable for cultivation (UN Office for the Coordination of Humanitarian Affairs 2010: 8–9), thus preventing the local population from having access to these lands and therefore violating its right to food. The figures given by the UN in this respect are quite revealing – 61per cent of the inhabitants of the Gaza Strip and 79 per cent of the Palestinian herding population in Area C in the West Bank[10] are food insecure. Almost 6 per cent of children between six months and five years of age living in these territories suffer from acute malnutrition and 28 per cent suffer from growth deficiency as a result of malnutrition (UN Office for the Coordination of Humanitarian Affairs 2010: 4).

Added to this initial observation is the fact that the wall brings about increasing difficulties in access to water resources. In 2003 the Special Rapporteur on the right to food warned that by building the fence, Israel would annex most of the western aquifer system (which provides 51 per cent of the West Bank's water resources) (Ziegler 2009: para. 5). Several Palestinian researchers also pointed out that the path of the wall coincidentally

---

himself and of his family, including food [...]" (U.N.G.A. Res. 217 A (III), 10 Dec. 1948). However the Declaration is not legally binding.

7 Committee on Economic, Social and Cultural Rights (hereinafter referred to as CESCR), General Comment No. 12 on the Right to Adequate Food, 12 May 1999, Doc. E/C.12/1999/5, para. 6.

8 Ibid., para. 15.

9 Report of the Special Committee to Investigate Israeli Practices Affecting the Human Rights of the Palestinian People and Other Arabs of the Occupied Territories, 22 August 2003, Doc. A/58/311, para. 26.

10 According to the terms of the Oslo Accords of 1994, the West Bank has been divided into three zones. Area A (approximately 4 per cent of the West Bank), is completely under Palestinian civilian and military control. Area B (27 per cent of the West Bank) is under Palestinian civilian control but Israeli military control. Finally, Area C which covers about 70 per cent of the West Bank is entirely under Israeli civilian and military control. Each new building, any repair work, crop cultivation or harvesting requires prior authorization from the Israeli authorities.

followed the contours of the water-bearing basins and water tables of the region and allowed Israel to incorporate most of the western water-bearing basin.[11] In its July 2004 advisory opinion, the International Court of Justice underlines this loss of water resources and assimilates it to a violation of the right to an adequate standard of living.[12] Indeed, as the Committee for Economic, Social and Cultural Rights points out, "the right to water clearly falls within the category of guarantees essential for securing an adequate standard of living, particularly since it is one of the most fundamental conditions for survival" (CESCR 2003: para. 3). This legally binding right[13] includes "the right to maintain access to existing water supplies necessary for the right to water, and the right to be free from interference, such as the right to be free from arbitrary disconnections or contamination of water supplies" (CESCR 2003: para. 10).

Therefore, the occupied territories of the West Bank and the Gaza Strip enjoy renewable and abundant water resources by comparison with most of the Middle East. The Jordan basin, the ground water in the West Bank and the Gaza coastal water table represent the three large water-bearing zones in these territories. Indeed these water resources have been exploited – even over-exploited[14] – by Israel for the needs of its population and to supply settlements in the occupied territories. Since 1967, these water resources have been controlled exclusively by the Israeli army. Palestinians are not allowed to build water supply plants without the Army's permission[15] and almost 200,000 people do not have access to running water (Amnesty International 2009). While this situation is not caused by the wall, it has been seriously aggravated by its construction.

One last individual right connected to natural resources and liable to be violated by the building of the wall is finally the right to property. As the Palestinian territories are considered as territories under foreign occupation, they are subject to the Regulations concerning the Laws and Customs of War on Land, annexed to the Fourth Hague Convention of 1907. Article 46 of these Regulations states that "private property […] must be respected" and "cannot be confiscated", while Article 52 expressly forbids requisitions in kind unless they are actually required for the needs of the occupying army. Although Israel is not a party to The Hague regulations, the International Court points out that their provisions apply because of their customary nature.[16] Consequently, the Israeli army's seizure of land to build the wall is contrary to international law. The Court deems in fact that "the construction of the wall has led to the destruction or requisition of properties under conditions which contravene the requirements of Articles 46 and 52 of the Hague Regulations of 1907".[17]

---

11   See the research studies of the Palestinian Hydrology Group for Water and Environment Resources Development (http://www.phg.org/). Also Tamimi 2004.

12   I.C.J., 9 July 2004, note 4 above, para. 134.

13   This is recalled by the UN Human Rights Council in its resolution A/HRC/15/L.14 (30 September 2010). A little earlier, the General Assembly had recognized "the right to safe and clean drinking water and sanitation as a human right that is essential for the full enjoyment of life and all human rights" (UN Doc. A/RES/64/292, 28 July 2010).

14   According to studies carried out by the United Nations Environment Programme (UNEP), the underground water taken from the West Bank and Gaza exceeds the available resources (See UNEP 2000: 166).

15   Military Order No. 92 of 15 August 1967 on water resources and water use in the occupied West Bank; Military Order No. 158 of 30 October 1967 amending the law on supervision of water in the West Bank; Military Order No. 498 of 4 November 1974 on water in the Gaza Strip.

16   I.C.J., 9 July 2004, note 4 above, para. 89.

17   I.C.J., 9 July 2004, note 4 above, para. 132.

The regrettable lack of international protection of the rights of access to and use of possessions prevents the International Court of Justice from pursuing its reasoning regarding the lawfulness of another consequence of the building of the wall. This edifice separates 400,000 Palestinians from their property, now situated on the other side of the wall (Courbe 2005). In the Loizidou vs. Turkey judgment rendered in 1996,[18] the European Court of Human Rights had been referred to by a female Cypriot citizen who had been refused access to her property situated in the northern part of the island which was under the control of the Turkish army and, since 1974, had been separated from the Greek part of the island by the Green Line. Without referring to the obstacle created by the wall, the European court had stated that

> as a consequence of the fact that the applicant has been refused access to the land since 1974, she has effectively lost all control over, as well as all possibilities to use and enjoy, her property. The continuous denial of access must therefore be regarded as an interference with her rights under Article 1 of Protocol No. 1 [to the European Convention on Human Rights].[19]

There is no doubt that this Protocol is inapplicable to the Palestinian situation[20] but given the disturbing similarity between events, it is regrettable that international law has nothing to say on this point. The process of the Europeanization of law – including international law – may remedy this in the future.

Aside from this last detail, it must be acknowledged that individual rights linked to natural resources are recognized on an almost universal level either because of their customary nature or because of massive adherence of States to the conventions which proclaim them. It is not always the case regarding collective rights which grant access to natural resources not to individuals but to peoples.

The Violation of Collective Rights

In its advisory opinion referring to the wall in Palestine, the International Court of Justice did not limit itself to a study of Israeli's obligations in accordance with the international law of human rights nor with international humanitarian law. It also studied to what extent the erection of the wall contravened the right of peoples to self-determination as set out in the first article of the United Nations Charter, reaffirmed by the General Assembly's resolution 2625 (XXV) and underlined by Article 1(1) of both International Covenants of 1966 which lays down that "All peoples have the right of self-determination. By virtue of that right they freely determine their political status and freely pursue their economic, social and cultural development". Based on these texts, the Court establishes that the building of the wall in the West Bank violates the right of the Palestinian people to self-determination.

---

18 ECHR, 28 November 1996, Loizidou v. Turkey (Merits), App. No. 15318/89, Rep. 1996-VI, p. 2216.

19 Ibid., para. 63. Article 1(1) of Protocol No. 1 interpreted by the European Court reads that "Every natural or legal person is entitled to the peaceful enjoyment of his possessions. No one shall be deprived of his possessions except in the public interest and subject to the conditions provided for by law and by the general principles of international law".

20 Especially as Protocol No. 1 is only open for signature by members of the Council of Europe, unlike other Council of Europe conventions open to non-European States.

Indeed, the position of the wall can be largely explained by Israel's desire to protect the settlements set up in violation of international humanitarian law.[21] The erection of the wall therefore attempts to consolidate an illegal situation and "thus severely impedes the exercise by the Palestinian people of its right to self-determination, and is therefore a breach of Israel's obligation to respect that right".[22]

That being said, the Court confines itself to the political meaning of the right of peoples to self-determination which allows them to free themselves from foreign domination and to choose their own political status.[23] However, surprisingly enough, the International Court of Justice does not take into account the economic aspect of this right which had been asserted nevertheless by the first article of the 1966 International Covenants and in several resolutions of the UN General Assembly.[24] In accordance with these texts, self-determination implies that the peoples concerned "may, for their own ends, freely dispose of their natural wealth and resources [...]. In no case may a people be deprived of its own means of subsistence".[25] The African Charter on Human and Peoples' Rights goes even further by acknowledging that peoples have "a right to a general satisfactory environment favourable to their development" (Art. 24). This last right goes beyond the principle of permanent sovereignty over natural resources as set out in the 1974 Charter of Economic Rights and Duties of States, the implications of which were clearly visible in the context of decolonization. The assertion of a genuine right of peoples to development seems to give rise to the concept of "the right to sustainable self-determination" (Corntassel 2008: 105–32) which is not without importance in the context of free access to natural resources.

However, the African Charter cannot be applied in any of the cases examined here. None of the States responsible for the controversial walls – Morocco included – is a signatory to this convention.[26] But the provisions of the 1966 Covenants are binding and impose certain restrictions, the scope of which still remains undefined. Insofar as the peoples of Palestine, Western Sahara and even Kashmir have the right to self-determination,[27] the principles attached to this right in terms of the free use of their natural resources are applicable to them. For the Palestinian people, this implies not only the right to access to and free use of the lands from which they have been expelled by Israel but also the right to full use of

---

21 I.C.J., 9 July 2004, note 4 above, para. 119–122.

22 Ibid., para. 122.

23 U.N.G.A., Res. 1514 (XV) of 14 December 1960, Declaration on the Granting of Independence to Colonial Countries and Peoples ; Res. 2625 (XXV) of 24 October 1970, Declaration on Principles of International Law Friendly Relations and Co-operation among States.

24 Notably Res. 1803 (XVII) of 14 December 1962 concerning the Permanent Sovereignty over Natural Resources, and Res. 3201 (S-VI) of 1 May 1974 containing the Charter of Economic Rights and Duties of States.

25 Art. 1 (2) common to both International Covenants of 1966. These rights are also recognized in Articles 21 and 22 of the African Charter on Human and Peoples' Rights.

26 Morocco is the only State from the African Continent not to have ratified the Charter and not to be a member of the African Union, precisely in order to protest about the admission of the Sahrawi Arab Democratic Republic (SADR) as a member of the regional organization.

27 See U.N.G.A., Res. 3236 of 22 November 1974, Question of Palestine; Res. 35/19 of 11 November 1980, Question of Western Sahara, Doc. A/RES/35/19. The recognition of the Kashmiri people is more uncertain. In several resolutions (Res. 47 of 21 April 1948, 51 of 3 June 1948, 80 of 14 March 1950, 91 of 30 March 1951, 122 of 24 January 1957), the Security Council asserts that "the final disposition of the State of Jammu and Kashmir [under Indian occupation] will be made in accordance with the will of the people expressed through the democratic method of a free and impartial plebiscite conducted under the auspices of the United Nations". Pakistan regularly refers to these resolutions as a way of establishing the Kashmiri people's rights to self-determination.

the groundwater resources present in occupied Palestinian territory.[28] It is also possible to add the right to access to and free use of the fishing produce from the coastal areas along the Gaza strip. In this case, it is not the wall but Israeli-imposed restrictions which prevent Gazan fishermen from reaching the fishing waters (UN Office for the Coordination of Humanitarian Affairs 2010: 11). Similarly, the Kashmiri people could legitimately claim control of the water resources of Kashmir which are extremely important given the situation of water stress throughout the region – indeed, most of the local waterways spring from the Siachen Glacier. However, India seized military control of Siachen in 1984 and reinforced her position by the erection of the wall in 2004.

As for the Sahrawi people, the free use of the natural resources of Western Sahara represents important financial interests, insofar as these resources include not only the phosphates from the mines in Bou Craa[29] and the fisheries from the Atlantic coast but also the offshore and onshore oil fields and uranium found in the phosphate deposits (Haugen 2007: 72–81). The "Sand Wall" thus separates the so-called "useful Sahara" under occupation by the Moroccan army from the free Sahara under the control of the Sahrawi Arab Democratic Republic (SADR). Several resolutions of the General Assembly of the United Nations state that the Sahrawi people are the sole owner of its natural resources.[30] Consequently, the licences granted by Morocco to foreign companies for onshore drilling in Western Sahara are in conflict with international law (Corell 2002). For the same reasons, in April 2009 the Security Council officially sanctioned the Declaration setting up an exclusive economic zone for Western Sahara whereby the SADR asserted its sovereignty over maritime areas and reiterated that no fishing activities in the Sahrawi maritime zone could be carried out without the agreement of the SADR government.[31]

Thus, the premise that the walls erected in the occupied Palestinian Territories, Western Sahara and Kashmir are in violation of the fundamental rights of peoples and individuals to access to natural resources, is borne out by the study of international documents. That being said, the prevailing status quo in these different situations reveals how impossible it is for the peoples concerned – and also for the international community – to assert these violated rights. From this point of view, international law appears improvable so that it might effectively guarantee both peoples and individuals the rights to access to the natural resources that they need.

---

28 Resolution 60/183 of the General Assembly "1. Reaffirms the inalienable rights of the Palestinian people and the population of the occupied Syrian Golan over their natural resources, including land and water; 2. Calls upon Israel, the occupying Power, not to exploit, damage, cause loss or depletion of, or endanger the natural resources in the Occupied Palestinian Territory, including East Jerusalem, and in the occupied Syrian Golan" (Permanent sovereignty of the Palestinian people in the Occupied Palestinian Territory, including East Jerusalem, and of the Arab population in the occupied Syrian Golan over their natural resources, 31 January 2006, UN Doc. A/RES/60/183).

29 The phosphate deposits in Bou Craa spread over 200 miles^2 and are very cheap to extract as the seams are close to the surface. The site, which is controlled by the OCP (Office Chérifien du Phosphate) today supplies 10 per cent of Morocco's total production.

30 See e.g. Res. 63/102 of 18 December 2008.

31 Report of the Secretary-General on the situation concerning Western Sahara, 13 April 2009 (Doc. S/2009/200).

Improving International Law to Guarantee Access Rights to Natural Resources

Despite the fact that they are proclaimed in international texts or recognized as international customs, access rights to natural resources may not be truly exercised by their entitled owners unless they have real and satisfactory guarantees.

The first of these guarantees lies in the ability to appeal effectively to a judge (whether national or international) in a case of violation of these rights. Although recourse to a judge is encouraged as a peaceful means of settling disputes, this possibility still seems too uncertain as a way of implementing access rights to natural resources. Consequently, the effectiveness of these rights may not be really guaranteed except by the prior strengthening of their justiciability (A) and by the concomitant development of alternative, coercive means (B).

Strengthening the Justiciability of the Proclaimed Rights

The implementation of the proclaimed rights implies not only their affirmation in texts which are legally binding and opposable to States but also the possibility of invoking these rights before judicial or quasi-judicial bodies which can determine their contents in a specific case and decide on the measures to take to compensate for the damage caused by their possible violation.[32] The justiciability of a right grows as the right itself and the correlative duties of States are defined more precisely. It also varies according to the efficiency of the judicial system under consideration, be it national or international.

The question of the justiciability of the rights to food and to water is the subject of a prolonged doctrinal debate. These two rights are implicitly set out in the 1966 International Covenant on Economic, Social and Cultural Rights, but their direct applicability in the internal legal orders of the States parties remains uncertain. Indeed, the Covenant does not set out in concrete terms the modalities for its application in national legal orders. None of its provisions oblige the States parties to incorporate it completely into national law or to grant it a particular force within that law. Nevertheless, in its General Comment Number 9 on the domestic application of the Covenant, the Committee on Economic, Social and Cultural Rights states that

> the Covenant does not negate the possibility that the rights it contains may be considered self-executing in systems where that option is provided for [...] It is especially important to avoid any a priori assumption that the norms should be considered to be non-self-executing. In fact, many of them are stated in terms which are at least as clear and specific as those in other human rights treaties, the provisions of which are regularly deemed by courts to be self-executing. (CESCR 1998: para. 11)

In practice, the case of South Africa which formally included in its 1996 Constitution the right to water as a human right and whose Constitutional Court expressly recognized the justiciability of economic, social and cultural rights,[33] is often quoted as an example, but it

---

32 Concerning the notion of justiciability, see Addo 1992: 96–7; Scheinin 2001: 53.

33 Constitutional Court of South Africa, 4 October 2000, Grootboom and others v. Government of the Republic of South Africa and others, Case n° CCT 11/00: "socio-economic rights are expressly

must be admitted that States not attributing any real effect to the International Covenant on Economic, Social and Cultural Rights are still in the majority.[34]

When dealing with rights to water and to food, it is necessary to point out that their contents have been progressively clarified either by the Committee itself [35] or by successive UN Special Rapporteurs on the right to food. Consequently, the argument which consists of dismissing the direct effect of these two rights because of their overly general formulation may henceforth be set aside. On the other hand, the International Covenants on Economic, Social and Cultural Rights neither organizes an individual's or a State's right to action, nor imposes sanctions following a possible violation of these two rights. Unlike the UN Human Rights Committee, which oversees States' observance of duties arising from the International Covenant on civil and political rights and can hear complaints from individuals,[36] the Committee on Economic, Social and Cultural Rights is not (yet) a quasi-jurisdictional body.[37] For the time being, the rights to water and to food may only be effectively brought before the International Court of Justice or even before the Human Rights Committee, which protects the right to food, using the expedient of the right to be treated with humanity and dignity and not to be subjected to cruel, inhuman and degrading treatments[38] or by virtue of the rights of minorities to their own culture.[39]

The question of the justiciability of the right of peoples to self-determination and of its corollary, the right of peoples to freely use their natural resources, is presented in very different terms in view of the collective nature of this right but also – and above all – because of its sensitive nature. The Human Rights Committee's General Observation Number 12 referring precisely to the right to self-determination as proclaimed in the first Article common to both 1966 Covenants, carries the obvious marks of the subject's sensitive nature.[40] Indeed, the unanimous doctrine declares that this general observation is deceptive, since it provides no details as to the beneficiaries, content or extent of this right (see Nowak 2005: 9; Decaux 2010: 91) – although such details could have strengthened its effectiveness. The aporia of the Committee's position regarding the extent of the First Article is also due to its unchanging jurisprudence, according to which the claim of a violation of this provision may not be open to individual communications, within the meaning of the

---

included in the Bill of Rights; they cannot be said to exist on paper only […]. These rights (DESC) are, at least to some extent, justiciable".

34 For a study on the justiciability of the right to food, see Golay 2009.

35 See the above-mentioned General Comments 12 and 15.

36 Nevertheless, this function is restricted by the fact that the Human Rights Committee can only make observations, not issue enforceable decisions which would have the force of res judicata.

37 On 10 December 2008, the UN General Assembly adopted an optional Protocol to the International Covenant on Economic, Social and Cultural Rights which allows individuals or groups of individuals claiming to be victims of a violation of any of the economic, social and cultural rights set forth in the Covenant, to submit communications before the CESCR (Doc. A/RES/63/117). However, this protocol will come into force only when it is ratified by 10 States Parties to the Covenant. On 1 September 2011, it had been signed by 36 States but ratified by only 3 (http://treaties.un.org/Home.aspx).

38 H.R.C., Communication No. 458/1991, Womah Mukong v. Cameroon, 21 July 1994, Doc. CCPR/C/51/D/458/1991 ; H.R.C., Communication No. 763/1997, Lantsova v. Fédération de Russie, 26 March 2002, Doc. CCPR/C/74/D/763/1997, para. 9.1.

39 H.R.C., Communication No. 511/1992, Länsman et al. v. Finland, 8 November 1994, Doc. CCPR/C/52/D/511/1992, para. 9.5.

40 H.R.C., General Comment No.12 on Article 1 (The right to self-determination of peoples), 13 March 1984, Doc. HRI/GEN/1/Rev.9.

Optional Protocol to the Covenant. Indeed, this Protocol only gives communication rights to "individuals" with a view to lodging a complaint about an infringement of their rights. The right of peoples to self-determination is a collective right conferred upon peoples as such, and not upon the individuals making up these peoples.[41]

The possibility of relying on the principle of peoples' sovereignty over their natural resources therefore remains very unsettled, especially as the jurisprudence of the International Court of Justice appears irresolute in this matter.[42] At the moment, the African Court on Human and Peoples' Rights appears to be the most appropriate international jurisdiction for applying the various aspects of peoples' rights, particularly because of the extended locus standi before the Court and the Commission which preceded it. Even in its collective form, the "right of peoples" is, by virtue of real actio pupularis (De Schutter 2010b: 701), as justiciable as any other right recognized by the Charter.[43]

One final point should be made in order to determine the real efficiency of access rights to natural resources. It concerns the international responsibility of States, builders of the walls restricting these rights. As soon as the justiciability of these rights is recognized by the deciding judge, the consequences of the incurred responsibility are easy to define. The State which committed an internationally illicit act must remove the wall, the construction of which infringes international law.[44] Yet, as Professor Tomuschat remarks in a statement referring precisely to the subject, "no wall has come down as a result of its international illicitness" (Tomuschat 2010: 182). Israel has not complied with the recommendations of the International Court of Justice.[45] This underlines the weakness of the law of international responsibility and points to the urgency of developing other means of applying pressure.

Developing the Use of Alternative Means of Pressure

Several methods are possible in an attempt to compensate for the inadequacies of the international responsibility of States when access rights to natural resources are violated. Although different, they all demonstrate by their implementation a real political will on the

---

41 H.R.C., Communication No. 167/1984, 26 March 1990, Chief Bernard Ominayak and the Lubicon Lake Band v. Canada, Doc. CCPR/C/38/D/167/1984, para. 13.3.

42 I.C.J., 21 June 1971, Legal Consequences for States of the Continued Presence of South Africa in Namibia (South West Africa) notwithstanding Security Council Resolution 276 (1970), Advisory Opinion, I.C.J. Reports 1971, p. 16 ; I.C.J., 16 October 1975, Western Sahara, Advisory Opinion, I.C.J. Reports 1975, p. 12 ; I.C.J., 30 June 1995, East Timor (Portugal v. Australia), Judgment, I.C.J. Reports 1995, p. 90 ; I.C.J., 9 July 2004, Legal Consequences of the Construction of a Wall in the Occupied Palestinian Territory, Advisory Opinion, I.C.J. Reports 2004, p. 136 ; I.C.J., 22 July 2010, Accordance with International Law of the Unilateral Declaration of Independence in Respect of Kosovo, Advisory Opinion, I.C.J. Reports 2010.

43 See e.g. African Commission on Human and People's Rights, Communication No. 155/96, 27 October 2001, The Social and Economic Rights Action Center and the Center for Economic and Social Rights v. Nigeria; African Court for Human and Peoples' Rights, 4 Feb. 2010, Case 276/2003, Endorois Welfare Council v. Kenya.

44 I.C.J., 9 July 2004, note 4 above, para. 163 (3).

45 Neither has it complied with those of the General Assembly which, taking note of the I.C.J. advisory opinion regarding the Palestinian wall, adopted resolution ES-10/15 of 2 August 2004 "demand[ing] that Israel, the occupying Power, comply with its legal obligations as mentioned in the advisory opinion" (Doc. A/RES/ES-10/15).

part of the international community. Only a concerted reaction can in fact put an end to the building of illegal walls.

The first of these solutions as an alternative to referring to a judge, would lead different international and regional organizations to become more involved in the resolution of conflicts relating to the walls. Above and beyond the role of mediator often carried out by these organizations or their representatives (with varying degrees of success) they could act in a compelling way within their own area of competence, with the object of inciting States to act in accordance with their international duties. Regional organizations could thus give effect to the principle of self-determination of peoples whose rights are violated, by recognizing them effectively as peoples and by granting legitimacy to the authorities representing them. The Organization of African Unity, which became the African Union in 2004, admitted the Sahrawi Arab Democratic Republic as a full member in 1982, causing Morocco to leave the organization in 1985.[46] Another possibility would be for these regional organizations to adopt targeted sanctions against political or military leaders or companies contributing to the restriction of access to natural resources.[47]

Nevertheless, the UN remains the international organization with the greatest capacity for action in this field. The General Assembly regularly proclaims the rights of the Palestinian and Sahrawi peoples[48] but these resolutions are unenforceable. At best, it can set up subsidiary bodies responsible for applying its resolutions, following the example of the Committee on the Exercise of the Inalienable Rights of the Palestinian People[49] or more recently the United Nations Register of Damage Caused by the Construction of the Wall in the Occupied Palestinian Territory.[50] As for the Security Council, it has based its actions to date on Chapter 6 of the Charter thus applying non-enforceable methods for the peaceful settlement of the situation.[51] Chapter 7 has never been invoked to resolve the Palestinian, Sahrawi and Kashmiri conflicts even if the occupation of Palestinian territories was declared contrary to international law in 1967, the invasion of Western Sahara was condemned

---

46   However the African Union's position is not shared by all the member states, some of which do not recognize the SADR. Similarly, the Arab League upholds Morocco's territorial integrity and does not recognize either the Polisario Front or the SADR, even though the Palestinian Authority is one of its members.

47   Within the EU, the European Council may thus decide to adopt by a qualified majority "restrictive measures [...] against natural or legal persons and groups or non-State entities", following a joint proposal from the Union's High Representative for Foreign Affairs and Security Policy and the European Commission (Art. 215(2) of the Treaty on the Functioning of the European Union).

48   See note 41 above.

49   U.N.G.A., Res. 3376, 10 November 1975. The Committee is required to monitor the situation in Palestine, to submit reports and make suggestions to the General Assembly or to the Security Council and to further the spread of information regarding its recommendations through NGOs in particular.

50   U.N.G.A., Res. ES-10/17, 24 January 2007. This office, placed under the authority of the UN Secretary General, is responsible for the upkeep of the UN Register of Damage caused by the Construction of the Wall and will remain open for the registration of claims as long as the wall remains on Occupied Palestinian Territory.

51   For Western Sahara, see e.g. resolutions 1754 (2007), 1783 (2007), 1813 (2008), 1871 (2009), 1920 (2010) and 1979 (2011). For Palestine, see resolutions 242 (1967), 338 (1973), 1397 (2002), 1515 (2003), 1850 (2008) and 1860 (2009). For Kashmir, see resolutions 47(1948), 51(1948), 80(1950), 91(1951), 122(1957) stating that "the final disposition of the State of Jammu and Kashmir will be made in accordance with the will of the people expressed through the democratic method of a free and impartial plebiscite conducted under the auspices of the United Nations" (Res. 122(1957)).

in 1975 and the withdrawal of Indian and Pakistani troops was called for in 1948.[52] The possibility of having recourse to Chapter 7 to bring about a military intervention appears illusionary faced with the contradictory geopolitical interests of the leading powers in these regions and, with regard to Western Sahara, because of the low intensity of the conflict (see Zoubir, Darbouche 2008: 91–105). On the other hand, recourse to Chapter 7 would be conceivable to establish international criminal tribunals to judge war crimes committed in the occupied territories[53] or to appeal to the International Criminal Court, assuming that it is competent in the matter.[54]

The Security Council's timid intervention, whether it is justified or not, creates situations of stalemate in the different conflicts and the growing pauperization of the Palestinian and Sahrawi populations, a state of affairs due largely to the difficulties of access to their natural resources and sometimes aggravated by the setting up of a targeted blockade. The disastrous humanitarian situation in which these populations can find themselves raises the question of the relevance of a "right of humanitarian intervention" which would allow the implementation of the "responsibility to protect" threatened populations, enshrined in 2005 by the General Assembly of the United Nations.[55] For the moment, the implementation of this responsibility remains hypothetical insofar as it would open the way for an authorized "right to intervene" which would contravene the principle of territorial sovereignty and the exclusive nature of State jurisdiction. On the other hand, without going as far as interference, it would perhaps be possible to establish one alternative to the responsibility to protect, which would take the shape of a duty of solidarity or aid in extreme situations. The Committee on Economic, Social and Cultural Rights considers this in its General Observation Number 12,

---

52 See U.N.S.C. Res. 242(1967), 380(1975) and 47(1948), respectively.

53 The status of the Palestinian, Sahrawi and Kashmiri territories needs to be defined beforehand. Indeed, the applicable law varies according to whether the territory in question is "occupied" or "disputed". While the international community unequivocally recognizes the occupation of the Palestinian territories and therefore the enforcement of international humanitarian law to these territories – although this is disputed by Israel – Kashmir and Western Sahara, on the other hand, are considered more as disputed territories. Nevertheless, the situation on the ground and especially the presence of 450,000 Indian soldiers in Jammu and Kashmir and of 120,000 Moroccan soldiers in Western Sahara de facto make these territories appear as occupied.

54 The I.C.J. is competent to try persons presumed guilty of war crimes. By "war crimes" the Statute of the Court defines "grave breaches of the Geneva Conventions of 12 August 1949", including "Extensive destruction and appropriation of property, not justified by military necessity and carried out unlawfully and wantonly" (Art. 8(2)(a)(iv) of the Rome Statute, Doc. A/CONF,183/9). However, the I.C.J. only has jurisdiction over crimes committed by a national of one of the signatory States, or those committed on the territory of a signatory State. But, as of 1 September 2011, neither Israel, nor India, nor Morocco belongs to the Rome Convention. Nevertheless, by virtue of Article 13(b) of the Rome Statute, the Security Council can submit a case to the Court under Chapter 7 of the Charter, this resolution then applies to all Member States of the UN, including those which did not ratify the Statute of the I.C.J. This is the situation for crimes committed in Darfur which are being investigated by the Chief Prosecutor of the I.C.J. even though Sudan did not sign the Rome Convention.

55 The 2005 World Summit Outcome states that "the international community, through the United Nations, [has the responsibility] to help to protect populations from genocide, war crimes, ethnic cleansing and crimes against humanity. In this context, we are prepared to take collective action, in a timely and decisive manner, through the Security Council […], should peaceful means be inadequate and national authorities are manifestly failing to protect their populations […]" (UN Doc. A/RES/60/1). The fact that the West bank and the Gaza Strip are occupied territories gives rise to the possibility of the Palestinian population being considered indeed as a victim of "war crimes", and thereby fulfilling the conditions required for a concerted intervention by the international community.

when it states that "States have a joint and individual responsibility, in accordance with the Charter of the United Nations, to cooperate in providing disaster relief and humanitarian assistance in times of emergency [...]" (CESCR 1998: para. 38).[56]

The implementation of such a duty could have particularly applied to Egypt, which refused for a long time to open the wall which bars entry to its territory at the southern end of the Gaza Strip, in spite of the Gazan population's disastrous humanitarian situation. Quite the opposite in fact. In order to cut off the galleries which run under the frontier and which undoubtedly allow Hamas to supply itself with arms – but also permit the population to obtain basic supplies such as food, medicine, petrol and building materials – the Egyptian government began in late 2009 to build another underground steel wall under the frontier, designed to go 60-feet deep into the ground (Helfont 2010: 432–3). If a duty to assist oppressed peoples had been established, there is no doubt that the building of this new wall could have involved Egypt's international responsibility.[57]

To avoid humanitarian disasters in the territories concerned, supply operations are carried out for the most part by NGOs under insecure conditions as the Israeli army's bloody boarding of the Mavi-Marmara carrying foodstuffs to the population of Gaza in 2010 tragically revealed. In Western Sahara, the Norwegian NGO, Western Sahara Resource Watch – largely financed in all probability by the Algerian government – approaches multinational companies investing in the zone to make them aware of the situation of the Sahrawi people. This strategy appears particularly fruitful. Since 2002, several companies involved in fishing, mining and drilling for oil have reassessed their activities on the Sahrawi territory and have cancelled contracts signed with Morocco.[58] A few gas and oil companies have even signed drilling and operating contracts with the SADR.[59] Moreover, in 2004, the US excluded products from Western Sahara from its free-trade agreements signed with Morocco – in the same way as the free-trade agreements between the EEC and Israel excludes products from the Occupied Palestinian Territories.[60] Strangely, however, the European Union remains deaf to the arguments of the Norwegian NGO which began a campaign in 2006 to prevent the signature (in 2006) and the renewal (in 2011) of the EU–Moroccan Fisheries Partnership Agreement which allows European fishermen to have access to the Moroccan and Sahrawi fishing grounds in exchange for subsidies to Morocco. Although the European Parliament's Legal Service warned in a confidential legal opinion that fishing carried out by European boats under the EU–Morocco agreement covering

---

56 More circumspect, the Special Rapporteur on the right to food asks "whether States are under an obligation to provide international assistance, including food aid, in certain circumstances, or at certain levels" (De Schutter 2009: para. 5).

57 After the fall of Mubarak's regime, the new Egyptian government decided in May 2011 to reopen its border crossing into Gaza.

58 To give a few examples, oil companies such as Kerr McGee (US), TGS-Nopec (Norwegian), Fugro (Dutch), Total-Fina-Elf (French) which had signed contracts with Morocco for the exploration and exploitation of petroleum resources along the coasts of Western Sahara, decided to withdraw from the territory as of 2003, following WSRW information campaigns. In 2007, the Norwegian shipping company Arnesen Shipbrokers stopped shipping out phosphates from the territory. In August 2010, the US fertilizer company The Mosaic Company, announced the suspension of its importations of phosphates from Western Sahara.

59 HAUGEN Hans Morten, "The Right to Self-Determination and Natural Resources: The Case of Western Sahara", Law, Environment and Development Journal, 2007, 79–80.

60 As the Court of Justice of the European Union recalls in the Brita GmbH v. Hauptzollamt Hamburg-Hafen judgment (Case C-386/08, 25 February 2010).

the Western Sahara's waters is in violation of international law,[61] the 2006 agreement was renewed and even extended on 25 February 2011. This reveals the little importance attached to the obligation of consulting the Sahrawi people on the use they wish to make of their own resources,[62] an obligation which nevertheless lies with all the States of the international community.

References

Addo, M. 1992. Justiciability Re-examined, in *Economic, Social and Cultural Rights. Progress and Achievement* edited by R. Beddard, D. Hill, New York, St Martin's Press, 96–7.
Amnesty International. 2009. *Troubled Waters. Palestinians Denied Fair Access to Water*, Amnesty International Publications, 125.
CESCR. 1998. *General Comment No. 9 on the Domestic Application of the Covenant*, 3 December, Doc. E/C.12/1998/24.
CESCR. 1999. *General Comment No. 12 on the Right to Adequate Food*, 12 May, Doc. E/C.12/1999/5, para. 6.
CESCR. 2003. *General Comment No. 15 on the Right to Water*, 20 January, Doc. E/C.12/2002/11.
Constitutional Court of South Africa. 2000. *Grootboom and others v. Government of the Republic of South Africa and others*, Case n° CCT 11/00, 4 October.
Corell, H. 2002. *Letter from the Under-Secretary-General for Legal Affairs, the Legal Counsel, addressed to the President of the Security Council*, U.N.S.C., 29 January (Doc. S/2002/161)
Corntassel, J. 2008. Toward Sustainable Self-Determination: Rethinking the Contemporary Indigenous-Rights Discourse, *Alternatives: Global, Local, Political*, 33, 105–32.
Courbe, J.-F. 2005. Les conséquences du conflit sur la situation économique et sociale des territoires palestiniens occupés, *Confluences Méditerranée*, 55.
De Schutter, O. 2009. *The Role of Development Cooperation and Food Aid in Realizing the Right to Adequate Food: Moving from Charity to Obligation*, Report of the Special Rapporteur on the Right to Food, H.R.C., 11 Feb. Doc. A/HRC/10/5.
De Schutter, O. 2010a. Access to Land and Right to Food, *Interim Report by the Special Rapporteur on the Right to Food, submitted in accordance with General Assembly Resolution 64/159*, 11 August, UN Doc. A/65/281, para. 3.
De Schutter, O. 2010b. *International Human Rights Law. Case, Materials and Commentary*, Cambridge, Cambridge University Press.

---

61 The legal opinion pointed to the illegality of the agreement on the grounds that the Sahrawi population was never consulted and never received any compensation for the use of its fisheries resources. It therefore calls upon the European Commission to suspend or modify the EU–Morocco agreement. This opinion was sent to the European Parliament in July 2009 but was only made public in February 2010. It should be noted that, for similar reasons, the Legal Affairs Committee of the European Parliament has also questioned the legality of a Draft agreement between the EU and Morocco which makes provision for the partial liberalization of trade in agricultural and fisheries products. The draft was concluded between the European Council and Morocco on 13 December 2010 but still needs the approval of the European Parliament.

62 See U.N.G.A., Res. 2229 (XXI) of 20 December 1966; I.C.J., 16 October 1975, Western Sahara, Advisory Opinion, I.C.J. Reports 1975, para. 55 et seq.

Decaux, E. 2010. Article 1er, in *Le Pacte international relatif aux droits civils et politiques. Commentaire article par article* edited by E. Decaus, Paris, Economica, 2010.

Golay, C. 2009. *Droit à l'alimentation et accès à la justice. Exemples au niveau national, régional et international*, Rome, FAO, 68, available at: http://www.fao.org/righttofood/publi09/justiciability_fr.pdf (accessed 14/11/11).

Haugen, H.M. 2007. The Right to Self-Determination and Natural Resources: The Case of Western Sahara, *Law, Environment and Development Journal*, 79–80.

Helfont, T. 2010. Egypt's Wall with Gaza and the Emergence of a New Middle East Alignment, *Orbis*, 54, Summer, 432–3.

I.C.J. 2004. *Legal Consequences of the Construction of a Wall in the Occupied Palestinian Territory, Advisory Opinion, I.C.J. Reports 2004*, 9 July.

Mouillard, S. 2010. Israël va construire un nouveau mur à la frontière égyptienne, *Libération*, 11 January.

Novosseloff, A. 2007. La construction du mur: de la protection à la séparation, *Questions internationales*, november–december.

Nowak, M. 2005. *U.N. Covenant on Civil and Political Rights. CCPR Commentary*, 2nd ed., Kehl am Rhein, Engel.

Report of the Special Committee to Investigate Israeli Practices Affecting the Human Rights of the Palestinian People and Other Arabs of the Occupied Territories. 2003. 22 August, Doc. A/58/311, para. 26.

Scheinin, M. 2001. Economic and Social Rights as Legal Rights, in *Economic, Social and Cultural Rights. A Textbook*, edited by Eide A., Krause, C., Rosas, A., The Hague, Kluwer Law International.

Stroobants, J-P. and Perrier, G. 2011. Le projet de mur à la frontière entre la Grèce et la Turquie embarrasse Bruxelles, *Le Monde*, 7 January.

Tamimi, A.R. 2004. *Le mur de l'eau*, 16 August, available at: http://www.france-palestine.org/article541.html (accessed 14/11/11).

Tomuschat, C. 2010. Murs et responsabilité des Etats, in *Les murs et le droit international*, edited by Sorel, J-M., Paris, Pedone, 171–82.

UN Office for the Coordination of Humanitarian Affairs, World Food Program. 2010. *Between the Fence and a Hard Place: The Humanitarian Impact of Israeli-Imposed Restrictions on Access to Land and Sea in the Gaza Strip*, August, available at: http://reliefweb.int/node/364799 (accessed 14/11/11).

UN Office for the Coordination of Humanitarian Affairs (Occupied Palestinian Territories) 2010. *The Humanitarian Monitor*, July, available at: http://reliefweb.int/node/365659 (accessed 14/11/11).

UN Office for the Coordination of Humanitarian Affairs, World Food Program. 2010. *Between the Fence and a Hard Place: The Humanitarian Impact of Israeli-Imposed Restrictions on Access to Land and Sea in the Gaza Strip*, August, 8–9, available at: http://reliefweb.int/node/364799 (accessed 14/11/11).

UNEP. 2000. *L'avenir de l'environnement mondial 2000: GEO-2000: rapport du PNUE sur l'environnement*, Bruxelles, De Boeck Université.

Zieglet, J. 2003. The Right to Food. Addendum: Mission to the Occupied Palestinian Territories, *Report by the Special Rapporteur on the Right to Food*, 31 October, Doc. E/CN.4/2004/10/Add.2, para. 49.

Zoubir, Y. and Darbouche, H. 2008. Conflicting International Policies and the Western Sahara Stalemate, *International Spectator*, 43, 1 March, 91–105.

Chapter 11
Border Fences as an Anti-Immigration Device: A Comparative View of American and Spanish Policies

Said Saddiki

The functions of international borders, as well as other components and symbols of the nation-state, have changed substantially due to the development of the political community. At the inception of the nation-state, borders were viewed in military term as "strategic lines to be militarily defended or breached" (Andreas 2003: 81). Before the end of the nineteenth century, most states, in Europe and North America, took a more or less "hands-off" attitude towards the immigration movement. Nevertheless, especially with the increase in the number of people crossing their international borders, control over cross-border movement became a central concern of nation-states.

Throughout history, nations have developed their immigration policies in-line with the development of the number and type of immigrants. According to the Westphalia model of sovereignty, migration control had been seen as the "reserved domain" of a nation-state and a quintessential act of its sovereignty. Consequently, states traditionally enjoy exclusively the right to pass immigration laws regulating the movement of people across their border, and decide which of them to admit, how many and from where.

Immigration policies and border control systems have undergone a number of significant reforms during the last two decades in response to the steady growth in the number of immigrants and the development of the means used by smugglers. The common denominator of new immigration strategies taken by host countries during the last two decades is the linking of immigration policy and border control management on the one hand, and immigration policy and security issue on the other hand. Additionally, tightening border control and enhancing judicial measures related to irregular immigration are the major means by which the immigrant-receiving countries try to assert national sovereignty as a response to their decreasing powers to control the flow of money, ideas, information and all kinds of virtual interactions which have slipped more and more from their authority.

Regardless of the differences in the history and volume of immigration in the US and Spain, their similar immigration policies and border control systems make them worth studying as a comparative case study. Militarization and fencing of their international southern borders remains the cornerstone of their strategy to keep unwanted immigrants out of their territory.

One of the questions that may excite researchers in the field of immigration is the gap between the declared intent of border control systems and their long-term humanitarian and geo-political impacts. For this, the chapter, first, presents a brief historical overview of the immigration and the development of immigration regulation in the US and Spain, and second, tries to compare the border control systems adopted as a part of a multifaceted "anti-illegal immigration" policy led by the two countries. So, to what extent could these strategies achieve their goals in two similar regional contexts marked by the paradox of inclusion and exclusion?

Different Immigration Histories

The United States has a long history of immigration, has attracted immigrants from all over the world since the first European settlers arrived on American shores, and today has one of the world's highest migration rates. However, it is accurate to say, from a legal point of view, that the Declaration of Independence in 1776 and the Treaty of Paris in 1783, which accorded to the US recognition as a nation, is the beginning of the immigration to the United States. Immigration flows have been a major source of US population growth, and have greatly enriched its culture and history. The United States remains home to the largest number of international migrants in the world. Today, according to the US Census Bureau (2010 American Community Survey), there are 36.7 million foreign-born persons legally residing in the US, making up 12 per cent of the nation's population,[1] and more than half (58 per cent) have not got American citizenship. Approximately, half of them were born in Latin America, and almost one-third were born in Mexico. Whereas, Spain was a sending country of migrants until recently, and approximately two million Spanish citizens live abroad. During the last half of the nineteenth century and the first half of the twentieth century, some 5 million Spaniards emigrated to South America; and during the 1960s and 1970s between two to three million Spaniards emigrated to other European countries especially to France, Germany and Switzerland. Since its accession to the European Community in 1986, Spain witnessed significant economic growth associated with rebuilding the infrastructure of the country, which required a large number of foreign workers. Since that time, Spain has increasingly become a country of destination rather than a sending or transit country.

The number of immigrants registered as living in Spain grew very slowly throughout the 1980s and 1990s, but this number increased, according to some reports, more than sixfold over the last 10 years (for example: S.A. 2010). In the mid-1990s, there were around half a million foreign nationals in Spain. In 2001, immigration had increased by 23.8 per cent and the foreign population in Spain numbered over one million people (Pinyol 2007). Between 2000 and 2004, the immigrant population multiplied by more than three, from 0.9 million to nearly 2.8 million. Moreover, this influx of immigrants was greater than the number of those legalized, leading to the appearance of a group of people (more than 0.8 million in 2004) in an irregular situation, working in the underground economy (Office of the Presidency of the Spanish Government 2005: 19). In June 2007, there were around 3,500,000 foreign people with residence visas in Spain (Pinyol 2007: 2). In 2008, the foreign-born population accounted for 14.1 per cent of the total Spanish population, compared to 4.9 per cent in the year 2000. This was the highest rate of growth of the foreign-born population over a short period observed in any OECD country since the Second World War (OSCE 2010: 240). In 2009, some 5.6 million non-Spaniards were registered as living in the country, accounting for 12 per cent of the population, an increase of 400,000 on 2008

---

1 According to the International Organization of Migration, in 2010 immigrants make 13.5 per cent of the US population; and the net migration rate between 2005 and 2010 was 3.3 migrant(s)/1000 population (available at: http://www.iom.int/jahia/Jahia/activities/pid/1392, accessed February 6, 2011).

(S.A. 2010). Concerning net migration[2] in the framework of the EU, since 1998, Spain has become the leading net migration country in the region, accounting for 35 per cent in 2003, followed by Italy with 28 per cent, while Germany ranks fourth, after the United Kingdom (International Organization for Migration 2008). However, the country's foreign population still represents relatively low numbers compared to other European states (8.8 per cent of the population in 2007) (Ministerio de Trabajo 2008: 383).

Immigration flows to the US are not related to temporary circumstances, and have never ceased since the first white man set foot on North America soil. All statistics,[3] in recent decades, indicate that more than 1.5 million new immigrants settle in the country every year. For Spain, immigration is both a new phenomenon and temporary related to a short period of the country's economic boom of the 1990s.

The two countries, as all host countries, have faced new aspects of international immigration including irregular immigration, unaccompanied immigrant children, irregular immigrant women, economic refugees and so on. Irregular immigration has long been a phenomenon in the US, especially since the latter half of the twentieth century, whereas Spain did not experience the phenomenon until the beginning of the 1990s when this new aspect of immigration started to appear especially at its Mediterranean coasts and the frontiers of Ceuta and Melilla.

In general, there is convergence in the estimates of the number of irregular migrants in the United States. For example, the Department of Homeland Security estimates that the unauthorized immigrant population living in the United States decreased to 10.8 million in January 2009 from 11.6 million in January 2008. Between 2000 and 2009, the unauthorized population grew by 27 per cent. Of all unauthorized immigrants living in the United States in 2009, 63 per cent entered before 2000, and 62 per cent were from Mexico (US Department of Homeland Security 2010: 1). While a report by the Pew Hispanic Center put the estimate at 11.1 million unauthorized immigrants living in the country in March 2009, a number that declined by about a million since 2007 (Passel, Cohn 2010: i). Approximately 80 per cent of them are of Hispanic origin. It should be noted that Mexico is no longer the only major country of origin of irregular migration to the US, but also a transit country for irregular migration from Latin America. Although, Spain remains the main destination for irregular immigration in Southern Europe, it cannot be compared quantitatively and qualitatively with the US in this area. Irregular immigration to Spain is a new phenomenon which started to appear with the emergence of the "Fortress Europe" strategy associated with the closure of external EU borders and very restrictive immigration legislations. In 2003 it was estimated that over one million irregular immigrants were in Spain (OECD 2004). According to the International Organization for Migration, the overwhelming majority of irregular migrants in Spain come from Latin America (at 20 per cent, Ecuadorians were the largest group, followed by Colombians (8 per cent) and Bolivians (7 per cent)). Eastern Europeans, especially Romanians (17 per cent), were also present in significant numbers, as were Moroccans (12 per cent) (IOM 2008: 210).

There are substantial differences between the US and Spain in the economic aspects of immigration due to their special size of economy and labour market. The United States is

---

2 Net migration is the difference between immigration into and emigration from the area during the year (net migration is therefore negative when the number of emigrants exceeds the number of immigrants). See European Commission, *Policy Plan on Legal Migration*, COM (2005) 669, December 21, 2005, 26.

3 Especially censuses conducted by the US Census Bureau.

the top immigration host country in the world with 42.8 million immigrants, while Spain ranks seventh with 6.9 million. This is reflected clearly in number of immigrants who cross the international border of the two countries every year. For example, in 2010, the Mexico–United States border was the top migration route with 11.6 million, whereas the Spain–Morocco route was not ranked among the top 31 routes of migration in the world in 2010. In the same period, the United States was the top remittance-sending country at US$ 48.3 billion. The largest part of this remittance was sent to Mexico, which ranked in the same period the third top remittance-receiving country at US$ 22.6 billion. While, Spain was ranked in the same year as the seventh remittance-sending country in the world with US$ 12.6 billion, an important proportion transferring to Morocco, as the 18th remittance-receiving country, which received in the same period US$ 6.4 billion from its expatriates all over the world (World Bank 2010: 1–15).

The 2007/2008 global financial crisis has created serious damage to some host immigration countries especially the US and Spain where the crisis began earlier. One of the immediate effects of this crisis touched the labour market, mainly low-skilled immigrant workers. In Spain, since the beginning of the 1990s, immigrants had been seen to play a leading role in the country's economic growth. Regardless of some critics, Spain's governments during the last two decades tried to integrate new immigrants into the socio-economic system. However, since the financial crisis, the integration process of immigrants in Spain, unlike the US, has rapidly dropped. This change in Spain's immigration policy is embodied by some initiatives aimed to reduce the number of immigrants living in the country. In this context, the Spanish Socialist Workers' Party government proposed in September 2008 a Voluntary Return Plan, which allows unemployed immigrants (except citizens of EU countries) to return to their homelands and collect their unemployment benefits early. On the other hand, undoubtedly, the economic downturn due the current global financial crisis has to some extent reduced the flows of irregular immigrants to the US and Spain. The high rate of unemployment associated with the current crisis in these countries has convinced many people in Africa and Latin America that immigration is not the best option at least during the current crisis.

From "Open-Border" Policy to Anti-immigration Legislation

As immigration to the United States is much older than the immigration to Spain, the regulation of the phenomenon is also much older in the former than the latter. The regulation of immigration to the US dates backs to the end of the eighteenth century, specifically 1798, with the adoption of three important Acts concerning the status of aliens in the United States (Naturalization Acts, Alien Friends Act and Alien Enemies Act). In 1891, Congress passed the Immigration Act, which was considered as the first comprehensive immigration law for the United States. Subsequently, US lawmakers adopted many acts to the immigration influx and the status of aliens in the country. The Immigration and Nationality Act (INA), also known as the McCarran–Walter Act, which was created in 1952, had restricted immigration into the United States. According to the US Citizenship and Immigration Services, the INA collected and codified many existing provisions and reorganized the structure of immigration law. The Act has been amended many times over the years, but is still the basic body of immigration law. Thus, it can be said that the United States is one of the largest countries that has a variety of instruments in the migration field. Until recent decades, the American government had not seen immigration as a serious threat, and had not paid much attention to the issue. For example, the platform of the Republican Party did not even mention immigration control until 1980, and only four years later did it affirm the country's right to control its borders and express concern about illegal immigration (Nevins quoted in Andreas 2000: 86). The large number of immigration laws aimed at preventing irregular immigrants characterizes the last decade of the twentieth century and the first decade of the twenty-first century. The Immigration Reform and Control Act (IRCA), adopted by Congress in 1986, which introduced sanctions for the first time for knowingly hiring irregular aliens, and increased border enforcement. This Act can be considered the beginning of stringent legislative policy. The Illegal Immigration Reform and Immigrant Responsibility Act (IIRIRA) released in 1996 was another step to place further restrictions on regular and irregular immigration by making for example the access to welfare benefits more difficult for legal aliens; and to tighten border control by allocating $12 million for a 14-mile triple fence along the US–Mexico border from San Diego eastward.

As mentioned above, the regulation of immigration in Spain is recent compared with the United States. Until the mid-1980s, Spain had neither an immigration policy nor an immigration law. The Organic Law on the Rights and Liberties of Foreigners in Spain (known in Spain as LOE after the Ley Organica sobre Derechos y Libertades de los Extranjeros en España), adopted on 1 July 1985, was the first comprehensive Spanish immigration law, and the beginning of modern Spanish immigration policy. This coincided with the entry of Spain to the European Community. Since that time, Spain's immigration laws, as many observers noted (for example: Calavita 1998: 543), have gone hand in hand with the process of European integration. According to its Preamble, the LOE had the dual purpose of guaranteeing foreigners' rights and controlling "illegal" immigration (op. cit.). The LOA has been criticized by many commentators for its generality and imprecision.

Since its creation in 1985, Spanish immigration policy has undergone many transformations, consistent both with shifting domestic political circumstances and the common EU immigration policy. In 1996, Spain adopted the Regulation for Foreigners (RF), which recognized more rights to foreigners, established the status of "permanent residents", and established annual quota for foreign workers. One of the most important points of this legislation is to grant more social rights without inquiry into immigration status (Gonzalez, Bride 2000: 170). In 2000, the Organic Law on the Rights and Liberties of Foreigners in Spain and Their Social Integration, commonly referred to as LO 4/2000, passed to replace the LOE. The new law, which was deemed by some to be "the most liberal law on the rights of foreigners in Europe" (Gonzalez, Bride 2000: 171), contained several provisions that enhanced immigrants' rights and broadened the access to social services. Moreover, it extended access to public health and education facilities to irregular immigrants. So, with the new law, "the key to accessing these rights was not legal status, but registration in the local municipality, as a de facto resident" (Calavita 2005: 30). This legislation had not been without controversy. It was fiercely opposed by the Prime Minister Anznar's government at the time, which abrogated many of its most generous provisions only months ago with the new law LO 8/2000 referred to by someone as the "Counter-Reformation". The law 8/2000 was considered as a much more restrictive law and it reduced the immigrants' rights that were recognized by previous laws especially the LO 4/2000. Concerning irregular immigrants, it eliminated most of their right to social services, and denied their rights of assembly, collective bargaining, striking, and joining labour unions. According to its preamble, law 8/2000 was designed to bring Spain into compliance with the EU agreement at Tampere (Finland) in 1999 and the Schengen Agreement, which the Popular Party claimed had been violated by the permissiveness of law 4/2000

(Calavita 2005: 33). From January 2000 until November 2004, the Spanish immigration law changed four times and four regularization processes were established. These changes were due to the complexity and lack of political consensus on passing migration laws, and to the irregularity that characterized migration flow to Spain (Pinyol 2007: 3).

It is worth mentioning that Spain's policy of immigration is closely related to those of the EU that led since the beginning of the mid-1990s a common strategy of "externalizing" immigration control. This strategy has "involved two main components: First was the exportation of classical migration control instruments to sending or transit countries outside the EU […]. The second element […] comprised a series of provisions for facilitating the return of asylum seekers and illegal migrants to third countries" (Boswell 2003: 622). Although, the securitization and Europeanization of immigration issue, which gave rise to the idea of "Fortress Europe", aimed at keeping out "undesirable" immigrants and refugees, it has not stopped irregular immigration flows, rather, it has led to changed routes and tools used by immigrants and smugglers as an unexpected opposite result.

One of the most important current aspects of international immigration is the link between immigration on the one hand and both security and criminality on the other hand in the national policy of host countries. This aspect has been more obvious especially after 9/11 events, so that irregular immigration has been presented as a possible national security threat. Mathew Coleman documented two significant recent shifts in US immigration policing in conjunction with the border militarization process. First, lawmakers since the mid-1990s have sought to bind immigration control to criminal law enforcement, such that a criminal conviction can be used as grounds for deportation from the US. He also argued that this mode of immigration governance means that immigration law is ultimately exempted from judicial review, even as it works largely on the basis of criminal law. Second, there has been a concerted effort on the part of lawmakers and the Bush administration, particularly since 9/11, to use local proxy forces – or non-federal delegates – to enforce immigration law. Coleman concluded that together, the criminalization of immigration law, as well as the enrolment of proxy immigration officers at sub-state scales, constitutes a new localized or rescaled geopolitics of immigration policing (Coleman 2007: 56). In sum, since the 9/11 attacks, several legislative measures have been taken to tighten security control on the US borders with Mexico and Canada. Furthermore, in the immediate aftermath of these events, some American politicians called for severe restrictions on immigrant admissions to the United States, and many "anti-illegal" immigration groups have taken advantage of the opportunity to raise the ceiling of their demands.

In Spain, since 2000 especially after the event that took place in the region of El Ejido in February of the same year, immigration has started becoming politicized with a debate on immigrants' rights, but also with the criminalization of immigration, and a debate on identity and law and order that has generated a great deal of populist, xenophobic rhetoric (Zapata-Barrero 2003: 2). The emergence of immigration as one of the key subjects of contemporary public political and social discourse in Spain since 2000 has occurred in a climate of constant tension and confrontation between the principal social and economic stakeholders and those from government, who, to electoral ends, have linked immigration with crime (Zapata-Barrero 2003: 30). This political debate on the immigration issue was undoubtedly related to the rise of right-wing parties in Europe that considered non-European immigrants as cultural and social threats. These anti-immigration sentiments intensified especially after the 9/11 events and the attacks of Madrid on 11 March 2004.

It is clear that, even if the historical context of immigration regulation in the US and Spain is different, the objective of immigration policy in the two countries is almost the same. But there is a significant difference in the capacity to absorb new immigrants. The US receives each year thousands of immigrants from all corners of the world, while Spain is fed up with all kinds of new immigrants, especial after the financial crisis hitting the country during recent years.

Construction of Border Fences: A Militarization of Immigration Control

Spain started to fence its *de facto* border with Morocco in Northern Africa, as part of a new comprehensive "anti-illegal" immigration policy, relatively early compared with the United States. The two countries made the fight against irregular immigration the major purpose of their policy which aims to militarize their southern borders.

With the exception of the short territorial boundaries of Ceuta and Melilla and their Moroccan hinterlands, the border between Spain and Morocco, whether on the Mediterranean or the Moroccan Atlantic coast opposite the Spanish Canary Islands, is a maritime one. Since controlling a maritime border is fundamentally different and more demanding because it requires surveillance of an area, as opposed to a line in the case of land borders (Carling 2007: 324), Spain and the EU adopted since the late 1990s, two complementary strategies to prevent the influx of African immigrants. On the one hand, Spain started to construct high barbed wire fences along the frontiers of Ceuta and Melilla. On the other hand, the EU, including of course Spain, has invested a lot of money to strengthen maritime border control and created some integrated systems of external maritime surveillance by using very advanced technology.

Ceuta and Melilla are the two most important enclaves in Northern Morocco controlled by Spain since the end of the "reconquista". Melilla was the first to fall under Spanish rule in 1497, and Ceuta, which had been seized by Portugal in 1415, was transferred to Spain under the Treaty of Lisbon in 1668 (Saddiki 2012: 51). Throughout Spain's prolonged occupation of Ceuta and Melilla since the fifteenth and seventeenth centuries, Morocco has never ceased to call for the restoration of the two enclaves and other rocky islands which are still controlled by Spain in Northern Morocco (Saddiki 2012: 51).

Since 1986, with Spain's entry into the European Community (later EU), the two enclaves have been considered to be EU territories, and the front line of what became known later as "Fortress Europe". In 1993, the fencing of the enclaves' perimeters started on the pretext of preventing irregular immigration. Starting in this year, the Spanish government has not ceased to strengthen and renovate these fences by using new advanced technologies including infrared cameras, optic and acoustic sensor devices, watchtowers, and radar systems.

Because of the unique geographical location of the two enclaves as *de facto* EU territories in North Africa, they have become during the last two decades the destination of thousands of Sub-Saharan African immigrants. Irregular immigrants prefer this direction because they can reach "European soil" once they enter the enclaves even if they are still in Africa, and it is a less costly and less risky route than riding the waves of the Mediterranean or Atlantic to an unknown fate.

Needless to say, the fences of Ceuta and Melilla were built to prevent Sub-Saharan African immigrants not Moroccans because of two reasons: firstly, according to the Agreement on the Accession of Spain to the EC, inhabitants of Tetouan and Nador, the two Moroccan provinces adjacent respectively to Ceuta and Melilla, are exempted from visa requirements which allows them to cross back and forth the enclave's border,[4] but they are not permitted to enter the Spanish mainland. Secondly, Moroccans from outside these two provinces, if they overstay the visa period or enter the enclaves irregularly can simply be expelled under the Agreement of Return signed between Morocco and Spain in 1992.

Although those involved in the 9/11 attacks did not enter the country illegally, the US government used terror and security threats to justify the construction of the fence along its border with Mexico. This is not the case with the fences of Ceuta and Melilla, which were built only – at least officially – on the basis of the prevention of irregular immigration. Even if the 3/11 attacks in Madrid had a great impact on the formulation of the new EU security strategy,[5] they did not have a significant impact on Spanish efforts to strengthen the fences of the two enclaves, because these border fences have already being constructed within different context and goals.

In the early morning of 28 September 2005, more than 700 Sub-Saharan-African immigrants tried to climb over the fence of Melilla using makeshift ladders. About 14 immigrants died in this tragic attempt to reach the enclave. The event deeply shocked the public and stressed once again the importance of a collective approach in tackling irregular immigration as a transnational issue. Although, the event required the serious involvement of transit countries, especially Maghreb countries, the EU and Spain continue to give preference to the unilateral and security initiatives based on the militarization of EU territorial and maritime borders, which had already demonstrated its inability to cope with transnational irregular immigration flows. Even when it comes to the "calculated" involvement of the transit countries as one of the applications of the externalization of borders control, the EU intends to use these countries as police or buffer zones.

In addition to the stated objective of stopping irregular immigration, the construction of the fences of Ceuta and Melilla reflects other long-term goals related to the disputed status of the two enclaves. The construction of the fences is one of many other measures aimed at consolidating the current status quo of occupation as a key element of Spain's comprehensive strategy which has taken several forms and steps: building border fences, delineating unilaterally the *de facto* Morocco–Spain "borders", granting autonomous status to the two enclaves, passing restrictive immigration laws, and visits by Spain's king and ministers to the enclaves.

It is worth mentioning that, the fences of Ceuta and Melilla are built on disputed territory between Morocco and Spain. Morocco considers Ceuta and Melilla to be occupied Moroccan land, and since independence, especially after 1975, it has sought to recover both cities and some small Mediterranean islands claimed by Morocco as integral parts of its territory. Furthermore, the Moroccan government has always objected to the construction of these fences. But with regard to the US–Mexico border fences, since they are built on American territories, regardless of the criticism they have attracted, remain legitimate under international law because it is not unlawful for a State to establish fences or walls on its own territory to control access to its territory.

---

4   Since June 2006, this privilege has been extended by the Spanish Government to the people of Al-Hoceimea.

5   Immediately after the Madrid attacks, the European council adopted on 25 March 2004, the "Declaration on Combating Terrorism" in which the Council identified the EU common measures to combat terrorism, including strengthen border control, sharing of intelligence, preventing the financing of terrorism, establishment of the position of a counter-terrorism coordinator, and the cooperation with other international partners.

In the US, although, the federal government funded the construction of fences around some southern border cities (Nogales, San Ysidro and El Paso) before the 1990s, it started seriously building fences and escalating control measures along its borders with Mexico in 1994 under Clinton's administration, as a comprehensive policy. The border south of San Diego, which has been identified as an area of high human smuggling and drug trafficking, was the first borderland to be fenced. Republican representative Duncan Hunter, the former Chairman of the House Armed Services Committee, played a significant role in the construction of the first security fence (14 miles/23 km) on the US southern border separating San Diego Country and Tijuana (Mexico).

After 11 September 2001, irregular immigration was soon placed in the same category as terrorism and security threats, including drug trafficking and organized crime. Thus, the border security and the hardline policy against irregular immigration became a key element of the US war on terror. One of the repercussions of the 9/11 attacks on the US border control system, is the creation of the Homeland Security Department (HSD) and the transformation of responsibility for border security from the Department of Justice to the Department of HSD and abolition of the Immigration and Naturalization Service.[6] Shortly after the creation of the Homeland Security Department in 2003, the Border Patrol was directed to formulate a new "National Border Patrol Strategy" that would better reflect the realities of the post 9/11 security landscape. The Border Patrol's strategy (National Border Strategy 2005: 2) consists of five main objectives:

- establish substantial probability of apprehending terrorists and their weapons as they attempt to enter illegally between the ports of entry;
- deter illegal entries through improved enforcement;
- detect, apprehend, and deter smugglers of humans, drugs, and other contraband;
- leverage "Smart Border" technology to multiply the effect of enforcement personnel; and
- reduce crime in border communities and consequently improve quality of life and economic vitality of targeted areas.

On 26 October 2006 President George W. Bush signed into law the Secure Fence Act of 2006 (P.L. 109–367), which has been deemed the most important law concerning the reinforcement of border control. George W. Bush, President of the United States at the time, considered the law as "an important step toward immigration reform" that "will help protect the American people". The Secure Fence Act of 2006 aimed to tighten border security by building 700 miles of double-layered fencing on the US–Mexico border. Further, the law authorized more vehicle barriers, checkpoints, and lighting to help prevent people from entering the country illegally; as well as authorizing the Department of Homeland Security to increase the use of advanced technology such as cameras, satellites, and unmanned aerial vehicles to reinforce the infrastructure at the border. The main goal of the law is to help secure America's borders to decrease irregular entry, drug trafficking, and security threats.

The financial cost of the project has increased from year to year. Appropriations for the Department of Homeland Security for the fiscal year 2007 provided $1.2 billion for the installation of fencing, infrastructure, and technology along the border; $31 million of this total was designated for the completion of the San Diego fence (Haddal, Kim,

---

6 The Homeland Security Act (Public Law 107–296), passed by Congress and signed by the President in November 2002.

Garcia 2009: 37). Appropriations for fencing and other border barriers have increased markedly since the plan entered into force from $6 million in fiscal year 2002 to $647 million in fiscal year 2007. The fiscal year 2008 appropriation, according to Customs and Border Protection, included $196 million for fence construction (Haddal, Kim, Garcia 2009: 37).

In general, the construction of border walls and fences leads to diplomatic tensions between neighbouring countries, because it is usually viewed as an unfriendly action by targeted countries. The construction of the fence along the US–Mexico border elicited a lot of controversies at both internal and external levels. Immediately prior to the 9/11 attacks, the US and Mexico were on the verge of an historic opportunity to rewrite immigration laws and fundamentally alter the migratory relationship between the two nations, regularizing the status of millions of undocumented immigrant workers living in the United States. At that promising moment, unexpected events happened on 11 September 2001, which caused a deterioration of relations between the two countries with more focus, especially from the American side, on national security concerns and to look at security from a regional perspective (Waslin 2003: 10–12). Mexico opposed the US plan to build more separation fences along the border between the two countries, considering them as the opposite direction to the regional integration process in the NAFTA region. Felipe Calderón, President of Mexico, stated that

> it is deplorable to go ahead with this decision of the wall at the border [...]. The wall will not solve any problem. Humanity made a huge mistake by building the Berlin Wall and I believe that today the United States is committing a grave error in building the wall on our border. It is much more useful to solve common problems and foster prosperity in both countries.

Even if the events of 9/11 were neither connected to Mexican nationals nor those who committed the attacks entered American territory illegally from Mexico, their long-term effects on US–Mexican migration relations and the regional integration process will last for decades.

Virtual Fence: Technology in the Face of "Non-traditional Threats"

To adapt to the information age, governments, whether in developed or developing counties, have made great efforts during recent decades to incorporate new information and communication technologies (ICTs) into their security policy. Today, border management and administration of immigration are high-tech fields especially in the Global North.

Both the US and Spain not only built physical fence along their southern borders, but also adopted a virtual system to control their borderlands. The latter system, known as a virtual wall or virtual fence, has grown significantly in the post-9/11 era as a preferred policy by some countries in Europe and North America in their response to transnational security threats. Josiah Heyman distinguishes between two meanings of this virtual system, one narrower and one broader. The narrower meaning of the virtual wall refers to the use of advanced surveillance and computer technologies to border law enforcement, by utilizing for example ground-level radar to detect the movement of people and define their direction of travel in the vicinity of the border. More broadly, the virtual fence, according to Josiah Heyman, points to the massing of police forces, including military and intelligence agencies, in the border region (Heyman 2008: 305). The virtual fence in the narrow sense is the first-generation of applying military technology to the border control system which has shown its ineffectiveness especially with intelligent use of developed technology and different styles of camouflage by smugglers and irregular immigrants. The broader meaning refers to total virtual militarization of the border to detect with high accuracy all kind of cross-border infiltrations around the clock and whatever the weather conditions.

The search for technological solutions to border control has been present in the debate over new immigration laws adopted by the US over the last decade. The Border Protection, Antiterrorism, and Illegal Immigration Control Act of 2005 (H.R.4437), passed by the House in December 2005, and the Comprehensive Immigration Reform Act of 2006 (S. 2611), passed by the Senate in May 2006, both have provisions requiring implementation of new technologies to support border control efforts at and between ports of entry, particularly along the US–Mexican border (Koslowski 2006).

The US virtual border fence is largely linked to the "Secure Border Initiative" (SBI) launched by the Department of Homeland Security (DHS) in November 2005. Through SBI, the DHS intended to enhance surveillance technologies, increase staffing levels, enforce immigration laws, and improve the physical infrastructure along the US borders with Mexico and Canada (US GAO 2010: 1) in order to prevent transnational security threats and reduce irregular immigration. As a part of SBI, the Secure Border Initiative Network (SBInet) is a multibillion dollar programme initiated in 2006 which involves the acquisition, development, integration, deployment, and operation and maintenance of surveillance technologies to create a virtual fence along the border as well as command, control, communications, and intelligence (C3I) technologies to create a picture of the border in command centres and vehicles (US GAO 2010: 1). The primary goal of SBInet is to strengthen the DHS's ability to control thousands of miles of American international frontier.

The US virtual border fence was very costly financially. According to the US Government Accountability Office, for fiscal years 2006 through 2009, the SBI programme received about $3.6 billion in appropriated funds. Of this amount, about $2.4 billion has been allocated to complete approximately 670 miles of vehicle and pedestrian fencing along the roughly 2,000 miles of border between the United States and Mexico (US GAO 2009: 4). Adam Comis, press secretary for the House Homeland Security Committee, stated that the cost of the entire south-western virtual fence project [if it was not stopped] is estimated to be about $6.7 billion by 2014 (US News and World Report 2011).

Although, the US government spent too much money to make technology take the place of a physical fence, the SBI did not achieve the desired results. For example, many of the sensors have proved difficult to maintain in a variety of weather conditions and they do not have the ability to differentiate animals from humans (Koslowski 2006). In fact, the ineffectiveness of the US virtual border fence programme takes many aspects. Smugglers and irregular immigrants developed many ways to circumvent the virtual fence along the US international border especially in the south. Sophisticated long and deep tunnels dug secretly under the US–Mexico border used for smuggling drugs and immigrants remain the big challenge which still escapes the control of the virtual control system.

After the many failures of the current US virtual border fence, former Homeland Security Secretary Janet Napolitano on 11 January 2011 cancelled the Secure Border Initiative-network (SBInet) programme. Napolitano justified the decision by technical problems suffered by the programme, cost overruns ($1billion) and schedule delays since its inception in 2005. At the same time, Napolitano announced a "new border security technology plan" along the border that is tailored to the technological needs of each border region, including commercially available mobile surveillance systems, unmanned aircraft systems, thermal imaging devices, and tower-based remote video surveillance systems.

In the European context, during the last two decades, the EU has taken many integrated initiatives to digitalize its border control system with the aim of controlling cross-border movement and preventing external security threats. The incorporation of ICTs by the EU is applied in at least two ways. First, they have been rolled out to "harden" or fortify security at the EU's external border. The Schengen Information System (SIS) and the Spanish government's Integrated System of External Surveillance (*Sistema Integrado de Vigilancia Exterior* – SIVE) clearly exemplify this strategy. The second strategy has involved deploying other kinds of ICTs to externalize cross-border control beyond the EU perimeter (Shields 2010: 255). Under the second strategy, the EU Council adopted in 2004 the Visa Information System (VIS)[7] – a system aimed at recording the biometric identifiers of visa applicants to facilitate the exchange of visa data between Member States, which will enable authorized national authorities to enter and update visa data and to consult these data electronically.

In Spain, as well as in other EU countries, the digital surveillance of irregular immigration is now a central part of all successive governments' agenda. The SIVE is one of the largest surveillance systems in Europe aimed at surveying the Spanish maritime areas targeted by irregular immigrants. The SIVE was first applied in 1999 around the strait of Gibraltar, where the majority of irregular immigrants were arriving at that time. Spanish government has subsequently extended the SIVE to the east and to the west to cover respectively the whole of Cadiz province in 2004, the entire Andalusia coast in 2005, and finally the Canary Islands. The SIVE has been gradually implemented by developed technologies of border control and management, including long-distance radar systems, advanced sensors can detect heartbeats from a distance, thermal cameras, night viewfinders, infrared optics, helicopters and patrol boats.

Spain's virtual fence, as with the American one, required a large budget funded partly by the EU. For the period 1999 to 2004, the SIVE was allocated 150 million euros, which means about 1,800 euros for each immigrant that was eventually intercepted during the five-year period in question (Carling 2007: 325). This elevated cost was justified by the necessity to adapt to the standards demanded by the European Union.[8] Despite the high financial and logistical costs, Spain's virtual fence system has not achieved significant results in preventing irregular immigrants, who risk their life by sailing across the Mediterranean and the Atlantic Ocean on rickety boats even directly from remote western African beaches in Senegal and Mauritania. Jørgen Carling argued that the development of the SIVE has not only led smugglers to adopt new routes, but has also resulted in technical and organizational changes on the part of the smugglers (Carling 2007: 327). Carling explained this conclusion, based on some previous studies, in four points as follows: first, smugglers have developed new boats purpose-built for smuggling instead of fishing boats. Second, in order to increase the profit by doubling the number of passengers on each journey, now smugglers use larger pateras and rubber boats (zodiacs). Third, they organize collective journeys including group of pateras which spread out when they approach the coast. This makes it difficult for the Guardia Civil to intercept all the boats that have been detected

---

7 See Council Decision of 8 June 2004 establishing the Visa Information System (VIS) (2004/512/EC).

8 As the former Spain's Minister of the Interior, Jaime Mayor Oreja, stated in a comment on the programme.

by the SIVE. Fourth, the SIVE programme makes immigrant's journey, especially those who lack nautical skills, more dangerous, while the smugglers run no risk of arrest by Spanish authorities (Carling 2007: 327). Additionally, in reaction to sophisticated virtual control systems applied in the western Mediterranean and the Atlantic Ocean, immigrants try to reach European soil from eastern Maghrebi coasts (from Algeria, Tunisia, and Libya) especially to the Italian islands of Lampedusa, Pantelleria, Linosa and Sicily. Moreover, it must be stressed that irregular immigrants who enter Spain and the US, as well as other host countries, by sea remain in the minority in regard to the total number of irregular immigrants entering those countries.

In both cases, Spain and the US, many humanitarian and human rights organizations and local politicians criticize the construction of virtual security walls due to their inefficiency and high financial and humanitarian costs. Opponents argue that these large amounts of money invested in building more physical and virtual walls between nations to control cross-border flows would be better spent on development assistance to the countries of origin.

Conclusion

Despite considerable efforts taken by the US and Spain aimed at preventing irregular border crossings, the decline in the number of new immigrants to the two countries during the last couple years is due not only to the border control systems or fences, but also to the current international economic and financial crisis that has affected to a large extent the labour market, especially low-skilled immigrant workers.

In fact, the inefficiency of restricted immigration policies and intensified border controls in preventing new immigrants from trying to reach their El Dorado lies mainly in neglecting the root causes of the phenomenon. It is argued that much of the money spent on fencing and militarizing the borders should go towards promoting comprehensive development in the countries of origin. Today, it is largely argued that the construction of walls around developed nations is not a solution to the immigration issue. As Bernard Kouchner (October 10, 2005), the founder of *Médecins Sans Frontières* and France's former health minister, said: "to close the door does nothing. They go through the window. They break the door".

References

Andreas, P. 2000. *Border Games: Policing the US – Mexico Divide*, Ithaca and London, Cornell University Press.
Andreas, P. 2003. Redrawing the Line: Borders and Security in the Twenty-first Century, *International Security* 28 (2): 78–111.
Boswell, C. 2003. The "External Dimension" of EU Immigration and Asylum Policy, *International Affairs* 79 (3): 619–38.
Calavita, K. 1998. Immigration, Law, and Marginalization in a Global Economy: Notes from Spain, *Law & Society Review* 32 (3): 529–66.
Calavita, K. 2005. *Immigration at the Margins: Law, Race and Exclusion in Southern Europe*, New York, Cambridge University Press.
Carling, J. 2007. Migration Control and Migrant Fatalities at the Spanish–African Borders, *International Migration Review* 41 (2): 316–43.

Coleman, M. 2007. Immigration Geopolitics beyond the Mexico–US Border, *Antipode* 38 (1): 54–76.

European Commission. 2005. *Policy Plan on Legal Migration* COM (2005) 669, 21 December.

Gonzalez, L.E. and Bride, R.M. 2000. Fortress Europe: Fear of Immigration? Present and Future of Immigration Law and Policy in Spain, *UC Davis Journal of International Law and Policy* 6 (2): 153–91.

Haddal, C.C., Kim, Y. and Garcia, M.J. 2009. *Border Security: Barriers Along the U.S. International Border*, RL33659 Washington DC, Congressional Research Service, 16 March.

Heyman, J. McC. 2008. Constructing a Virtual Wall: Race and Citizenship in U.S.–Mexico Border Policing, *Journal of the Southwest* 50 (3): 305–34.

International Organization for Migration. 2008. *World Migration Report 2008: Managing Labor Mobility in the Evolving Global Economy*, Geneva.

Koslowski, R. 2006. Immigration Reforms and Border Security Technologies, *Border Battles: The U.S. Immigration Debates*, New York, Social Science Research Council, available at: http://borderbattles.ssrc.org/Koslowski (accessed 10/11/11).

Kouchner, B. October 10, 2005. Interview on the French National Radio Europe 1, transcribed by the Newspaper Le Nouvel Observateur, available at http://tempsreel.nouvelobs.com/monde/20051010.OBS1631/migrants-dans-le-desert-l-appel-de-kouchner.html (accessed 11/05/14).

Nevins, J. 1998. "Illegal Aliens" and the Political Geography of Criminalized Immigrants, paper presented at the annual meeting of the Association of American Geographers, Boston, 8 March.

Office of the Presidency of the Spanish Government. 2005. *Convergence and Employment: The Spanish National Reform Programme*, Madrid, Ministerio de la Presidencia.

Organization for Economic Co-operation and Development. 2004. *International Migration Outlook*, Paris, SOPEMI.

Organization for Economic Co-operation and Development. 2010. *International Migration Outlook*, Paris, SOPEMI.

Passel, J.S., Cohn, V. 2010. U.S. Unauthorized Immigration Flows are Down Sharply since Mid-Decade, *The Pew Hispanic Center*, 1 September.

Pinyol, G. 2007. The External Dimension of the European Immigration Policy: a Spanish Perspective, paper presented at the conference on The Euro-Mediterranean Partnership (EMP): Perspectives from the Mediterranean EU countries, Rethymnon, Crete. 25–27 October, available at: www.idec.gr/iier/new/EN/PINYOL per cent20Paper.pdf (accessed 11/11/11).

S.A. 2010. Spain sees sixfold increase in immigrants over decade, *The Guardian*, Monday 8 February.

Saddiki, S. 2012. Les clôtures de Ceuta et de Melilla: Une frontière européenne multidimensionnelle, *Revue Études internationales* 43 (1): 49–65.

Shields, P. 2010. ICTs and the European Union's Evolving Border Surveillance Architecture: A Critical Assessment, *Observatorio (OBS*) Journal* 4 (1): 255–88.

US Department of Homeland Security, Office of Immigration Statistics. 2010. Estimates of the Unauthorized Immigrant Population Residing in the United States: January 2009, available at: http://www.dhs.gov/xlibrary/assets/statistics/publications/ois_ill_pe_2009.pdf (accessed 10/11/11).

United States Government Accountability Office. 2009. *Secure Border Initiative Fence Construction Costs*, Washington DC, 29 January.

US News and World Report. 2009. Officials Ready to Build Virtual Fence Along Border, available at: http://www.usnews.com/science/articles/2009/05/08/officials-ready-to-build-virtual-fence-along-border (accessed 19/02/11).

Waslin, M. 2003. The New Meaning of the Border: US–Mexico Migration Since 9/11, paper prepared for the conference on Reforming the Administration of Justice in Mexico, Center for US–Mexican Studies, University of California, San Diego, May 15–17, available at: http://escholarship.org/uc/item/3dd8w0r6 (accessed 10/11/11).

World Bank. 2010. *Migration and Remittances Factbook 2011*, 2nd edition, Washington, The World Bank.

Zapata-Barrero, R. 2003. EU and US Approaches to the Management of Immigration: Spain, in *EU and US Approaches to the Management of Immigration: Comparative Perspectives,* edited by J. Niessen and Y. Schibel, Brussels, Migration Policy Group.

Zapata-Barrero, R. 2008. Perceptions and Realities of Moroccan Immigration Flows and Spanish Policies, *Journal of Immigrant and Refugee Studies* 6 (3): 382–96.

Chapter 12
Walls, Sensors and Drones: Technology and Surveillance on the US–Mexico Border

Rodrigo Nieto-Gomez

No policy idea is more central to the politics of border security than the deployment of tactical infrastructure (the so-called "border fence" or "border wall") between Mexico and the United States. These barriers play a dominant role in the construction of the geopolitical representations that define the border security environment in North America and are the most visible, photogenic, concrete and controversial consequence of contemporary geopolitical conflicts in the borderlands.

Two fundamentally different kinds of technologies are also being tested and deployed as part of the homeland security effort, and are as important to the construction of the deterrence-based "system of systems" of the border as the physical barriers:

1. the so-called virtual walls (systems formed by a combination of sensors and optical surveillance technologies); and
2. the recent addition of a fleet of Unmanned Aerial Vehicles (UAV), allowed to fly in the border zones for the first time inside the Continental United States, and the use of Air Force operated Tethered Aerostat Radar Systems (TARS).

Physical barriers, virtual fences, radars, cameras and UAVs were framed in the Secure Fence Act of 2006 as essential systemic components to obtain operational control of the border region against trans-border threats, yet the politics involved in their deployment are very different. While sometimes these technologies play complementary functions supporting each other, frequently their deployment is presented as an either/or proposition (virtual wall vs. physical wall, UAVs vs. virtual wall, etc.) This provides policymakers with alternative tools to respond to the competitive demands of different sectors of public opinion and stakeholders that advance the following opposed goals for border security policies:

- More border deterrence against all clandestine actors, including economic migrants.
- Less border enforcement and a comprehensive immigration policy that is less offensive to the identity of local communities and the Hispanic population of the United States.
- Less visually and politically offensive tactical infrastructure, while still maintaining the current deterrence model.
- Infrastructure that is deployed somewhere else, but "not in my backyard".
- More cost-effective spending.

This chapter analyzes some of the political implications of the use and deployment of these technologies, as well as the tactical and aspirational roles they play. It will also study the multi-scalar identity conflicts they have provoked between local, regional and federal spheres. By studying the technology adoption process in the context of the discourse that surrounds it, we can better understand how technological innovation contributes to shape the geopolitical conflict at the edge of the state.

Building a Wall to Reshape a Policy: The System Architecture of America's Force Multipliers

The walling of the southern border is such a powerful geopolitical representation in the contemporary American security narrative that it is relatively easy to forget that – in this immense linear territory – the security landscapes like those of operations "Hold the Line" (El Paso, TX) or "Gatekeeper" (San Diego, CA) are recent occurrences in a border territory that for a very long time was imagined as remote, unpopulated and mostly unaltered by big infrastructure projects.

All that changed in the nineties when border security was "rebooted" around the concept of deterrence, making the deployment of technological infrastructures to influence and change the behavior of clandestine actors the central component of policies and territorial planning for the border region.

Walls, sensors, drones and other border technologies are all the result of acts of volition on the part of policymakers responding to the adaptation of clandestine agents whose business model is to defy and exploit border interdictions. Policymakers aspire to impose behavioral changes on these human networks by introducing to the border ecosystem a series of technological changes meant to multiply the capacity and effectiveness of border authorities. The stated goal is absolute "operational control" of the border, defined by law as the "prevention of all unlawful entries into the United States, including entries by terrorists, other unlawful aliens, instruments of terrorism, narcotics and other contraband" (H.R. 2006). The "zero risk" objective to prevent 100 percent of unlawful entries will theoretically be attained because of the environmental design taking place around the border landscape, building infrastructures that ultimately should deter all illegal activities in the borderlands.

These walling acts of volition have allocated billions of dollars in resources to attain this seemingly impossible goal, creating in the process a new security and defense market to use corporate innovation against the clandestine networks. This private/public research and development effort culminates in an escalating deployment of security systems at the borderline. Walls, sensors and drones have different specifications and different political functions, even if all of them share the objective of bringing governance and operational control to the border spaces, and ultimately creating a deterrence-based "system of systems".

The physical barriers (walls or fences) are undoubtedly the most visible component of the border deployment. In fact, they are meant to be highly visible in opposition to sensors or UAVs that depend on stealth capabilities to remain effective. The visibility of walling technology fulfills a communication role beyond their tactical value, transmitting two complementary messages to the North American continent:

1. To Mexico and Central America, the tactical infrastructure projects a deterrence message. Through their deliberately frightening appearance, border barriers are supposed to influence the behavior of clandestine actors by dissuading them from trying to break the interdiction and cross the border illegally. After a tactical infrastructure has been deployed in one sector, the resulting menacing landscape is not an unintended consequence, but a central objective of the deployment. This

accidental adaptation of the "crime prevention through environmental design" (CPTED) meme ignores the elements of reinforcement of positive behaviors so important in the original model (Jeffery and Zahm 1993). The defensible space this infrastructure creates in the borderlands depends only on its capacity to deter, using surveillance, enforcement and flow control technologies.

2. To the rest of the territory of the United States, border fences are meant to transmit a reassuring message of governmental effectiveness in dealing with the "border problem". At the same time, its technological design perpetuates the framing of the border region as a space of threat because a siege mentality is an unavoidable complement to strategies of fortification.

Martha Pollak claims that during the Middle Ages "siege warfare ... became a mark of advanced civilization. It was a systematic and demanding way of fighting that required careful planning and detailed organization" (Pollak 2000: 645). Building and maintaining walls – as well as fighting to penetrate them – requires a permanent innovation effort that takes place in the boundary area, making it a territory where competitive conflict and friction cannot be ignored or forgotten, and clandestine innovation is incentivized. Fortifications memorialize the role of the border as the protective envelope of the Westphalian state, but also as a conflict zone, in the landscape. These kinds of border fortifications also incite the creativity of clandestine actors, anchoring them near the barrier to study its weaknesses and then exploit them for their own benefit. The Trojan Horse was deployed at the gates of the wall of the city of Troy.

The border infrastructure as we imagine it today is a relatively recent policy event in the geopolitical history of the US–Mexico border. Even if since the nineteenth century fences at the borderline have been used to demarcate private property and limit the movement of cattle, the border wall only acquired the central role it has today in the security discourse during the first term of the Clinton administration in the 1990s (Andreas 2000: 199). The terrorist attacks of September 11, 2001 and the increase of drug related violence in Mexico's border areas since 2007 only reinforced previously existing walling patterns by giving them two new security contexts: The "war against terror" and the possibility of "spillover" violence from Mexico into the United States.

Before the Clinton administration decided to make the infrastructure-heavy deterrence model the centerpiece of the United States border policy, the southern border was secured in a profoundly different way, less technologically dependent and with a smaller footprint in the landscape of the border spaces.

Historically, the Border Patrol deployed its agents in the border zone around farms, ranches and the border cities considered to be gathering towns for clandestine migrants, with the objective of capturing them after they illegally crossed the border (Maril 2006). The Border Patrol Agents followed the tracks of clandestine migrants in the middle of the desert, trying to find and arrest them inside American territory.

In this operational design, the immigrants had a role akin to that of an infiltrating force behind enemy lines that had to be tracked as prey, while the Border Patrol had the role of a skilled predator in a very complicated "hide and seek game" being played in the immensity of the American borderlands.

This approach demanded two complementary sets of skills from the border agents: a geographic understanding of the territory of the sector in which they operated, and the knowledge of a good desert tracker (to follow the trail left by the clandestine immigrants during their trip). The only "force multipliers" were those of any law enforcement agent operating anywhere else in the United States: transportation (a motorized vehicle or horse), a weapon and a police radio. They did not have access to any kind of environmental design other than some rudimentary fencing; thus the landscape remained mostly undisturbed.

The Border Patrol units were highly mobile as they would travel from one extreme to the other of their sector while following the trails of groups of immigrants, learning about the most used migration routes and raiding places known to be frequented by clandestine migrants.[1]

Under this strategy, the main metric used to measure the success of the Border Patrol and its agents was the number of clandestine immigrant arrests. The more immigrants captured, the more effective the tactical deployment was considered to be. President Nixon's "war on drugs" increased the smuggling value of the Mexican territory by squeezing the Caribbean routes and sending part of that traffic to Mexico. It is one more iteration of what border theorists call today a "balloon effect": putting pressure on one part of the system (the balloon) increases the pressure somewhere else, redirecting conflict from one region to the other (Madsen 2007: 280–98). When this happened, the Border Patrol applied the same metrics to its strategy against drug smuggling, and again the number of arrests and the number of tons of drugs seized were used as the main measure of success until the 1990s.

Between 1993 and 1995, a multi-scalar chain of events triggered an important transformation in the American strategy against clandestine migration and drug smuggling, giving the concept of a border barrier the dominant role it has today in the contemporary border security discourse.

At the federal scale, the debate surrounding the signature of the North American Free Trade Agreement (NAFTA) re-centered the attention of American public opinion on the Mexican–American border. The complicated process needed to get the treaty approved weakened the Clinton administration and made it very vulnerable to criticism that denounced the limited efforts and involvement of the federal administration to counter illegal immigration and "fix the border" (Cornelius 2005: 775–94). As a consequence, the White House looked for novel policies to reinforce its border security credentials. A local "experiment", taking place at the regional (sectoral) scale, would provide the desired innovative approach.

In 1993, Silvestre "Silver" Reyes, chief of the El Paso sector, convinced a then reluctant Immigration and Naturalization Service (INS) to run a pilot program to modify the central objective of the border security deployment in his sector, shifting from the old strategy of tracking and arresting clandestine actors inside US territory to a frontal deployment of force in a highly visible linear configuration designed to enforce a blockade at the border, in approximately 32 linear kilometers adjacent to the metro zone of the border city of El Paso.

The change was profound. While the original tactical approach to border security was based on the use of strategic depth, and the Border Patrol deployed most of its limited resources inside the American territory with little to no surveillance in the border line itself, prevention through deterrence redirected and concentrated those same resources from the interior of the territory to its edge, introducing the use of tactical technologies to build a fortified line.

While the previous strategy depended on the "stealth" capabilities of the Border Patrol agents to move in the desert and track the unauthorized migrants without being noticed, the new strategy was based on high visibility operations to deter the crossings. This placed

---

1   Border Patrol Agent who requested to remain anonymous. Personal interview. May 2007.

most human resources and technology in highly visible locations that durably transformed the landscape, rendering it menacing at that particular point.

As originally conceived, the border blockade was a three-pronged approach that combined barriers, sensors and aerial surveillance in the following way (Bean, Chanove, Cushing, De la Garza 1994):

1. A highly visible deployment of law enforcement officers placed in the border line. Border Patrol vehicles were parked with their high beams on, pointing at Mexico. They functioned as observation outposts, human sensors and elements of deterrence. While "sitting on an X", as the maneuver became known among Border Patrol agents, no mobility was allowed, replacing mobile patrols with static, visible surveillance.
2. Four helicopters provided aerial surveillance of the 32 kilometers where the strategy was being tested.
3. Finally, a rapid response team was formed to maintain and repair the preexisting 14 kilometers of fencing infrastructure where clandestine migrants had pierced it. No hole should go un-repaired for more than 24 hours. In the years that followed, this fence was replaced by a more complex linear fortification system.

The El Paso sector pilot project articulated for the first time the systemic use of three of the most important kinds of technologies that shape the current border security technology-based response: (1) a physical barrier of linear configuration as the central component of a deterrent system; (2) a series of agents that were at the same time part of this barrier (their positions were static while "sitting on the X"), but also functioned as "human sensors"; and (3) the use of aerial surveillance to bring situational awareness to the law enforcement agents.

The innovative model of operation "Hold the Line" (its original name, "Blockade", was deemed politically problematic) changed the relation of the federal government of the United States to the border space, introduced the use of technology for environmental design between points of entry, and made the transformation of the border landscapes an intended consequence of the deterrence-based model. It also replaced the previous centrality of the human component in the border security strategy with stationary technology for surveillance and deterrence. While "sitting on an X", an agent had no use for the tracking and geographic knowledge that previously used to be his or her most valuable skill.

The most disruptive thing that operation Hold the Line did was to completely change the value proposition. When the Clinton administration repackaged the El Paso sector blockade experiment under the umbrella policy of prevention through deterrence, it also modified the criteria employed to measure the success of operations between points of entry. The new deterrence-based strategy completely reversed the measures of success that, until then, were being used by the Border Patrol to evaluate performance. The success of the blockade-based model was and still is measured not by the number of arrests, as was the case before, but by the decrease in the number of arrests compared to previous years. In the prevention-through-deterrence model, fewer arrests are interpreted as "deterred" clandestine actors (mostly economic migrants).

As the number of arrests in the El Paso sector decreased, the operation was regarded as a resounding success. Silvestre Reyes was elected congressman in 1996, and in 1995 the Clinton administration made prevention through deterrence the centerpiece of its policy to "fix the border", elevating the pilot program in El Paso to the rank of central strategy for the Border Patrol.

Hold the Line was extended over several kilometers, and operations Gatekeeper (in California) and Safeguard (in Arizona) were implemented following the same principles. The process continued, and after 9/11 and the passage of the Secure Fence Act of 2006 (that authorized the construction of hundreds of kilometers of new barriers and the installation of sensors and the use of UAVs) the walling of the whole US–Mexico border was durably framed as an essential condition to securing the homeland (H.R. 2006).

While the previous strategy left the border zone landscape practically undisturbed, the system architecture of prevention through deterrence requires a level of territorial planning never before seen in the borderlands. This security-based transformation of the environment modifies the landscape in profound ways, as it entails the deployment of manned walling systems and stadium floodlights in the middle of the desert, the creation of "no man's lands" or buffer zones, the construction of surveillance towers, the installation of motion sensors and even the use of irrigation canals as ditches to slow and ultimately deter the movement of clandestine actors (Cornelius 2001: 661–85). Modern border systems still include a combination of these technologies, and the only important addition has been the use of aerial unmanned technology.

The type of physical barrier the Department of Homeland Security (DHS) deploys depends on the environment in which it is built and the objectives for that territory: urban, rural or remote (H.R. 2007). The most complex ones are in reality complete security deployments with at least two fences, powerful floodlights, internal roads and buffer zones in between the two fences. They are permanently manned and labor intensive.

These kinds of systems are the most expensive, both in terms of construction costs and operation. They are mainly used in high-density urban areas where the clandestine migrant can reach the "vanishing point" (the place where he or she can blend with the local population and become undetectable) in a very short amount of time.

A system like this is the heart of operations like Hold the Line, Gatekeeper and Safeguard. This type of barrier is highly visible to clearly project its deterrence message. Construction of this barrier in densely populated urban zones – that once represented traditional clandestine immigration routes – is also used as a tool of strategic communications, to alter the public perception of the border as a conflictive environment where the state was unable to impose the rule of law. These barriers are as much tools of political discourse as they are a tactical infrastructure.

At the peripheries of cities and in rural zones where the vanishing point might be hours away from the border, the type of barrier used is the one referred to as a "pedestrian fence" that provides strategic depth to the Border Patrol.

These fences are built to prevent the clandestine passage of pedestrians in well-known immigration corridors, but they do not have the level of complexity of the urban walls. Although the first barriers of this kind were built during the 1970s, the DHS has been working to create modern, cheaper and more effective pedestrian fencing systems.

In the rural and remote environments where the vanishing point might be days away from the border, "vehicle fences" are preferred. This kind of fence is intended to prevent the illegal crossing of cars and pickups, and although vehicle fences do not prevent the passage of pedestrians, limiting the motorized mobility of clandestine actors provides a mobility advantage to the Border Patrol, and more time to effectuate an arrest. These walls are installed mostly in isolated areas of the border where, without a vehicle, the vanishing point is measured in days of walking before a clandestine actor can blend with the American population.

Border barrier technology is far from being homogeneous and systematically designed. Until 2006, when the fence lab was created at the Texas Transportation Institute at Texas A&M to evaluate the performance of the fencing technology, the rules and specifications used to decide what kind of barrier should be built in the different sectors did not exist, and no real process of territorial planning had been employed to organize the effort to transform the security landscapes of the border zone, at the scale of the whole border.

As the territorial planning process to wall the American border became more centralized at the national scale, the criteria employed to evaluate and deploy the technology provoked a multi-scalar conflict between the local communities and their more nuanced representations regarding the border as a space of threat, and the federal administration that authorized the Border Patrol to securitize the border space by transforming it in ways no other federal law enforcement agency would be allowed to do, anywhere else.

With a technological deployment that visually cuts in half the El Paso/Juarez bi-national metro area, the blockade of prevention through deterrence in that zone sends two very different messages, depending on the scale, using the same technology:

1. At the national scale, the federal administration framed the border barriers (both physical and virtual) as core elements of the American security and defense system to protect the nation against the threats of exogenous asymmetrical agents. In Buzan's terms, border technology broadcasted a non-verbal *speech act* to securitize the politics of the border spaces (Buzan, Waever, De Wilde 1998).
2. At the local scale, some important stakeholders perceived, in this securitization move targeting their regional space, an imposition of central authority that ignored the bi-national identity of the local communities. They also expressed concern over the consequences the technology deployment would have on the way of life of local border inhabitants.

Raul Salinas, Mayor of the City of Laredo, TX published an article in 2008 in the United States Conference of Mayors newspaper stating that:

> It is not just Laredo that handles 13,000 trucks a day. Nuevo Laredo, my neighbors to the south for over 150 years, is an extension of the cultural, historical, and business ties that have defined the two cities as one community – Los Dos Laredos. And now someone wants me to place a fence in the middle of this community like a 21st Century version of Berlin.
>
> Let me make it clear. Neither the TBC [the Texas Border Coalition] nor I are opposed to the nation securing its border. We think such security is an imperative. (This should come as no surprise since so many of us have dedicated our lives to law enforcement. In my case, I served five years as a Capitol Hill Police officer and more than 20 years as an FBI agent.) We just believe there are better ways to achieve it.
>
> For instance, rather than divide my community in two, we have proposed to the Department of Homeland Security that we widen the Rio Grande River and build up the river bank on the US side. The result would be a physical barrier higher than anything the DHS is suggesting, but like many of you that have pursued waterfront development, our barrier

would serve as the base of our Riverwalk. The net result of inviting local input would be to a superior barrier with enhanced security; not an offensive wall that divides me from my neighbors to the south. (Salinas 2008: 3)

Since the construction of the wall for the Laredo/Nuevo Laredo region was announced by DHS in 2007, the city council has used all available legal tactics to fight the construction of this infrastructure.

Laredo is just one among the many cities that have fought against the deployment of border walling technologies in their local environment. The city council of Eagle Pass, TX approved a resolution to deny all necessary permits for the construction of the wall in municipal lands adjacent to the Rio Grande. The city of Brownsville used its police department to deny access to the barrier builders. Brownsville's mayor framed the construction of the fence as an "us versus them" issue (Ahumada 2007a):

Why try to force [on] us your way of thinking when you don't even live here ... It's not affecting you. And, if you're so worried about whatever you're worried about, why not build a fence around your state.

He also described this opposition as a conflict between different geographic regions of the United States (Ahumada 2007b):

[the border wall] symbolically it's the wrong message to send to our neighbors ... It's being built to appease middle America.

This local authority targeted one "geographical" region that is defined by a set of values and not by territoriality, in his criticism of the border infrastructure: the "middle America", far from the border deployment, but also far from the shared identity of the border communities. The multi-scalar conflict is thus framed around this question: what could the predominantly white American heartland know about the challenges and cooperation mechanisms developed by twin towns in the borderlands like Brownsville that (like many other border towns) is more than 80 percent Mexican-American?

This is why it is possible to affirm that the opposition to the deployment of border technologies is more than just a Not In My Backyard (NIMBY) phenomenon. Instead, it has been framed by local authorities as a threat against the regional identity of the border communities, their relation with their southern neighbor and their interaction with the rest of the geography of America, in particular with the American heartland.

These regional leaders oppose the prevention-through-deterrence walling infrastructure from a social identity perspective. The walling technology is perceived as an unfair policy that sacrifices the binational identity of the local communities. This technology is used to eliminate perceived threats against a population that does not care about border interactions because they live far from the border and do not suffer the consequences of the transformation of the border landscapes.

It is important to accentuate that the opposition against this securitization move comes not from fringe sectors of the political landscape, but from elected officials and other prominent local leaders who see in the deployment of border technologies a projection of power by the federal government against their local sphere. The Texas Border Coalition – which has been the main face of the opposition against the construction of the border wall in

Texas – represents 30 border municipalities, 21 chambers of commerce and 18 commissions for the economic development of the border region.[2]

At the heart of this clash between the local and federal spheres is a conflict of symbols between the informal trust mechanisms that the local border communities have developed with the Mexican populations at the other side of the border, and the reciprocal mistrust that exists at the federal scale between Mexico and the United States. As border walls play the role of unilateral conflict resolution mechanisms, the citizen bilateralism of the local communities is in direct opposition to the federal government's objectives.

In El Paso, the environmental design of Hold the Line transformed the landscape in a permanent way. Floodlights, double fencing, buffer zones, surveillance towers, border patrols (and even the rapid waters of the threatening water canal) give to this border a menacing appearance that is not compatible with the nature of the shared identity between the communities of El Paso and Juarez (formerly named "El Paso del Norte").

As stated before, this threatening appearance is not a secondary, undesired effect of the frontal deployment, but one of its central design components. Prevention through deterrence logically requires the obstacles to crossing the border to present a frightening image to achieve deterrence objectives. While this image is clearly projected to the local population of law abiding citizens, smuggling mafias have learned how to exploit the limitations of the technology and not be afraid of it. The net flow of clandestine distribution chains has remained mostly unaltered.

The physical barriers are just one part of the "system of systems" deployed with the final intent of gaining operational control of the border region. Other systemic components are designed not to limit the free movement of clandestine actors in between points of entry, but to create a common operational picture using surveillance technology to provide operational control capabilities to the DHS. Observation towers and motion detectors in remote and low population density zones also provide strategic depth to the border deployment.

Because the use of this surveillance technology requires only minor alterations of the border landscapes, these technologies received the informal name of "virtual fences". They promised the policy maker a more cost-effective alternative to the highly controversial walling technology, with most of its advantages and almost none of its local flaws.

Do Good Sensors Make Good Neighbors? SBInet and the Politics of Virtual Fences

When border security strategies moved away from the tracking capacities of agents as the most critical component of the system to the use of technological force multipliers as the backbone of the whole strategy, innovation cycles became central to the construction of border security policies. In an environment like this, the technological performance of the infrastructure has direct consequences in the homeland security narrative. The rise and fall of SBI (Secure Border Initiative) and SBInet is probably the best example of this change.

SBInet was one of the most ambitious deployments of surveillance technology ever tried in the borderlands. The "virtual fence/wall", built and tested between 2006 and 2008, was meant not only to complement the physical barrier technologies, but also to become a viable alternative to them.

The SBI project was created to research, develop and prove the viability of a tactical "system of systems" to gain operational control of the Mexican–American border. By

---

2   The website of the organization is: http://www.texasbordercoalition.org (accessed 21/12/2013).

combining off-the-shelf surveillance technologies (sensors, cameras, radars and telecom systems in Border Patrol vehicles) and walling tactical infrastructures (pedestrian and vehicles fencing), SBI was supposed to demonstrate how a networked technology response was a cost-effective approach to provide operational control of the border region, giving to the Border Patrol a definitive tactical advantage over clandestine actors (Stana 2008). From 2006 to 2009 "the SBI program received about 3.6 billion in appropriated funds" (Stana 2008: 4).

The information technology component of SBI was named SBInet. Closed down in 2011 after multiple governmental and external reports concluded that the project had been a management failure, its cancellation has called into question the contractor's model used to manage it, in which a private corporation played the central role in the research, development and implementation process of the deployment of the border technology. For Papademetriou and Collet,

> [The contractor's] failure to understand the complexities of border management can ultimately push costs up for government clients while undermining the value of the technologies implemented. The troubled SBInet program, for example, had more external consultants than agency officials working on it (especially Border Patrol officials), and concerns were raised from the outset as to the relative inexperience of the consortium of private-sector companies (led by Boeing) in the field of border control. (Papademetriou 2011)

In 2011, Secretary of Homeland Security Janet Napolitano canceled SBInet, stating that the program "cannot meet its original objective of providing a single, integrated border security technology solution" (Napolitano 2011). Despite the rise and fall of SBInet, the Department of Homeland Security has continued on its path to develop, combine and integrate technological systems to use as force multipliers in the borderlands, including a reinforcement of the CBP's Unmanned Aerial Vehicle program.

Because its cancellation raised questions about the management style, but not about the technology-based response to border security, SBInet remains relevant as one of the most systemic trials to integrate different technological approaches to border security. Its managerial failure is also a cautionary tale regarding the challenges of cost-effective technology acquisition for the multi-billion dollar border security market.

Given the significant number of information technologies employed in its design, SBInet was often referred to by the media as the "virtual wall/virtual fence". In reality, this pilot program included a series of tactical infrastructures, among which different types of physical fences were tested and deployed. However, while walling technology was part of the "technology mix", the most ambitious components of SBInet included the use of surveillance technology like stationary radars, infrared and optical sensor towers, motion detectors and cameras.

The SBInet contract was awarded in 2006 to the aerospace and defense company Boeing. Treated as a single research, development and implementation project, SBInet was the most ambitious effort to that date to provide operational control of the border zone. While Boeing subcontracted many of the different aspects of the project, the company was responsible for managing this key component of the new border policy.

In 2006, Boeing initiated the construction of "Project 28", a prototype of a "virtual fence" in the Tucson sector near the communities of Arivaca and Sasabe, AZ built around one of the most popular smuggling corridors. The backbone of "Project 28" was formed by nine antennas deployed to monitor the territory using motion sensors, radars, cameras (regular and infrared) and motion detectors to complement the visual information obtained by the surveillance towers.

The SBInet "system of systems" needed to fulfill four basic requirements to obtain operational control of the border territory (Department of Homeland Security 2006):

1. Detection. Using one of its multiple information sources, a system must detect all possible security breaches in the territory between points of entry. This information is then transmitted in real time to the Command and Control Center and to the terminals installed in the Border Patrol Vehicles, creating a common operational picture of the threat.
2. Identification. Once a possible clandestine crossing is detected, the system's Artificial Intelligence (AI) should be able to autonomously discern between different possible scenarios depending on the agents involved: cattle, clandestine immigrants, drug dealers or possible terrorists.
3. Risk Analysis. During this step, the system AI should provide enough information and analysis to determine who and what is crossing, if it is an illegal activity, how many individuals are involved, what they are doing and what kind of risk they pose to law enforcement agents.
4. Response. To respond efficiently to the threat and "resolve" the illegal crossing, while protecting the lives of the involved agents, the system should provide cost effective alternatives from which the decision maker can choose to deploy the available resources in the area.

Covering 28 miles of the US–Mexico border, this prototype was meant to serve as a proof of concept (POC) to demonstrate the viability of the technological approach to border enforcement. Instead, SBInet "proved too expensive, vulnerable to technical failures, and insufficiently sensitive of the requirements of the Border Patrol agents on the ground" (Koslowski 2011).

UAVs have been framed since the official cancellation of the project as a more cost-effective alternative to the virtual fence. Mark Borkowski, DHS executive director of SBInet mentioned that, while the use of UAVs was not contemplated as part of the SBInet plans, "the department is now considering expanding its drone fleet to beef up border security" (Borkowski 2010). The ultimate oversight authority for the virtual technology deployment decided to frame the expansion of the UAV fleet as a competitive alternative and not a complement to the virtual wall. The predator drone the CBP uses as its primary drone in the border region is produced by General Atomics and not Boeing, who had the failed SBInet contract. Therefore, this change in the technology mix affects negatively the role of one border security innovator, while benefiting another.

The cancellation of SBInet and its Project 28 represents the failure of the most comprehensive effort by the DHS to upgrade the principles of the prevention-through-deterrence model using twenty-first-century networked technology as the backbone of the process. It affected the trajectory of the border strategy, slowed the deployment process and changed the priority given to the different elements, reinforcing the UAV program as an alternative to the failure of the sensor based "virtual fence".

The project also demonstrated that surveillance technologies might not provoke the identity based opposition of physical walls, but these technologies are not excepted from creating multi-scalar geopolitical conflicts between the federal and local scales, this time in the name of privacy rights.

Arivaca is a little community in the Tucson sector, seventeen kilometers inland from the Mexican–American border. Because the village found itself inside the zone of Project 28, as it sits near one of the most important smuggling corridors of North America, the town became one of the hot spots for the NIMBY opposition to the virtual fence. Although Arivaca is not adjacent to the border, one of the nine high tech surveillance towers was placed in a small hill that dominates its whole geography, against the will of the local inhabitants.

The emplacement of the "spy tower", as the citizens of Arivaca frequently referred to the Project 28 technology, allowed it to observe almost every street of the small town. Although the system was designed to be deployed in uninhabited areas of the immense border territory, this particular tower was installed in an inhabited community and provoked a strong NIMBY reaction against it. The inverse relation between the size of the community and the level of sophistication of the surveillance technology created an increased sensation of being observed, described by the inhabitants as akin to "being always in a reality show".[3] Emilie Livezey popularized the term NIMBY in 1980 to refer to an opposition against a development not because of the development itself, but because of the undesirable byproducts it produces "in your backyard" (Livezey 1980).

This NIMBY protest against the surveillance technology is different from the previously described opposition to the physical walls of the Texas Border Coalition or the mayors of Laredo or McAllen, based on a strong identity sentiment against the walling technology itself. The citizens of Arivaca were mostly opposed to a byproduct of the border wall – their loss of privacy – not the physical infrastructure.

The tower did transform the landscape of Arivaca, and what made its deployment more puzzling to the local community was that the objective of this particular tower was to give to Project 28 some strategic depth beyond the border line; it was installed by the contractor not to observe the border, but to observe the interior territory of the United States, around the town. Its emplacement near the Sasabe smuggling corridor made sense at the system scale, but not to the local inhabitants who perceived that the only objective of the "spy tower" was to spy on them, violating their privacy rights.

NIMBY opposition to surveillance technology is not an exclusive phenomenon of the border zone, but as privacy concerns increase and surveillance technologies are seen as the central problem, surveillance innovation in border environments has become a key battlefield for privacy right advocates who frame this increased surveillance deployment as a threat that has to be opposed, in order to avoid the same technology trickling down to affect the rest of the country.[4] Once again, innovation and technology specifications drive border security politics well beyond the border.

Even after the termination of SNInet, the use of force multipliers (technological means to increase the success rate of the Border Patrol agents) is still at the core of most border security debates. Therefore, the process of environmental design of the border landscapes has also continued. Current and planned force multipliers bring to the borderlands a level of technification never seen outside theaters of operations (TO), making the edge of the state a territory of high technological experimentation for security and defense innovation, and

---

3 Results and comments obtained during one of the author's geographic field research studies in the Project 28 deployment zone in 2007.

4 The ACLU refers sarcastically to the border region as a "constitution free" zone, were surveillance violates in their opinion constitutional protections (see ACLU).

a showroom for the multibillion dollar markets for fortification, surveillance and robotics technologies. The classification of the borderlands as an innovation sandbox for defense technologies can be easily demonstrated by three facts already discussed in this chapter:

- High tech walls have modified the border landscape in ways no other law enforcement agency would be allowed to do anywhere else.
- Surveillance towers "spy" on border communities like Arivaca, AZ with state of the art surveillance technology never before used outside military environments.
- Drones are authorized to fly in the borderlands for the first time ever inside the continental United States.

The border regions of North America have become the space where some the most promising interdiction and surveillance technologies can be tested and "de-weaponized" to render them acceptable to civilian environments far from the battlefield and usable in the western world, expanding exponentially their potential markets. Because of this, barriers, sensors and drones complement and frequently compete to become the dominant technology. As most of these deployments can be placed in the "early adopter" column of Geoffrey Moore's model for technology adoption (Moore 1999), the American borderlands are now a key "target market" for those innovators trying to cross the chasm that divides early adopters from the pragmatist majority. Technologies successfully adopted in the borderlands of North America will definitely have a competitive advantage when marketed in other border spaces around the world, and in other law enforcement and surveillance markets in western societies.

In the territories where the technology has been deployed in permanent ways under the prevention-through-deterrence model, border security has become a "total activity" as the presence of law enforcement agents and security infrastructure becomes constant and highly visible, modifying in a permanent way the landscape and the human behavior of people living near the border line, and creating conflict between the local and federal scales.

Imaginary Politics: Pivot Technology to Rule the Border Deployment and Control the Discourse

Immigration and demographic studies have proven that migrants "deterred" by the frontal technology deployments from crossing a "prevention trough deterrence enabled" sector did not cease in their effort to gain access to American territory, and instead looked for crossing points that offered less resistance. Demographers call this displacement of routes a "balloon effect" in which the pressure applied to one part of the balloon sends it to another sector where the deployment is less effective. In information technologies, we call this "hacking": a permanent adaptation process to find the path of least resistance by constantly probing the security technology to identify a weakness in the design of the system, and then exploiting it.

This process has reoriented migration routes to dangerous zones of the borderlands where the immensity of the unpopulated territory makes operational control very expensive to obtain in any sustainable way. This hacking of the border security system has enabled criminal networks to maintain smuggling avenues and the clandestine population unchanged. In fact, given the increased risk of death associated with the new routes found during this adaptation process, clandestine migrants increased the amount of time they remain illegally in the United States from months to years, ending the so-called circularity in migration patterns that used to follow the seasonal rhythms of the agricultural and construction industries (Cornelius 2011).

In many ways, these technology deployments made the immigration "problem" worse. On the one hand, the barriers were effective enough to redirect the flow of migrants to more dangerous zones, making the flow less visible, but the technologies were neither comprehensive nor adaptive enough to avoid being constantly hacked by capable clandestine actors. On the other, the hardship of the border trip encouraged migrants to remain in United States territory for longer periods of time. When this happened, migration networks that used to be seasonal became permanent, and Hispanic migrants lost any incentive to remain near the American side of the border after crossing, as they were no longer able to shuttle between the two countries. Because of this, immigration patterns changed inside of the United States as new migrants decided to move with the labor market beyond the border zone. The Hispanic population skyrocketed in areas of the United States that were previously "immigration free", and this amplified in a vicious cycle the identity conflicts that put pressure on the political system to reinforce the border deployment, perpetuating the process (Massey 2005: 1250–60).

Peter Andreas has described these immigration and border control policies as a "border game" that operates primarily in the field of symbols and representations. According to him, the original main objective of the border deployments was not to reduce but instead to redirect the immigration flows to areas with less visibility, in order to influence perception. In this view, producing a winning appearance provided a viable alternative to actually solving the "border issue" (Andreas 2000). Two main arguments give credibility to Andreas' hypothesis:

1. At least until the arrival of the counter-terrorist border of the post 9/11 world, the way the Border Patrol operated in the borderlands had its biggest impact in the terrain of image and perception, as in reality no clandestine flows (drugs or labor) have ever been durably interrupted, even after Operation Blockade and its sister deployments Gatekeeper (in California) and Safeguard (in Arizona) were fully implemented.
2. The construction and deployment of border technologies in the urban territories gave a powerful argument to the federal administration in proving its commitment to "solve the border problem" even if no fundamental patterns were altered.

As border walls are technology infrastructures that in their most advanced environmental design are both visually impressive and simple to understand, they produce a powerful and photogenic statement about the commitment of the United States to enforce the border management laws with a zero tolerance approach to clandestine activities in the borderlands. If their deterrence capabilities can and have been questioned by opponents, scholarly analysis and governmental reports, their usefulness as aspirational technologies that affect border discourse is unquestionable.

Although Peter Andreas is right to emphasize that prevention through deterrence has a clear symbolic component, two observable systemic patterns of the technological deployment demonstrate why their usefulness for the federal government is more than just aspirational.

1. The geographic expansion pattern. Since the first components of the border fence were built in the 1920s, and especially since 1995 and the arrival of prevention through deterrence, the deployment of tactical infrastructure has been driven by an escalation dynamic that in many ways feeds on itself. As the deployment of technology at one point of the border redirects parts of the previously existing clandestine smuggling networks to new areas that were not affected by clandestine activities before, the attention of stakeholders also shifts to new border regions. This frequently culminates in a new border deployment in a new zone, redirecting the flows once again to a new territory in what has become a pattern.
2. The iterative innovation pattern. Border innovation dynamics have created a symbiotic ecosystem between clandestine border actors and law enforcement agencies. Smuggling organizations are encouraged to improve the performance of their technological approaches to pierce the border fortification, while the DHS and its contractors are also repetitively forced to improve their designs and find better force multipliers to remain effective. The constant wave of symbiotic technological adaptation between law enforcement agencies and clandestine actors produces an escalation process.

Because of these two iterative patterns, the border security deployment cannot be labeled exclusively as an aspirational technology. Since 1995, the border enforcement infrastructure has grown in size and complexity every year, and not one linear meter has been disassembled (the only exception was a section of the fence that was built by accident on the Mexican side of the border region).

The border deployment has behaved like a "slippery slope" policy, escalating in little steps each time in size and complexity and never backtracking. Viewed through the lens of innovation theory, governmental border technology follows a clearly defined sustaining path, with successive waves of technologies improving incrementally the quality of the deployment. On the other hand, clandestine actors produce both incremental and disruptive technology paths, as they frequently outdate their own technologies to defeat the technology-dependent interdictions (Christensen 2000).

It is possible to imagine a scenario were, because of these two patterns, the aspirational design might be only a provisional state of the border system. At one point, the sustaining growth of the technology deployment and its constant improvement could attain a tipping point where the whole border – and not only individual sectors – becomes so hard to cross illegally that the deterrence effect is obtained at the systemic level. Under this scenario, it is not that the technology deployment is not effective; it is just that it is not yet completed.

In many ways, this is the scenario under which the DHS operates, constantly improving border technologies and deploying them in new zones (Haddal 2010: 54). To be clear, even in this scenario, an effective border system does not presuppose a cost-effective one.

But it would be a mistake to ignore an alternative scenario, in which the adversarial forces that oppose the border deployment also get a vote. Nothing in this ecosystem decreases the incentive to innovate for clandestine actors. Therefore, an effective system will not be effective for too long, if the adaptive clandestine actors are not deterred to innovate. As smuggling "industries" are in fact dependent on the solidity of the interdiction to maintain their business model, an effective border fortification increases the incentives to penetrate it.

The famous X Prize foundation induces "radical breakthroughs" by "creating and managing large-scale, high profile, incentivized prize competitions that stimulate investment in research and development".[5] In many ways, border deployments have created a similar environment – a dark X Prize – that incentivizes clandestine actors to permanently disrupt the border environment. As new border technologies become known and understood, clandestine innovators find new ways of piercing them to win a great "prize": unrestricted access to a series of multibillion dollar industries that are well worth any research and development effort. The more the DHS invests to keep the pace in the geographic and innovation races, the more incentives clandestine actors have to keep disrupting the border environment (as that know-how becomes more valuable if the technology is effective) in an escalation process that makes the illegal activities sustainable, while those of the DHS are not. Federal budgets for border security cannot keep growing indefinitely, but the prize to pierce the interdiction is more valuable the harder it gets to do it.

Conclusion

Long gone are the geopolitical representations of the spaghetti westerns where the border deployment consisted of not much more than a remote outpost, constantly being challenged by Mexican bandits at the heart of the pristine Chihuahuan desert, near the Rio Grande. Instead, the dominant narrative of the Mexican–American border of today makes it an imagined place where border fortifications alternate with empty territories to form a flawed and unfinished technological deployment of force multipliers, ineffective only because power struggles and poor managerial choices – like SBI – have failed to finish this project.

Different technological mixes are still being tested to improve the environmental design of the borderline, and barriers sensors and UAVs are being recombined in different proportions to keep looking for "operational control", the holy grail of border management and security.

This innovation cycle has created a market were inventors are now trying to develop technology solutions to the "border problem" as it has been defined by the current political environment. But the cycle works the other way around too, as the capabilities and limitations of the developed technology influence in return the political environment, creating a reinforcing loop.

This is why it is so important to have a correct definition of the problem: As innovators see in the big problems of today the big markets of tomorrow, the definition of the problem today triggers invention cycles for years to come. As SBI demonstrated, once billions of dollars have been invested in one accepted technology development path, the barriers to exit "trap" policies and policy makers inside the framework of the specifications of that technology.

Because border technologies are not designed in a vacuum and they are just one more element of the geopolitics of the borderlands, technology adoption should be considered in the context of other affected territories, other alternative technologies and other concerned actors. As walls are a controversial and expensive technology that impacts the relation of the United States with its neighbors and the identity and way of life of the local binational communities, the tradeoffs of physical barriers should also be factored as part of the technology assessment. Deployment should be optimized by a rigorous cost-effective analysis that determines if and when such walls are the optimal solution to a problem,

---

5   X Prize foundation "about" webpage. Retrieved from: http://www.xprize.org/about/who-we-are (accessed 25/12/2013).

despite the geopolitical conflicts they provoke. Sterling proposes three metrics to evaluate the effectiveness of fencing deployments:

1. How do borders influence and threaten a rival's perceptions and behavior?
2. To what extent do the strategic defenses of one country impact the military balance in current and long-term relations?
3. In what ways do the defenses influence leadership and popular attitudes impacting policy choices? (Sterling 2009: 309)

His evaluation criteria are based on a military defensive environment designed to oppose a symmetrical enemy, because this was the original context for fortification technologies. Defining the threat, the rival, the military "balance" and the popular attitudes vis-à-vis clandestine actors is more complicated in an asymmetrical environment where Mexico is not an adversarial nation, but an important trading partner of the United States via the legal points of entry of this conflicted border. But the three questions do offer a good starting point to evaluate the cost-effectiveness of the technology while deciding if this deployment should be complemented and/or replaced by other technologies in other territories.

An opportunity-cost assessment of border technologies requires a clear definition of the threat by policymakers, because the different clandestine behaviors that today are confronted almost exclusively at the borderline are in fact shaped by networks that extend well beyond the border region. The fight against these clandestine activities should be done at the system level and not just at the scale of the border region, and strategies that work against one definition of the threat and one network might not have any effect against the others. For example:

- If the threat is defined as economic illegal migration, border security solutions should evaluate also workplace enforcement; technologies to improve Immigration and Customs Enforcement (ICE) capacities; biometrics (including the possibility of a "smart" national ID card required during the hiring process); the creation of seasonal labor markets to reestablish circularity; as well as the facilitation of legal migration to end the incentives that fuel the illegal labor market.
- If the threat is drug-related violence in the borderlands, then collaborative enforcement options that partner bureaucracies on both sides of the border should be evaluated too. If they are considered to be a cost-effective approach, then the consequences of antagonistic representations created by walling technologies should be also considered, as there is an opportunity-cost associated with the mistrust fortifications memorialize in the border landscape. Walls create a unilateral response to a given problem while making bilateral responses to the same problem more difficult to negotiate.
- If the threat is drug consumption and the associated health risks, then prevention through education of consumers might be a more effective approach than prevention through deterrence in the border spaces. Legalization, treatment, and research and development of new and safer recreational drugs using FDA approved clinical trials should also be part of the technology mix assessment.

Independently of the definition of the threat, adoption plans should consider the potential opposition and the effects at the local scales of the technology deployment. As demonstrated, there are different kinds of opposition to a technology deployment; identity-based opposition and NIMBY opposition are not the same nor should they be treated in the same way. A NIMBY opposition to the border fence opposes the emplacement, but not the idea. An identity-based opposition questions the geopolitical representations and symbolic nature of the deployment, and the existence of the technology itself.

Also, the zero-risk goal of the border technology security system is ill defined because governmental resources are finite and trade-offs have to be made. It encourages a border narrative where the desired final state is unattainable as the border cannot be protected all the time, everywhere, against all possible kinds of new exploits, known and unknown. Effective fencing legislation should reflect this fact, and adopt accordingly a realistic risk management approach. Homeland Security literature has developed tools like Model Based Risk Analysis (MBRA) to create a risk-informed decision-making process that is intrinsically cost-effective (Lewis 2011 and 2009). By studying all components of the affected network, risk management tools can guide optimal non-politicized strategies to decrease risk, if the definitions of threat and risk are unambiguous.

Finally, the politics of border enforcement should consider scientific approaches (game and prospect theories are two possibilities) to study the consequences of current innovation patterns in the present and future behavior of clandestine border agents. By influencing the incentive system, the current technology has "gamified" (Sy 2011) the border environment, creating a sort of "dark X-prize" where clandestine actors are challenged under the following "competition rules": Whoever is capable of finding a way to "exploit" or "hack" the border security deployment in its current form by smuggling a relatively small amount of easily transportable chemical products will be awarded billions of dollars after every successful run.

The fiercest competition in the deployment of border security technologies is not happening among security and defense contractors (i.e., Boeing vs. General Atomics), but among them and the clandestine actors who have proven to be more adaptive by developing cost-effective counter-technologies. The incentives to innovate are too high for organized crime to ignore, and they increase with the effectiveness of the border enforcement. For a border security technological deployment to be successful, governmental technologies would have to be more disruptive and faster to adapt than the research and development cycles of those trying to exploit them. Today, that is certainly not the case.

References

ACLU. ACLU fact sheet: U.S. "Constitution free zone". Available at: http://www.aclu.org/technology-and-liberty/fact-sheet-us-constitution-free-zone (accessed January 25, 2012).

Ahumada, P. 2007a. Texan Mayors Oppose Plan for Border Fence. *NPR*. Available at: http://m.npr.org/news/front/15315131?page=4 (accessed January 5, 2012).

Ahumada, P. 2007b. Border Fence Stirs Mixed Emotions. *NPR*. Available at: http://www.npr.org/templates/story/story.php?storyId=15034078 (accessed January 5, 2012).

Andreas, P. 2000. Border Games: Policing the U.S.-Mexico Divide. *Journal of Policy Analysis and Management*, 21.

Bean, F., Chanove, R., Cushing, R., et al. 1994. *Illegal Mexican Migration and the United States/Mexico Border: The Effects of Operation Hold the Line on El Paso/Juárez*. Austin, TX: US Commission on Immigration Reform.

Borkowski, M. 2010. Interview reproduced in Strohm, C., Homeland Security Officials Weigh More UAV Border Patrols. *Government Executive*. Available at: http://www.govexec.com/defense/2010/06/homeland-security-officials-weigh-more-uav-border-patrols/31757/ (accessed January 25, 2012).

Brent, S. 2009. *Do Good Fences Make Good Neighbors? What History Teaches us About Strategic Barriers and International Security.* Washington, DC: Georgetown University Press.

Buzan, B., Wæver, O., De Wilde, J. 1998 *Security a New Framework for Analysis*. Boulder, CO: Lynne Rienner.

Christensen, C.M. 2000. *The Innovator's Dilemma: When New Technologies Cause Great Firms to Fail*, Kindle Edition.

Cornelius, W. 2005. Controlling "Unwanted" Immigration: Lessons from the United States, 1993–2004. *Journal of Ethnic and Migration Studies*, 31 (4), 775–94.

Cornelius, W.A. 2001. Death at the Border: Efficacy and Unintended Consequences of US Immigration Control Policy. *Population and Development Review*, 27 (4), 661–85.

Department of Homeland Security. 2006. *SBInet: Securing U.S. Borders Factsheet*. Washington, DC: DHS.

Haddal, C. 2010. *People Crossing Borders: An Analysis of U.S. Border Protection Policies*. Washington, DC: Congressional Research Service.

H.R. 2006. 6061–109th Congress: Secure Fence Act of 2006. Available at: http://www.govtrack.us/congress/bills/109/hr6061 (accessed March 24, 2012).

H.R. Committee on the Judiciary. 2007. Past, Present and Future: A historic and Personal Reflection on American Immigration: Hearing before the Subcommittee on Immigration, Citizenship, Refugees, Border Security, and International Law of the Committee on the Judiciary, House of Representatives, One Hundred Tenth Congress, 1st session, March 30, 2007. Washington, DC: US Government Printing Office.

Jeffery, C.R., Zahm, D.L. 1993. Crime Prevention Through Environmental Design, Opportunity Theory, and Rational Choice Models. *Routine Activity and Rational Choice Advances in Criminological Theory* edited by R.V. Clarke and M. Felson, Transaction Publishers.

Koslowski, R. 2011. *The Evolution of Border Controls as a Mechanism to Prevent Illegal Immigration*. Migration Policy Institute. Available at: http://www.migrationpolicy.org/pubs/bordercontrols-koslowski.pdf (accessed January 25, 2012).

Lewis, T.G. 2009. *Network Science: Theory and Applications*. John Wiley & Sons.

Lewis, T.G. 2011. *Bak's Sand Pile*. Monterey, CA: AgilePress.

Liverzey, E. 1980. *Hazardous Waste*. Boston, MA: Christian Science Monitor.

Madsen, K.D. 2007. Local Impacts of the Balloon Effect of Border Law Enforcement. *Geopolitics*, 12 (2), 280–98.

Maril, R.L. 2006. *Patrolling Chaos: The U.S. Border Patrol in Deep South Texas*. Texas Tech University Press.

Massey, D.S. 2005. Backfire at the Border: Why Enforcement without Legalization Cannot Stop Illegal Immigration. *Russell The Journal Of The Bertrand Russell Archives*, 59 (29), 1250–60.

Moore, G. 1999? *Crossing the Chasm: Marketing and Selling Technology Project*, Kindle Edition.

Napolitano, J. 2011. Written statement by the Secretary of Homeland Security, cited in Homeland Security Scraps Border Fence. *The Wall Street Journal*. Available at: http://online.wsj.com/article/SB10001424052748703959104576082132545578242.html?mod=rss_US_News (accessed January 25, 2012).

Papademetriou, D.G., Collett, E. 2011. *A New Architecture for Border Management*. Washington, DC: Migration Policy Institute.

Pollak, M. 2000. Representations of the City in Siege Views of the Seventeenth Century. In *City Walls: The Urban Enceinte in Global Perspective* edited by J.D. Tracy, Cambridge, MA: Cambridge University Press, 605–47.

Salinas, R. 2008. Laredo Mayor Advocates Long-Term Solution to Immigration, Homeland Security Challenges on US–Mexico Border. *The United States Conferences of Mayors*. Available at: http://usmayors.org/usmayornewspaper/documents/06_02_08/pg3_laredo1.asp (accessed March 12, 2012).

Stana, R.M. 2008. *Secure Border Initiative: Observations on the Importance of Applying Lessons Learned to Future Projects: Congressional Testimony*. Washington, DC: GAO. Available at: http://books.google.com/books?hl=en&lr=&id=fg5SVXzL59cC&pgis=1 (accessed January 5, 2012).

Stana, R.M. 2009. *Secure Border Initiative Fence Construction Costs*. Diane Publishing. Available at: http://books.google.com/books?hl=en&lr=&id=EZb5-SIuITYC&pgis=1 (accessed January 5, 2012).

Sy, S. 2011. *Gamification by Design*. O'Reilly Media, Inc.

Chapter 13
Technologies, Practices and the Reproduction of Conflict: The Impact of the West Bank Barrier on Peace Building

Christine Leuenberger[1]

In the Age of Walls

After the fall of the Berlin Wall in 1989, an era of open geographical spaces and unparalleled physical and electronic mobility seemed to replace a world divided along ideological and political lines. The post-1989 global dissemination of capitalist forms of governance produced unprecedented wealth, unmatched economic opportunities and stark inequities (Sassen 2006). The ever-increasing prevalence of uneven economic developments between the North and the Global South has spurred a proliferation of border barriers that have led to a "strict hierarchization" of global flow. While the free movement of goods, services, and of a privileged global citizenry is encouraged, for the underprivileged, dispossessed, and poor the borders have hardened (Rosiere 2011). At the same time, states increasingly face a new set of problems – waves of immigration from the economic periphery to the center, illegal activities along their borders, and a rise in ethnic violence. In response, politicians, policy makers and security forces have reverted to the historically widespread strategy of constructing "strategic defense systems" such as barriers, walls, and fences (Sterling 2009). Underlying the proliferation of border technologies is the assumption that they can inhibit immigration and illegal activities (such as smuggling and drug trafficking), create security, curb terrorism, and minimize ethnic violence. The post-1989 hopes for freedom and mobility have therefore gone hand in hand with a "new age" of walls (Borges 2007).

Since 1990 numerous barriers have been built, or proposed, in and between various countries including, between Mexico and the United States, the United Arab Emirates and Oman, India and Pakistan, Morocco and the Spanish cities of Ceuta and Melilla, and around neighborhoods in Baghdad (Iraq) and Padua (Italy). The West Bank Barrier, which has been under construction since 2002 by the Israeli government and separates Israel from Palestinian territories, is one of the more controversial such projects. Like other barriers around the world, the West Bank Barrier doesn't provide a symmetrical division between separate societies, cultures, and ethnicities. Rather, the social and cultural spaces of both Palestinian and Israeli society intermingle, forming "a giant web" (Boeri 2003: 53) of interrelated, but disconnected, ethno-social spaces. Palestinian and Jewish villages may

---

[1] I am grateful to the Fulbright Scholar Program for the Middle East, North Africa, Central and South Asia Regional Research Program's support (grantee no. G48413539), the Fulbright Specialist Program (grantee no. 88100362) and the National Science Foundation (award no. 1152322), and I am indebted to numerous respondents for their time and insights.

reside side by side, yet despite their physical and spatial proximity they are frequently separated from one another by walls and fences.[2]

The intermingling of ethno-social spaces and the attempt to separate them with barriers is a recurring feature not only between nation-states, but also ever more within cities. In the Italian city of Padua, barriers contain and sustain homogenous neighborhoods; in the Iraqi Green Zone in Baghdad, fortresses separate the American military from the local population; and in Californian suburbs, gated communities preserve the neighborhood within, whilst guarding against the unwanted other from without. Similar mechanisms have been observed in the Brazilian city of Sao Paulo, where the increasing mix of social classes in the same geographical spaces, the upsurge in crime and fear of crime since the 1980s has led to a proliferation of walled-off communities, secured apartment complexes, security posts, and private guards to enforce rules of exclusion and inclusion (Caldeira 1996).

Strategies of exclusion have also remade American cities. For instance, in Los Angeles "social polarization and spatial apartheid are accelerating" (Davis 2003: 528). Various social problems ranging from unemployment, budget crises, and the deterioration of public spaces in the 1980s led to new strategies of physical segregation in downtown Los Angeles: "Foot traffic in the new financial district was elevated above the street on pedways whose access was controlled by the security systems of individual skyscrapers" (Davis 2003: 529). Meanwhile gang violence could continue unabated underneath, separated off from the elevated privatized spaces of business. This has resulted in the multi-tier geography of Los Angeles, or what Mike Davis calls, various "social control districts" (Davis 2003: 532) in which architecture has merged with law enforcement and land-use planning. Accordingly:

> The border is everywhere, around every public and private property and infrastructure, splintered into a variety of local and regional fortification and security apparatuses, that are exemplified in today's road-blocks, check-points, fences, walls, CCTV systems, safety zones, mine fields, and killing zones. (Weizman 2004: 2)

Israel and the Palestinian Territories contain many closure and bordering mechanisms around buildings, neighborhoods, communities and territories. Israel/Palestine thus provides an exemplary case for studying social interconnectedness and mechanisms for separation in multicultural and multifaceted societies. Israel's policies of separation and their effect on an ever more complex social fabric may provide insights into general processes underway from Morocco to Mexico.

Walls as Objects: Theory and Methods

Social theorists have long argued that objects can summon, embody and sustain various meanings that are not inherent in their materiality, but are socially produced and consolidated. Studies in the sociology of knowledge have shown how society, knowledge, and institutions together produce "reality" and its associated "problems" and "meanings" as seemingly relevant, self-evident and inevitable (Berger and Luckmann 1984). Constructivist studies of

---

2 How the intermingling of Jewish and Palestinian populations on both sides of the Green Line (the internationally recognized 1949 armistice line) between Israel and the West Bank may impact the two-state solution see Weizman 2004. For maps on the ethnic distribution in the West Bank see http://www.btselem.org/English/Maps/Index.asp (accessed March 26, 2010).

social problems propose that "problems" are not "out there", but are constituted by claim-makers who often call upon various cultural, scientific and political resources as well as on material objects, such as Columbine High School or the Berlin Wall to evoke powerful images of social ills, creating the contours of widely recognized social problems such as school violence or social dislocation (Holstein and Gubrium 2000; Leuenberger 2006; 2011a). While such works speak to the social construction of problems, meanings, and realities, border studies scholars have increasingly focused on how spatiality and borders are socially produced, not only within border areas, but also through social practices, legislations and discourses that permeate societies. Indeed, bordering mechanisms and their impact reside within a complex network of institutional practices and narrative frameworks across different spaces, in which people perform notions of territoriality, cultural identities, and power relations (Paasi 2005; Brunet-Jailly 2011). While Border Studies provides valuable conceptual tools to understand the social and spatial production of boundaries, Science Studies adds to our understanding of modern borders as large technological systems. These works deal with such issues as how society, culture, and politics co-produce differences in the design, function, meaning, and use of technologies; the role of material infrastructures for governance; and how technological changes are not "neutral" processes, but always rearrange social relations. Studies of the social consequences of technologies – whether they are telephones, electronic media, or washing machines – show that their effect is neither deterministic nor inevitable (Alatout 2009; Bijker et al. 1987; MacKenzie and Wajcman 1999; Pfaffenberger 1990; Westrum 1991; Wetmore 2009; Winner 1986; Zureik et al. 2010). Rather, the introduction of telephones could unite as well as divide communities. Electronic media can link people in far-flung places, but may also create psychological distance by eliminating the need for face-to-face interaction.

By combining the conceptual tools of the sociology of knowledge, constructivist studies of social problems, Border Studies and Science Studies, my aim is to understand how particular social practices and discursive repertoires sustain particular meanings, functions, and consequences of the West Bank barrier. While policy-makers, politicians and economists have tackled the economic, political and security consequences of constructing barriers, the social consequences of technological systems that enforce long-term separation have received only scant attention from policy analysts and journalists (Nunez-Neto and Garcia 2007). Yet, the recent proliferation of barriers as a way to tackle contemporary social, political, and economic problems makes analyses of their impact all the more pressing.

The research reported here was commenced in 2008 and draws on a data corpus that includes 52 qualitative in-depth interviews (conducted in 2008 and 2010) with a range of professionals, citizens, academics, and politicians; participant observations; and a collection of academic, popular, and media sources, as well as archival materials. By triangulating interview data, ethnographic observations, and published and archival sources the aim is to capture various commonly shared discourses amongst Israelis and Palestinians about the barriers' impacts, functions, and social consequences and analyze how the barrier enhances or constrains various forms of interaction.

Discursively Constructing the Barrier

The philosopher John Austin has pointed out that we always do things with words. The terms used to describe the West Bank barrier are iconic examples for performing cultural meanings and political stances. Its Israeli proponents call it the "Security-" or "Anti-Terrorist Fence" to signify permeability, transparency, movability, security and good neighborliness. Its Israeli opponents and Palestinians, however, describe it most often as the "Apartheid-", "Segregation-", "Separation-", "Colonization-", "Demographic-" or "Annexation Wall". The term "wall" evokes negative connotations associated with dictatorial power and permanent separation. While protagonists use the descriptors "fence" versus "wall" politically to denote different meanings of the barrier, in modern high-tech border systems the difference between walls and fences are increasingly being erased. As physical barriers become linked to virtual barriers, such as electronic warning devices, surveillance systems, radar, ground sensors and remote control cameras, both, walls and fences, inhibit trespassing equally effectively (Rosiere 2011).

The international community, too, struggles to find the appropriate term to describe the barrier. In a 2004 advisory opinion, the International Court of Justice (2004) declared, what it referred to as the "Wall", to be illegal under international law, whilst the BBC and Human Rights Groups frequently use the "Separation-", or the "West Bank-" "barrier" as acceptable generic descriptions (BBC News 2006). Such idioms, ranging from "walls", "fences" to "barriers", disclose their perceived functions, purposes, and consequences, and divulge particular ideological alliances. As the barrier is constructed, its diverging meanings become built into the discursive repertoires of these divided communities.

Within Israel, there are two predominant, yet conflicting, discursive repertoires that pertain to the barrier's function, purpose, and effect. On the one hand is the widely shared "security" discourse, that is informed by the rise of right-wing ideologies since the 1970s, and is sustained by the philosophical tenants of the political party Likud and settlers' interest groups, such as the Yesha Council and Gush Emunim.[3] Accordingly, concerns about Israel's security and sustainability as a Jewish state in a "bad neighborhood" (Interview DI) predominate. On the other hand, the "peace camp", which is represented by such non-governmental organizations (NGOs) such as Peace Now, B'Tselem, and Ir Amin[4] provide an alternative discursive repertoire. They are concerned with such issues as finding a peaceful resolution to the Israeli–Palestinian conflict, Israel's compliance with international law, and the humanitarian impact of the barrier. These two political stances of the "right" versus the "left" respectively, inform whether the barrier is understood as manifesting either Israel's security policy or its occupation and annexation of Palestinian territories.

In Palestine, the barrier is less of an object of internal political debate. Instead, there is a wide consensus that it functions as a tool of colonization, occupation, annexation and ethnic separation. The International Court of Justices' Advisory Opinion on the "Wall" as illegal also serves as a resource to point to it negative social consequences and its propensity to annex Palestinian land and water resources. Furthermore, the day-to-day impacts of various Israeli closure mechanisms (of which the barrier is an integral part) on Palestinians' livelihood, communities, and freedom of movement provide for shared experiences that inform everyday, academic, and political discourses. In the following I will first focus on how Israelis from the right and from the left political spectrum contest the barriers' function, and account for its construction and purpose.

---

3 For more information concerning the Likud party see https://www.likud.org.il/en/, the Yesha Council http://www.myesha.org.il/ and Gush Emunim http://www.knesset.gov.il/lexicon/eng/gush_em_eng.htm (accessed 4/30/2013).

4 For more information on Peace Now see http://peacenow.org.il/eng/; B'Tselem http://www.btselem.org/; Ir Amin http://eng.ir-amim.org.il/ (accessed 4/30/2013).

Israel's Barrier: Where Security, Demography, and Geography Collide

The Israeli Ministry of Foreign Affairs affirms that 97 percent of the barrier consists of a fence and 3 percent of a concrete wall. While walls were constructed in certain high-density population areas (such as cities or along highways) in order to prevent shooting and sniper attacks, the barrier is mostly a fence system (that is usually 45–70 meters wide including a patrol road, sand tracks, a ditch and outer fencing on each side). For the Israeli government, the purpose of the "fence" "is ... security" and is a direct "response to suicide bombers who enter into Israel", and therefore the "security fence" is allegedly nothing like the Berlin wall (UN OCHA 2007: 46).[5] It is instead presented as a temporary, rather than a permanent defense measure, that can be moved or destroyed after peace negotiations.[6] The Ministry of Foreign Affairs, the mainstream media, and public discourses tend to correlate the construction of the barrier with improved security and feelings of safety within Israel (Bimkom and B'Tselem 2005). According to one politically right-leaning psychologist: "In Israel most of the people will say ... it defends us. Our children are defended ... And statistically it is true" (Interview G).

For another interviewee, Israeli security also trumps any "inconvenience" to Palestinians, as "the fence" "prevents bombers" (Interview WD). When attacks do occur within Israel, they are frequently blamed on the yet unfinished barrier and they generate calls to finish it promptly in order to increase security still more (Interview D). The "security fence" thus "exists as a metaphor in the minds of Israelis, a kind of prophylactic against the HIV of terrorism" (Grant 2004). However, Israeli critics who query their governments' policies and who are often active in "left-wing" NGOs, question the barriers' ability to increase security (Bimkom and B'Tselem 2005). For instance, for one peace activist the claim that "the wall" is about security is "a lie", instead she asserted that it provides a means to annex Palestinian lands (Interview RM). Political preferences and assessments of the barrier's purpose and ability to increase security are thus inevitably entwined. Yet, not only the barriers' effectiveness remains contested, but also its history and function.

The construction of a barrier has long been part of Israeli debates. Original critics, such as former Israeli Prime Minister Ariel Sharon, opposed a barrier for it would divide "Greater Israel" (which includes Israeli and Palestinian lands). However, concerns grew that the rapidly increasing Palestinian population constituted a "demographic time bomb", who may not win the war through military might, but through its fertility rates. Such fears consolidated calls to "disengage and separate" from the Palestinians. These kinds of demographic anxieties have long informed various governmental and settlement policies, that were to "aid Jews in conquering the Promised Land" (Soffer 1989: 91). Yet, when such policies could not tip the demographic imbalance, ideas of ethnic separation and Palestinian autonomy gained currency. In 1989 the demographer Arnon Soffer predicted: "There is no answer other than a territorial solution of one kind or another ... it will be necessary to compromise over the Occupied Territories in Judea, Samaria, and the Gaza Strip" (Soffer 1989: 104). For him, a "hard" border was to not only improve Israel's security, but was also to ensure a Jewish majority within Israel by excluding densely populated Palestinian areas.

---

5   See also Israeli Ministry of Foreign Affairs www.mfg.gov.il (accessed 10/12/2008).

6   For the historical meaning and political consequences of border fences in Israel see Bimkom and B'Tselem 2005; UN OCHA 2007.

It was not until 2002 – the height of the second Intifada[7] – that the then Prime Minister Ariel Sharon succumbed to political pressure to build a "security fence".[8] When complete, the barrier is projected to be 721 km long (of which 525 km is to be within West Bank territory) and will be more than twice as long as the internationally recognized Green Line, the 1949 armistice line, between Israel and the West Bank. While the building and routing of the barrier happened largely "behind closed doors without any possibility of public debate" (B'tselem 2002: 2; 2003), different interest groups nevertheless examined to what extent various factors, other than security, might have determined the barrier's construction and routing. Whilst some cite a range of security, demographic, and topographical issues, others argue that the barrier was constructed so as to annex Palestinian land and water resources, and include Jewish settlements within Israeli territory while excluding densely populated Palestinian areas.[9] Yet others point to legal rulings, political pressure from other countries (notably the United States), Israeli political parties, and lobbies representing Jewish settlers, as well as economic interests of Israeli real-estate developers as having co-determined the barrier's route (Bimkom and B'Tselem 2005; UN OCHA 2007).

Debates about which criteria – security, water aquifers, or settlements – most importantly impacted the routing of the barrier become inevitably entwined with political stances. For many "right-leaning" protagonists the barrier not only signifies an increase in Israel's security, which reflects the shift of Israeli public opinion to the political right after the second Intifada, but also ensures Israel's survival as a Jewish state and assures Jewish land-claims. According to such right-wing expansionist discourses, which seemingly address issues of security, demography and Jewish land claims, the barrier solves various problems: it increases Israel's security and sustainability. Nevertheless, the barrier can rapidly become mired in controversy. Various Israeli, Palestinian, and international interest groups argue that, not security imperatives, but other factors, including economic, demographic and territorial interests co-determined the construction and routing of the barrier. While the predominant "security discourse" inside Israel can quickly yield to political disagreements, Palestinian observers construct the barriers' meanings and consequences in vastly different ways.

Palestinians Encircled by a Wall System

Palestinians, like Israelis, use various terms to refer to the barrier. However, unlike Israelis, who express their political polarization by referring to it as either a "fence" or a "wall", for Palestinians the wall is never a fence, but always a "wall".[10] The "wall" is the summation of various other exclusionary Israeli policies and is part of an extensive "wall system". Exclusionary policies include restrictive permit systems that are administered by the Civil Administration's District Coordination and Liaison Office (DCL) that regulates Palestinians access to Israel and movement across the West Bank. Magnetic cards that allow bearers to enter Israel require special security clearance; identity cards, blue for Israelis, and orange or green for Palestinians, are also a vital means of identification. Such forms of identification

---

7   The term "intifada" means "shaking", which for many Israelis implies a Palestinian war against Israel, and to Palestinians signifies a popular uprising against an occupying regime (Prime 2003).

8   For a detailed barrier route see http://www.btselem.org/English/Maps/Index.asp (accessed 3/25/2012).

9   For information on Jewish settlements and their legal status see Ayoub 2003; UN OCHA 2007; Gisha (available at http://www.gisha.org, accessed 6/11/2009).

10   For how wall grafitti becomes a form of political activism see Leuenberger 2011b; Peteet 1996.

help govern the populace and administer their movement around the West Bank and into Israel. These kind of bureaucratic hurdles are complemented by a "wall system", that includes (as of 2012) over 530 closure mechanisms,[11] including manned checkpoints, temporary roadblocks and physical obstacles, Israeli-controlled no-go areas, as well as the "Forbidden Road System" (which consists roads primarily for Israeli use to which Palestinian access is regulated or prevented). As a result, the West Bank if fragmented "into a series of Palestinian enclaves. Each Palestinian enclave is geographically separated from the other by some form of Israeli infrastructure including settlements, outposts, military areas, nature reserves and the Barrier" (UN OCHA 2007: 70). The West Bank has thus become "physically partitioned into two separate but overlapping national geographies" and ethno-social spaces (Weizman 2004: 18).[12]

Sociologists of technology have pointed out that for new technologies to be useful, they have to be compatible with already existing technological systems and infrastructures, which inform their design and function (Star 1999). The barrier, too, has been the summation of exclusionary mechanisms, which comprises existing bureaucratic and material barriers, including a "sequence of convoluted boundaries, security apparatuses, and internal checkpoints" inside the West Bank (Weizman 2004: 5; Zink 2009). Its embeddedness within control and closure mechanisms already in place, provides it with its very power to administer population flows.

Interviewees attest to how the "wall system" channels their movements, governs their actions, and administers their everyday activities. A psychologist, who crosses checkpoints daily maintained:

> [we live] in one big prison or several big prisons adjacent to each other … you need a permit to move from one wall to another, from one prison to the other. (Interview AS)

A psychoanalyst also argued that Palestinians experience a constant sense of living "in prisons because they can't move" (Interview H). For an environmental analyst, seeing the wall makes him feel like "I am in a jail" (Interview JI). Similarly, an unemployed nurse stated: "we are living in a prison without a jailer" (Interview N). Such widespread feelings of encirclement are tied to a perceived powerlessness in the face of Israeli policies and military occupation.[13] For one city mayor: "the occupier … wants to control every breath that you are going to take, every single movement, everything – all aspects of life. This is occupation" (Interview J).

For Palestinian interviewees the wall "has nothing to do with security" (Interview AS), but serves as a tool to colonize, annex, segregate, and separate. A psychologist argued that the wall's deviation from the Green Line, its inclusion of Jewish settlements and exclusion of Palestinian population centers, is "everything. Its Apartheid, its separation … and its annexation" (Interview S). For a religious scholar, it is about land grab in line with the "old Zionist position 'maximum land, minimum people'" (Interview AS). For a city mayor, the

---

11 For updates see maps and reports on closures and access, available at UN OCHA http://www.ochaopt.org/maps.aspx?id=106 (accessed 04/27/2013).

12 For how such separate national geographies inform Israeli map-making practices see Leuenberger and Schnell 2010.

13 According to international law, the Palestinian Territories are under Israeli occupation. The Israeli government, however, contends that due to Israel's need for self-defense and its replacement of Jordanian rule over the West Bank, its presence in the West Bank has a unique legal character (Ayoub 2003).

wall and checkpoints, also don't secure, but endanger Palestinians as they are subject to violence, humiliation and aggression. He contended that the barrier cannot secure Israel either as it is built "inside Palestinian territories" (Interview J), placing Palestinians (whom, according to the security rationale, the wall is supposed to exclude) on both sides of the barrier. Also, determined "wall jumpers" can find alternate ways to enter Israel. Even children who live east of the wall in East Jerusalem regularly find ways to avoid checkpoints in order to get to school west of the wall:

> on the way back from school they go through the sewage [system] ... there is a shortcut through the sewage ... there [are] school kids coming from the other side of the wall ... they meet inside the sewage. (Interview AS)

Not only does the wall not provide security, but, according to a professor, it serves: "one side at the complete expense of the other side" (Interview A) as it affects economic, social, and cultural ties between Palestinians across the West Bank. For instance, for West Bank Palestinians, East Jerusalem had been their economic, social and cultural center. The barrier and the concurrent permit regime, however, have severely restricted their access to a range of educational, health care, and religious institutions in Jerusalem. Moreover, as a result of the closures and the West Bank's territorial fragmentation, social contacts inside the Palestinian Territories have been ever harder to maintain. Consequently, traditional social networks weakened, leading to what one professor of education maintained was a loss of "the sense of connectedness, the sense of community, the sense of sharing social, religious and cultural activities" (Interview A). The loosening of social bonds has allegedly gone hand in hand with a rise in atomization and individualism and an upsurge in social problems, crime, and violence in a society that was traditionally maintained and controlled by powerful extended family networks and clans. The territorial fragmentation thereby purportedly challenges the very "essence" of Palestinian society (Interview A). Unlike Jewish Israelis who's support for the barrier tends to be split along political fault lines, Palestinians are inclined to agree that the "wall system" impacts their livelihood, economy, and society negatively. Their experiences of closure mechanisms across the West Bank has provided for a repertoire of common understandings that inform their popular, academic, and political discourses. Within these discourses the barrier signifies a range of social problems ranging from repression, humiliation, and occupation to a profound sense of social, cultural and economic dislocation.

From Mental Walls to Physical Divides

Throughout history, the construction of walls and barriers has usually been the summation of various policy measures that had been provoked by enduring conflicts (Sterling 2009). The West Bank barrier is not only part of an extensive system of exclusionary policies and physical infrastructures, but it is also symptomatic of a long-standing "culture of conflict" (Bar-Tal 2009). Indeed, the barrier has become the very site of its institutionalization and material manifestation. As Peter Berger and Thomas Luckmann (1984) point out, institutionalization provides a way to deal with prevalent issues and problems, yet their sedimentation will make them more resistant to change. Not only has the barrier often not been moved despite court orders to do so, but also, as the politics of the conflict have been designed into its very structure, it is ever harder to overcome its in-built premises of conflict, mutual suspicion, and cultural incommensurability. For a Palestinian psychologist, it is thus less the physical wall that is most consequential for Israeli–Palestinian relations, but what has led to its construction: "the historical conflict and the conflict resolution efforts and the failure of these efforts and all the blood that [flowed] between them" (Interview AS). This long history of conquest, war, and occupation has given rise to damaging ethno-cultural stereotypes and discursive repertoires that are used to reflect on the barrier's structure and social impact. Such categories have also become part of conceptual toolkits used to make sense of the others' actions, behaviors, and intentions.

According to social psychologist Daniel Bar-Tal (2008), homogenizing stereotypes of Arabs have long informed the arts, schoolbooks, as well as the media in Israel. Arabs are frequently portrayed as hostile, barbaric, hateful, bad, primitive, dirty, fanatical, exotic, retrograde, untrustworthy and as endangering the existence of Israel. Also for many Israelis "Palestinians are interested in killing Jews for the sake of killing Jews ..." (Mitchell 2001: 11). Palestinian stereotypes of Israelis are equally widespread, with Israelis often "depicted in the worst language possible" (Sabella 1994). They are portrayed as "vile characters thirsty to kill the Arab ... without any justification" (El-Deek 1994). A Palestinian psychoanalyst also maintained "Palestinians ... never meet a usual Israeli ... they have just met soldiers ... or policeman". As a result, many assume that Israelis are "enemies" that only "terrorize and steal" (Interview H). Also the 2001 Mitchell Report concluded that Palestinians and Israelis:

> expressed concerns about hateful language and images emanating from the other, citing numerous examples of hostile sectarian and ethnic rhetoric in the Palestinian and Israeli media, in school curricula and in statements by religious leaders, politicians and others. (Mitchell 2001: 17)

Both sides have often experienced conflicts over history, land, and its ethnic imprinting[14] on a most personal level. Consequently, not only have "negative psychological projections become the norm" (Sabella 1994), but continuing hostilities have also encouraged distrust and the dehumanization and delegitimization of "the other" (Bar-Tal 2008). An Israeli psychiatrist and human rights activist, who had visited Israeli soldiers and their Lebanese prisoners of war during the first Lebanon war, expressed her concern about the dehumanization of "the other" as follows:

> it is so cold up there ... and those tents [were] open and the wind is [blowing] and the prisoners hardly have a ... cover ... and I said 'how come those prisoners are [in] those conditions? They might freeze to death!' and one of the soldiers told me, in the most sincere way, 'Palestinians – they don't suffer from cold. They are not like us'. (Interview M)

The mounting dehumanization of the other has also led to either side failing to appreciate the others problems, concerns, and suffering (Mitchell 2001). For the Israeli psychiatrist then, it is this "mental wall" that has now become a physical reality (Interview M). Indeed, already in 1923, the Zionist Vladimir Jabotinsky, suggested that Jewish settlers construct an "Iron Wall". The aim was to develop a "strong power in Palestine that is not amenable

---

14 See Adwan and Bar-On 2004; Falah 1996; Klein 2004. For NGOs, that raise awareness about diverse historical narratives, see Zochrot: Remembering (available at http://www.zochrot.org/index.php?lang=english, accessed 10/06/09); Prime: Peace Research Institute in the Middle East (2003).

to any Arab pressure" (Jabotinsky 1923). Rather than negotiate with Arabs, Jews were to disengage from them in order for the Zionist mission to succeed. Treatises, by early Zionists, contemporary politicians, and scholars, have thus pointed to a cultural gulf between Jews and Arabs and hereby also helped to sediment perceptions of socio-cultural differences (Rabinowitz 2010). While the fall of the Berlin Wall in 1989 gave way to what Germans call "the wall in the head" (Leuenberger 2006), in Israel and Palestine, enduring "mental walls" have now sedimented into material structures.

The partitioning of the land through walls, checkpoints and no-go areas, in conjunction with travel restrictions that prevent Palestinians and Israelis from entering each other's territories, channels them into separate, but often parallel ethno-social spaces. Most Israelis (unless they are peace activists or security and military personal serving in the West Bank) don't tend to travel to Palestinian controlled areas as Israeli law prohibits them from doing so. At the same time, Palestinians require special permits to enter Israel or cross Israeli-controlled areas within the West Bank. These closure mechanisms and policies[15] provide various institutionalized spaces in which Israelis and Palestinians may still meet. These interactional and geographical spaces are highly circumscribed. They mainly include potential friction points: such as checkpoints and West Bank areas, where Palestinians don't tend to meet Israeli civilians, but soldiers, police- and military units, and Jewish settlers.

Checkpoints as Spaces of Separation

The most common "contact zone" between Israelis and Palestinians are checkpoints. According to Yehudit Keshet, checkpoints "embody the occupation" (2006: 4; Zureik et al. 2011). They are emblematic of state surveillance and they signify Israeli control of the West Bank. Indeed:

> Israel is best described as the 'state of the checkpoints', the occupied territories are the 'land of the checkpoints', the Israelis the 'owners of the checkpoints', and the Palestinians 'the people of the land of the checkpoints'. (Zureik et al. 2011: 28)

By 2012, there existed within the West Bank over 530 staffed and unstaffed closure mechanisms ranging from roadblocks, fixed and temporary checkpoints, barrier gates, and crossing terminals into Israel. While Palestinians traveling between various Palestinian-controlled areas, may cross manned or temporary roadblocks and checkpoints in order to reach schools, work, medical facilities, or attend social functions, those with permits to enter Israel (and the Israeli-controlled territory between the Green Line and the barrier) will often cross the more modern infrastructurally complex terminals that resemble international border crossings. Such terminals consist of long metal corridors leading to electronic turnstiles. After the first set of turnstiles, queuing continues for more turnstiles after which soldiers in bulletproof cubicles give instructions through microphones to walk through a metal detector and place belongings onto an x-ray machine. Subsequently, attending Israeli soldiers or security guards check permits, IDs and biometric data.

---

15 Closure policies and their associated infrastructures of separation commenced in 1991 and have been continuously reinforced throughout the West Bank since the second Intifada in 2000 (Keshet 2006).

The introduction of technology in the terminals, from scanners, to x-ray machines and biometric cards, appears to be "neutral and scientific" and was intended to humanize the design of the checkpoint (Zureik et al. 2011: 31). However, the technology, such as bulletproof windows separating soldiers or private security guards from checkpoint crossers, embody mistrust and the potential for violence. By designing technology to prevent aggression it becomes the very signifier of conflict, occupation, and power inequities. According to a Palestinian scholar, the interactions at such checkpoints consist of "zero communication". Moreover, it is there that:

> people realize we have this kind of arrangement precisely because of the occupation ... the Palestinian always sees the soldier as soldier – as part of the occupation ... In fact every time you go through the checkpoint it reinforces the feelings, your worldview, your understanding of the occupation. (Interview MAS)

It is these spaces that have become the public theater of the conflict where not individuals, but collectivities, confront each other through bullet-proof windows, where M16s confront "civic resistance", where Palestinian van drivers and porters, at times, resist the occupation by moving the roadblocks at night, where a Palestinian coffee seller refuses the request of an Israeli soldier to provide free coffee (Hammami 2004). The checkpoint, as a stage for "civic resistance", can also turn into the site of violence. During the second Intifada, checkpoints became the public spaces of hostilities and turned into "a factory for suicide bombers" (Reeves 2002). Also Israeli Prime Minister Ehud Olmert commented that roadblocks and checkpoints worsen relations between the two people and can become a "boiling pot that can explode" (Verter 2008). Checkpoints thus become rallying points not only for civic resistance, but, at times, they can also become targets for collective political action.

Checkpoints, as interactional spaces, may not only become the focus of resistance and violence, but more often than not, can also bring about a range of bureaucratic and interactional contingencies,[16] such as unpredictable delays or refusals of passage. According to an Israeli psychiatrist and human rights activist, delays can entail that:

> people can [stand for] hours – half a day with their best clothing and shiny shoes and children ... and they will get dirty and wet – summer or winter, summer from sweating, winter from everything, and schlepping ... heavy things ... the way they will appear after this waiting ... they are looking like trash. (Interview M)

Not only do such situations turn Palestinians into the seemingly dirty and possibly aggressive enemies that have been written about in Israeli textbooks, but the power inequities underlying checkpoint interactions can also become a mechanism for dehumanizing the other. As the Israeli psychiatrist observed: "[the fact that] I can trash you, I have the gun and ... the power – and you don't ... makes you trash" (Interview M). The likelihood for unpredictable, contingent and arbitrary actions and behaviors is all the greater given the kind of security and military personnel that are most often at potential friction points, such as checkpoints: young recruits with no or little experience in conflict management (Mitchell 2001). Instead, for them, checkpoints can provide a chance to test their personal

---

16 See Keshet 2006; Machsomwatch available at http://www.machsomwatch.org/en/reports (accessed 4/30/2010), Physicians for Human Rights available at http://www.phr.org.il/default.asp?PageID=4 (accessed 4/30/2010).

limits far from oversight. Boredom, fear, or peer pressure may impact soldier's judgments, behaviors, and actions (Grant 2003). As "being tough" is frequently associated with a "quiet sector", transgressions can become the norm. While new recruits are frequently overly polite, they quickly learn "how to work at the checkpoint" (Furer 2003). An array of techniques to establish crowd control, including delays, intimidation, humiliations, and violence are likely to ascertain an environment of conformity. Consequently, checkpoint passage, delays, closures, and questioning can be arbitrary.

At remote rural checkpoints in particular, Palestinians fear being humiliated or abused, and therefore often avoid crossing checkpoints altogether. A Palestinian professor recounted that:

> they intend to humiliate you in front of others. They humiliate you in front of your children. So you lose your motherhoods, your parenthood. So the children know you are worthless now because you cannot even protect yourself ... what is fearful is that Israelis are living in a world of impunity. They can do whatever they want ... this is fearful if you know you can do whatever you want and you can get away with it. (Interview A)

Also Israeli human rights organizations have commented on the "culture of impunity" pervading checkpoint interactions and have criticized perpetrators' lack of accountability for transgressions.[17] Likewise, in 2004, Israeli Chief of Staff Gabi Askenazi expressed his concern that "the IDF will lose its humanity because of the continued fighting" (Harel 2008). To be sure, social-psychological experiments ranging from the Stanford Prison experience to the Milgram experiments have revealed how power inequities can often inadvertently impact social relations negatively. Israeli critics are indeed concerned that working at checkpoints may challenge soldiers' ability to adhere to the rules of engagement and can foster behavioral patterns that may be carried into civilian life. Also Israeli soldiers have termed the potential psychological damage incurred from working checkpoints as "checkpoint syndrome" or the "mental scratch", and concerned citizens have expressed trepidations about the occupation's long-term psychological consequences on Israeli society (Furer 2003; Levy 2003).

It is technologically mediated spaces, such as checkpoints, that become sites for potential confrontation, fear, and violence, as the social interactions that they afford, enhance the "othering" of the other. Certainly, as Eyad Hallaq (2003) points out, they "invariably serve to ... increase the space, physically and conceptually, between neighbors". While the technological mediation of mundane interaction often remains unnoticed, the design, operation, and infrastructure of technological systems, nevertheless, crucially mediates and constrains certain forms of interaction. To be sure, checkpoints, as technologically facilitated platforms, enable forms of interaction that reinforce perceptions of power inequity and the threatening potential of "the other". Consequently, Palestinians and Israelis, shielded from each other by bulletproof glass, are likely to continue to perceive the other as a threat to their own security and livelihood.

---

17 See e.g. Yesh Din http://www.yesh-din.org/site/index.php?page=index&lang=en&id= (accessed 4/30/2010); Btselem http://www.btselem.org/English/ (accessed 4/30/2010).

Separation and its Impact on Cross-community Interaction

Not only do Palestinians and Israelis predominantly meet at potential friction points, but the barrier and closure policies have also impacted cross-border cooperation. With the signing of the Oslo Accord in 1993, Israeli, Palestinian and international NGOs increasingly promoted trans-border collaborations. Also the Mitchell Report (2001) recommended cross-community cooperation by non-state actor as a policy towards peace as it tends to increase willingness by both sides to continue dialogue and participate in future projects.[18] However, ever more stringent closure policies have negatively impacted cross-border friendships, professional alliances, and cooperation between Israeli and Palestinian NGO's (Panorama 2007). A Palestinian professor, who had worked with an Israeli colleague maintained that, as a result of the closures, joint projects have become ever more difficult to execute:

> The Israeli occupation policy ... means that, after 2000, they are not allowing Israelis to enter Area A or Area B, the Palestinian controlled areas, ... we [the Palestinians] need permits to go to Israel ... [consequently] on many occasion we met at the checkpoints where [name of Israeli colleague] comes from East Jerusalem side and me from Bethlehem and ... we ask the soldiers if he can step just – bypass 2–3 meters after the post and I approach him and we can meet there and we did some meetings ... discuss business, issues, sign checks, plan programs. (Interview A)

Palestinians need to apply for permits to enter Israel, and Israelis' restricted access to Palestinian-controlled areas within the West Bank, has severely curtailed possible meeting places. Consequently, respondents increasingly rely on virtual forms of communication, ranging from Skype to e-mail, in order to maintain contact and cooperation. Yet, the Palestinian professor explained that, after his Israeli partner developed a debilitating health condition, and face-to-face meetings gave way to virtual communication, something was irretrievably lost:

> I cannot see [him] so we keep communication through email and through phone calls mostly and that actually puts a lot of burden on you ... it dries [up] the relationship ,,, the wall ,,, creates a lot of (distanciation) – the others become far away – you lose the sense of who they are. (Interview A)

While the introduction of the telephone in rural communities did historically unite people in far-flung places, by replacing face-to-face interaction, it could also diminish a sense of community (Fisher 1994). Indeed, the Amish forbid telephone usage in individual homes for fear that their widespread availability could negatively affect their society (Wetmore 2009). Similarly, Palestinians' and Israelis' increasing use of various forms of virtual communication at the expense of face-to-face meetings is frequently experienced as an impoverishment that nonetheless has become a necessity, due to travel restrictions, permit refusals, and checkpoint delays. Yet, various NGO's working towards a peaceful resolution to the Israeli–Palestinian conflict continue to regularly bring together Israeli and Palestinian cultural, academic, and business leaders. Given the restrictive permit regime,

---

18   For information on the willingness of different professional groups to cooperate, and reasons for Palestinians greater reluctance to engage in joint projects, see Panorama 2007.

however, some Palestinian participants often can't attend, and those with permits are frequently delayed at checkpoints. During one such meeting in 2008, a West Bank politician arrived late. She said, what had become a standard expression for anyone trying to cross checkpoints: "the checkpoint was bad this morning". Indeed, while:

> in Britain people ask about the weather ... it's a daily thing ... how's the weather? ... In Palestine they ask about the checkpoint. How was the checkpoint? How was the checkpoint when you came home today? ... It's become like a reference point for our life because ... more than 50 percent of Palestinians go through these checkpoints every single day. (Interview AS)

As a result, Israeli and Palestinian academics, peace activists, and NGO representatives repeatedly point out that the closure policies impact cross-border cooperation to such an extent that it is easier to meet in Turkey, Jordan or Germany. A Palestinian psychoanalyst put it succinctly:

> Even to meet to talk about peace – it is not easy ... how can we encourage people to make peace, to live together, if we are putting all these obstacles and barriers and walls between them? (Interview H)

Conclusion

Policy makers have erected barriers since at least 1990 BCE. Athens's Long Walls, Hadrian's wall, and the Great Wall of China are just a few of the many walls that were built in order to solve regional disputes. Their recent reemergence across the globe as a favored policy to ward off illegal immigrants, control unlawful activities in border areas, calm ethnic tensions, and preempt terrorism make it all the more urgent to evaluate their strategic, social, and cultural consequences. Brent Sterling (2009) points out that, throughout history, such "strategic defense barriers" have had a range of short-term effects. They enabled wall-builders to deter enemies, place field-forces elsewhere, limit their own and increase their attackers' losses, provide them with time to mobilize allied support, enhance their people's sense of security (although as politicians tend to exaggerate a barrier's strength, subjective feelings of security often don't match up with their "objective" ability to provide security), and mark their intentions and territorial claims. Then again, "strategic defense systems" have usually been attacked in the long-run. While they may delay or displace aggression at first, motivated adversaries eventually find other avenues of attack. What is more, with barriers in place, its builders often become complacent. They frequently fail to perceive their own vulnerabilities and they tend to take riskier actions that may exacerbate adversarial relationships. Moreover, already built "strategic defenses" not only tend to hamper peace negotiations (because changing their lines carries political weight and weakened adversaries are less inclined to negotiate), but also, existing barriers frequently remove policy makers' incentives to come up with alternate policies for defense, negotiations and peace.

Nevertheless, given the long history of conflict in the land between the Mediterranean Sea and the Jordan Valley, many Israeli voices make a case for division as essential for eventual rapprochement. As one right-leaning Israeli academic put it:

we don't want them and they don't want us. [There is] a hundred years of hatred ... Let's first have 40 years of separation and peaceful separation ... and [then] we might mingle together. (Interview B)

Also, the Israeli novelist A.B. Yehoshua contends that separation is necessary in order to "distinguish the two people as a necessary preliminary to eventual cohabitation, [and] ... political integration" (Boeri 2003: 53). Yet, the weight of research on the social effects of closure mechanisms as a way to separate people and territories indicate that successful instances of partitions as a form of rapprochement are at best tenuous (Shirlow 2003; Davis 1998; Pain 2000). Historically, defense barriers not only hampered peace-building efforts in the long-term, but they also tended to "agitate rather than soothe relations" (Sterling 2009: 315). Closures and exclusionary mechanisms mostly don't reduce, but create fear, enhance social exclusion, and encourage "mutual suspicion and a profoundly anti-communitarian fortress mentality" (Davis in Pain 2000: 371). Indeed, segregation enforced by visible security measures, humans or non-humans, ranging from security guards, watchtowers to barriers, have often not deterred aggression, but become the very site of tension, crime, and attacks toward the other side. Israel's secret service Shin Bet has also pointed out that the "fence" creates hostilities and fuels attacks (Haaretz 2008). Moreover, the barrier becomes the emblem of the conflict. While for Israelis, the wall conceals the "other" and becomes "a symbol and realization of the impossibility of identifying with Palestinians" (Marton and Baum 2005: 216), for Palestinians, it becomes the menacing symbol of Israeli domination and ill intentions. In Ireland, too, the walls (known as the Peace Lines) have reconfigured social relations. While social groups, that didn't sever, but maintained, social ties to people from the other side were generally less fearful of the other and did not display "ethnosectarian" consciousness and animosities, for most people the walls have become "the malevolent face of the people who live on the other side" (Shirlow 2003: 81).

Yet the effects of technologies of closures are intimately linked to the meanings they acquire. To be sure, the West Bank barrier embodies various meanings and signifies different social problems for diverse social groups. The terms used to describe the barrier hereby speak to the many ways in which it can be understood. Indeed, it is a "wall" that infringes international and human rights law, a "fence" that increases Israel's security, or a "colonization wall" that annexes Palestinian lands. But walls matter only because we make them matter. The walls' various meanings – ranging from exclusion, defense, security, domination, annexation to repression, become enacted and maintained daily. It is not their materiality that inherently excludes or separates; rather it is policies and social practices that enforce their intended social effect. Consequently, the materiality of borders and border regions is only significant in terms of the ways bordering practices are performed. The fact that Palestinians and Israelis meet mainly at potential friction points, such as checkpoints, and are increasingly unable to engage in cross-border cooperation reinforces the cultural gulf between them. The policy of separation and its material manifestation in walls and fences therefore enables and constrains certain types of social practices and interactions that tend to maintain, institutionalize, and legitimize long-standing mistrust, hostility, and animosity between the two sides. It also fosters perceptions of difference in communities on either side. Narratives about "others" on the alternate side of the barrier being different from "us" on this side, whether they are Bedouins, West Bank or Gaza Palestinians, Israeli Arabs or Jewish Israelis, have become ever more widespread.

Closure technologies are not only enacted and performed, but they also embody certain technical, economic, organizational, political, and cultural aspects. Indeed in order "to predict the influence of a given technology on a society" we need "a good theory of how that society works" (Pfaffenberger 1990: 396). The socio-cultural environment can impact the design and dominant meaning of the technology. The building of a barrier as a response to a "culture of conflict" not only effects a rival's understanding of its adversaries' intentions, but certain social concerns and political beliefs become built into its very design and function. The social effects, meanings, and consequences of the West Bank barrier are also to be understood as an integral part of a system of exclusionary measures that operate through a range of institutions and practices, ranging from restrictive permit regimes to checkpoints. Nonetheless, policies of separation that are enforced by high technology are fraught with danger:

> As other people recede in physical distance, signals reminding us that they are human become fainter. We are more likely to treat another as an abstraction, a number, a case, which provides for both a greater degree of stereotyping and fantasy and a greater callousness in regard to others' suffering. (Westrum 1991: 269)

The use of technologies such as smart weapons and missile delivery systems in remote theaters of war also create distance between agent and victim, which may lower feelings of responsibility, increase possibilities for technologically mediated crime, and insulate perpetrators from the consequences of their own actions (Warburg 2003; Gusterson 1991; Petley 2003). Closure technologies, too, can produce psychological distancing. Indeed, the West Bank barrier system makes others' individualities socially invisible, yet, at the same time, making them "socially visible" only as part of a collective otherness, that is threatening, unfriendly, and dangerous (Hagan 2008). For a Palestinian environmental analyst, therefore, "this wall is creating a psychological barrier that will last forever between us and the Israelis" (Interview I), not least because the closures make the possibility for rapprochement and for encountering the others' humanness increasingly remote.[19] Yet, for Genghis Khan "the strength of walls depends on the courage of those who guard them" (Sterling 2009: 319). Social practices may maintain the status quo, but they can also mitigate or reimagine certain technical systems. After all, in rural America, the early Model T was frequently used to power washing machines (Kline and Pinch 1996). Maybe walls, and their meanings and functions, can also be reimagined, and practices of exclusion may give way to performances of inclusion. During a political demonstration in 2004 one demonstrator started to climb the wall in Abu Diss.

> The audience gasped in awe as in just a few seconds the courageous climber was standing up on the wall ... After a moment of silence, dozens of people lined up below him and quickly followed his example. Suddenly stripped of a whole layer of beliefs and psychological investments, the massive concrete construction flickered and shifted meaning ... For a brief moment, the wall was just a wall. (Marton and Baum 2005)

---

19 Studies concerned with the long-term effects of exclusionary practices across the globe and in Israel/Palestine in particular point to their propensity to radicalize populations (Bar-Tal 2009; Gamson 1995; Jerusalem Media and Communications Center (JMCC) http://www.jmcc.org/ (accessed 4/30/2010).

References

Adwan, S. and D. Bar-On. 2004. Shared History Project: A PRIME Example of Peace-Building Under Fire, *International Journal of Politics, Culture and Society* 17(3): 513–21.

Alatout, S. 2009. Walls as Technologies of Government: The Double Construction of Geographies of Peace and Conflict in Israeli Politics, 2002–Present, *Annals of the Association of American Geographers* 99(5): 956–68.

Ayoub, N. 2003. The Israeli High Court of Justice and the Palestinian Intifada, Ramallah: Al-Haq – Law in the Service of Man.

Bar-Tal, D. 2008. Das Bild der Araber in der israelisch-jüdischen Gesellschaft, in *Zwischen Anti-semitismus und Islamophobie: Vorurteile und Projektionen in Europa und Nahost* edited by J. Bunzl and A. Senfft, Hamburg, Verlag, 195–227.

Bar-Tal, D. 2009. Open Letter from Daniel Bar-Tal on Gaza War. 16 February.

BBC News. 2006. Israel and the Palestinians: Key terms. October 12. Available at http://news.bbc.co.uk/newswatch/ukfs/hi/newsid_6040000/newsid_6044000/6044090.stm#barrier (accessed 06/10/2009).

BBC News. 2009. Israel: "No need to finish" West Bank barrier, May 19 (accessed 5/29/2009).

Berger, P., T. Luckmann. 1984. *The Social Construction of Reality: A Treatise in the Sociology of Knowledge*, London, Penguin.

Bijker, W.E., T.P. Hughes, T.J. Pinch (eds). 1987. *The Social Construction of Technological Systems: New Directions in the Sociology and History of Technology*, Boston, MIT Press.

Bimkom and B'Tselem. 2005. Under the Guise of Security: Routing the Separation Barrier to Enable the Expansion of Israeli Settlements in the West Bank, Jerusalem, Bimkom and B'Tselem.

Boeri, S. 2003. Border-Syndrome: Notes for a Research Program, in *Territories* edited by A. Franke, E. Weizman, S. Boeri, R. Segal, Berlin, K.W. and Verlag der Buchhandlung Walter König.

Borger, J. 2007. Security fences or barriers to peace? *The Guardian*, April 24.

Brunet-Jailly, E. 2011. Special Section: Borders, Borderlands and Theory: An Introduction, *Geopolitics* 16(1): 1–6.

B'Tselem: The Israeli Information Center for Human Rights in the Occupied Territories. 2002. The Separation Barrier: Position Paper September 2002, Jerusalem, B'Tselem.

Caldeira, T.P.R. 1996. Building Up Walls. The New Pattern of Spatial Segregation in Sao Paulo, *International Social Science Journal* 48/1(147): 55–66.

Davis, M. 2003. Beyond Blade Runner: Urban Control. The Ecology of Fear, *Criminal Perspectives: Essential Readings* 23 (Open Magazine Pamphlet Series): 527–41.

El-Deek, J. 1994. The Image of the Israeli: Its Evolution in the Palestinian Mind, *Palestine-Israel Journal: Psychological Dimensions of the Conflict* 1(4), available at http://www.pij.org/index.php (accessed 5/2/2010).

Falah, G. 1996. The 1948 Israel–Palestinian War and its Aftermath: The Transformation and De-Signification of Palestine's Cultural Landscape, *Annals of the Association of American Geographers* 86(2): 256–85.

Fisher, S.C. 1994. *America Calling: A Social History of the Telephone to 1940*, Berkeley, University of California Press.

Furer, L.R. 2003. Checkpoint Syndrome, *If Americans Knew*, available at http://www.ifamericansknew.org/cur_sit/checkpoints-articles.html (accessed 5/18/2009).

Gamson, W.A. 1995. Hiroshima, the Holocaust, and the Politics of Exclusion: 1994 Presidential Address, *American Sociological Review* 60(1): 1–20.

Grant, L. 2003. What the war does to us, *The Guardian*, November 29.
Gusterson, H. 1991. Nuclear War, the Gulf War, and the Disappearing Body, *Journal of Urban and Cultural Studies* 2(1): 28–39.
Haaretz, 2008. Shin Bet: Separation Fence Fueling Attacks by Easy Jerusalem Arabs, *Haaretz*, September 24.
Hagan, J., W. Rymond-Richmond. 2008. The Collective Dynamics of Racial Dehumanization and Genocidal Victimization in Darfur, *American Sociological Review* 73(6): 875–902.
Hallaq, E. 2003. An Epidemic of Violence, *Palestine-Israel Journal: Two Traumatized Societies*, 10/4, available at http://www.pij.org/index.php (accessed 1/21/2009).
Hammami, R. 2004. On the Importance of Thugs: The Moral Economy of a Checkpoint, *Middle East Report* 231: 26–34.
Harel, A. 2008. Analysis: Israeli security forces losing control in the West Bank, *Haaretz*, July 30.
Holstein, J.A. and J.F. Gubrium. 2000. A Constructivist Analytics for Social problems, in *Challenges and Choices: Constructivist Perspectives on Social Problems* edited by J. Holstein and G. Miller, Hawthorne, Aldine de Gruyter, 187–208.
International Court of Justice. 2004. *Legal Consequences of the Construction of a Wall in the Occupied Palestinian Territory: Advisory Opinion*, July 9, available at http://www.icj-cij.org/docket/index.php?pr=71&p1=3&p2=1&case=131&p3=6 (accessed 11/06/2009).
Jabotinsky, V. 1923. *The Iron Wall*, available at http://webcache.googleusercontent.com/search?q=cache:xJZYWrMsMZ4J:www.informationclearinghouse.info/article14801.htm+jabotinsky+iron+wall&cd=5&hl=en&ct=clnk&gl=us&source=www.google.com (accessed 7/23/2011).
Keshet, Y.K. 2006. *Checkpoint Watch: Testimonies from Occupied Palestine*, New York, Zed Books.
Klein, M. 2004. Jerusalem without East Jerusalemites: The Palestinian as the "Other" in Jerusalem, *The Journal of Israeli History* 23(2): 174–99.
Kline, R. and T. Pinch 1996. Users as Agents of Technological Change: The Social Construction of the Automobile in the Rural United States, *Technology and Culture* 37: 763–95.
Leuenberger, C. 2006. Constructions of the Berlin Wall: How Material Culture is Used in Psychological Theory, *Social Problems* 53(1), 18–37.
Leuenberger, C., I. Schnell. 2010. The Politics of Maps: Constructing National Territories in Israel, *Social Studies of Science* 40(6): 803–42.
Leuenberger, C. 2011a. From the Berlin Wall to the West Bank Barrier: How Material Objects and Psychological Theories can be Used to Construct Individual and Cultural Traits, in *After the Berlin Wall: Germany and Beyond* edited by K. Gerstenberger, J. Braziel, Palgrave, Macmillan.
Leuenberger, C. 2011b. The West Bank Wall as Canvas: Art and Graffiti in Palestine/Israel, *Palestine–Israel Journal: Jerusalem – In the Eye of the Storm*, 17(1&2), available at http://www.pij.org/details.php?id=1350 (accessed 06/22/2011).
Levy, G. 2003. Daily Dehumanization, *Haaretz*, December 21.
MacKenzie, D. and J. Wajcman (eds). 1999. *The Social Shaping of Technology*, London, Open University Press.
Marton, R. and D. Baum. 2005. Transparent Wall, Opaque Gates, in *Against the Wall* edited by M. Sorkin, New York, The New Press.

Mitchell, G.J. 2001. Sharm El-Sheikh Fact-Finding Committee Report – Mitchell Report (downloadable from http://en.wikipedia.org/wiki/Mitchell Report_%28Arab %E2%80%93Israeli_conflict%29) (accessed 4/24/2010).

Nunez-Neto, B., M.J. Garcia. 2007. Border Security: Barriers Along the U.S. International Border, *CRS Report for Congress*, Washington, DC, Congressional Research Service.

Pain, R. 2000. Place, Social Relations and the Fear of Crime: A Review, *Progress in Human Geography* 24(3): 365–87.

Panorama. 2007. *Mapping of Mainstream Israeli and Palestinian Organizations Willing to Engage in Dialogue*, Jerusalem, Panorama: The Palestinian Center for the Dissemination of Democracy and Community Development.

Paasi, A. 2005. Generations and the "Development" of Border Studies, *Geopolitics* 10: 663–71.

Peteet, J. 1996. The Writing on the Walls: The Graffiti of the Intifada, *Cultural Anthropology* 11(2): 139–59.

Petley, J. 2003. War Without Death: Responses to Distant Suffering, *Journal for Crime, Conflict and the Media* 1(1): 72–85.

Pfaffenberger, B. 1990. The Harsh Facts of Hydraulics: Technology and Society in Sri Lanka's Colonization Schemes, *Technology and Culture* 31(3): 361–97.

Prime: Peace Research Institute in the Middle East. 2003. *Learning Each Other's Historical narrative: Palestinians and Israelis*, Beit Jallah, PNA: A Prime Publication.

Rabinowitz, D. 2010. Oriental Othering and National Identity: A Review of Early Israeli Anthropological Studies of Palestinians, in *Across the Wall: Narratives of Israeli-Palestinian History* edited by I. Pappe, J. Hilal, London, I.B. Tauris, 45–73.

Reeves, P. 2002. Hated checkpoints top list of Palestinian targets in *The Independent*, February 22, available at http://www.independent.co.uk/news/world/middle-east/hated-checkpoints-top-list-of-palestinian-targets-661631.html (accessed 5/16/2009).

Rosiere, S. 2011. Teichnopolitics: The Politics of Border Closure, *Si Somos Americanos. Revista de Estudios Transfronterizoa* XI/1: 151–93.

Sabella, B. 1994. Palestinian–Israeli Enmity: The Process of Transformation, *Palestine-Israel Journal: Psychological Dimensions of the Conflict* 1(4): available at http://www.pij.org/details.php?id=693 (accessed 4/28/2013).

Sassen, S. 2006. *Territory, Authority, Rights: From Medieval to Global Assemblages*, Princeton, Princeton University Press.

Shirlow, P. 2003. "Who Fears to Speak": Fear, Mobility, and Ethno-sectarianism in the Two "Ardoynes", *The Global Review of Ethnopolitics* 3(1): 76–91.

Soffer, A. 1989. Demography and The Shaping of Israel's Borders, *Contemporary Jewry* 10(2): 91–105.

Star, Susan Leigh. 1999. The Ethnography of Infrastructure, *American Behavioral Scientist* 43(3): 377–91.

Sterling, B.L. 2009. *Do Good Fences Make Good Neighbors? What History Teaches Us about Strategic Barriers and International Security*, Washington, DC, Georgetown University Press.

UN OCHA. 2007. *The Humanitarian Impact on Palestinians of Israeli Settlements and other Infrastructure in the West Bank*, Jerusalem, UN OCHA.

Verter, Y. 2008. PM to IDF commanders: Think of Palestinian suffering at roadblocks, *Haaretz*, November 4.

Warburg, J.P. 2003. The age of meta-war: the distancing effects of techno-weaponry and a sanitized global media are altering the structural basis of modern warfare, *Arena*

Magazine, April 1, available at http://www.arena.org.au/2003/04/the-age-of-meta-war/ (accessed 4/30/2010).

Weizman, E. 2004. The Geometry of Occupation, Centre of Contemporary Culture of Barcelona, conference lecture at the cycle "Borders". CCCB, March 1, available at http://www.cccb.org/en/edicio_digital-selection_of_texts_on_public_space_and_ the_city_made_available_from_its_documentary_collection-10392.

Westrum, R. 1991. *Technologies and Society: The Shaping of People and Things*, Belmont Ca, Wadsworth.

Wetmore, J.M. 2009. Amish Technology: Reinforcing Values and Building Community, in *Technology and Society: Building Our Sociotechnical Future* edited by D.G. Johnson, J.M. Wetmore, Boston, MIT Press, 297–318.

Winner, L. 1986. Do Artifacts have Politics, in *The Whale and the Reactor: a Search for Limits in an Age of High Technology*, Chicago, University of Chicago Press, 19–39.

Zink, V. 2009. A Quiet Transfer: The Judaization of Jerusalem, *Contemporary Arab Affairs* 2(1): 122–33.

Zureik, E., D. Lyon, and Y. Abu-Laban (eds). 2010. *Surveillance and Control in Israel/ Palestine: Population, Territory and Power*, London, Routledge.

Chapter 14
Towards a High-Tech "Limes" on the Edges of Europe? Managing the External Borders of the European Union

Vincent Boulanin and Renaud Bellais

Introduction

The increase in human and economic flows that characterizes globalization is pushing states to reconsider their traditional border management policies according to the following contradiction. In an economic context where the economic success of a state is closely related to its participation in free trade, the permeability of its borders to flows of goods and people is essential. On the other hand, security considerations related to terrorism, organized crime or illegal immigration invite states to seal their borders by increasing controls.

The position of the European Union (EU) illustrates this dilemma. The desire to control the "illegal" flow of people or goods seems inconsistent with the desire to remove border control protocols to boost trade inside and outside the Union. With the creation of the Schengen zone, EU member states chose on the one hand to abolish borders between them to facilitate the free movement of goods and people and, on the other, to entrust the EU with the responsibility to strengthen the Union's external borders. The rise of border management at the community level materialized concretely with the creation of a dedicated institution, a border management agency, named Frontex.

The following chapter proposes to uncover the constitutive logic and driving strategy of the EU's external border control policy by articulating the research question in two dimensions. First, we propose to use the literature on international public goods to analyse and question the creation of Frontex as the outcome of a collective policy. The issue here is whether Frontex is adequately conceived and equipped to deal with its mission. This analysis will lead us in the second section to question why technology plays a central role in the EU's strategy to counter illegal immigration and illicit trafficking. This study emphasizes the role of the industry in shaping the very technical dimension of the EU's security and border control strategy and, more broadly, the impact of technology on the border as both a tool and as a space of political control.

Undertaking Border Management at the European Level

If external security is the responsibility of national states, the increase in human and economic flows makes the national level less and less relevant to control flows at political borders. Socio-economic dynamics have led national administrations to rethink border management as an international public good at the European scale, hence the development of a regional agency named Frontex.

Border Management as an International Public Good

In a pure Hobbesian tradition, assuring security is the first *raison d'être* of the modern state. The provision of security (not only military, but also economic or social) in modern states has been historically structured with a strong division between the inside and the outside. As Freund puts it (Freund 1965: 40),

> the specific purpose of the political or the common good consists on the one hand in strengthening of external relations, which corresponds to the safety and protection according to Hobbes and the other in maintaining order and the establishment of reasonable living conditions, which corresponds to inner peace in the prosperity according to Hobbes.

From that perspective, the border, as geographical and political marking of sovereignty, is a key component in the definition of a political entity, and border security and border control are key concerns to the survival this political entity.

From the point of view of economic theory, border security can be seen as a public good. A public good is distinguished from private goods by two main criteria: non-rivalry and non-exclusion (Samuelson 1954). A good is "rival" when its purchase or use by a person permanently excludes any other use by another person. A public good such as external security can, however, be consumed by as many people as there are potential users, at no additional cost. A good is said to be "non-exclusive" when its owner cannot prevent or exclude another economic agent who refuses to pay the required price from using this good. Both criteria correspond to border management. Once set up, border management benefits all people living in a given territory at the same level; and it is difficult, if such a good is privately provided, to force people to pay a price in return.

When these two criteria are met (or even when one of them is present), it is very likely that market mechanisms fail to supply such goods. As noted by the Greffe (1994: 20), one needs then "to mobilize an entrepreneur of a rather special type, one who will agree to invest in only public interest, even at a loss with the resources it can withdraw resources from other members of the community. This particular entrepreneur is the state". Regarding border security, there is little doubt that such activity belongs to the state's sovereign missions. One could however consider that today national state is not the most or only relevant political level of intervention. However, if one frames border security as an international or transnational public good, other geographical and political levels can be relevant.

A State can focus its control only on its physical borders, but this control will be limited or illusory if a given state is unable to control flows that can pass through the border. With globalization and the improvement of the means of transport, trans-boundary flows are increasing and many of them are driven by dynamics that emerge (far) beyond national borders. One needs to anticipate movements and understand them as a whole, especially when it concerns illegal trafficking. Border control related to illegal trafficking can presuppose a change of scale in the response, from the national to the regional level.

For example in the area of commercial goods, increasing flows makes it more difficult to preserve intellectual property rights – conventional means of control are not sufficient to counter the violations of these rights (European Commission 2010). An effective strategy requires a change of scale, allowing an increase in collective resources as well as a better understanding of the phenomenon, in particular to avoid circumvention of border control policies. Speaking of circumvention strategies, illegal immigration represents a very problematic issue particularly because of the risks taken by immigrants to cross borders.

Table 14.1 **Illegal immigration in Europe (detections or cases as reported by Member States)**

	2009	2010	2011	2012	2013
Clandestine entries at BCPs	700	242	282	599	599
Illegal entries between BCPs	82,368	104,056	141,051	72,437	107,360
Facilitators	6936	8629	6957	7720	6902

Note: BCP = border-crossing point.
Source: Frontex, *FRAN Quarterly*, issues from July 2010 to April 2014, Warsaw.

The Frontex statistics above show that circumvention of barriers is massive and growing. Attempts to cross official points of entry are of marginal concern since the main flows of illegal trafficking pass between these entry points of the borders, where barriers are weaker.

As the flow of mass immigration penetrates though "weakness points" on territories such isolated islands located near areas of emigration (e.g. Canary Islands, Malta, Greek islands, Italian islands), European states are inclined to look for new approaches to monitor these areas as well as adapt barriers and border policies, especially in cooperation with other states. Recent events shed light on the importance of greater transnational cooperation. Over the period from 1 January to 13 February 2011, approximately 5,526 migrants arrived on the Italian island of Lampedusa, off the coast of Tunisia.

Not only are local (or national) resources insufficient to deal with such flows, but also the structuring of policies on a national grid does not enable tailored responses to changes in migration flows because the information arrives too late to allow national border authorities to anticipate these changes. Between the discovery of potential immigrants in the national political space and the implementation of response, time is often too short for effective action. To anticipate these flows states have to elevate their actions of border control beyond the national border and engage a more internationalized policy in cooperation with other states, be it other hosting countries or those countries that are starting points of emigration (Frontex 2010a).

The inadequacy of national frameworks to deal with massive immigration and various forms of trafficking leads to a reconsideration of the need of control in a broader perspective, that is, at the regional level. This change of perspective invites going beyond the traditional approach to public goods and their related policies by using the concept of regional or international public good. Originally developed by Inge Kaul at the UNDP on issues related to development and health, an international public good is defined as a public good whose social or economic nature goes beyond existing political boundaries (Kaul et al. 2003). It has the same characteristics as the public goods as defined by Samuelson (1954) but it covers a geographical area that goes across national borders, resulting in a regionalization or globalization of the problem and its management. One meets here a major challenge that could be presented as follows: how to assure the optimum supply of border control as an international public good?

Alternative Aggregation Technologies of Public Supply

Because public goods are defined as non-rival and non-exclusive, there is a market failure to provide those goods, as no private agent will be encouraged to produce them. Indeed,

Table 14.2 Alternative aggregation technologies of public supply

Supply technology	Examples
Summation: public good level equals sum of individual contributions	curbing air pollution reducing global warming cataloguing species
Weakest-link: only the smallest effort determines the public good level	containing river blindness maintaining the integrity of networks limiting the spread of insurrections
Best-shot: only the largest effort determines the public goods level	finding a cure for AIDS neutralizing a pest engineering the next green revolution
Weighted sum: each country's contribution can have a different additive impact	cleanup of sulphur emissions monitoring the planet from different vantages controlling a pest

Source: Todd Sandler, *On Financing Global and International Public Goods*, Policy Research Working Papers 2638, Washington, World Bank, July 2001.

if there is no rivalry, it is difficult to set or to justify a price (for lack of balance in the market), and if there is no exclusion it is difficult to charge users – who can act as "free riders". Government intervention solves this problem because of its ability to collect taxes. Therefore the free-riding dilemma no longer exists as state provision, publicly funded through taxes, turns free riders into "forced passengers".

This solution works on a national scale because there is a state structure that can impose consumption by raising taxes. In the case of international public goods this possibility is rarely or never possible in the absence of a supranational government or institution having its own resources. The question then is to understand the economic effectiveness of the different potential collective solutions for supplying an international public good. Cornes and Sandler (1996) present a literature review of different possible production technologies to supply international public goods. Four aggregation technologies of public supply are possible (see Table 14.2 for empirical illustrations).

The first aggregation technology is the summation, where the level of public good results from the sum of the contributions of each state. In this aggregation technology, the risk that states behave as free riders is very high. Due to the lack of supranational structure, there are no incentives for states to provide the optimal level of efforts to deal with flows at the regional level, especially for states that are indirectly exposed. As a result, the level of effort will remain inadequate, sub-optimal to meet the expected outcomes at both national and collective levels. Moreover, this technology does not provide satisfying results due to the difficulties of coordination or lack of will for collective action that combines the efforts of different countries, caused by the absence of a supranational structure to organize them. The solution can be to create an ad hoc multinational structure to make the richest country provide the collective public good.

The second aggregation technology is the weakest link. In this case, the smallest effort made by a country determines the level of effort of other countries. Once again, the level of shared effort may be lower than what is needed to optimally produce the international public good. In addition, the actions and commitments depend solely on the goodwill of contributors. If an agency is set up to channel capacity, its action is limited due to its limited resources or its inability to influence states. However it can improve coordination, which is not the case for the summation, since this dimension has the advantage of being inherently present through this aggregation technology.

The third aggregation technology is the best shot. Here, only the largest effort of production determines the level of public good, i.e. a single country bears most of the effort. It is still likely that the overall level of effort remains below the optimum because that country has little incentive to pay for the others. Production can also be unevenly distributed regionally, since it is in the country's interest to focus its efforts where its interests are. Again, the establishment of a supranational structure is a way to allocate resources efficiently and/or to encourage other countries to contribute. The most involved country has an interest in involving others via the development of partnerships. However, it is very likely that the others will act as free riders.

The fourth aggregation technology is the weighted sum. The contribution of each country may differ depending on its interest in the production of the public good in question. For example, Austria may be indirectly affected by issues related to maritime safety in Europe, but having no navy or coastal areas, this country is less inclined to contribute to a common European policy in this matter than, e.g., Italy and the United Kingdom. The fact that participants have greater benefits than others explains the distortion of efforts. These distortions lead the way once again to free riding because it is very difficult to have a match between the expected utility of one country and its actual level of effort, bringing one back to the difficulties met with the "best shot" technology. Regulation can be implemented if a multinational structure is in place, especially for revealing information on the involvement of countries and the adequacy of their efforts and on the profits they can make on the international public good.

These four aggregation technologies show that the effectiveness of the response depends, in the worst case, on coordination of efforts and, in the best case, on the establishment of a multi-institution or supra-national government to support the provision of international public good.

EU's Institutional Response: The Creation of Frontex

To deal with border management at the EU level, a dedicated agency, Frontex, was set up in 2004. Its mission is to manage operational cooperation at the external borders of the member states of the EU. The Agency's mission is to conduct operations with member states (mainly ensuring the coordination of their operations) and to propose solutions to increase the effectiveness of borders management policies in both defining the required resources at the national level and setting up additional means at the European level.

By construction, Frontex corresponds to the fourth kind of aggregation technology, the weighted sum, enhanced with a (light) supranational coordination. Such institutional creation reflects in a way a non-choice, since member states keep their national policies. Additionally if the need for a collective approach led them to accept a supranational "layer", they have *ab initio* limited the power of this supranational agency over national policies. One can clearly perceive this limitation in the reports of the European Parliament on Frontex, especially when they call for more financial and human resources and greater responsibility for the agency. The budget of Frontex has grown rapidly since its creation and most of its resources are allocated to operations conducted under the auspices of the agency. However it also appears that its means are truly insufficient vis-à-vis the tasks allocated to the agency.

This collective solution is not without consequences for the representation of the strategies to implement. Because of its limited budget, Frontex ends up mainly playing an important role in coordinating responses and defining how to upgrade existing national resources. Being unable to acquire its own surveillance systems and to make decisions that supersede national policies, the agency has positioned itself as very much of a technical advisor vis-à-vis national authorities. Thus Frontex has developed a technocratic vision of border control and leverages on technical and technological standards to influence national border control policies.

As described in its annual report (Frontex 2010b: 3), "FRONTEX's vision is to be the cornerstone of the European concept of integrated border management", focusing on four dimensions:

- Vigilance: intelligence and operational information for a better understanding of border areas;
- Action: playing a key role in the implementation of a "European concept of integrated border management, especially in the field of border control measures;"
- Interoperability: "promoting the harmonization of doctrines, needs, administrative and operational procedures and technical solutions" at the national, European and international level; and,
- Performance: for a greater efficiency of resources.

The definition of standards and upgrading of national resources is indeed the most natural way for Frontex to carry out its missions without questioning the role of the member states. The agency has developed a technology-driven approach that, up to a certain point, resembles the "limes" developed by the Roman Empire, that is, the quest for impassable borders and walls protecting Europe against barbarians.

Such an approach then raises the question of the role of the private industrial sector in providing technical solution for border control and security.

The Defence Industry and the Border Security Agenda of the European Union

The literature on the EU border policy widely acknowledges how technology is meant to be a central component in the approach of the EU regarding border security and border management. That the private industry, and the defence industry in particular, played a key role in shaping the EU agenda on that matter, however, has received less coverage. The following section will present to what extent private industrial actors have been involved in drafting the research agenda of the EU on security, which deals widely with border security.

The Defence Industry, a Privileged Partner in the Security Research Programme of the EU: A Framework of Analysis

The EU's border policy has to be understood in the wider context of the EU's security policy. It is indeed linked on the agenda of the Union to the deployment of a (in)securitization process that establishes a continuum between terrorism, organized crime and illegal immigration (Bigo, Tsoukala 2008). The border is considered by member states as a key element of the security architecture of the EU in dealing with these issues. It is in that light that the study opens up the security policy of the EU and its security research programme conducted under the 7th Framework Programme. In order to understand why technology seems to play a central role in the EU's vision of security, one needs to look specifically at the role the defence industry had in the conception and development of this programme. The level of participation of the defence industry in the genesis of the EU's security research programme can be analysed using Charles O. Jones's (1970) sequential analysis of public policies. Jones identifies five stages: the agenda setting, policy formulation/adoption (depicted here as the development of the programme), implementation, evaluation and termination of the programme.[1]

Setting the Agenda

The "agenda setting" stage is the phase during which the needs and the agenda of a policy (here, the research programme) are defined (Muller 2010: 24–5).

In 2003, following the release of its security strategy "For a Secure Europe, in a better world", the European Commission decided to start a research programme on security. In that framework, the Commission gathered a "Group of Personalities", whose role would be to identify the needs and research priorities and make concrete recommendations for the design of the research programme. This group was mainly composed of actors from the defence realm, be they institutional, from the research field, or from industry, including the four main European arms producers (EADS [now Airbus group], BAE Systems, Thales and Finmeccanica) as well as Ericsson, Indra, Siemens and Diehl.[2]

The arms-producing companies have been visibly associated with the agenda setting process and their influence has been remarkable if one considers the recommendations formulated by the Group of Personalities. First, the Group of Personalities clearly promotes "technology" as a central component to the EU's security strategy, "as a force to enable security for Europe". The key argument being the following: "Technology itself cannot guarantee security, but security without the support of technology is impossible" (Group of Personalities 2004: 6). Such promotion of technology is typical of the intellectual paradigm that dominates the defence sector. For example, in the American context in particular, the arms industry offers to respond to each kind of threat with a specific and adapted technology.

Secondly, the report of the Group of Personalities underlines that many possible synergies could be found between the civil industry and the defence industry (Group of Personalities 2004: 12). In terms of industrial know-how, some military technologies have found civilian commercial applications and on the other hand, military network-centric systems are largely developed on civilian commercial technologies. The technological needs of police forces and military forces are also said to be increasingly overlapping (Group of Personalities 2004: 12). The report takes, for instance, the case of UAVs, insinuating that the latter can be used both for border surveillance by customs authorities and crisis management mission or surveillance mission abroad by military forces (ibid.). Announcing that there is more and more of a "continuum" between the technological base of defence and civil security applications, the Group of Personalities recommended the EU support a greater integration of the defence and security technologies, in particular by favouring the

---

1   The last stages are not covered here since the EU security research programme was supposed to come to an end in 2013, that is two years after this chapter was drafted.
2   For a full report on the role of the defence industry in the "Group of Personalities" see: Ben Hayes, *Arming Big Brother*, TNI Briefing Series, 2006/1, Amsterdam, Transnational Institute.

development of sophisticated security goods and services and by taking specific measure to support the European defence industrial base (Group of Personalities 2004: 20).

These recommendations, which are largely favourable to the defence sector, were for the most part retained by the Commission and integrated into a policy paper setting the agenda of the security research programme entitled *Security Research: The Next Steps* (European Commission 2004). The participation of the defence industry in shaping the European programme did not come to an end with the agenda-setting phase. Arms-producing companies took part in developing the research programme itself.

Development of the Programme

The development phase is the stage during which the problem is addressed and methods and solutions to deal with it are designed and promoted (Muller 2010: 24–5).

One of the final recommendations presented by the Group of Personalities in its report was indeed to set up an advisory board, on the model of the Group of Personalities that would supervise the development of the research programme: the European Security Research Advisory Board (ESRAB). The latter would gather 50 actors from the demand and the supply sides to develop the research agenda and supervise the implementation of the research programme according to the roadmap drafted by the Group of Personalities. As for the latter, the private sector side of ESRAB was largely composed of arms-producing companies, mostly those who were part of the Group of Personalities. The recommendations addressed by ESRAB regarding the FP7 were also tainted by a remarkable "defence approach".

For each of the four key security missions identified (protection against terrorism and organized crime; border security; protection of the critical infrastructure; and restoring security in crisis situations), the ESRAB recommended to tailor the research agenda according to a capacity-based approach (ESRAB 2006: 6). This concept was directly borrowed from the defence world. It was first used to describe the shift in the armament doctrine of the US administration in the 1990s following the fall of the Soviet Union. Facing a strategic uncertainty created by the disappearance of a recognizable enemy, the US decided to move from a threat-based approach to a capacity-based approach. Since one cannot predict any clear threat, one needs to prepare for every kind of possible threat. Such an approach has been the object of much criticism, especially in Europe, as its tends to disconnect technological development from actual military "needs" (Desportes 2009) and fuel technologism, i.e. research of a tool for itself independent from the real and identifiable needs of the military. Technological development being turned into a goal in itself, the research and the defence industry are driven by techno-industrialist logic (Galbraith 1978). It could be noted in light of this that ESRAB pointed out two generic objectives: respond to security needs and develop the global competitiveness of European technological supply (ESRAB 2006: 6). Technological development, especially in a transatlantic perspective, was presented as an issue in itself.

Eleven functional capacities have been identified and five of them are particularly of interest regarding border security: detection, identification and authentication; situation awareness, including surveillance; information management; communication; training and exercises. The kinship with the military capacities encapsulated under the acronym C4ISR (Command, Control, Communication, Computer, Intelligence, Surveillance and Reconnaissance) is striking. The technological solutions concerned with these capacities are for a large part born into systems produced for military uses – for example, satellite based surveillance systems, UAVs, secured communication systems, sensors and target reconnaissance systems – highlighting the increasing overlap between defence and civil security needs. Further, ESRAB supports and motivates such integration.

The arms industry's footprint on the development of the research programme is clearly visible. The capacity-based approach that structures the research agenda recalls to a great extent the logic that dominates arms procurement in the USA and the EU. Consequently, it is not fundamentally surprising to note that the actual implementation of the research programme largely benefits arms producers.

Implementation

The implementation phase is the stage during which decisions are made and applied and the means to do so coordinated (Muller 2010: 24–5).

Looking at the various projects funded under the framework of the Preparatory Action for Security Research (PASR 2004–2006) and of the 7th Framework Programme between 2007 and 2009 (although the FP7 goes on until 2013), arms-producing companies seem to have benefited to a great extent from allocated research credits.

As Ben Hayes reported, out of the 24 projects funded under the PASR, 17 were led by companies operating mainly in the defence sector. EADS, BAE Systems, Finmeccanica and Thales, the four companies sitting on the Group of Personalities, were here strongly represented (Hayes, 2004), in particular on key projects.

With projects such as SENTRE[3] (Security Network for Technological Research in Europe) led by the Aerospace and Defence Industry Association of Europe (ASD) and ESSRTRT (European Security: High Level Study of Threat Responses and Relevant Technologies) led by Thales, the arms industry identified and developed under the PASR concrete needs of the security research programme of the FP7. It is also worth mentioning that arms-producing companies led the projects dealing specifically with border security. One could mention here three significant projects:

- STRABORSEC (Standards for Border Security Enhancement) led by Sagem Defense et Sécurité (Safran)[4] proposed to developed technical standards for interoperability in the domain of border security;
- BORDER SECURITY UAV[5] led by Dassault Aviation with the participation of Alenia Aeronautica (Finmeccanica), SAAD and Thales, looked at how to use UAVs for border surveillance;
- SOBCAH (Surveillance of Borders, Coastline and Harbours) led by Galileo Avionica (Finmeccanica) with the participation of Patria, Thales, Indra and Rheinmetall, dealt with the interoperability of the maritime and land surveillance systems.

One can make a similar appraisal by looking at the projects funded under the actual FP7 phase. Even if the ratio of projects led by arms-producing companies is lower than under the PASR, the arms industry remains a pampered beneficiary of the credits allocated up until 2009. Out of the 45 projects funded in 2009, 17 were led by companies operating mainly in the defence realm, and five were led by companies operating mainly in the security sector. The other non-industrial defence related agents, such as the research agencies of the

---

3 ftp://ftp.cordis.europa.eu/pub/fp7/security/docs/sentre_en.pdf.
4 ftp://ftp.cordis.europa.eu/pub/fp7/security/docs/straborsec_en.pdf.
5 ftp://ftp.cordis.europa.eu/pub/fp7/security/docs/bs-uav_en.pdf.

Dutch (TNO) and Swedish (FOI) Ministries of Defence, though not taken into account here, also led significant projects. The border security related projects in the FP7 are also mainly led by arms-producing companies. Without going into detail, one also could refer to projects such as AMASS the automated maritime surveillance systems led by Carl Zeiss, EFFISEC (Efficient Integrated Security Checkpoint) led by Sagem Défense et Sécurité, WIMA²S (Wide Maritime Area Airborne Surveillance) led by Thales.

Using Charles O. Jones's framework of analysis of public policies, it appears clear that the arms industry has played a central role in shaping and monitoring the EU's security research programme. And more importantly for this chapter, arms-producing companies are the first beneficiaries of funding allocated to research on border security. The significant influence of these companies is not really surprising. On the one hand, arms companies already have privileged relations with public authorities, and they benefit from the lack of expertise of the Commission on security issues. As they are already operating security-related activities under the responsibility of Defence Ministries, it is easy for them to appear as natural interlocutors. There is also little doubt that security-related R&D can appear as an alternative funding channel for European arms-producing countries that need to support their defence industrial bases. On the other hand, security markets related to border security or counter-terrorism represent interesting opportunities in the context of a declining defence market.

Impacting the Actual EU Border Control Agenda: The Case of EUROSUR

The case of the European external border surveillance system (EUROSUR) proposed by the Commission in 2008 shows that solutions developed by the defence industry in the framework of the security research programme have largely retained the attention of top-level EU policy makers. EUROSUR, which is still in a project phase, consists of setting up "systems of systems" to monitor and react to illegal immigration and trafficking at the Union's southern and eastern maritime borders and is based on a "situation awareness" model.[6]

Even though the actual proposal of the European Commission does not mention credits allocated to projects under the framework of the security research programme, there is a clear link between the three phases of the EUROSUR project and some solutions developed by arms-producing companies within the FP7.

The first phase, which plans to interconnect and rationalize border surveillance systems at the national level recalls to a great extent the previously mentioned projects STRABORSEC and EFFISEC presented by Sagem Défense et Sécurité, projects which promote the standardization and the integration of biometric identification and surveillance systems. Echoing the WIMA²S project promoted by Dassault Aviation, the second phase on the improvement of the performance of surveillance tools at the EU level clearly forecasts and promotes the use of UAVs even if drones are currently not allowed to fly in European airspace (European Commission, 2008: 8–9). The third phase on the creation of a common monitoring and information-sharing environment for the EU maritime domain appears to be a carbon copy of the OPERAMAR project led by Thales.

The EUROSUR project witnesses the adhesion of the Commission to a technologically driven approach regarding border security that has been clearly promoted by arms-producing companies under the framework of the security research programme. In such a

---

6 http://europa.eu/legislation_summaries/justice_freedom_security/free_movement_of_persons_asylum_immigration/l14579_fr.htm#, accessed on March 3, 2011.

context, it could be relevant to raise the question of whether it would be appropriate to use here the notion of a "security-industrial complex". A proper academic study revisiting and using the theoretical and conceptual contribution on the military–industrial complex on this specific case would be very welcome here.

In the following section we move to another analytical level to show that the solutions proposed by arms-producing companies tend more broadly to deeply modify our relation to borders as space and tools of control.

The Arms Industry's Technological Solutions and Their Implications on Borders

The different technologies promoted by arms-producing companies could be sorted according to various categorization criteria. Here four generic categories have been selected according to their function in the border security apparatus:

- spatial surveillance;
- detection, identification and authentication of flows of goods and people (concerning primarily biometric recognition systems);
- information management (database or information management software that is, for example, used to manage biometric information on migrants);
- integrated systems (systems of systems, combining different functionalities).

All these different kinds of technologies developed for border security and border management are not neutral, whether as geographical elements or as political tools of control. Let us focus on the influence of the surveillance systems and then on the detection, identification and authentication technologies.

Toward a Thickening of the Border, from Border-lines to Border-spaces

The surveillance technologies promoted for border security are said to allow a ubiquitous monitoring of the border, i.e. monitoring the border to its full length and depth.

In that perspective, the EU-funded research project TALOS offers the development of an automated surveillance system based on UAV and UMV platforms that would open the way to the creation of a virtual barrier. The idea is that authorities could remotely follow and stop illegal or unauthorized passage at the border, anywhere on the border and at any time, in particular, in deserted areas or regions difficult to access. That is, such automated systems tend to dematerialize the border as a physical line and barrier (i.e. no need to raise walls or fences) to better reaffirm symbolically the border's presence. With these systems there should be no grey zone, spatial discontinuities in the political and territorial marking. The border as a spatial marking between an inside and an outside should be ultimately monitored.

The question of whether these surveillance systems are really efficient and useful could, however, could also be raised. The world of military technologies has shown that every new technological *dispositif* (apparatus) calls for new bypass methods, and that concrete use of the technologies contradicts the original objective. As Hélène Perrin reported, the development of high-tech surveillance systems at the US–Mexican border, has paradoxically reinforced, instead of reduced, the role of migrant smugglers on illegal immigration. As it is more difficult to cross the border now, illegal immigrants to the US have become more dependent on smugglers, who are the experts in bypassing the security systems (Pellerin 2004: 81). Moreover, it has been argued that if surveillance systems can be used to prevent humanitarian catastrophes – e.g. locating and intercepting makeshift boats used by migrants to cross the Mediterranean before they sink – then these systems encourage migrants to take more risks in more dangerous itineraries via unmonitored routes.

The thickening of the border is another geographical implication of the surveillance solution put forward by arms-producing companies. The various surveillance systems they developed for air, land or maritime monitoring in defence settings tend to develop, extend and grade spatially the border as the point of control. With these systems, border control and monitoring, especially with the use of drones or satellites, are no longer limited to borderlines *per se*, but extended to border-spaces or buffer zones.

The case of the southern EU maritime border is here an interesting case. Spain acquired a surveillance system called SIVE (*Sistem Ingrado de Viligancia* or the Integrated External Surveillance System) to detect boats of migrants off African shores. This is an example of an increasing distancing and thus re-territorialization of border control. Such a system allows states to go beyond the traditional legal and territorial frameworks of border control. With this system surveillance is carried out at different levels and in different layers: surveillance starts already in the country of departure of the migrants or traffickers and moves to the actual border of the monitoring country to end inside its national territory.

One could pinpoint that this logic of the re-territorialization of border control is not only the consequence of technological evolution. It is a strategy more widely supported by the EU and its member states. For example, under the supervision of Frontex, a Rapid Border Intervention Team operates directly in the territorial water of Mauritania and Senegal. More broadly, the EU tends to outsource its border control by inviting transit or departure countries to contain the flows at the source. The case of Morocco is a good example here (Belguendouz 2005). The EU funds, trains and equips Morocco border officials in order to share the burden of its immigration control policy directly with North African countries.

While the surveillance technologies focus on borders as space and tools of control, the detection, identification and authentication technologies propose to control the flows themselves.

Paradox of the Reaffirmation and Deletion of the Border as the Centre of the Dispositif to Deal with Undesirable Flows

Tracing and identification technologies make it possible to monitor directly the flows of goods and people, whether inside or outside the borders. Regarding immigration, biometrics technologies coupled with data management and storage systems offer the ability to distinguish between undesired migrants, potentially risky travellers and "bonafide" travellers – i.e. travellers that do not represent any risk. Data mining on people's pasts (e.g. frequent itineraries, immigration record,[7] foods and habits) or the use of biometry to check body identities allow border control authorities to conduct pro-active and discriminating controls according to risk profiles. Part of the success of these technologies is due to the fact that instead of globally slowing down the circulation of goods and

---

7   The EU has several databases related to immigration: two on entrances and denial of access inside the Schengen area (ISI, SIS II); one on granted and denied visas (VIS); one containing biometrics data on illegal immigrants (EURODAC); and one on the authenticity of travel documents (FADO).

services, they develop different speeds. Controls being more targeted, they affect only certain categories of people.

For Ayse Ceyhan, the success of rapid development of biometrics technologies has to be seen in the wider context of a new form of modernity (Ceyhan 2006), a "liquid modernity", a term originally theorized by Zygmun Bauman (Bauman 2000). This version of modernity challenges the classical political role of borders, causing states to have to deal with contradictory forces in terms of border control. On the one hand, states are invited to open up the border to flows of goods and people as national economies are increasingly interdependent within globalization. On the other hand, security imperatives framed by professional unease call for greater and stronger border control practices. This dilemma appeared clearly in the USA following 9/11. When Washington decided that border control between the USA and Canada should be greatly strengthened for security reasons, the US business sector warned it would negatively impact the free-circulation of goods and thus the commercial balance of the USA inside NAFTA (Ceyhan 2004). In that context, tracing and identification technologies appear to states as highly valuable tools, as they propose to better monitor the flows without turning the border into a indiscriminating watertight wall.

Tracing and identification strategies allow, especially regarding immigration, an upstream selection and identification, directly when a traveller applies for a visa at an embassy or checks in at the airport. These technologies allow states to externalize and distance their border control. The border becomes, then, the last point of control instead of the first. On other hand, tracing and identification technologies also make it possible to identify migrants (e.g. those that have overstayed their visas) and individuals with an at risk profile (e.g. traffickers) inside borders.

With these technologies, the border loses its fundamental functions of filtering and identification point. One ends up facing the following paradox: the reaffirmation of the border in its role of filter fuelled by the increasing securitization of illegal immigration and terrorism requires paradoxically a de-territoralization and virtualization of its control prerogatives. The border ceases to be the centre of the border control apparatus but rather one component of a much broader and dynamic and pro-active *dispositif*. Benjamin Muller argues in light of this that these technologies push a paradigm shift that makes one speak more and more of border management instead of border security (Muller 2010: 8–24).

Border security technologies promoted by arms-producing companies to ensure border security tend to transform the border in contradictory ways. The surveillance technologies propose to monitor and improve the security of borders along their length and depth, making it virtually watertight. Geographically speaking these technologies transform the border into a buffer zone. On the other hand, the tracing and identification technologies make the border thinner for some and thicker for others. With border control being virtualized and developed beyond the actual border checkpoint, the border loses its strategic significance in the security *dispositifs* and tends to be reduced to its primary function of geographic marking.

Conclusion

This chapter has looked at why and how the EU has elaborated a collective policy to manage its external borders. All things considered, it clearly appears that controlling the external border of the EU is considered by EU institutions and the member states as a collective issue that calls for common and coordinated solutions. A mission-based agency, Frontex, was created with that view in mind.

The first part of the chapter has shown however that due to its limited budget and prerogatives, this agency uses mainly technology and technical standards to coordinate and have an impact on national border control policies. This technical "approach" is on the other side supported and reinforced by the significant role played by arms-producing companies under the framework of the EU research programme on security, partly at the request of the European Commission. These companies lobby on the role that their technologies could play to ensure border security. These technologies – whether they are surveillance, identification or detection technologies – could themselves deeply transform the role of the border both as space and as a tool of control, that is, how borders are defined, perceived and managed.

Technology tends to be the central point of the EU's border security *dispositifs*, partly as a consequence of the belief that every security issue can be solved with technical solutions. The central role granted to technology to make the EU's external borders more secure echoes in some way the "limes" strategy of the Roman Empire. As the "limes" of its time, technology is expected to give the EU the ability to have full and encompassing control over the border. The history of the "limes" or other "ligne Maginot" has shown however that this feeling of security is to a great extent illusory and that purely technological solutions do not exist.

References

Bauman, Z. 2000. *Liquid Modernity*, Cambridge, Polity Press.
Belguendouz, A. 2005. Expansion et sous-traitance des logiques d'enfermement de l'Union européenne: l'exemple du Maroc, *Cultures & Conflits*, 57.
Bigo, D., Tsoukala, A. 2008. Understanding (In)security, in *Terror, Insecurity and Liberty* edited by Bigo, D., Tsoukala, A., London, Routledge.
Ceyhan, A. 2004. Sécurité, frontière et surveillance aux États-Unis après le 11 septembre 2001, *Cultures & Conflits*, 53.
Ceyhan, A. 2006. Enjeux d'identification et de surveillance à l'heure de la biométrie, *Cultures & Conflits*, 64.
Cornes, R., Sandler, T. 1996. *The Theory of Externalities, Public Goods and Club Goods*, Cambridge, Cambridge University Press.
Desportes, V. 2009. Armées: "technologisme" ou "juste technologie"?, *Politique étrangère*, 2.
ESRAB. 2006. *Meeting the Challenge, The European Security Research Agenda*, Luxemburg.
European Commission. 2004. *Security Research: The Next Steps*, Brussels, COM (2004)590.
European Commission. 2008. *Examen de la création d'un système européen de surveillance des frontières (EUROSUR)*, Brussels, COM(2008)68.
European Commission. 2010. *Report on EU Customs Enforcement of Intellectual Property Rights 2009*, Brussels, Taxation and Customs UE.
Freund, J. 1965. *Qu'est-ce que la politique?* Paris, Le Seuil.
FRONTEX. 2010. *Annual Report 2009*, Warsaw.
FRONTEX. *FRAN Quarterly*, Warsaw, Risk Analysis Unit, 1, all issues from July 2010 to April 2014.

Galbraith, J.K. 1978. *Le nouvel État industriel, Essai sur le système économique américain*, Paris, Gallimard, 1979.
Greffe, X. 1994. *Économie des politiques publiques*, Paris, Dalloz, Précis.
Group of Personalities. 2004. *Research for a Secure Europe*, Luxemburg.
Hayes, B. 2006. Arming Big Brother, Amsterdam, Transnational Institute, *TNI Briefing Series*, 2006/1.
Jones, C.O. 1970. *An Introduction to the Study of Public Policy*, Belmont, Duxbury Press.
Kaul, I. et al. 2003. *Providing Global Public Goods, Managing Globalization*, New York, Oxford University Press.
Muller, B.J. 2010. *Security, Risk and the Biometric State: Governing Borders and Bodies*, PRIO New Security Studies, New York, Routledge.
Muller, P. 2010. *Les politiques publiques*, Paris, Presses Universitaires de France, Que sais-je?
Pellerin, H. 2004. Une nouvelle économie politique de la frontière, *A contrario*, 2.
Preuss-Lausinotte, S. 2005. L'Union européenne et les technologies de sécurité, *Cultures & Conflits*, 64.
Samuelson, A. 1954. The Pure Theory of Public Expenditures, *Review of Economics and Statistics*, 36(4), 381–9.
Sandler, T. 2001. *On Financing Global and International Public Goods*, Washington, World Bank, Policy Research Working Papers 2638.

Chapter 15
Towards the Wall between Nogales, Arizona and Nogales, Sonora

Irasema Coronado

This chapter unfolds with: (1) an introduction and brief history of the border wall issue; (2) identification and classification of political actors in Nogales, Arizona and Nogales, Sonora; (3) elite responses to the border wall issue; and (4) analysis of bi-national and political dimensions of this issue and its impact on the two communities. Stoddard, Martinez and Martinez Lasso (1979) in their study of El Paso-Cd. Juárez examined public opinion of community leaders vis-à-vis the "tortilla curtain" [the building of a fence between the cities] as well as to determine the bi-national border linkages created around the issue. The authors concluded that although the leaders of El Paso and Cd. Juárez did not agree in their assessment of the Immigration and Naturalization Service (INS) fence project, community leaders did agree that border cooperation is a requisite for the survival of both border communities (Stoddard, Martinez, and Martinez Lasso 1979: 40).

The Nogales, Arizona steel wall was imposed by federal mandate and caused community divisiveness, sectors of Ambos Nogales, supported or bemoaned the steel wall. Broader bilateral issues such as illegal immigration, drug trafficking, environmental problems and border crime, impact border communities in ways unique to them. Leaders in border communities are cognizant of their economic interdependency, especially people in the business sector. Nogales, Arizona's economy relies heavily on Mexican consumers. According to Louis Valdez, Nogales, Arizona's mayor from 1994–1996, 60 percent of sales tax revenue derives from sales to Mexican nationals (Louis Valdez, personal interview, December 5, 1994).

The US experiences anti-immigrant sentiments, periodically, and in the 1980s, these focused on immigrants coming over the border. Ronald Reagan's statement that " we have lost control of our borders" (Martinez 1988: 1) coupled with perception that Mexican immigrants were entering the US to take advantage of social welfare benefits, led to viewing immigration, especially from border regions, as a national security problem. In Nogales, Arizona, however, residents make a clear distinction between illegal immigrants and bona fide shoppers, who enter without legal documents. Nogales, Arizona has the reputation of being the easiest port of entry into the United States without documents, according to Steve McDonald of the US Border Patrol (Steve McDonald, personal interview, October 13, 1993).

Border Wall History

Steve McDonald, Border Patrol (BP) spokesperson justified construction of steel walls: "… this fence is a relatively inexpensive, practical response to issues such as cross-border crime, illegal immigration and drug trafficking" (Brooks 1992: B1). In 1990, San Diego, California erected initial steel reinforcements. Subsequently, San Luis, Nogales, Naco, and Douglas, Arizona were earmarked as recipients of 3.2 meter-tall steel planks to reinforce their chain link fences. In November, 1992, the fence dividing San Luis and Rio Colorado, Sonora and San Luis, Arizona was reinforced with steel mats (Brooks 1992: B1). Active Duty US Marines placed impenetrable, steel planks from Persian Gulf War military operations to reinforce the original chain link fence. This appeared inconsistent with NAFTA's trade openings.

In January 1992, federal law enforcement officials discussed the steel wall construction and the Nogales Chamber of Commerce voiced no opposition to the plan, according to Steve McDonald, the Border Patrol spokesperson (Vandervoet 1993: 1, 14). Fred Johnson, Nogales Chamber of Commerce Executive Director, stated: "… it's an option we could look into depending on how it's done – if it could be cleaned up to something that doesn't look like junkyard fencing" (Brooks 1992: B1). This statement led to criticism of the Chamber of Commerce for simultaneously promoting free trade and building steel walls. By March 1993, viable oppositions organized against and for four miles of steel wall construction in Nogales, Arizona. Residents felt the wall's presence would damage bilateral relationships, prevent existing communication and goodwill in Ambos Nogales and anger Mexicans, stymieing environmental, crime and drug trafficking negotiations. In the US it was also perceived as an aid in ending illegal immigration and crime. Sherrie Nixon, community activist and Democratic Party member, stated it was not a proper way to control illegal immigration and that less drastic, more accessible measures should be taken. Nixon added that this measure went against free trade principles, and could affect the relationship between the two countries. Mexican officials defended the US right to protect its boundaries, but lamented the steel wall construction as an anti-Mexican sentiment and assault on human dignity. Debate was inflamed when rumors surfaced that the steel planks were radioactive, or contaminated by chemical or biological weapons.

In the following section, political actors and their responses to the measure are classified into the following categories regarding steel wall-building in Nogales, Arizona: official proponents, economic antagonists, and national security advocates; and in Nogales, Sonora: diplomatic opponents, unofficial proponents, economic proponents, and security advocates; lastly, human rights advocates against the wall are addressed.

Nogales, Arizona; Official Proponents of the Wall

US Border Patrol (BP)

The US BP was an official proponent of steel reinforcement. Chain link fencing underwent frequent repairs since people found creative ways to cut, tear, or shred it. According to BP spokesperson, Steve McDonald, as quickly as holes were repaired, new ones appeared. Occasionally, holes were so big that cars could cross through. Benny Barron, a US BP agent, said 50 percent of drug shipments entering the US through Mexico are introduced through "holes" and that 70 percent of US illegal aliens, including those incarcerated in US jails, are Mexicans who entered through fencing-holes.[1] For all these reasons, he believed it was necessary to build steel walls to reduce crime and drug trafficking rates (de Viana Amador 1993).

---

1 Statistical verification proved difficult, though Maria Jimenez from American Friends Services Committee (AFSC), claims that only one-third of all illegal aliens enter through southern borders. The remaining two-thirds – "visa abusers" – entered legally but stay with expired visas.

BP agents complained that near the border they risk being hit with rocks thrown by Mexican children, especially from Buenos Aires,[2] and taunting by children sent as pawns by *polleros*[3] in order to distract the agents, and allow flows of illegal aliens to enter. Therefore, BP was an official wall proponent for obvious reasons. However, the wall was not perceived as a panacea to illegal immigration and drug trafficking problems.

US Customs

US Customs was an official proponent of the wall, however Fred Lawrence, local Customs District Director, expressed concern that it would not fully address the problem of illegal immigration and drug trafficking. Between April 2 and April 6, 1993, US Customs maintained surveillance and videotaped three fence-holes in order to count illegal entries during 24-hour periods. Fred Lawrence conducted the survey to increase understanding of the problem. The number of illegal entries varied from 1,199–1,664 during a 24-hour period. According to the newspaper *Nogales International*, Lawrence reiterated that he did not conduct the survey to be critical of the BP or Immigration and Naturalization Service (INS), but "just to say our current system is a farce". Lawrence said additional BP agents were needed, as well as a steel wall. Lawrence added that a steel wall would only slow down illegal immigration (Gómez 1993: 14). US Customs and the BP were competing for both recognition and resources from the federal government in the war against drugs. Officially, US Customs had to support the border fence project since some of the money was channeled through their office.

Immigration and Naturalization Service (INS)

INS was an official proponent of steel wall construction. On April 12, 1994, the newspaper *El Diario de la Frontera* reported that a Nogales, Sonora woman was charged with assaulting a US INS federal officer during illegal entry through a fence-hole. The agent asked the woman to go to back through the hole. She responded that she was coming for shopping. He followed her and grabbed her shoulder, at which point, she turned and slapped him, breaking his glasses and scratching his face. Six other agents came to his aid and were able to finally detain and handcuff the woman, who was taken to Tucson to appear before a federal judge (Ruedaflores 1994: B1).

Such incidents occur frequently, crystallizing the importance people place on shopping in the US, and the necessity of obtaining necessary documents to cross legally. Additionally, according to both the BP and the INS, people who are arrested are processed and quickly returned to their port of entry. Penalties for entering illegally are non-existent; crossers acknowledge they have no documents, are taken to BP for processing and returned to Mexico. The lack of penalty (monetary/detention), the relative ease of US entry through holes, and the difficulty in obtaining a border-crossing card are factors that explain the illegal entry problem. According to Susan Ponce, INS officer for Nogales, Arizona:

---

2 The Buenos Aires Neighborhood Association's position on the border wall issue will be discussed in the second part of this chapter.

3 *Polleros* earn their living by transporting people without documents into the US. *Polleros* have been known to exploit, rob, victimize and abandon many of their clients in the southern Arizona desert, where they perish.

At one time we were able to expedite 30 [border crossing cards] a day, due to limited personnel. Now, we are able to process 100 [border-crossing cards] a day, and in April, we will be able to process more [border-crossing cards], since we will get more staff and will be open longer hours, from 8:00 a.m.–8:00 p.m. (Silva 1993: A1)

The INS, though an official proponent of the wall, acknowledged that issuing border-crossing documents to everyone is bureaucratic and time-consuming and that better, more expeditious service could be provided.

Nogales Police Department

The Nogales Police Department was officially supportive of steel wall construction, but has long criticized BP agents for poorly patrolling the border area, "The new wall alone can't stop crime. What type [of fence] and what material they use is only as good as how well they monitor that area", said Captain Miguel Baldenegro of the Nogales Police Department. Baldenegro added that illegal aliens commit 90 percent of Nogales' crime[4] (Brooks 1992: B1). According to Santa Cruz County Sheriff, Antonio Estrada, 80 percent of the 90 people detained in the county facility at the time of interview were of Mexican origin. The detainees are usually charged with drug trafficking, robbery and assault, usually committed in proximity of the border (Eddie Rosas, personal interview, September 3, 1994).

The Nogales, Arizona Police Chief, Eddie Rosas, believed one way to solve all problems around the fence is for BP to do its job: "It does not matter how big, or strong they make the wall, people will still come through, and one way to make sure that they don't come through is for the BP to patrol the border area" (Eddie Rosas 1994). According to him, the Border Patrol's mission had changed drastically since it was given a lead role in the war on drugs. "Now the BP is rewarded for catching drugs, but see, they have to let the drugs through the fence first, in order for them to make a bust". Eddie Rosas claimed that several times BP was more concerned with detention of drug trafficking than of illegal aliens.

We have called BP often. On some nights, we get a whole lot of illegal people by the railroad tracks waiting for the train to come by to jump on. We can't arrest them because they are not doing anything wrong. We can call the BP five or six times to come pick them up, and they don't show up. Sometimes they tell us that they are too busy waiting for a load.

Rosas added that there were too many agencies and bureaucracies on the border: US Customs, INS, the Border Patrol, the Drug Enforcement Agency (DEA), the Federal Bureau of Investigations (FBI), the Santa Cruz County Sheriff's Department, the Arizona Department of Public Safety, and the Nogales Police Department. "Everyone wants to get credit for catching big loads of drugs and no one wants to work together", he said.

Crime is extremely important in this border community because individuals who commit crimes in either country cross the border, avoiding capture or detention. With increases in drug trafficking, it is common to hear gunshots, day or night, on the border (Buck Clarke, personal interview, May 23, 1995). In an *El Diario de la Frontera* article, the border-region was described as having a "lack of adequate police vigilance, and the anarchy that exists in

---

4   The figure was not confirmed.

that place that is controlled by *polleros* and *malvivientes*[5] (Rivadeneira 1993: A1). Clearly, the border fence crosses an area of high crime, much of which goes unreported.

In summary, federal and local law enforcement agencies, are involved in jurisdictional, bureaucratic and budgetary conflicts over the border. As Eddie Rosas stated, "everyone wants credit for the work that they are doing on the border. By and large, most of the federal and local law enforcement agencies officially support the construction of the steel wall, however, there are unresolved issues and conflicts within the agencies".

Economic Antagonists

Downtown Merchants

Perhaps Arizona's most vocal wall opposition came from downtown merchants, who rely on sales to Mexican nationals. The Downtown Merchants Association included retailers in family-owned and-run businesses. Due to "downtown's" proximity to the border, undocumented people favor businesses there.

Downtown merchants distinguish between illegal immigrants who stay in the US to work and undocumented "shoppers". According to the merchants, undocumented "shoppers" walk through the chain link fence, makes purchases in downtown, and return to Mexico that same day. They claim that the "shopper", employed in Mexico, relies on the US economy to meet basic food and clothing needs because it is less expensive and you can buy better quality items. According to the US BP, 80 percent of the people deported at Nogales, are from Nogales, Sonora (de Viana Amador 1993); merchants reiterated this, bolstering their argument that undocumented people are local.

Downtown merchants and Chamber of Commerce spokespersons expressed the following concerns to the southern Arizona Congressional delegation: (1) shoppers are unable to meet strict INS requirements to obtain border-crossing cards; (2) waiting times to obtain a border-crossing card is approximately nine months, once necessary paperwork is submitted to INS;[6] and (3) bona fide shoppers are consumers-different from illegal aliens-because they return to Mexico.

Downtown merchants recommended expediting the process of obtaining crossing cards; reinforcement of the border wall coupled with the difficulty in obtaining a border-crossing card would adversely impact the city's economy. While undocumented shoppers enter without the benefit of documents, Nogales, Arizona's economic elite does not perceive them as criminals. Rather, they are people who have cash to purchase US consumer goods, contributing to the city's economic wellbeing.

Downtown merchants suggested to INS, BP, and Congressional delegation that BP checkpoints be positioned on Nogales' outskirts, approximately 21 miles out, not downtown. They complained vehemently when BP patrolled close to the fence, causing businesses to lose customers. Nogales, Arizona residents and documented "shoppers"

---

5   *Malvivientes* comes from Spanish words, mal, bad and vivir, to live. Literally translated "bad livers", *malvivientes* includes vagrants, petty criminals, deviants.

6   A special internship program was established in May of 1995, whereby University of Arizona students worked with INS to process applications. The waiting time to obtain a crossing card was reduced to three months. Fred Johnson, Chamber of Commerce Executive Director, and Carlos Ramirez, Assistant Port Director and INS supervisor, termed the internship program a "great success" during interviews.

with cars do not shop downtown, but drive three miles north to a shopping center housing national retail chains.

Downtown merchants were adversely impacted with wall-construction. Their involvement was due to the economic impact on their livelihood. As economic antagonists, they constantly reiterated the "shoppers" financial contribution to Nogales' economy; they said sales declined 90 percent in December 1992 due to import restrictions imposed in Mexico by the Secretaría de Hacienda y Crédito Público. Previously, one could import merchandise worth $200 duty free into Mexico but that amount was reduced to $50. The coupling of the import tax and the steel wall was detrimental to many downtown businesses and subsequently many closed.

In summary, downtown merchants argued for expediting border-crossing cards, border enforcement moving north, free entrance within the city limits without BP harassment and ceasing steel wall construction. The merchant's view of "shoppers" is linked to their mutually beneficial economic relationship. Merchants contended that if INS facilitated the issue of border-crossing cards, the problem of illegal entry by shoppers would be eliminated. The border wall construction would adversely affect people conducting legitimate business in the community. Clearly downtown merchants were motivated by profit, hence, their classification as economic antagonists.

Chamber of Commerce

The Chamber of Commerce, another economic antagonist, initially appeared to support the border wall measure, but later revised their position. Fred Johnson, Chamber of Commerce Executive Director, clarified that he is against illegal immigration and a proponent of expediting border-crossing cards, facilitating legal entry. Johnson, a legal entry advocate, contends that the INS should expedite border-crossing cards. "Until every Mexican national who wants a legal document to enter this country legally, [gets one] not until then, should we put up the steel wall" (Fred Johnson, personal interview, December 12, 1994). The Chamber of Commerce (personal interview, December 12, 1994) proposed the issue of special immigration permits for shoppers as an alternative to the inconvenience of curtailing crossing.

The crux of the issue in Nogales, Arizona became the distinction between bona fide shoppers and illegal immigrant, the Downtown Merchants and the Chamber of Commerce worked jointly to address this. Additionally, the Chamber of Commerce convened business and political leaders and government officials of Ambos Nogales on March 15, 1993 to discuss the issue. In attendance was the former mayor of Nogales, Arizona, José Canchola, and Mario de la Fuente Manríquez, City Council and International Affairs Committee member, simultaneously representing the mayor of Nogales, Sonora. Captain Alfonso Novoa, Director of Public Security for Nogales, Sonora, voiced concern over the limited role that his agents could play in law enforcement activities close to the border "since the area is a federal zone and federal agents should be in charge there". Also in attendance was José Marrufo, a US BP agent who argued that illegal alien and drug trafficking problems had overrun the agency. José Marrufo insisted that the steel wall was necessary and justified and reminded people that in 1957, Congress mandated that the BP would be in charge of maintaining the border, but that the mandate was extremely difficult to meet, therefore the steel wall was required. INS representative, Susan Ponce, stated that she would look into temporary visas enabling undocumented shoppers' legal entry (Silva 1993: A1).

Fred Johnson added that several *maquiladoras* (foreign-owned assembly plants, taking advantage of tax benefits and cheaper Mexican labor) had joined the effort by allowing their workers time off to get documentation together for obtaining their border-crossing cards. These efforts, according to Fred Johnson, were fruitful:

> One of the managers told me that the workers were so grateful for this. One particular woman, after she got her border-crossing card, went up the manager and said 'thank you, now I do not have to suffer the indignities of having to go through the holes with my children, thank you'. (Fred Johnson, personal interview, December 12, 1994)

In summary, the Chamber of Commerce, due to its economic interests lobbied extensively to expedite border-crossing card processing, though they never vocally opposed steel wall construction. Instead they opted to work constructively in order to help people cross the border legally. Additionally, a faction of the Chamber of Commerce was opposed to the wall for aesthetics reasons.

Aesthetically-pleasing Wall Contingency

From the Chamber of Commerce membership a group emanated that were not necessarily opposed to the wall, but concerned with the urban blight eyesore that the rusty steel planks created. This group of people was concerned with the city's image and the tourist reaction to the wall. The Chamber of Commerce and Associated Engineers submitted alternative plans: while still a wall, it was aesthetically pleasing ("No se extenderá" 1993: A3). The wall was far from being "aesthetically pleasing" and this particular group lobbied extensively for an "aesthetically pleasing" fence, one that could perhaps be decorated with flowers, or painted by children on both sides. This group was not opposed to the fence. In December 1993, Hank Tintos, city council member, stated that in the most urban area of the city, the steel wall planks would be replaced with a "more aesthetic fence" (Silva 1993). Victor Sesteaga, also a Nogales city council member wanted "something far more presentable, especially at the port of entry, so that the tourists do not see something so ugly" (Victor Sesteaga 1994).

The aesthetically-pleasing fence was never built, despite the fact that US Customs had received the funding for it; it is not clear why the border fence in the downtown was not beautified. In summary, the "aesthetically pleasing wall contingency" counts among economic antagonists, since members were concerned about the city's image and the effect on tourism.

National Security Advocates

Court Street Neighborhood Association

The Court Street Neighborhood Association was a national security proponent of the steel wall. They are concerned about crime alongside illegal immigration and fully supported construction of a more effective barrier. They are one of the most vociferous organizations voicing concerns about public safety and illegal immigration. The border is close to Court Street, among the oldest residential areas in Nogales, Arizona. Though the border does not cross it, the neighborhood is used as a thoroughfare for those entering illegally. Court Street residents complained repeatedly of people hiding, defecating and urinating in people's yards. Additionally, residents reported burglaries, missing laundry from clothes lines, and entries into homes where only food, clothes and shoes were taken. Dr Mark Silverman headed this organization, a small but loud minority which is racially motivated, according to some observers. "Not only are they against the illegals, they are anti-Mexican as well".[7]

One of the most interesting aspects of the Court Street Neighborhood Association was the fact it built a coalition with the Buenos Aires Neighborhood Group in Nogales, Sonora, despite the fact that the Court Street Neighborhood Association is comprised mostly of upper middle class Anglos and the Buenos Aires Neighborhood is among its city's poorest. Both groups shared similar concerns: crime, intrusions, missing clothes, fear for safety, drug trafficking, and stray bullets and therefore, were able to work together in promotion of the steel wall. Their transcendence of ethnic and economic differences in the promotion of their cause begs further study.

Rio Rico Neighborhood Association

Another vocal organization was the Rio Rico Neighborhood Association. This association, a national security proponent of wall construction was extremely supportive of the wall due to public safety concerns. Rio Rico, Arizona is a predominately Anglo residential area eight miles north of Nogales, Arizona. Homes there are located on large lots. Residents include maquiladora managers who work in Nogales, Sonora. Undocumented immigrants who have successfully evaded Border Patrol agents sometimes walk north through Rio Rico. Residents complained that illegal aliens have broken into their homes. The Justice of the Peace in Santa Cruz County, Mary Helen Maley, stated that "over 50 percent of my case load involves undocumented people. They are not bad people, but in their attempts to try to enter the US without any money they resort to stealing/shoplifting in order to eat" (Mary Helen Maley, personal interview, November 25, 1994). She supported the steel wall "because we needed something, the wall could serve as a barrier to commit crimes, it would keep people out of jail, keeping in mind that the legal can come". Her position reflects the Chamber of Commerce position, of which she was a member.

Ethnic and class divisions indicated that this group is not only anti-Mexican, but also anti-Mexican-American. Several US Customs, INS, and BP agents reside in Rio Rico; residents bus their children to a school 30 miles north to Sahuarita in Pima County, rather than send them to local schools with a predominant Mexican-American student body. The community protested when a lower income development was built on the west side of Rio Rico across Interstate 19. "On the east side, where the Anglos live, is Rio Rico, and on the west side, we call it Rio Pobre[8] that is where the Mexican-Americans live, and of course they are not as well off" (Alma Barajas, personal interview, November 13, 1994). The Rio Rico Neighborhood Association's pro-wall stance and concerns regarding public safety coupled with anti-immigrant sentiments resonated well.

Diplomatic Opponents

Mexican Consulate

Officially, the Mexican Consulate in Nogales, Arizona could not issue a statement opposing the wall. Consular officials immediately informed the Secretaria de Relaciones Exteriores

---

7   This statement was made by two of the interviewees, both Anglo.
8   Translation: Pobre means poor in English.

(SRE) of the impending plan for a steel wall. The Mexican consulate official reiterated commitment to protect Mexicans in the US, and lobbied for cooperation between countries. Privately, the consul did state:

> The border wall issue is a policy of the president of the United States to exclude the immigrant, the Hispanic. The anti-immigration climate is strong especially against the Mexicans; the border is very big. The Border Patrol has only two categories, the Mexican and the Other Than Mexican (OTM). Mexicans do the hard work in this country, picking onions, lettuce, etc.; this enables the growers to make a profit because they hire Mexican workers. The Mexican pays taxes and does not use public services simply because they are afraid of being detected and returned. Mexican labor makes this country great. Additionally, the US wants to enhance trade and sell things to them like hamburgers, televisions, clothes, etc. anything to make a profit for North Americans. You also have to blame the 'Sacadolares';[9] they do not reinvest in the country. (Raúl López Lira, personal interview, May 23, 1995)

The Mexican Consulate in Tucson, Arizona appeared less concerned with protocol. On March 21, 1993, Luis Enrique Castresana, Mexican Consul there, said the wall could affect international relations and that measures were inconsistent with the new trade era that both countries were entering. He added that the INS idea that the wall would help to protect the lives of the undocumented was false (Brooks 1992: 81). The Mexican Consulate, working through diplomatic means, could not officially condemn the US for building the steel wall, since the US is a sovereign nation; their criticism of the wall was tempered. However, in private, Mexican Consulate officials expressed opposition.

Mexican Immigration Service

The official response of the Mexican Immigration Service according to spokesperson, Raúl Ernesto Osete Espinoza de los Monteros, was that the US was a sovereign nation, and therefore, had every right to protect its boundary. Raúl Osete stated that during the expansion of the port of entry in 1994, representatives of US Customs and INS had worked together with his office to expedite the flow of traffic amidst construction. He added that: " ... the INS spokesperson actually came to visit me a few times; we had lunch and I consider her a friend" (Raúl Osete, personal interview, June 6, 1994). He felt that the wall not only served as a physical barrier, but acted as an impediment to good communication and relations between cities, and indeed countries. According to Raúl Osete, "The increase in the flow of illegals through the holes is really only 'local traffic', people who cross daily to shop" (Charles 1993: 3). Raúl Osete demonstrated great sympathy for the local "shopper" because he said they are "usually poor people who just go over to buy milk for their kids".

---

9 Sacadolares means "take out dollars", the term is used to describe Mexicans who make profit in Mexico and invest it in dollars in the US, rather than Mexican banks; this affects the Mexican economy since there is no reinvestment in the country.

Unofficial Proponents

Mexican Customs

All federal Mexican agencies respected the US decision to protect their boundary and simultaneously lamented the construction of the steel wall. As mentioned previously, the Secretaría de Hacienda y Crédito Público [hereafter Mexican Customs] imposed a $50.00 limit on tax-free imports; anyone entering Mexico must pay 32 percent import taxes on pricier purchases. This measure was not well received by Mexican shoppers, especially at Christmas. In December, Mexican workers receive an *aguinaldo*, equivalent to a month's salary. Many look forward to spending their *aguinaldo* in the US. With imposition of the tax, undocumented shoppers who relied on their access to the US economy had to make several trips a day returning to Mexico with only $50 worth of merchandise each time. This policy led to an increase of illegal crossings, not to mention the inconvenience. Downtown merchants provided receipts to customers reflecting a lower price on an item so as to avoid paying a higher import tax for those entering Mexico legally. Mexican Customs agents who customarily collected taxes as well as a *mordida*[10] noticed declines in the amount of duties collected. Returning Mexicans reentered through holes, to circumvent taxes, especially if their purchases exceeded $50.00. Mexicans have relied on televisions, electronics, washers, and refrigerators sold in the US.

People reported assaults during return trips through the holes with their merchandise. Delinquents and bandits would take small televisions, electronics from people circumventing Mexican Customs. Victims were reluctant to report incidents to local authorities for fear they would be arrested for smuggling. In summary, Mexican Customs agents were supportive of the steel wall measure because they would be able to collect duties as well as *mordidas*.

City of Nogales, Sonora Public Security

The city of Nogales public security officials were unofficial wall proponents. Local law enforcement officials were extremely frustrated with the lack of law enforcement in the border region. Just as Nogales, Arizona's police were frustrated with law enforcement personnel at the border, so were counterparts in Nogales, Sonora. According to the local public security spokesperson, the immediate boundary line is considered federal property in Mexico and therefore, the city police have limited jurisdiction in the area. Often *polleros* have assaulted and stolen from desperate immigrants attempting to enter the US. Once in, the *polleros* have led people astray and abandoned them once they pay a fee, sometimes in the middle of the Sonoran Desert. Women sometimes experience sexual violence from *polleros*. Human rights organizations and law enforcement agencies document abuses. However, prosecuting *polleros* is difficult since they use aliases, working through intermediaries to avoid detection. *Bandidos*[11] are another group of delinquents who victimize illegal border-crossers. Often *bandidos* set up a toll entrance at the chain link fence and charge $1.00 or $2.00 for crossing into the US. Should an illegal immigrant not pay the money, he/she is usually beaten or not allowed to cross. Additionally, small time drug dealers conduct

---

10 *Mordida* literally means "a bite", but implies that someone has bribed an official. Border residents refer to "*la mordida*" as a quasi-tax.

11 *Bandidos* do not enter the United States; they rob, extort, and victimize illegal aliens in Mexico.

business near the fence. They entice people who are desperate, and short on funds to take across marijuana or other drugs for $10.00 or $20.00.

Nogales, Sonora public security personnel indicate that people report these incidents, but are unable to make arrests, or enforce laws. Additionally, *bandidos*, *polleros* or drug dealers can cross to the US to avoid apprehension if police are close-by. Law enforcement agencies on both sides expressed frustrations over the unlawfulness in the fence's proximity, and the potential for an international incident such as law enforcement agencies entering another nation's sovereign territory. Therefore, officially, local law enforcement agencies in Nogales, Sonora support reinforcement of the fence to deter crime.

Economic Proponents

Nogales, Sonora Merchants

Nogales, Sonora merchants on the one hand were extremely upset with the construction of the steel wall seeing it as an assault on Mexicans. On the other hand, Nogales, Sonora merchants anxiously awaited the building of the steel wall because store owners would have a captive market and their businesses would flourish. If anyone stood to gain economically from the wall in Nogales, Sonora, it was local businesses. The President of the National Chamber of Commerce in Nogales, Sonora, Francisco Partida Gómez, stated that "the reinforcement of the chain link fence with steel mats will benefit businesses in this city". He added that 80 percent of all businesses in Nogales, Sonora were small businesses, and that only 20 percent of businesses belong to national chains. "The country can be enhanced by shopping here and purchasing national products" (Reyes and Lutz 1993: A5).

Nogales, Sonora residents expressed their concerns that local merchants would take advantage of the situation and increase prices. During Joel Bojórquez's show on Radio XENY, both consumers and business owners called in to express their concerns. Francisco Partida Gómez stated that if Mexican businesses did not provide customers with good products at reasonable prices, the wall would not deter the consumer from entering the US and finding the merchandise he/she wanted at a price they could afford. Partida Gómez was calling on all merchants to not take advantage of the wall issue to increase prices and compromise quality. This was an indication that merchants were taking on a pro-consumer stance and were hoping to lure customers.

Human Rights Organizations

Human rights organizations opposed the steel wall. Southern Arizona Legal Aid Spokesperson, Alma Barajas, was one of the few local voices in Nogales, Arizona expressing opposition to the wall; she claimed the undocumented would be more vulnerable to BP abuses in remote places. Such local voices were not united, nor did they form coalitions. Tucson-based human rights organizations were more often quoted in the press than local groups. Members of La Mesilla Organizing Project, a Tucson-based group documenting civil and human rights violations, Hermanos Contra el Muro,[12] The Border Rights Coalition, etc. were opposed to the wall, but not headquartered in Ambos Nogales.

---

12   Translation: "Brothers Against the Wall".

Jesus Romo Véjar, former Mexican Consulate legal counsel in Nogales, Arizona and a member of Grupo La Mesilla said Mexico was more concerned about "better treatment of its exports than its people" and was responsible for human rights violations. According to him, "the steel wall is in contradiction with the substance of the Free Trade Agreement ..." (Lopez 1993: Al). Jesus Romo mentioned six border patrol agents were under investigation for collaborating with drug traffickers or stealing drugs (de Viana Amador 1993: A10) and believes that the BP is hypocritical because they support the wall, but are involved in drug trafficking.

Except for a few isolated activists in Nogales, Sonora who openly stated that the wall was an insult to human rights, no organized group took an open, formal stance on the issue, locally. The State of Sonora Human Rights Protection office, did not issue statements against the wall; the State's relationship with Arizona is good, with the governors meeting frequently.

Teresa Leal, an independent activist in Nogales, Sonora called for an immediate economic boycott of all Nogales, Arizona business in response to the proposed wall. She stated that "... that way, the businesses and the city hall in Nogales, Arizona would learn how valuable the Mexican really is to their economic livelihood". Maria Guerrero, Partido Revolucionario Institucional (PRI – Institutional Revolutionary Party) member, and Director of Grupo Dignidad[13] did not support the economic boycott because she believed it would affect the poor in Nogales, Sonora. The rich in Nogales, Sonora could buy in local stores, but the poor could not afford their high prices. That bi-national human rights groups were unable to coalesce is interesting – divisiveness in Nogales, Sonora precluded the organization of a viable human rights, bi-national coalition.

In summary, the steel wall issue raised difficult political, economic, and human concerns. That local law enforcement agencies on both sides are rendered ineffective actors is concerning. Competing interests between federal bureaucracies, especially in the US, leads to ineffective policies and rivalries that preclude people from working together to solve immigration, crime and drug-trafficking problems. The economic impact that "shoppers" have on the US economy affects businesses and Nogales' tax base, while adding a burden to the poor who maximize bi-nationally. Simultaneously, Mexican's preference for the US shopping affects Sonoran businesses, and subsequently the Mexican economy, negatively. Border residents holding public and private, political and economic, and social and humanistic viewpoints were divided on the steel wall. The following section focuses on how elites responded.

Nogales, Arizona Elite Responses to the Wall

Juan Lichter

Juan Lichter, city council member, described the steel wall as "una cosa horrorosa para las dos naciones".[14] He added that "illegals" damage the US because they learn to abuse the welfare system. Juan Lichter believes the problem is in Mexico, which should pay better wages and raise the living standards; that way no one will come to the US. According to Lichter, Mexicans emigrate out of need, not desire, or for political reasons. Lichter

---

13 Translation: "Dignity Group".
14 Translation: "A horrible thing for both nations".

emphasized that he did not actively or publicly participate in the wall debate, adding, "There is no greater country than this and we all want to come here" (Juan Lichter, personal interview May 22, 1994). He differentiated between legal immigrants who come to the US to work, and recent arrivals taking advantage of social services. Perhaps his point of view reflects the fact that Lichter's business is not dependent on Mexican shoppers, but influenced by prevailing anti-immigrant sentiment, even while he is an immigrant himself.

Hank Tintos

During the wall debate, Hank Tintos was president of the Nogales-Santa Cruz Chamber of Commerce. Privately, he believed that the wall insulted Mexico, that if you really like your neighbors, you do not put up a steel wall. He reiterated that the wall was conceived by outside forces from Washington, DC. He was part of the aesthetically pleasing fence contingency and met with people from Nogales, Sonora including Mario de la Fuente over the issue.

> I am against the steel wall; even though the safety and well-being of my family is at stake, I am against it. Instead, we need to find common ground solutions; the steel wall is not the solution. We need to increase cooperation between law enforcement agencies, such as Grupo Beta, the Border Patrol; there needs to be better constant communication, and genuine cooperation by both sides. The image of the Border Patrol in Mexico is bad; we all need to work together genuinely and cohesively. (Hank Tintos, personal interview, January 7, 1995)

Hank Tintos' response demonstrates genuine public safety concerns but that border cooperation is important among law enforcement agencies. Publicly, Hank Tintos was not an outspoken critic.

Fred Johnson

Fred Johnson described a community meeting whereby the BP and other federal agencies were soliciting public input on the wall as a pseudo-democratic exercise; community input was not changing the steel wall issue's outcome. Johnson said the meeting was orchestrated by federal agencies in collusion with known community supporters, who controlled the agenda.

> The Board of Supervisors was like a lynch mob group; they shouted at Mayor Canchola and would not let him make a statement at that meeting, because they knew that he was against the steel wall. We tried to organize a group to propose an acceptable alternative, a substantial strong fence that is secure but aesthetically attractive fence that will also provide security. We had over 1,300 signatures on a petition for a better-looking fence. We had a real problem with these rusty lining mats going through the city. We would have a city with a 10-foot wall and pole vaulters and ladder makers. There was also a small group of activists on the east side of the city who were racially and from a security point of view motivated to pursue this (Court Street Neighborhood Association). None of us is supportive of illegal immigration. The meeting ended up being a shouting match, and was quickly adjourned. (Fred Johnson, personal interview, December 12, 1994)

Fred Johnson, an important political actor involved in the wall issue, lobbied extensively to promote legal crossings. His attitude is indicative of a law-abiding advocate working legally to permanently address illegal immigration through issuance of border-crossing cards.

Steve Colantuoni

According to Steve Colantuoni, people in Nogales have a "Mexicancentric" view of immigration while on the East Coast, where he originates, people from Haiti, Cape Verde, Angola, Portugal etc. live, illegally; Colantuoni added that Americans were upset about fraudulent welfare abuse that was sometimes exaggerated and racist. He said countries can only respond to so many people, and that the US has the right to build a wall. Immigrants by nature are not slouches, but motivated people who get up and move – he didn't want to sound like a *pinchi gringo*[15] "I am not stomping down on Mexicans who only want to improve themselves. But I think that Mexicans should go protest their own government, instead of blaming the 'gringos' for being racist" (Steve Colantuoni, personal interview, May 19, 1995).

Colantuoni evoked former governor of Baja California Norte, Ernesto Ruffo's, note that the illegal immigration is not the problem of Americans, but rather of Mexicans since people leave Mexico because of low wages, and a low living standard, compounded by political negligence, corruption, and centralism. Steve Colantuoni concluded by affirming that immigration is good for the country, and noted Mexico's treatment of Guatemalan immigrants.

Steve Colantuoni's position reflects a broader view of the immigration problem: though he supported the wall, he felt Mexico had to address economic and political problems. Steve Colantuoni's job luring transnational corporations to Nogales, Sonora perhaps influences his viewpoint.

Robert Rojas

Robert Rojas, Nogales City Council member, mentioned troubling experiences with the wall.

> At first I was against the wall, as was the city council. Later on I started looking at the community without thinking about myself; I put myself in another position. I needed to speak for the majority. I am the voice of the people – what I hear is what I react to. We realized that we had no process of finding out what the community wanted. I acted for myself and asked the community, the people, 'what do you think about the wall?' I learned that the main reason people supported the wall was for security reasons. We have lived here on the border all of the time; we knew each other. There are 350,000 inhabitants in Nogales, Sonora; we do not know our neighbors. After we voted (against the wall) we got the feedback from the community. The community was for the wall. There was a lot of confusion about our direction on the council; do we change our mind? Are we losing face? We had to because of our constituents. (Robert Rojas, personal interview, December 9, 1994, Nogales, Arizona)

---

15   Translation: "Damned American".

For political reasons, Robert Rojas changed his mind on the wall. He knew that the city would lose sales tax revenue, a serious consideration for him as a city council member, however, he has higher political aspirations and wanted to remain in the voters' good graces.

Mike Hein

Mike Hein was surprised at the intra-ethnic conflicts he found in the community. His experience in an academic environment, which he labeled "politically correct" led him to believe that there would be great affinity between Mexicans and Mexican-Americans. "I found a lot of racism, US Mexican-Americans to Sonorans. I can't believe they refer to them as 'wets'" (Mike Hein, personal interview, December 9, 1994). Mike Hein added that the wall was a "Washington, DC thing", that the city lobbyist there was behind it. He added that US Customs had received a $500,000.00 check for the decorative fence, and was supposed to schedule planning with the Army Corps of Engineers but never did.

Mike Hein's ability to view the border wall issue from a variety of perspectives crystallized the issue's complexity; he was aware of the conflicting emotions that the wall posed.

> People here talked out of all sides of their mouths: 'We do not want to lose sales tax revenue, we want to be reelected, we need shoppers, we want safe neighborhoods, we want the wall, but make it pretty, we don't want the wall because it will offend Mexico, we need the wall to keep out drugs and illegal aliens who abuse social services, and those poor immigrants, they work so hard. We also need to protect crossers [shoppers] from other aliens'. We need the border patrol to effectively control the border, then merchants complain when they patrol in the border area. It was really frustrating to hear all of the inconsistencies. (Mike Hein, personal interview, December 9, 1994)

Mike Hein felt that US government's responsibilities are to protect the border, and that the Mexican government could increase the $50.00 tax-free limit so that people without documents would not have to cross over as often to shop.

Mary Macías

Mary Macías, former mayor of Nogales, Arizona never publicly participated in the debate and her point of view was not reflected in community discourse surrounding the border-wall. "People cross illegally because it is prohibited; people like doing what is not allowed legally; tear down the fence" (Mary Macías, personal interview, December 12, 1994).

Only two respondents in Ambos Nogales suggested the fence be torn down: one was Mary Macías, the other was José López Garcia, in Sonora.

Nogales, Sonora Political Elite Responses

Abraham Zaied

The mayor of Nogales, Sonora during (1994–1997) when the wall was built, was respectful of the US government's decision to build the steel wall. He stated that "it was the right of any nation to protect their boundaries, and if building a wall is what they need to do they should be able to ..." He did not understand why people would enter the country illegally: "our government has worked very hard to create jobs, people should just stay here" (Abraham Zaied, personal interview, January 5, 1995).

Abraham Zaied's opinion regarding the steel wall is reflective of the majority elite response in Nogales, Sonora: US right to protect its boundaries was the usual response during the interview. Disdain for people entering the US illegally was common among elite respondents in Nogales, Sonora – if they were *gente decente*[16] they would cross legally. Zaied mentioned that in order to obtain a crossing card, people must be law-abiding citizens and there were good reasons if a person could not obtain a border-crossing card.

Ana Lilia Gutiérrez

Ana Lilia Gutiérrez, Partido Acción Nacional (PAN – National Action Party) mayoral candidate, and former city council member, said she respected the US's right to protect boundaries. However, she criticized her compatriots asking, "When are these people going to understand that they are not wanted there?" She evoked Proposition 187 and anti-immigrant hysteria in the press/media. Gutierrez commented "of course, the government here is to blame because of the lack of jobs and the low wages". Ana Lilia Gutierrez while criticizing Mexico, bemoaned the people who left.

Daniel Tavares

Former City Council member and PAN activist Daniel Tavares, responded emphatically, "I am not enamored with the US. However, I understand and respect their right to defend their border. Why people would want to go there I do not know, even though some members of my family live there. Why go and subject yourself to abuse?" (Daniel Tavares, personal interview, January 6, 1995).

His response demonstrated deference to the US and reproach for fellow citizens who opted to emigrate. Both Ana Lilia Gutierrez and Daniel Tavares probably reflected the official PAN platform regarding immigration. Their views are very similar to Steve Colantuoni who referred to Ernesto Ruffo's position on illegal immigration – the Mexican political system was to blame.

José López García

José López García's view point on the wall was unlike other response in Nogales, Sonora.

> Here on this border, Mexicans live on one side and Mexicans live on the other side. I think that the Mexicans who live on the other side can help to bring about change on this side. Why is the US building a wall now, if half of Mexico is already there? The US opens its borders when it needs cheap labor. I think that the wall issue has an ideological component to it because the US is beginning to see that they will be unable to control the Mexicans who live in the Southwest. If I had my way I would ensure that the border did not exist, borders should disappear between peoples. (José López García, personal interview, June 1, 1995)

---

16 Translation: "Decent people".

This perspective reflects José López Garcia's bi-national linkages and his global approach to problems. Critical of US foreign policy, he believes that Mexican-Americans are exploited and discriminated against in the US.

Francisco Mendívil

Francisco Mendívil's position vis-à-vis the wall reflected both his business interests and concern for immigrants who rely on work in the US for their livelihood; clearly, he had mixed feelings.

> I see the wall issue as an advantage for our businesses simply because it allows us to sell more in the country. From the point of view of human dignity, it is denigrating. On one hand they want us when they need workers; on the other they stop us at their leisure, open the doors when they want and close them when they want. I think that this situation should be handled by both governments; in the case of Mexico, they should dialogue profoundly and deeply to settle this situation for good. (Francisco Mendívil, personal interview, June 29, 1995)

Héctor Mayer

Héctor Mayer criticized fellow Mexicans for immigrating illegally into the US. He acknowledged that it was difficult for people to find work in Mexico but felt that if they really looked, they could find work. He also felt that people entering illegally were deviants, criminals, or drug traffickers since any law-abiding citizen could obtain border-crossing documents and enter through the front door.

> 'Have you ever tried to immigrate into Mexico?' If you think that entering the US is a complicated matter, you should try immigrating into Mexico. I do not blame the US for building walls; I am sure that if they do nothing, more people from Mexico are going to go there. (Hector Mayer, personal interview, May 8, 1994)

Concluding Analysis

The steel wall issue raised concerns in both communities, reflecting many bi-national dimensions. Though in this research quantification and enumerating public perceptions of the issue is difficult, some generalizations follow. Economic interests divide at the border. In Nogales, Sonora merchants would have an economic advantage because the wall precludes people from entering illegally to shop. Mexican merchants could take advantage of the situation, increasing prices. Nogales, Arizona merchants would lose customers; the city would have less sales tax revenue to collect, and subsequently that shortfall would mean a decrease in city services; ultimately, the steel wall contributed to the partial demise of economic activity downtown and several businesses closed.

The poor in Nogales, Sonora would suffer most since many rely on cheaper US products for their daily consumption. This, in turn, could affect life-quality as they spend more money on less goods shopping in Mexico. Economics aside, many Mexicans saw the wall as an assault on their dignity. People's feelings were hurt that their neighbor would put up a wall to keep them out. While Mexico is at a disadvantage, occupying a subordinate position vis-à-vis the US government, elites generally acknowledged that the US had a legitimate right to build a steel fence and enforce immigration laws.

Anti-immigrant sentiment within Mexico was frequently expressed. Though interviewees acknowledged that people entered the US without legal documents because they needed work, the Mexican elite who held legal documents to cross, could not understand why people could not obtain border-crossing cards. Statements like "As far as I am concerned only criminals and drug dealers go through the holes" or "*la gente decente* have a passport to enter legally", or "people should get necessary paperwork in order" were common.

Obtaining legal documents is costly, time-consuming, and a lengthy process. INS acknowledges their backlog in application processing. Additionally, requirements are difficult for poor people to meet: INS requires proof of mortgage, rent receipts, and checking or savings accounts passbooks which the poor cannot provide. For example, squatters do not own the land they live on and don't pay rent. Since the dwelling is not "theirs", they cannot prove that they own a home, nor do they have rent receipts to demonstrate that they pay rent. Furthermore, in Mexico checking and saving accounts are costly and poor people deal only in cash. Clearly, in US immigration policy, the border-crossing card requirements are oriented towards middle and upper classes, not the poor. Moreover, since there are no penalties for illegally entering and people are willing to be voluntarily deported, the poor would rather put up with potential inconvenience than attempt to meet legal requirements.

Some respondents in Nogales, Sonora indicated that people crossing illegally deserve the ill treatment they get from law enforcement because they broke the law. A few respondents in Mexico defended BP, or INS actions, indicating their job justified it, even when immigrants were abused or beaten. Human rights organizations advocate respecting people's dignity; law enforcement officials can detain and deport suspects while not resorting to bodily force. A contradiction exists within NAFTA; while promoting free movement of goods and services, they prevent the movement of people. Human rights activists predict that with the steel wall, human rights abuses will increase because immigrants will be forced into remote areas. The BP and immigrants will then be in isolated areas where abuses are more likely to occur unreported.

Nogales, Sonora respondents wondered why people want to go to the US in the midst of anti-immigrant sentiment. Other respondents were envious of immigrants because they had the "guts" to leave Mexico, indicating it was only normal to want to migrate to the US. Some classified immigrants as traitors, wondering why they leave to earn dollars. Statements, such as: "immigrants leave just so that they can earn dollars though they compromise their dignity in the process" and "it is not fair; they should stay here and suffer with the rest of us", were common. One source said if anyone was a traitor to the country, it was the *sacadolares*, people with Mexican businesses, who do not reinvest their money in Mexico but deposit it in US or European banks.

Mexican political and economic systems were blamed as the cause for emigration: Mexico's low wages and dim prospects for better lives is responsible. Mexican respondents also defended the US: "The US should not be blamed; Mexico is to blame for the influx of people entering the US". Lupita Aguirre, PRI city council member in Nogales, Sonora, respects the US decision to build a wall, adding, "entering the US illegally is like entering someone's home without permission" (Guadalupe (Lupita) Aguirre, personal interview, June 8, 1995).

Why some choose to emigrate and others do not, is a question that requires substantial research: however, emigration helps Mexico substantially. For example, remittances sent by Mexicans back to Mexico for their families is the third largest source of dollars for the country, thereby helping the economy. México would likely be faced with greater economic and political pressures if emigrants were unable to leave the country. In reality, if Mexicans wanted to improve their life chances, it was much more feasible to emigrate into the US than to challenge or contest existing political and economic structures.

Legalizing crossing into the US by all Mexican nationals might decriminalize the border however, Mexicans employed in the US would still be involved in illegal activity. Mary Helen Maley stated, "There is one thing that needs to occur in order to ensure that the border area is safe; and that is to promote legal crossings by expediting the issuance of border-crossing cards". Yet others feel "expediting" documents can dilute rigorous controls that keep out undesirable people and facilitate the entry of people who could potentially work illegally in the US.

Border residents have differing viewpoints regarding the wall. While people openly state, "None of us is supportive of illegal immigration" (Fred Johnson interview 1994), the wall issue divides the community simply because individuals are personally divided emotionally, economically and nationally. In the same breath, interviewees stated, "the wall is an insult to Mexican people; you can't blame people for coming over here – salaries in Mexico are terrible.

Nonetheless, cross-border cooperation, in the midst of this adversity, is noteworthy. Colonia Buenos Aires residents working with residents of the Court Street and the Rio Rico Neighborhood Associations represents a unique example of grassroots, cross-border cooperation. These three neighborhood associations vehemently supported building the steel wall. Court Street and Rio Rico residents are predominately Anglo and of a higher socio-economic class; Buenos Aires residents are poor Mexicans, many of them lacking basic urban services. Notwithstanding linguistic, ethnic, cultural, and economic differences, these organizations brought attention to the border crime they experience. At the neighbor-to-neighbor level, a better understanding of the complexity of the problem exists than at other levels.

Another example of cross border cooperation and linkages evolved in the following manner: the Downtown Merchants and the Chamber of Commerce lobbied the Arizona Congressional Delegation, the Congressional Delegation requested INS to expedite issuing border-crossing cards, and the Chamber of Commerce asked the Maquiladora Association to give workers time to complete the process. Whether the Maquiladora Association did this to benefit workers or downtown merchants is unclear, but this cooperation benefitted both parties. The wall issue served as a catalyst to promote cross border cooperation.

Interviews

Aguirre, Guadalupe (Lupita). Personal interview, June 8, 1995, Nogales, Sonora.
Barajas, Alma. Personal interview, November 13, 1994, Nogales, Arizona.
Clarke, Buck. Personal interview, May 23,1995, Nogales, Arizona.
Colantuoni, Steve. Personal interview, May 19, 1995, Nogales, Arizona.
Estrada, Antonio (Tony). Personal interview, October 17, 1994, Nogales, Arizona.
Gutierrez, Ana Lilia. Personal interview, January 13, 1995, Nogales, Sonora.
Hein, Mike. Personal interview, December 9, 1994, Nogales, Arizona.
Johnson, Fred. Personal interview, December 12, 1994, Nogales, Arizona.
Lichter, Juan. Personal interview, May 22, 1995, Nogales, Arizona.
Lopez Lira, Raul. Personal interview, May 23, 1995, Nogales, Arizona.

Lopez Garcia, José. Personal interview, June 1, 1995, Nogales, Sonora.
Macias, Mary. Personal interview, December 12, 1994, Nogales, Arizona.
Maley, Mary Helen. Personal interview, November 25, 1994, Nogales, Arizona.
Mayer, Hector. Personal interview, May 8, 1994, Nogales, Sonora.
Mendivil, Francisco. Personal interview, June 29, 1995, Nogales, Sonora.
Osete, Raul. Personal interview, June 6, 1994, Nogales, Sonora.
Partida Gomez, Francisco. Personal interview, January 10, 1995, Nogales, Sonora.
Rojas, Robert. Personal interview, December 9, 1994, Nogales, Arizona.
Rosas, Eddie. Personal interview, September 3, 1994, Nogales, Arizona.
Sesteaga, Victor. Personal interview, December 13, 1994, Nogales, Arizona.
Tavares, Daniel. Personal interview, January 6, 1995, Nogales, Sonora.
Tintos, Hank. Personal interview, January 7, 1995, Nogales, Sonora.
Valdez, Louis. Personal interview, December 5, 1994, Nogales, Arizona.
Zaied, Abraham. Personal interview, January 5, 1995, Nogales, Sonora.

References

Brooks, L. 1992. Steel wall creates own problems at border. *Arizona Daily Star*, March 7, B1.
Charles, R.E. 1993, February 24. Empieza el año y aumentan las deportaciones de EUA. *La Voz del Norte*, p. 3.
de Viana Amador, V.G. 1993. Acusa Romo Véjar a la Patrulla Fronteriza y a la Aduana de los EU de ser Corruptas. *Tribuna del Yaqui*, March 27, A10.
de Viana Amador, V.G. 1993. En un 50 por ciento cruzan cargas de narcóticos por "hoyos" de la línea. *El Imparcial*, June 2.
Gómez, A.P. 1993, April 21. Border Problems: Thousands cross through fence daily. *Nogales International*, p. 14.
Lopez, J.R. 1993. Interesa más a México el comercio que el trato en EU. *Diario de la Frontera*, March 3, Al.
Martinez, O. 1988. *Troublesome Border*. Tucson, AZ: The University of Arizona.
No se extenderá a Nogales, Ariz. La "Operación Bloqueo." 1993, April 30. *El Imparcial*, p. A3.
Reyes, O. and Lutz, R.M. 1993, March 14. Beneficiaría a comerciantes la nueva barda. *El Imparcial*, p. A5.
Rivadeneira, R. 1993, January 31. Problemas en la Línea. *Diario de la Frontera*, p. Al.
Ruedaflores, G. 1994, April 12. Golpea Mexicana a un Border Patrol. *Diario de la Frontera*, p. B1.
Silva, J. 1993, March 16. Oposición comercial a la malla de acero. *Diario de la Frontera*, p. Al.
Silva, J. 1993, October 26. Cambia actitud del SIN en Arizona. Diario de la Frontera. p. Al.
Silva, J. 1993, December 10. Se aprobó el proyecto del cerco ornamental propuesto por la cámara de comercio; inversión de 350 mil dólares. *Diario de la Frontera*, p. Al.
Silva, J. 1994, April 12. Ineficaz el "muro de acero." *Diario de la Frontera*, p. Al.
Stoddard, E.R., Martinez, O. and Martínez Lasso, M.A. 1979. *El Paso-Ciudad Juárez relations and the "Tortilla Curtain": A study of local adaptation to federal border policies*. El Paso, TX: El Paso Council on the Arts and Humanities.
Vandervoet, K. 1993, August 8. Mayor of Nogales, Arizona meets with Mexican President. *Nogales International*, pp. 1–4.

Chapter 16
Border Wall as Architecture

Ronald Rael

By some measures, the US Secure Fence Act of 2006 funded the single largest and most expensive building project in the United States of the twenty-first century. It finances approximately 800 miles of fortification dividing the US from Mexico at a cost of up to $16 million dollars per mile. Known as the Mexico–United States Barrier, the Great Wall of Mexico, border fence and border wall, the construction of this wall has transformed the large cities, small towns, and the multitude of cultural and ecological biomes along its path. It is a utopian scenario, engineered for a conceptual *tabula rasa* defined by Department of Homeland Security Secretary Michael Chertoff who was given unprecedented powers by President George Bush to waive any and all laws in order to expedite the wall's construction.[1] Ignoring the rich and diverse contexts found along the border not only raises critical questions of ecology, politics, economics, archaeology, urbanism and eminent domain (to name a few), it also radically redefines and transforms the territories of the *frontera*.

In many locations the wall is fabricated of steel, wire mesh, concrete, even re-purposed Vietnam-era Air Force landing strips (Figure 16.1). Elsewhere, it makes use of high-tech surveillance systems – aerostat blimps, subterranean probes and heat sensors. In all cases, the concept of "national security" governs and militates construction and design of the wall, and the success of the wall has been measured in the number of intercepted illegal crossings.

Border Wall as Architecture suggests that the wall, at such prices, should be thought of not only as security, but also as productive infrastructure – as the very backbone of a borderland economy. Indeed, coupling the wall with viable infrastructure – and this proposal focuses on water, renewable energy, and urban social infrastructure – is a pathway to security and safety in border communities and the nations beyond them. *Border Wall as Architecture* is a proposition for a wide array of retrofits and new schemes for the US–Mexico border wall that builds on existing conditions and seeks to ameliorate current problems created by the physical divider.

Over 700 miles of barriers have been constructed since 2006, at the cost of $3.4 billion. Additionally, the new wall has been breached over 3,000 times, incurring $4.4 million in repairs. The construction and maintenance costs are estimated to exceed $49 billion over the next 25 years and there are several hundred more miles of wall construction recently proposed.[2] Recent statistics show a 50 percent drop over the past two years in the number of people caught illegally entering the United States from Mexico. However, human rights groups put the number of deaths during attempted crossings at its highest since 2006 and

---

1 While there are a number of architectural definitions to define the barrier, Chertoff describes the intervention as a "tool" (Chertoff 2009: 42).

2 While it is difficult to accurately measure the exact scope and cost of the fence project, it has spanned more than 700 miles through four states and will cost as much as $49 billion over the expected 25-year life span of the fence according to a nonpartisan Congressional Research Service (see Hendricks 2007: B-1).

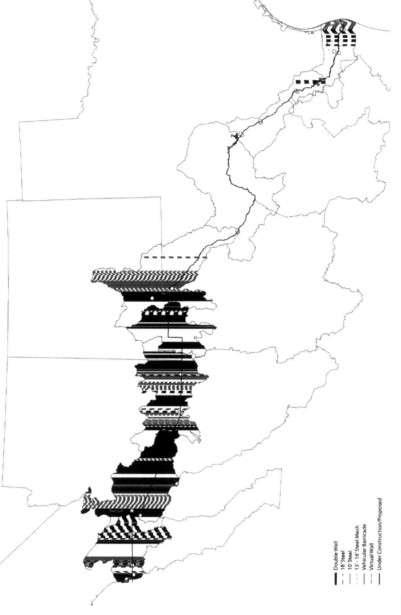

Figure 16.1 Different forms of barrier used along the US–Mexican border

almost 6,000 deaths have occurred since 1994.[3] It might also be noted that 30 laws were waived or suspended for the construction of the wall, including important environmental, wildlife and Native American heritage protections.

For the most part, architects and designers have stayed away from the border security issue. Ricardo Scofidio of Diller Scofidio + Renfro in New York said about architect's involvement in a border fence project: "It's a silly thing to design, a conundrum. You might as well leave it to security and engineers". Hamilton[4] architect Rem Koolhass had great interest in the related topic of the Berlin Wall and said of his studies of the wall (Hans 2003: 507–28):

> I had hardly imagined how West Berlin was actually imprisoned by the Wall. I had never really thought about that condition, and the paradox that even though it was surrounded by a wall, West Berlin was called 'free', and that the much larger area beyond the Wall was not considered free ... [and that] ... the Wall was not really a single object but a system that consisted partly of things that were destroyed on the site of the Wall, sections of buildings that were still standing and absorbed or incorporated into the Wall, and additional walls some really massive and modern, others more ephemeral all together contributing to an enormous zone. That was one of the most exciting things: it was one wall that always assumed a different condition.

The US–Mexico wall has created a similar territory of paradox, horror, transformation and flux, but at a much larger scale. It divides, or is proposed to divide rivers, farms, homes, public lands, cultural sites, wildlife reserves and migration routes and to cut through a university. And while the wall is always constructed on US soil, in many places, the border wall is constructed as much as two miles away from the actual territorial border. Currently, the land surrounding the border security infrastructure has lost its productive value. Removed from the market economy, it is essentially fallow. There are approximately 40,000 acres of US land that already do – or are planned to – lie on the Mexican side of the border wall – an area equal to twice the size of Manhattan.[5] This land has been isolated from US public access and economically neutralized. To counter this, the security infrastructure must be put to work through contextual engagement and investment. *Border Wall as Architecture* proposes a productive border through site specific but also modular solutions, retrofits and new schemes focused on the following areas: water infrastructure, renewable energy and social infrastructure. This proposal will also highlight some of the potential benefits these productive improvements can engender.

The border wall has already proven to be an effective, if accidental water collection system. Water from desert rains typically drain across the border – yet in areas such as the port of entry at Sonoyta, Mexico and Organ Pipe Cactus National Monument and in the Ambos Nogales (Arizona and Sonoma) the fence acts as a dam. It not only attempts to block northern flows of immigrants, the wall diverts water flows on both sides of the border

---

3 Deaths along the border are also difficult to account for. Many bodies have not been discovered and the cause of deaths vary and can be attributed to many factors (Hsu 2009).
4 William Hamilton, "A Fence with More Beauty, Fewer Barbs", *The New York Times*, June 18, 2006, sec. Week in Review.
5 This estimation emerged by calculating the total estimated area of US land that is south of the US–Mexico barrier using available maps of barrier locations.

Figure 16.2   Flooding in Nogales, Arizona caused by the border wall

into nearby cities, causing flooding and enormous environmental damage (Figure 16.2).[6] When water collection is considered pro-actively, it becomes a massive water collection system with transformative consequences for the desert communities along the border. For example, the city of El Paso levies storm water fees on all residents and businesses based on the amount of impervious surface that is located on a given property. These funds are then used to pay for a proposed system of storm water catchments to ameliorate the consequences of flooding in the rapidly growing desert city.

El Paso plans to raise $650 million for the entire project, which will distribute storm water catchments throughout the city. Dividing El Paso from Juarez is the large concrete basin defining the location where the Rio Grande/Rio Bravo River once flowed. By locating these catchments along the river, a linear park and riparian ecology will once again flow through the two cities (Figure 16.3). Locating additional rainwater collection shed roofs along the existing wall will increase the amount of water collected and also create cool, well shaded places where performances, markets and events could take place. Waterbanking the collected resource can lead to the eventual re-opening of the river to the city.

Creating a linear water park has important security implications as well. The purpose of wall construction is not to stop the flow of immigrants from the south, but to slow it down. According to the Department of Homeland Security, the wall gives border patrol agents only a few minutes more time to apprehend an illegal crossing (McLemore 2007).

---

6   In 2008 the border fence was responsible for causing 7-foot deep water levels in the cities of Nogales. See: (2008) report: Faulty design turned border fence into dam. *Arizona Daily Star* 15, August.

Figure 16.3   Water catchment wall, El Paso, TX

The department sees rivers as natural obstacles that also offer five minutes of added time to border patrol's advantage. A linear water park along the wall that meanders on both sides can create a doubly-secure linear tactical, social, ecological and hydrological infrastructure. Allowing the river to flow once again through the city, triples that security measure.

The New River is considered the most polluted river in the United States (Frisvold, Castwell 2000). It flows north from Mexicali, Mexico, and crosses the border at Calexico, California. The New River's toxicity is comprised of chemical runoff from the farm industry, sewage, contaminants – such as volatile organic compounds, heavy metals, pesticides – pathogens like tuberculosis, hepatitis, and cholera – as well as fecal coliform bacteria, which at the border checkpoint far exceed US–Mexico treaty limits. The New River then flows through the Imperial Valley, which is a major source of winter fruits and vegetables, cotton, and grain for both US and international markets. While the Secure Fence Act of 2006 was enacted, according to President Bush, to "help protect the American people" from illegal immigration, drug smuggling and terrorism, the New River represents a far more dangerous flow north from Mexico in need of containment (Bush 2006). A wastewater treatment wall located in the 2-mile long wasteland that buffers the dense border city of Mexicali from the agricultural Eden of the Imperial Valley is a solution to the "illegal entry" of toxins to the US. The pollution problem is expected to worsen as Mexicali's population, already 1.3 million, continues to expand without adequate infrastructure. For $33 million, the same cost as the wall that divides Calexico and Mexicali, it is possible to construct a wastewater treatment facility with the capacity to handle 20 million gallons/day of effluent from the New River (Figure 16.4).[7] This proposed facility is comprised of a linear pond filtration and

---

7   Calculations were based on the cost per square foot of recently constructed waste water treatment plants in the US.

Figure 16.4   Water treatment wall, Calexico, CA

purification system creating a secure and invaluable border infrastructure. The positive by-product of the wastewater treatment facility includes methane and water. The combination of methane and water is used to fuel the needs of a linear urban border park, running through the entire city providing a series of lit green corridors, and creating a healthy social infrastructure that join these growing border cities.

The greatest untapped potential for solar development in the United States lies along the US–Mexico border. Solar farms, in turn, are highly secure installations. Re-allocating funds used to construct and maintain the border wall for the construction of energy infrastructure along the border creates scenarios that in many instances are more secure than the existing wall, and also simultaneously provide solar energy to the energy hungry cities of the southwest. Consider the 100-mile stretch of border between Nogales, Arizona and Douglas, Arizona where 87 miles of border wall have been constructed at a cost of $333.5 million. Compare that figure to the cost of the largest solar farm in the world, the Olmedilla Photovoltaic Park in Olmedilla, Spain, which cost $530 million. For $333.5 million, 54 miles of profit generating solar farm can be constructed, 40-feet wide providing 60 megawatts of electricity, powering 40,000 households (Figure 16.5). Electricity is an important bi-national commodity and many border towns share electrical grids where electricity could be sold across the border. Transmission placed along the border make reliable electrical infrastructure for both nations to tap. This has important implications when it is understood that, according to the US Department of Energy, "one square foot of solar energy production along the border can power a dishwasher for 1 year"

Figures 16.5a and 16.5b   Solar wall

and in Germany, a country that is a leader in the new energy economy, the 5.3 gigawatts of solar farms they have built have generated 10,000 jobs (Solarbuzz 2011).

Further border improvements combine solar heat gain with water issues. In urban environments, the border wall is coupled with hot water production, creating low-cost

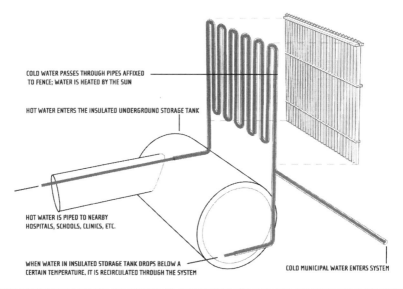

Figure 16.6 Solar hot water wall

additional resources that supplement the infrastructure of rapidly growing border cities. The massive steel walls are enormous heat absorbing agents, and they are retrofitted with panels that produce hot water, which is a much-needed amenity in border cities, and used in markets, clinics, hospitals and schools (Figure 16.6).

When solar energy is coupled with water collection, it also offers a key component for the establishment of life safety beacons along the border (Figure 16.7). The principal cause of death among migrants attempting to cross the border illegally is exposure to the elements, which causes heat stroke and dehydration (Eschbach, Hagan, Rodriguez 2001). Solar generated electricity powers life-safety beacons inform border patrol of both immigrants and American citizens who find themselves in danger in the harsh extremes of the southern deserts. The photovoltaic panels are designed to collect water runoff; to power atmospheric water extractors; or to pump water from wells or rivers that could be stored, purified and dispensed as needed to distressed crossers in the desert. Engaging the water dispenser or even approaching the life safety beacon alerts border patrol. Such devises gives wildlife access to water, as they often find themselves unable to travel their natural migration routes in search of it.

While most of this work has been focused on public utility-style resources, the importance of social improvements along the border should also be stressed. Sports, for example, are inherently social activities where networks between people with common interests are formed. The social capital produced by these networks is a core element in the fabric of communities: it produces safety and security, friendship and community, civic identity and economic value. Over time, social capital builds what may be termed "social infrastructure", a key element in the success and health of communities. One of the most devastating consequences of border wall security in its present state is the division of

Figure 16.7   Water and life safety wall

Figure 16.8   Family visits across the wall

communities, cities, neighbourhoods and families, and the erosion of social infrastructure (Figure 16.8).

Even so, sports have served as a way to cope with the realities of the wall. Volleyball is played using the fence as a net in several sites along the border and bi-national yoga classes have been held through the border wall as well (Figure 16.9). Using the border as an armature for a linear urban park through certain urban areas that is supplemented with green spaces, connected to schools and other parks offers pedestrian and bicycle routes through the city (Figure 16.10). The linear park, in turn, increases adjacent property values and the quality of life on both sides of the border while providing an important green corridor through the city.

The infrastructural improvements under consideration here play with the legislative hand the US has been dealt, working firmly within the complex and often labyrinthine fiscal, cultural and political realities of the border. The transformation of the border wall into a productive infrastructure that transcends security has important consequences on at least three fronts – improving the quality of life along the border, increasing security and creating jobs. Increasing the quality of life in Mexico is a step towards immigration reform. Border towns lack the infrastructure that allows them to be sustainable, healthy cities and infrastructural wall elements have the potential to provide city amenities amid urban growth. Infrastructural elements are highly secure facilities and profits from infrastructure development projects and infrastructural improvements to border cities will go a long way towards contributing to increased national security and immigration reform. The construction of large-scale infrastructure projects creates jobs, as do the manufacturing of the vital components that make up infrastructural technologies, which can be produced along the border.

Franklin Delano Roosevelt set out a course for US–Mexico relations at the onset of World War II with a vision of hemispheric security that was not beholden to a limited view of border fortification. He said, "*What I seek to convey is the historic truth that the United States as a nation has at all times maintained opposition – clear, definite opposition – to*

Figure 16.9   Yoga across the wall

Figure 16.10   Bike path and pedestrian wall

any attempt to lock us in behind an ancient Chinese wall" (Jan 6, 1941) (Roosevelt, in Grafton 1999: 93). Yet, the border fence in its current form recalls the inflexibility and ancient strategy of a wall as a singular means of security. Michael Chertoff, the architect of the existing wall said, "*A fence by itself is not going to work, but in conjunction with other tools, it can help*". There are many reasons to think that border security can be achieved – and will only be achieved – by employing a more multi-valent and flexible tool in the form of a vision of border infrastructure than has yet been imagined.

References

Arizona Daily Star. 2008. Report: Faulty design turned border fence into dam. *Arizona Daily Star*, 15, August.
Bush, G.W. 2006. *Introductory Speech at the Signing of the Secure Fence Act*, The Roosevelt Room, The White House, Washington DC, October 26.
Chertoff, M. 2009. *Homeland Security: Assessing the First Five Years*, Philadelphia, University of Pennsylvania, 2009.
Eschbach, K., J. Hagan, N. Rodriguez. 2001. *Causes and Trends in Migrant Deaths Along the U.S.–Mexico Border 1985–1998*, Center for Immigration Research, University of Houston.
Frisvold, G.B., M.F. Caswell. 2000. Transboundary Water Management Game-theoretic Lessons for Projects on the US–Mexico Border. *Agricultural Economics*, 24, 101–11. DOI: 10.1111/j.1574–0862.2000.tb00096.x.
Genova, J. 1995. *Wittgenstein: A Way of Seeing*, Psychology Press.
Hamilton, W. 2006. A Fence with More Beauty, Fewer Barbs, *The New York Times*, June 18.
Hendricks, T. 2007. Study: Price for border fence up to $49 billion: Study says fence cost could reach $49 billion/lawmakers' estimate falls far short of total, research service says. *San Francisco Chronicle*, January 8, B-1.
Hsu, S. 2009. Border deaths are increasing: Rise is despite fewer crossers, U.S. and Mexican groups say. *Washington Post*, September 30.
McLemore, D. 2007. Texas to see border fence construction next year despite opposition: Rio Grande set for 150 miles of barriers. *The Dallas Morning News*, December 5.
Obrist, H.U. 2003. Part 1: On Berlin's New Architecture, in *Interviews*, Volume I, edited by Thomas Boutoux, Milano, Charta, Fondazione Pitti Immagine Discovery, 507–28.
Roosevelt, F.D. 1999. Four Freedoms, January 6, 1941 in *Great Speeches*, edited by John Grafton New York, Dover Publications, 93.
SolarBuzz. 2011. *Fast Solar Energy Facts*, available at http://www.solarbuzz.com/FastFactsGermany.htm (accessed January 13, 2011).

Index

9/11 1–3, 13, 52, 60, 62, 69, 72, 74, 76, 79–80, 85, 87–8, 93–5, 97–8, 106, 138, 143–6, 148–50, 180, 182–4, 196, 204, 243

acoustic sensor device 181; *see also* technology
Acropol communication systems 148
Aeclesia Universalis 110
agriculture 46, 94, 108, 161–2, 204, 271
    agricultural lands 162
AIDS 234
Air Force Corps of Engineers 147
Alaska 92, 100, 147
Algeria 13, 37, 172, 187
AMASS 240
anti-illegal immigration 175, 180–81
anti-immigration 91, 118, 120, 175, 177–80, 183, 185, 187, 189, 255
anti-landing decree 71
anti-Mexican 248, 254
apartheid 123, 212, 214, 217
aquifer 93, 162, 216; *see also* water
Arab League 170
Arab Spring 19, 53, 149
Arizona Border Surveillance Technology Plan 148
Armenia 112
asymmetry 2, 86–8, 143, 145, 150, 197, 207
Austin, John 213
Australia 169, 67, 69–71, 75–6, 78
availability, principle of 79

Badie, Bertrand 1, 58, 106–7, 144
BAE Systems 149, 237, 239
Balibar, Etienne 1, 59, 123
bandidos 256–7
Bangladesh 5, 77, 105, 117–18, 121, 131–2, 146, 159
barbed-wire 105, 108–9, 117, 148–9, 159, 181
barrier
    defense 224–5
    multilayered 119
    physical 123, 145–6, 191–2, 196–7, 199, 206, 214, 255
    preventive 148
    virtual 148, 214, 241

barrier route 216
Bauman, Zygmut 61, 75, 146, 243
Bedouins 225
Belgium 33, 110
Berlin Wall 1, 122, 131–3, 137, 139, 148, 159, 184, 211, 213, 215, 220, 269
berm 105, 125–6, 131–2, 146, 149, 161
biological weapon 248
biometric data, *see* biometrics
biometric technologies, *see* biometrics
biometrics 31, 54–5, 67, 70, 75–7, 79, 186, 207, 220–21, 240–43; *see also* technology
Boeing 56, 148–9, 200–201, 208
border
    Alaska–Yukon 100
    bioborders 67, 78
    Canada–US 86, 91, 93, 98, 100
    closed 146–7
    de facto 3, 181
    smart 54, 70, 78, 183
    thicker 93, 96, 241–2
    US–Mexican 28, 30, 184–5, 199, 206
    waiting times 251
border barrier 2, 4, 118, 122–3, 127, 143, 145, 184, 192, 194, 197, 211
border city 194, 271
border communities 87, 94–5, 183, 198–9, 203, 247, 267
border control 11, 16, 19, 22, 27–32, 36, 39, 40, 52–3, 55–7, 67–72, 75–7, 79, 111, 125, 147, 175, 179, 181–3, 185–7, 200, 204, 231–3, 236, 240, 242–4
    management 175
border crossing 44, 55, 78, 85, 87, 89–90, 97, 99, 113, 119, 125–6, 147, 172, 187, 220, 233, 249–53, 260–65
    illicit 119, 125
border discourse 1, 143–5, 204, 208
border economy 90
border fence 1, 31, 108, 117–27, 137, 175, 177, 179, 181–3, 185, 187
    cost of 56–7, 119, 146, 148–9, 183, 185–6, 196, 205, 267, 271–2
    dismantling of 112, 125

border fortification 2, 54, 118, 144–8, 150, 193, 205, 206, 276
border industry, *see* border market
border market 147, 149
border patrol 85, 89–92, 118, 183, 193–7, 200–202, 204, 247–8, 250, 253, 255, 258–9, 261, 270–71, 274
border post 108, 110, 148
border region 28–9, 46, 87–9, 92, 96, 99–100, 138, 184, 191–3, 199–203, 205, 207, 225, 247, 250, 256
border security 67–70, 72–3, 75, 77, 79–80, 85, 89, 91–2, 145, 147–50, 183, 185, 191, 192, 194–5, 199–203, 205–8, 232, 236, 238–41, 243–4, 269, 278
   dispositive 244
border space 68, 93, 192–3, 195, 197, 203, 207, 241–2
border studies 117, 121–3, 125, 213
border wall 1–4, 103, 132, 135, 144–6, 150, 184, 191, 193, 198–9, 202, 204, 247, 249, 251–2, 255, 261, 267, 269–74, 276–7
border zone 54, 56, 70, 89, 93, 136, 147, 150, 191, 193, 196, 197, 200, 202, 204
bordering mechanism 212–13
borderlands 2, 85–91, 93–100, 119–22, 183–4, 191–3 196, 198–200, 202–4, 206–7, 267
   borderland culture 51, 70, 86–8, 94, 99–100, 150
borderless world 1–2, 67, 86, 111, 113
borderline 28, 67–8, 78, 87–8, 92, 121, 143, 192–3, 206–7, 242
borders
   institutionalization of 87–8, 96, 218
   militarization of, *see* militarization
   obsolescence of 107, 122, 144
   proliferation of 106, 211
   securitization of, *see* securitization
Botswana 105, 117, 131, 159
boundary line 86, 92, 256
boundary waters 93
Briand Kellog Pact 106
BRIC 87, 93, 95, 140, 150, 159, 212, 267, 274
British Columbia 92, 94–5, 99
Brownsville 198
buffer zone 68, 71, 144, 182, 196, 199, 242–3
B'Tselem 214–16
Bulgaria 1, 74
Burton, John 106
Brunei 105, 146

camouflage 185

Canada 1, 85–9, 91–100, 160, 169, 180, 185, 243
Canary Islands 27, 29–32, 34–8, 40–41, 43, 45–6, 59, 75, 181, 186, 233
Cape Verde 35, 37–8, 46, 260
Caribbean 34, 78, 80, 92, 194
Cassidian 149
CIA 68, 71
Central Asia 105, 120
Ceuta 30, 31, 40, 59, 105, 117–18, 131, 141, 146, 159, 177, 181–2, 211
checkpoint 117–20, 148, 183, 217–18, 220–26, 240, 243, 251, 271
Chemillier-Gendreau, Monique 136
China 1, 105, 117, 143, 145–6, 150
cholera 271
citizenship 14, 39, 95–6, 110, 176, 178
Clausewitz, Carl Von 60, 106
climate 67, 78, 149, 255
Clinton administration 193–5
closure technologies 226; *see also* technology
Coast Guard 18, 68
cocaine 120
Cold War 1–3, 63, 69–70, 105–7, 109, 111, 118, 143–4, 146–7, 149–50
Colorado 92, 248
common market 106
Conakry 37, 41, 45
constructivism 117, 122–3, 145, 212–13
Copenhagen School 57
corridor 87, 89, 92, 98–9, 196, 200, 202, 220, 272, 276
counter-terrorism 76, 182, 240; *see also* terrorism; wall, anti-terrorist
CRATE 53–4
crime
   organized 29, 75, 126, 132, 183, 208, 231, 236, 238
   transborder 31
crisis
   economic 27, 43, 45, 149–50
   financial 106, 178, 181, 187
   of 1929 107
cross-border cooperation 93, 223–5, 265
Cuba 1, 71
culture of conflict 218, 226
Customs and Border Protection 98, 149, 184, 200–201
Cyprus 2, 59, 105, 112, 131–2, 144

Danevirke 1
Dassault Aviation 239–40

death of migrants 21, 55, 59, 77, 203, 219, 267, 269, 274, 279
Declaration of European Identity 111–12
defence industries 147, 149–50
defence markets 147
dehumanization 219, 221
dehydration 40, 274
Delors, Jacques 111
Denmark 1, 111
Department of Energy 272
Department of Homeland Security, see Homeland Security
Department of Interior
    Italy 16
    Germany 20
    Libya 16
    Spanish 29, 38, 186
    United States 91
Department of Justice 183
Department of Public Safety 250
deportation 3, 13, 20, 41, 79, 94, 119, 180, 251, 264
detention 20, 44, 45, 71–2, 249–50
detention centre 13, 19, 41, 71, 147–8
deterrence
    fence as deterrent 195
deterritorialization 68, 80, 145
DHS, see Homeland Security
digitalization 79, 186
discrimination 17, 19, 21, 136
distress at sea 16–17, 22
DMZ, see Korean Demilitarized Zone
drones 16, 97, 143, 147–9, 191–3, 195, 197, 199, 203, 205, 207, 240–42
DRS Technologies 148–9
drug cartel 119
Drug Enforcement Agency (DEA) 250
drug-related violence 207
drug trafficking 31, **38**, 63, 91, 119–20, 126, 146, 183, 185, 194, 204, 211, 247–50, 252, 254, 256, 258, 261, 264, 271
drugs
    cocaine 120
    heroin 120
    illicit 120, 207
    marijuana 257
    war on 250

EADS 148–9, 237–9
East Germany 78
ECHR 17–18, 164
ecology 267, 270; see also environment
economic flows 28, 231

EFFISEC (Efficient Integrated Security Checkpoint) 240
Egypt 1, 13, 19, 145, 159, 172
Elbit Systems 148
Elias, Norbert 61, 63, 92, 107
enclave 59, 105, 133, 137, 146, 159, 181–2, 217
end of history 147
Enhanced Driver's License (EDL) 97
entry
    clandestine 32, 193–6, 201, 233
    illegal 19, 249, 252, 271
environment 4, 44, 46, 55, 62, 86–7, 91–3, 107, 121, 143, 147, 150, 163, 165, 172, 191–6, 198–9, 202–4, 206–9, 217, 222, 226, 240, 247–8, 261, 269–70, 273
ESSRTRT (European Security: High Level Study of Threat Responses and Relevant Technologies) 239
ESTA (Electronic System for Travel Authorization) 55
Europe, as Unidentified Political Object 111
European Commission 12, 19, 21, 52–3, 55–8, 170, 173, 177, 232, 237–8, 240, 244
European Parliament 21, 34–5, 38, 62, 112, 172–3, 235
European Union 13–14, 16, 19–20, 22, 27–9, 31, 33–9, 43–5, 51–8, 61–3, 71, 75, 78–9, 111–12, 139, 149, 170, 172, 186, 231, 236
Europol 79
EUROSUR 21, 52, 54, 55, 240
Evros 105
exclave 117
exclusion 3, 12, 114, 123–4, 176, 212
    exclusionary policies 124, 143, 212, 216–18, 225–6
externalization of borders 22, 28–9, 180, 182, 186, 243

FBI 68, 197, 250
fence
    aesthetical 253, 259
    barbed-wire 149, 181
    chain link 248, 251, 256–7
    double 105
    electric 79
    electronic barrier 55
    repairs on 149, 162, 195, 248, 267
    security 183, 215–16
    vehicle 196
fishing industry 17, 31, 161–2, 166, 172
fortification 1, 2, 105, 118, 121, 132, 143–8; see also border fortification

Fortress Europe 14, 28, 63, 177, 180–81
Foucault, Michel 61, 75
Framework Programme, European Union 237, 239
France 20–21, 29, 33, 55, 58, 60, 108, 110, 112–13, 132, 148–9, 160, 172, 176, 187
free trade 3, 108, 110–11, 172, 194, 231, 248, 258
Frontex 14, 17, 31, 34, 52–4, 60, 62, 69, 71, 75, 112, 231, 233–6, 242, 244

gas 161, 172, 226
gated communities 123, 212
gatekeeper 13, 120, 123, 125–6, 192, 196, 204
Gateway, Cascade 89–92, 99
Gaza 117, 120, 159–60, 162–3, 166, 171–2, 215, 225
Geneva Convention 138, 171
General Dynamics 149
Genko Borui 1
Georgia 105, 112
Ghandi, Indira 118
globalization 1–3, 11, 30–31, 42–3, 46, 54, 67–8, 78, 86, 95–6, 105–11, 113, 117, 122, 124, 139, 143–4, 150, 231–3, 243
Golan Heights 1, 149, 166
governance 69–71, 79, 99, 100, 107–8, 110, 180, 192, 213
Greece 1, 3, 14, 54, 105, 112, 131, 144, 145–6, 159
Green Line 105, 112, 133, 161, 164, 212, 216–17, 220
Green Zone (Iraq) 212
groomed sand cover 148
Group of Personalities, European Commission 237–9
Guantánamo 1, 71
Guardia Civil (Spain) 186
Guinea Bissau 41, 45

Habermas, Jurgen 125–6
Hague Programme 34, 52, 62
Hamas 172
hepatitis 271
Hispanic population 177, 191, 204, 255
Hobbes, Thomas 51, 61, 63, 105, 232
Homeland Security 54, 56, 68, 91, 92, 94, 147–9, 177, 183, 185, 191, 196–201, 205–6, 208, 267, 270
Hong Kong 1
human security 99, 231
Hungary 74
Huntington, Samuel 57

hydrological infrastructure 271; *see also* water infrastructure
Hypersecurity 80

identity card 216
IDF 1, 149, 222
Illegal Immigration Reform and Immigrant Responsibility Act (IIRIRA) 179
immigrant
    arrest 194
immigration
    illegal 12, 14–17, 31, 33, 36, 38, 51–2, 54, 56–63, 91, 118, 126, 146, 175, 179–81, 185, 231–2, 236, 247–9, 253, 259–60, 262, 265, 271
    irregular 13–14, 27, 30, 34–5, 39, 41, 45–6, 57, 175, 177, 179–83, 185–6, 271
Immigration and Custom Enforcement (ICE) 207
Immigration and Nationality Act 178
Immigration and Naturalization Service (INS) 194, 247, 249
immigration policy 11–14, 17–18, 22, 33, 39, 59, 96, 112, 127, 175, 178–81, 187, 191, 264
    procedures 72
    quota 13
Immigration Reform and Control Act 179
Imperial Valley 271
Imperium Mundi 110
India 1, 3, 19, 94, 105, 117–18, 120–21, 128–9, 131–2, 138, 143–6, 148, 150, 159, 161, 165–6, 171, 211
Indian tribes 138
infrared camera 181
Integrated Border Management (IBM) 52, 56, 58, 69, 71, 77, 100, 236
International Court of Justice 131–2, 134, 161, 163–5, 168–9, 214
International Joint Commission 236
International Union of Telecommunications 113
Interpol 12, 79
inter-subjectivity 109, 146
Intifada 159, 216, 220–21
Ir Amin 214
Iraq 77, 94, 105, 108, 112, 117, 131, 146, 148–9, 211–12
Ireland 42, 44, 225
Iron Curtain 105–6, 108; *see also* Berlin Wall
Israel 1, 3, 105, 109, 117, 120, 132–4, 136–8, 140, 145–6, 148–9, 159–66, 169, 171–2, 211–26
Israel Aerospace Industries 148

Israeli
  Arab 225
  Jewish 218, 225
Italy 13–21, 29, 42, 44, 59, 71, 113, 177, 187, 211–12, 235

Jabotinksy Vladimir 219
Jewish settlement 216–17
Johnson, Fred 248, 251–3, 259–60, 265
Joint Africa–EU strategy 39, 45
Jones, Charles O. 1–3, 144–6
Jordan 1, 145, 148, 160, 163, 217, 224

Kashmir 105, 131–2, 144, 159–61, 165–6, 170–71
Kazakhstan 120
Keohane, Robert 106, 144
Kirghizstan 105, 131
Kollsman 148
Korea
  North Korea 105, 146, 159
  South Korea 105, 145, 149
Korean Demilitarized Zone 105, 118, 145
Kouchner, Bernard 187
Kurds 198
Kuwait 105, 117
Kyushu 1

labour market 30, 42–4, 46, 123, 177–8
Lampedusa 16, 18–19, 21, 187, 233, 240–41, 243
law
  humanitarian 137, 138, 140, 164–5, 171
  international 13, 17, 30, 69–71, 78, 111, 131–7, 139–40, 160–61, 163–4, 166–7, 169–70, 173, 182, 214, 217
  labour 136
Lebanon 1, 145, 160, 219
legal personality 111–12
LG Electronics 149
liberalism 28, 111
Libya 13–19, 28, 36, 39, 71, 77, 187
Limbang 105
Lisboa Treaty 13, 39, 112, 181
Loizidou vs. Turkey 164
LORROS 148

Maastricht Treaty 12, 52, 112
Macao 1
Madrid attacks 180, 182
Maginot Line 2, 109
Malaysia 117, 131, 146
Mali 36–7, 41, 45–6
Malta 17–19, 21, 59, 233

Manley, John 94
maquiladora 252, 254, 265
Mauritania 28, 31, 35, 38–9, 41, 45, 186, 242
Médecins sans Frontières 187
Mediterranean Sea 11, 13–17, 19–22, 34, 53, 59–60, 71, 77, 80, 181–2, 186–7, 224, 242
Melilla 30, 31, 40, 59, 105, 117–18, 131, 146, 159, 177, 181–2, 211
mental walls 58, 63, 218–20
metal corridors 220; *see also* corridor
Mexican customs 256
Mexican Consulate 254–5, 258
Mexico 56, 77, 91–2, 96, 105, 118, 120, 131–2, 135, 138, 145–7, 149, 159, 176–80, 182–5, 191–6, 199, 201, 207, 211–12, 248–9, 251–2, 255–6, 258–67, 269, 271–2, 276, 278
migrants; *see also* immigration
  death 14, 16, 21, 55, 59, 77, 79, 182, 203, 219, 267, 269, 274
  irregular 13–16, 21, 27–30, 35, 40–41, 44, 46, 60–63
  smuggling 41, 77, 125, 241
  undocumented 13–14, 17, 22, 29–30, 32, 44–5, 57, 184, 251, 254
Migration Amendment Act 2011 71
migration, *see* immigration
migration routes 1, 14, 178, 194, 269
militarization of borders 28, 52–3, 60, 75, 91, 99, 106, 143–4, 147, 175, 180–82, 185
military expenditures 147
military–industrial complex 143, 146–7, 150, 241
Mitchell Report 219, 223
migrant smuggling 29, 41, 146, 241
mobile surveillance system 186
mobility 11, 14, 20, 22, 27–9, 38, 42–3, 46, 54, 56, 70, 75–6, 78, 91, 99–100, 195–6, 211
Model Based Risk Analysis (MBRA) 208
Mongol invasions 1
Morocco 2, 13, 28–9, 31, 33–7, 39–41, 77, 105, 117–18, 132, 145–6, 149, 159, 161, 165–6, 170–73, 178, 181–2, 211–12, 242
motion/metal detector 199–201, 220
Mozambique 1
Myanmar 117

NAFTA 68, 88, 96, 184, 194, 243, 248, 264
Napolitano, Janet 56, 185, 200
National Forest Service 91

National Parks Service 91
national security 12, 73, 98, 123, 137–8, 145, 180, 184, 247–8, 253–4, 267, 276
native reservation 160
natural resources 91, 159–61, 163–72
naturalization 178, 183, 194, 247, 249
neo-functionalism 111
NEXUS 97
NIMBY (Not In My Backyard) 198, 202, 208
no man's land 196
Nogales 147, 183, 247–65, 269–70, 272
nomads 14
nuclear power 144
Nye, Joseph 106

oil 161, 166, 172
Oman 105, 146, 211
OPERAMAR 240
operation Gatekeeper 192, 196, 204
operation Hold the Line 192, 195–6, 199, 208
optic device 181; *see also* technology
Organization of African Unity (OAU) 170
Ottoman Empire 112

Pacific Northwest border region 89
Padua 211–12
Pakistan 1, 37, 105, 117, 120, 131, 144, 146, 161, 171, 211
Palestine 77, 131–5, 137–40, 160–61, 164–5, 170, 212, 214, 219–20, 224, 226
Paris, Treaty of 176
Peace Arch crossing 89
Peace Lines 225
Peace Now 214
Persian Gulf 105, 248
personal state 11
phosphate 161, 166, 172
Plug-in Optronic Payload 148
Polisario Front 105, 146, 161, 170
polleros 249, 251, 256–7
ports-of-entry 247, 249, 253, 255, 269
post-modernism 68, 76, 96, 106, 109, 111–12, 117, 122–3, 126
post-positivism 117, 124
post-Westphalian world 12, 106
Preparatory Action for Security Research 239
profiling 19, 21, 72–4, 79, 94
proliferation of barriers 213
Punjab 144

Qatar 105

radar 31, **34**, 53, 56, 147–8, 181, 184, 186, 191, 200–201, 214
radar stations 148
Rajasthan 144
Rapid Border Intervention Team 38, 242
Ratheon Corp 149
Ratzel, Friedrich 30
Reagan, Ronald 247
re-bordering 95–6
Reclus, Elysée 113
reconquista 181
refugee 15–17, 29, 71, 79, 159, 160, 177, 180
refugee camps 159–60
regionalization 87–8, 111, 233
Remote Video Surveillance System 186
Renan, Ernest 60
residence permit 13, 20–21, 146, 176
Rhodesia 1
Ridge, Tom 94
Rien à déclarer 110
right of
    asylum 15, 17, 21–2, 29, 109, 146
    defence 18, 20, 22
    freedom of movement 12, 79, 107, 138, 160, 214
right to
    be free from hunger 161
    body integrity 74, 79
    education 136
    food 161–2, 168, 172
    health 136
    informational privacy 76–7, 79
    life 136
    normal family relationship 136
    personal security 136
    property 136, 161, 163
    safe and clean drinking water and sanitation 163
    water 161, 163, 167
rights
    economic 136, 165, 167, 169
    fundamental 14–17, 21–2, 72, 163, 166
    human 14–15, 17–18, 21–2, 29
    humanitarian 136, 137–8, 187
road-block 212
Roman Limes 1, 236, 246
    Antonine Wall 1
    Hadrian's Wall 1, 224
Rome convention 171
Roosevelt, Franklin Delano 276
Rosenau, James 107
Rousseau, Jean-Jacques 107

SAAB 239
Sao Paulo 212
Sahrawi Arab Democratic Republic 165–6, 170
satellite 31, **38**, 92, 123, 242, 238
SBInet Program 55–6, 119, 185, 200–201
Schengen Agreement 12–13, 20, 28, 31, 33, 35, 52, 62, 179
Schengen zone 54, 111, 231
Schmitt Carl 57–61, 65
Secure Fence Act 183, 191, 196, 267, 271
security; *see also* national security
  budget 149–50, 206
  heightened security 87–8, 148
security-industrial complex 146–7, 150, 241
security industry 143, 146, 150, 238, 241
security market 147, 149, 192, 200, 240
security narrative 63, 192, 199
Security Network for Technological Research in Europe (SENTRE) 239
securitization of borders 29, 72, 80, 94, 143–4, 147
self defence 138
self-determination 138, 159, 164–5, 168–70, 172
Senegal 28, 31, 35–9, 41, 45–7, 186, 242
Shalit, Gilad 120
Sharon, Ariel 215–16
Shin Bet 225
Sicily 16–17, 187
Siegfried Line 2
Sierra Leone 41, 45
Sinai 1
SIVE 33–4, 186–7, 242
small business 149, 257
Smart Border Initiative 54–5, 64
smuggling 30–31, 40–41, 91, 120, 123, 126, 145–6, 159, 183, 185–6, 194, 199–200, 202–3, 205, 208, 211, 256, 271; *see also* drug trafficking; migrants, smuggling
soft power 112
SOGEM 239–40
solar power 272–4
Sonoran Desert 91, 256, 258
South Africa 1, 160, 167
sovereignty 2, 11, 28, 30, 62, 70–71, 75, 78, 108, 134, 138, 139, 143–4, 165–6, 169, 171, 175, 232
Soviet Union 63, 111, 137, 238
Standards for Border Security Enhancement (STRABORSEC) 239–40
state
  failed 71, 78, 108
  nation 14, 68

prison 108
transit 96, 145, 176–7, 182
Strategies for Effective Police Stop and Search (STEPPS) 74
Sudan 171
surveillance 3, 13, 16, 21–2, 31, 33, 36, 38, 52–5, 57, 67–8, 70, 72, 75, 89, 90–92, 97, 117, 147–9, 181, 184–6, 191, 193–6, 199–203, 214, 220, 236–44, 249, 267
Surveillance of Borders, Coastline and Harbours (OBCAH) 239
surveillance system 21–2, 31, 33, 38, 52, 54–5, 147–8, 186, 214, 236, 238, 240–42, 267
Switzerland 112, 176
Syria 1, 94, 108, 112, 148, 149, 160, 166

Talarion 149
TALOS 241
technology 4, 12, 27, 31, 42, 46, 52–6, 58, 68, 70, 73–5, 77–9, 143, 146–9, 181, 183–5, 191–3, 195–208, 213, 217, 221–2, 226, 231, 234, 235–42, 244
territorial integrity 159, 170
territorial state 11, 106
territorial trap 2
terrorism 29, 31, 52, 60, 63, 68–76, 79–80, 120, 126, 131–2, 144–6, 161, 182–3, 192–3, 211, 215, 224, 231, 236, 238, 243, 271
  war against 60, 71–2, 80
Tethered Aerostat Radar Systems (TARS) 191
Texas Border Coalition 198–9, 202
TGS-Nopec 172
Thailand 117, 131, 146
Thales 149, 237, 239–40
thermal imaging device 186; *see also* technology
third-country national 18–19, 46, 54, 74, 79–80
threat, non-traditional 184
TORC2H 148
Total-Fina-Elf 172
towers, *see* watchtower
traffic 52, 73, 79, 89, 97–8, 194, 212, 255
travel documents 11, 62, 74, 79, 242
trespasser 118, 120–21, 125–7
tuberculosis 271
Tunisia 13, 19–20, 53, 77, 187, 233
Turkey 1, 54, 105, 108, 112, 131, 144–6, 159, 164, 224

UNCLOS 16
unemployment 42–5, 108, 178, 212
United Arab Emirates (UAE) 146, 211

United Nations 16, 71, 105, 108, 160, 163–6, 170–72
   charter 72, 106, 108, 164, 172
   general assembly 5, 263–6, 170–71
   secretary general 166, 170
   security Council 165–6, 170–71
United Nations Refugee Convention 16–17, 71
unmanned aerial vehicle 56, 183, 191, 200; *see also* drones
US Department of Energy 272
US–Mexican border 28, 30, 184–5, 199, 206
Uzbekistan 105, 131, 146

Valéry, Paul 107, 112
virtual barrier 132, 148, 184, 187, 191, 200–201, 241
Visa Information System (VIS) 12, 54, 76, 79, 186, 242
visas 3, 12–13, 19, 37, 54–5, 60, 68, 75, 77, 111, 123, 139, 146, 160, 176, 181–2, 186, 242–3, 248, 252

wall
   Advisory Opinion on the 131
   annexation 214, 225
   anti-terrorist 118, 120, 214
   apartheid 214
   Bagdad walls 132
   colonization 214, 225
   Great Wall of China 1, 117, 224
   high tech 148, 203, 214, 231
   of shame 106
   physical 191, 219
   sand 131, 146, 159, 166
   security 146
   separation 2–3, 120, 124, 132, 133, 143, 214, 225
   solar 273–4
   steel 172, 247–65
   steel plank 247–8, 253
   virtual 132, 148, 184, 191, 200–201
   system 216–18

war
   crimes 171
   gulf war 147, 248
   on drugs 96, 194, 249–50
   on terror 193
watchtower 148, 196, 199–203
water
   aquifer 93, 162, 216
   fishing waters 166
   flooding 93, 270
   catchment 270–71
   collection 269–70, 274
   flows 269
   infrastructure 269
   resources 162–3, 166, 214, 216
   table 163
   water-bearing basin 163
Weimar Republic 61
West Bank 117, 146, 159–64, 171, 211–14, 216–18, 220, 223–6
   Area A 162, 223
   Area B 162, 223
   Area C 162
West Bank barrier 161, 211, 213, 218, 225–6
Western Hemisphere Travel Intiative (WHTI) 96–7
Western Sahara 2, 41, 105, 131–2, 159–61, 165–6, 169–72
Westphalian order 108, 138, 175, 193
White House 194
Wide Maritime Area Airborne Surveillance (WIMA) 240
wildlife reserve 269, 274
World Heritage 92
World War I 68, 107
World War II 108, 121, 176, 276
world without borders, *see* borderless world

Yemen 105, 117–18, 131, 146
Yukon 92, 100

Zambia 1